PENNSYLVANIA GAZETTEER

PENNSYLVANIA GAZETTEER

American Historical Publications, Inc.
725 Market Street
Wilmington, Delaware 19801

PRINTED IN THE UNITED STATES OF AMERICA

©

Copyright 1989 by
American Historical Publications

L.C.# 85-30830

I.S.B.N.# 0-937862-81-9

Library of Congress Cataloging-in-Publication Data
Main entry under title:

Pennsylvania gazetteer.

1. Pennsylvania--Gazetteers. I. American
Historical Publications.
F147.P46   1986   917.48'003'21   85-30830
ISBN 0-937862-81-9

FOREWORD

A gazetteer is a dictionary of places. This is a (historical) gazetteer. Its primary function is to give detailed information on events that have occurred in this State and the people who have participated in them.

It is also intended to serve as a contemporary directory of certain basic reference data of frequent interest. Most prior geographical references were prefaced with lengthy explanations interpreting codes, abbreviations, keys and other space-saving, but confusing symbols. This gazetteer needs no such explanations. The abbreviations used have obvious interpretations.

Larger cities are, of course, covered extensively in general encyclopedias and numerous monographs. An important service offered in this gazetteer is in arranging material systematically and in providing information on the vast majority of places that are not well covered elsewhere.

The Biography Index should be of particular value for researchers in making readily accessible information on famous persons related to their places of origin or activity.

New editions are planned basis for updating material currently listed and for adding new information to expand the usefulness of the publication.

Acknowledgment is made to the many Chambers of Commerce in that have provided information, the many libraries and especially the Library of Congress for the use of its facilities. Credit is also due the U.S. Geological Surveys for reference to their most recently published material. Also to the U.S. Census Bureau for expediting the availability of the latest population data for our use. Considerable use has been made of the Federal Writer's Project State and City Guides and a special tribute is offered to the hundreds of celebrated writers who contributed to that unprecedented collection of Americana.

OTHER PUBLICATIONS AVAILABLE
BY AMERICAN HISTORICAL PUBLICATIONS, INC.

California Biographical Dictionary
California Gazetteer
Florida Biographical Dictionary
Florida Gazetteer
Illinois Biographical Dictionary
Illinois Gazetteer
Massachusetts Biographical Dictionary
Massachusetts Gazetteer
Michigan Gazetteer
Missouri Gazetteer
New Jersey Biographical Dictionary
New Jersey Gazetteer
New York Biographical Dictionary
New York Gazetteer
Ohio Biographical Dictionary
Ohio Gazetteer
Pennsylvania Biographical Dictionary
Pennsylvania Gazetteer
Texas Biographical Dictionary
Texas Gazetteer

INTRODUCTION:

PENNSYLVANIA

"THE KEYSTONE STATE"

Pennsylvania, the coal mine, the oil well, the steel mill of the nation, is a state unto itself. Although it was one of the thirteen original colonies, it isn't a New England state. Although it touches on Lake Erie, it isn't a Great Lakes or Midwestern state. And in spite of the fact that tobacco is grown on the farmlands around Lancaster, Pennsylvania has never been a Southern state. Yet it connects all of these regions which surround it, and the history of the nation has almost always been paralleled by the events taking place in Pennsylvania.

This is the nation's factory. There are other states with much more land and vaster resources, but Pennsylvania will be known as the place where urban-industrial America was born. Here Edison and Westinghouse perfected their electrical appliances, and here John D. Rockefeller and others controlled the railroads and the oil that powered them to carry the nation's goods. It was also in Pennsylvania that the first Bessemer steel was produced, revolutionizing all aspects of industry. And it was in Pittsburgh and other city factories where workers first joined hands in order to get a fair shake of the new wealth.

Pennsylvania was William Penn's promised land. His Friends envisioned a Utopia, and received instead an imperfect commonwealth. Today, the "Peaceable Kingdom" is often torn with dissension among various groups for various causes. The problems of unemployment, racial strife and aging cities has caused many people to leave Pennsylvania and so the population has risen only .2 percent since 1970.

Still, more programs than ever before help the poor, the minority groups and the renovation of older urban neighborhoods, while government officials have hopes of a brighter, more technological than industrial future for Pennsylvania. Pittsburgh looks better today than it did ten years ago as a result of this visionary outlook, and many people are finding non-farming ways to live in the less populated countryside of the state. (See **History** section).

The future of Pennsylvania is a subject of study in the coming decades. The outward appearances of the stte may change dramatically, but to get a picture of the heart of the commonwealth, one can't overlook the symbols created during its history.

State Symbols

THE NAME

Pennsylvania means "Penn's Forest Land," and was named by King Charles II in honor of William Penn's father, who had served at a high rank in King James' court. On March 14, 1681, when Charles signed the land grant making William Penn the leader of a vast tract of land in America, Penn wrote to his friend Robert Turner: "This day my country was confirmed to meet under the Great Seal of England, with large powers and privileges, by the name of Pennsylvania; a name the king would give it in honour of my father. I chose New Wales, being, as it is, a pretty hilly country, but Penn being Welsh for a head,...as Penn in Buckinghamshire, the highest land in England, (they) called this Pennsylvania..." Penn maintained afterward that the province's name meant simply, the "high or head woodlands," and he tried to downplay his role in the naming. "I much opposed it," he said. "And went to the king to have it struck out and altered, he said it was past...nor could 20 guineas move the under secretary to vary the name..."

Penn's reference to the "head woodlands" comes from a combination of two words from two different languages. *Penn* is an old Celtic term, meaning "a head" or "a headland," and *sylvania* is a Neo-Latin term meaning "relating to a forest," derived from the Latin feminine place name *sylva*, denoting "a wood forest."

The founder originally suggested *Sylvania* because of the forestland he found in the province, but the king prefixed it with *Penn,* much to his embarassment, as he says. In any case, Penn returned to his Quaker settlement soon afterwards, and no one ever tried to change the name to his suggestion of "New Wales."

THE NICKNAMES

Five nicknames have been used in reference to Pennsylvania, including the "Coal State," the "Oil State" and the "Steel State," the "Quaker State," and the "Keystone State." However, the currently established nickname remains the "Keystone State."

The "Coal State," the "Oil State" and the "Steel State" are all suggestive of the three largest commodities produced in Pennsylvania. The nickname "Quaker State" commemorates the fact that William Penn and his Society of Quakers were the first white settlers in this region, and from 1680, Penn was instrumental as a Quaker leader in attracting many more Friends to settle here.

The "Keystone State" is the more official sobriquet, probably because it relates to the first American government in Pennsylvania. The name is accounted for in two different ways.

The first is that when the government was moved to Washington, D.C. in 1790, in building the Pennsylvania Avenue Bridge over Rock Creek to the old city of Georgetown, the initials of the name of the State of Pennsylvania were put on the thirteenth, or key stone of the arch. Also, Pennsylvania was in a central position among the states when the first U.S. Constitution was adopted, and when Pennsylvania delegate John Morton became the thirteenth signer of the Declaration of Independence, he made the state "the keystone" in the federal arch. One of the earliest signs of Pennsylvania being known as the "Keystone State" is in the American Philosophical Society's halls in Philadelphia. There, a drawing of a stone arch representing the thirteen states show Pennsylvania in the keystone position.

STATE FLAG

Pennsylvania's state flag is composed of a blue field of the same color as the field in the U.S. flag, upon which is embroidered the state coat of arms.

The first flag bearing the coat of arms was authorized by the general assembly in 1799 and in 1871 Governor Curtin procured regimental flags bearing the arms of the Commonwealth. During the Civil War, many Pennsylvanian regiments carried flags modeled after the U.S. flag, but placed the state's coat of arms on the blue field in the place of the stars.

Introduction

This official description of the state flag was approved on June 13, 1907: "The flag...shal be blue,... and of the following dimensions and design; to wit, the length, or height of the staff to be nine feet, the fly of said flag to be six feet two inches, and to be four feet six inches on the staff; in the center of the flag there shall be embroidered in silk the same on both sides of the flag the coat of arms of the Commonwealth of Pennsylvania in proportionate size; the edges to be trimmed with knotted fringe of yellow silk, two and one-half inches wide..."

STATE MOTTO

Pennsylvania's State Motto, "Virtue, Liberty, and Independence," is specified in the original description of the obverse of the seal as being inscribed on a streamer held in the eagle's beak. It does not appear on the present seal, however. "Virtue" is a tradition of Pennsylvania's, dating from the time when the province passed out of the hands of the profligate Charles II of England into the possession of the great humanitarian William Penn. Pennsylvania has always been active in the struggle for freedom, hence the motto "liberty and independence."

STATE SEAL

The Pennsylvania state seal has two faces: the obverse, which has the more familiar face and the one most referred to as the "state seal;" and the reverse, or counter-seal, which is used less frequently.

When the Commonwealth was still a province of England, its seals were those of the Penn family. In 1776, at the state constitutional convention, the state seal was directed to be used by "all state commissions." By 1778, a seal similar to the present one was in use, and thirteen years later the general assembly gave it legal recognition. The official description of the seal was adopted in 1809.

The obverse of the seal shows a shield upon which are displayed a sailing ship, a plough and three sheaves of wheat. To the left of the shield is a stalk of Indian corn, and to the right, an olive branch. "And on the wreath of its colours a bald eagle—proper, perched, wings extended for the crest," according to the 1809 rules. Encircling the design is the inscription: "Seal of the State of Pennsylvania."

The reverse of the seal shows a woman representing Liberty trampling a lion representing Tyranny. The woman holds a wand topped by a liberty cap, another traditional symbol of freedom. This design is encircled with "Both Can't Survive," meaning Liberty and Tyranny.

Although the seal was modified by the introduction of scrollwork to the bottom of the circular seal in 1868, the essential symbols of the Commonwealth remained.

OTHER SYMBOLS

Two new symbols were added to the Commonwealth of Pennsylvania's roster in 1982. Milk is the state beverage as enacted by the general assembly on April 29, 1982 and the Pengift Crownvetch is the state beautification and conservation plant as enacted June 17, 1982.

Introduction

THE CAPITOL

An Act of April 14, 1897, supplemented by the Act of July 18, 1901, authorized the erection of the present building, which was rapidly constructed and dedicated by President Theodore Roosevelt on October 4, 1906.

The architect, commissioned in 1902, was Joseph M. Huston of Philadelphia. Designed in the classic style adopted from the architecture of the Italian Renaissance, the Capitol is 520 feet long and 254 feet wide. It covers 13 acres of ground and within its one-half mile circumference are 475 rooms. The exterior is of Vermont slate and rises five floors above the main floor. Above the center wing is a magnificent green dome of fine proportion, rising to a height of 272 feet.

Throughout the interior, the Capitol is furnished in marble, mahogany, bronze and tiling and adorned with appropriate decorations and by mural paintings by such well-known artists as Violet Oakley (see **Biographies** section). State records give the amount of over $10 million as the cost of the Capitol building, exclusive of furnishings.

Barnard group of statuary

Flanking the sides of the front entrance, facing west, are two heroic groups of statuary by the Pennsylvania-born sculptor George Grey Barnard. To the right as one faces this entrance is a group of men and women in attitudes representing the spiritual burdens carried by humans. the group to the left represents "work" and "brotherhood."

Bronze doors

At the center of the entrance are huge bronze doors, enriched with sculptured relief. These doors depict historic events in the state's life and recall Ghiberti's doors in the Baptistry at Florence, Italy. The leaves of this central door weigh one ton each and were cast in one piece.

Rotunda

The size and immense space within the Rotunda below the dome, the sweep of the grand staircase, the rich ornamentation of the walls and ceiling, all add to the monumental and inspiring effect of this focal point of the government of the Commonwealth.

Appropriately placed around this great rotunda, just under the main cornice, are the famous words of William Penn which outline his hopes for the new experiment in democratic government he was founding.

"There may be room there for such a Holy Experiment, for the nations want a precedent. And my God will make it the seed of a nation, that an example may be set up to the nations, that we may do the thing that is truly wise and just."

In the recessed arches and circular panels are paintings by the Pennsylvania artist, Edwin Austin Abbey, which commemorate the spiritual, intellectual and economic advances of the Commonwealth.

War record

Around the rotunda are six glass cases containing flags carried by Pennsylvania soldiers in the Civil and Spanish-American wars an an Honor Roll listing state employees in World War II.

The main corridor

Extending to the north and south are wide corridors. In the south corridor, to the right as one faces the staircase, are mural paintings by W.B. Van Ingen, a noted Pennsylvania artist, which represent various phases of the religious influences that are a part of Pennsylvania's history. Carved on the gilded capitals along these corridors are heads which represent outstanding individuals of the many nationalities that have contributed to the growth of Pennsylvania.

The senate chamber

North of the rotunda, off the second floor balcony, is the Senate Chamber, which is richly furnished and conveys a feeling of quiet dignity. In this room are paintings by Violet Oakley, one of Pennsylvania's most outstanding artists and a member of the Brandywine School of Artists. The paintings in front and to the left of the central niche represent "The Creation of the Union," and portray Washington and his troops marching through Philadelphia on their way to the Brandywine in 1777, and

Introduction

Washington presiding over the Constitutional Convention, Independence Hall, Philadelphia, in 1787.

To the right are paintings representing "The Preservation of the Union," which depict general Meade and his troops in camp before Gettysburg, 1863, and President Lincoln at the dedication of the National Cemetery at Gettysburg, 1863. In the panel above is represented Wiulliam Penn's vision of "International Understanding."

At the rear of the room are two other paintings by Violet Oakley, representing two old Quaker legends: one, the Open Latch String, and the other the Friend who purchased and set free a boatload of slaves. Just below the ceiling are circular stained glass windows by W.B. Van Ingen, symbolizing subjects such as Weaving, Temperance, Glass Blowing, Peace, Railroads, Militia, Legislature, History, Foundries and Architecture.

The house of representatives chamber

South of the rotunda, of the second floor balcony, is the richly decorated Chamber of the House of Representatives. This room is ornamented with a wealth of architectural detail and with stained glass windows and paintings.

The windows, by W.B. Van Ingen, depict outstanding Pennsylvania activities. The paintings in this room are by Edwin Austin Abbey. The largest of these paintings is the "Apotheosis," directly above the Speaker's platform, which portrays those prominent in the commonwealth's early history. To the left is a picture of "Penn's Treaty With the Indians," while to the right is shown the "Reading of the Declaration of Independence" at Independence Hall. To the rear of the chamber between the two entrances, is Abbey's picture of "Valley Forge," showing Baron Von Steuben instructig recruits. In the circular panel in the ceiling of the House is "The Passage of the Hours," another striking example of Abbey's symbolic art.

The appellate court room

This room on the fourth floor is dedicated to the use of the Supreme court and the Superior Court. It is approached by a corridor extending east from the rotunda. In this room of quiet dignity are displayed sixteen panels by Violet Oakley, portraying the evolution of law through the ages.

The governor's suite

This suite of richly furnished rooms is on the second floor of the south wing. The public reception room, paneled in English crotched oak, is enhanced by a series of mural paintings by Violet Oakley. These paintings portray events in the history of religious liberty in England and in the rise of the society of Friends. In addition, they show dramatic moments in the life of William Penn, culminating with his arrival in America on the ship *Welcome.*

The lieutenant governor's suite

In the front of the building and off the second floor balcony, over the main entrance, is the lieutenant governor's suite. The public reception room is of considerable interest because of its wainscoting of mahogany and the decorative leather surfacing the walls.

Capital group

Long ago it became apparent that ground was needed for a proper setting of the Capitol as well as additional buildings. The original park, a four-acre grant from John Harris, was increased to fifteen acres by 1873 at a cost of $36,400. Between the years of 1912-1919, the park area was enlarged to 45 acres through the purchase of the area included between the Capitol and the railroad and between Walnut Street and North Street. This area included 537 properties and with the removal of the buildings was acquired at a cost of over $2 million.

In 1916 architect Arnold W. Brunner and landscape architect Warren H. Manning were commissioned to prepare comprehensive plans for the future development of this area.

In 1941, surveys and studies were made for the acquisition of more property to the north, to provide space and a setting for additional buildings necessary to an expanded sphere of state services.

In 1943, the general assembly established a Capitol Park Extension Commission to examine and approve all acquisition proceedings involved in purchasing the north of the Capitol to Forster Street between Third and the railroad. The former Department of Property and Supplies was directed to acquire this property and $3 million was appropriated for this purpose. In 1945, an additional $6 million was allocated to acquire more land for the Capitol complex. Plans for the new State Archives and Museum Building as a memorial to William Penn were begun.

Sources: *The Pennsylvania Manual*, volume 105; *State names, Flags, Seals, Songs, Birds, Flowers, And Other Symbols*, by George E. Shankle (1938); and Gail Ackley, chief of Publications Planning, Editing and Assistance Division, Commonwealth of Pennsylvania.

•**AARONSBURG**, Village; Centre County; Pop. 500; Area Code 814; Zip Code 16820; Elev. 1200'; 30 m. NW of Lewisburg in central Pennsylvania; settled in 1775; named for *Aaron Levy*, who founded the town in 1786.

•**ABBOTTSTOWN**, Borough; Adams County; Pop. 689; Area Code 717; Zip Code 17301; Elev. 544'; S Pennsylvania; on Beaver Creek, was formerly a cigar manufacturing center.

Community Event - Indian Summer Bluegrass and Fiddlers Festival, Annual, September

•**ABERDEEN**, Unincorporated Village; Lackawanna County; Pop. 40; Area Code 717; Zip Code 18444; part of Madison township in NE Pennsylvania.

•**ABINGTON**, Township; Montgomery County; Pop. 59,084; Area Code 215; Zip Code 19001; Elev. 350'; SE Pennsylvania; Founded in 1714, when the Abington Presbyterian Church was built.

•**ACADEMY CORNERS**, Village; Tioga County; Pop. 50; Area Code 717; Zip Code 16929; 5 m. S of New York State Line in N central Pennsylvania; named for old Union Academy, which was established in this region.

•**ACCOMAC**, Village; York County; Pop. 50; Area Code 717; Zip Code 17406; S Pennsylvania.

•**ACKERMANVILLE**, Village; Northampton County; Pop. 350; Area Code 717; Zip Code 18010; Elev. 500'; 10 m. N of Easton in E central Pennsylvania.

1

•**ACME**, Village; Westmoreland County; Pop. 300; Area Code 814; Zip Code 15610; Elev. 1,920'; near Mount Pleasant in SE central Pennsylvania.

•**ACMETONIA**, Village; Allegheny County; Pop. 1,200; Area Code 412; Zip Code 15024; located near Pittsburgh in W Pennsylvania.

•**ACOSTA**, Village; Somerset County; Pop. 500; Area Code 717; Zip Code 15520; Elev. 1,880'; S Pennsylvania.

•**ADAH** (alt. ANTRAM), Village; Fayette County; Pop. 600; Area Code 412; Zip Code 15410; Elev. 920'; SW Pennsylvania.

•**ADAMS COUNTY**, County; S Pennsylvania; Area 526 sq. m.; Pop. 56,937; Seat Gettysburg; Established January 12, 1800; Named for *John Adams*, President of the United States.

Known as the place "where the apple is king," Adams County is a rich agricultural region. *President Adams* is said to have passed through the area on his way to the new capitol in Washington.

On January 22, 1800, after ten years of agitation, the western part of York County was erected into the new county of Adams. The name of Adams County seems to have special appropriateness from the fact that twenty-two years before, when the territory of the new county was yet a part of York County, *John Adams*, the Massachusetts statesman, lived and labored at York for six weeks as one of the leaders of the Continental Congress, which met there on September 30, 1777.

The surname Adams is derived from the Hebrew personal name Adam, which literally means "red earth."

•**ADAMSBURG**, Borough; Westmoreland County; Pop. 236; Area Code 417; Zip Code 15611; Elev. 1,200'; near Jeannette in SW Pennsylvania; named for *President John Adams*.

•**ADAMS DALE**, Village; Schuylkill County; Pop. 160; Area Code 717; Zip Code 17972; near Schuylkill Haven in E central Pennsylvania.

•**ADAMS HILL**, Village; Westmoreland County; Pop. 120; Area Code 412; Zip Code 15642; near E Pittsburgh in SW Pennsylvania.

•**ADAMSTOWN**, Borough; Berks and Lancaster Counties; Pop. 1,119; Area Code 717; Zip Code 19501; Elev. 500'; SE Pennsylvania. Adamstown has attracted a number of factories because the water that gushes from the base of a sandstone hillside here is so pure that it prolongs the life of their boilers. *William Bird*, an ironmaster, obtained a patent for 356 acres here in 1739; Adams Mill was included in the patent, but insufficient ore caused the abandonment of the mill.

•**ADAMSVILLE**, Village; Crawford County; Pop. 150; Area Code 814; Zip Code 16110; Elev. 1,040'; 15 m. SW of Meadville in NW Pennsylvania.

•**ADDISON**, Borough; Somerset County; Pop. 259; Area Code 814; Zip Code 15411; Elev. 2,026'; near Maryland state line and Youghiogheny Reservoir in S Pennsylvania; former toll house here was built for the National Road; mountainous farming region.

•**ADELAIDE**, Village; Fayette County; Pop. 150; Area Code 412; Zip Code 15425; near Connellsville in SW Pennsylvania.

•**ADMIRE**, Village; York County; Pop. 50; Area Code 717; Zip Code 17364; 10 m. W of York in SSE Pennsylvania.

•**ADRIAN**, Village; Armstrong County; Pop. 150; Area Code 412; Zip Code 16210; Elev. 1,080'; 10 m. N of Kittanning in W central Pennsylvania.

•**AIKEN**, Village; McKean County; Pop. 125; Area Code 814; Zip Code 16744; near Bradford in N central Pennsylvania.

•**AIRVILLE**, Village; York County; Pop. 85; Area Code 717; Zip Code 17302; Elev. 780'; 20 m. SW of Lancaster in SE Pennsylvania; is located near the Susquehanna River.

•**AKELEY**, Village; Warren County; Pop. 70; Area Code 813; Zip Code 16345; on Conewango Creek near New York state line in NW Pennsylvania.

•**AKRON**, Borough; Lancaster County; Pop. 3,471; Area Code 717; Zip Code 17501; Elev. 400'; SE Pennsylvania; was settled by Germans in the 1800s and was incorporated as a borough n 1884.

•**ALBA**, Borough; Bradford County; Pop. 222; Area Code 717; Zip Code 16910; Elev. 1,340'; N Pennsylvania.

•**ALBANY**, Village; Berks County; Pop. 1,109; Area Code 215; Zip Code 19529; SE Pennsylvania; named for *James II* whose Scottish title was Duke of Albany.

•**ALBERTS CORNERS**, Village; Luzerne County; Pop. 60; Area Code 717; Zip Code 18707; near Wilkes-Barre in NE central Pennsylvania.

•**ALBION**, Borough; Erie County; Pop. 1,818; Area Code 814; Zip Code 16401; Elev. 904'; NW Pennsylvania; was settled in 1815. Its early growth was assured when it became a station on the Erie Extension Canal. First known as Jackson Cross Roads.

> *Agriculture* - Varied farming
> *Industry/Mfg.* - Machine shop

•**ALBION**, Village; Jefferson County; Pop. 100; Area Code 814; Zip Code 15767; near Punxsutawney in W central Pennsylvania.

•**ALBRIGHTSVILLE**, Village; Carbon County; Pop. 150; Area Code 717; Zip Code 18210; Elev. 1,600'; on Muddy Run; approx. 15 m. N of Jim Thorpe in central Pennsylvania.

•**ALBURTIS**, Borough; Lehigh County; Pop. 1,428; Area Code 215; Zip Code 18011; Elev. 440'; near Allentown in E Pennsylvania.

•**ALDAN**, Borough; Delaware County; Pop. 4,671; Area Code 215; Elev. 120'; suburb of Chester in SE Pennsylvania.

•**ALDEN,** Village; Suzerne County; Pop. 800; Area Code 717; Zip Code 18634; E central Pennsylvania; suburb of Nanticoke and Wilkes-Barre.

•**ALDENVILLE,** Village; Wayne County; Pop. 50; Area Code 717; Zip Code 18401; Elev. 1,220'; on White Oak Pond near Honesdale in NE Pennsylvania.

•**ALDOVIN,** Village; Wyoming County; Pop. 100; Area Code 717; Zip Code 18657; 10 m. N of Tunkhannock in NE Pennsylvania near Lake Carey.

•**ALEXANDRIA,** Borough; Huntingdon County; Pop. 435; Area Code 717; Zip Code 16611; Elev. 700'; on Juniata River's Frankstown branch; in Appalachian Mountains and near Huntington in S central Pennsylvania.

•**ALFARATA,** Village; Mifflin County; Pop. 150; Area Code 717; Zip Code 16611; Elev. 700'; suburb of Lewiston on Juniata River in S central Pennsylvania; named for "Alfrata, the Maid of Juniata," heroine of a local folk song sung by *Mrs. Maria Dix Sullivan* :

> "Wild roves an Indian Girl-
> Bright Alfarata-
> Where sweep the waters of
> The blue Juniata.
> Swift as an antelope, through
> The forest going;
> Bright are her jetty locks,
> In wavy tresses flowing..."

•**ALFORD,** Village; Susquehanna County; Pop. 50; Area Code 717; Zip Code 18826; NE Pennsylvania.

•**ALICIA,** Village; Fayette County; Pop. 50; Area Code 412; Zip Code 15417; on Manongahela River near Brownsville in SW Pennsylvania.

•**ALINDA,** Village; Perry County; Pop. 50; Area Code 717; Zip Code 17040; near New Bloomfield and Harrisburg area.

•**ALIQUIPPA**, Borough; Beaver County; Pop. 17,094; Area Code 412; Zip Code 15001; Elev. 725'; W Pennsylvania. Named for an Iroquois Indian Queen, *Aliquippa*, who is said to have lived on the site of McKeesport in the 1750s. The name may mean "hat" in Iroquoian. *Aliquippa* was called "Queen of the Delaware", although she was probably Mohawk.
George Washington's Journal records a visit with the Queen when he presented her with a bottle of rum.

> *Agriculture* - Fruit, cattle farming
> *Industry/Mfg.* - Cement products, steel, dairy products
> *Chamber of Commerce* - PO Box 708

•**ALLANDALE**, Village; Cumberland County; Pop. 900; Area Code 717; Zip Code 17011; Central Pennsylvania; suburb of Camp Hill and Harrisburg.

•**ALLEGHENY**, Village; Allegheny County; Pop. 650; Area Code 412; Zip Code 15076; W central Pennsylvania; unincorporated suburb of Pittsburgh.

•**ALLEGHENY COUNTY**, County; SW Pennsylvania; Area 728 sq. m.; Pop. 1,605,133; Seat Pittsburgh; Established September 24, 1788; named for river, which was named for Allegiwi Indian tribe; Delaware word Oolikhanne meant "the best river."
County is heavily industrial, with steel and coal related manufactures important.

•**ALLEGHENY MOUNTAINS**, Mountain Range, W central Pennsylvania; Extends SW to NE, W of and parallel to the Blue Ridge Mountains. Highest point is Mt. Davis in Somerset County, at 3,213 feet.
The mountain range was named for the Allegiwi Indian tribe which once lived along its ridges and valleys. The name may have meant "people of the cave country.

•**ALLEGHENY RIVER**, River, Pennsylvania and New York; Flows NW and S 325 m. from source in Potter County, Pennsylvania, into southern New York, and then down through central and W Pennsylvania. Joins Monongahela River at Pittsburgh, becoming the source of the Ohio

River. Kinzua Dam in Warren County, Pennsylvania forms Allegheny Reservoir.
This wide and deep river was named for the Allegiwi Indians, or "cave-people" who once lived along the river banks and in the Allegheny Mountains. In 1754, Fort Trent was built at the confluence of the Monongahela and Allegheny Rivers; it was renamed Fort Duquesne two months later when the French took over. On this site, which eventually was gained by Americans, Pittsburgh was built.

•ALLEGHENYVILLE, Village; Berks County; Pop. 50; Area Code 215; Zip Code 19540; E Pennsylvania; suburb of Reading.

•ALLEMANS, Village; Clearfield County; Pop. 70; Area Code 814; Zip Code 16639; Elev. 1,778'; Central Pennsylvania.

•ALLEN, Village; Cumberland County; Pop. 400; Area Code 717; Zip Code 17001; Elev. 510'; near Harrisburg in S central Pennsylvania.

•ALLEN, Township; Northampton County; Pop. 1,856; Area Code 717; Zip Code 18067; named for *William Allen*, who was Chief Justice of Pennsylvania (1750-74) and received 3,000 acres here in 1748. He was related to the *Penns* by marriage.

•ALLENPORT, Borough; Washington County; Pop. 735; Area Code 412; Zip Code 15412; SW Pennsylvania.

•ALLEN'S CREST, Village; Lehigh County; Pop. 300; Area Code 717; Zip Code 18052; unincorporated suburb of Allentown.

•ALLENSVILLE, Village; Mifflin County; Pop. 350; Area Code 717; Zip Code 17002; Elev. 98'; 10 m. NE of Huntington in S central Pennsylvania.

•ALLENTOWN, City; Seat of Lehigh County; Pop. 103,758; Area Code 215; Zip Code 181 + zone; Elev. 364'; near Bethlehem and Easton in E Pennsylvania; incorporated as a borough in 1811 and as a city in 1867.

Originally known as Northampton Town, the city was first settled by German immigrants in the 1720s. *William Allen*, a son-in-law of *Alexander Hamilton*, moved here in 1735 when he was given a large tract of land by the *Penn* family. In the 1750s, Allen erected a hunting and fishing lodge here, but the town was not planned until 1762. During the Revolution, American arms and supplies were manufactured here. In 1777, the British began melting down Philadelphia's church bells in order to make more ammunition. The nation's Executive Council decided to send the Liberty Bell to the county church of Zion in Northampton Town for safekeeping. When Philadelphia was returned to the Americans, the Liberty Bell was returned to its original location; however, a Liberty Bell Shrine was erected at Zion church in 1958, with a full size replica of the bell.

In 1829, the Lehigh canal was built through town to Allentown in honor of *William Allen*. The mid to late nineteenth century was a time of booming industry; iron works, cement mills, and silk factories were important. Today's industries include electronic equipment, textiles, machine tools, and trucks.

POINTS OF INTEREST

ALLENTOWN ART MUSEUM- European and American paintings from 18th-20th century in permanent collections; changing exhibits.

LEHIGH COUNTY MUSEUM- Local history displays, including Indian artifacts.

SOLDIERS AND SAILORS MONUMENT- Monument to Civil War veterans.

TREXLER-LEHIGH COUNTY GAME PRESERVE- Herds of bison, deer, elk and other animals roam over 1,700 acres; 25-acre children's zoo.

TREXLER MEMORIAL PARK- Contains gardens, trout nursery, picnic areas; band concerts.

TROUT HALL- Oldest home in the city (1770), belonged to *Willam Allen's* son *James Allen*. Period rooms and museum.

ZION'S REFORMED CHURCH- The *Liberty Bell* was hidden in the church basement in 1777; the church now houses a full-size replica of the bell and historical and art exhibits.

8

Industry/Mfg. - Varied manufacturing, trade
and services.
Higher Education -
Muhlenberg College
United Wesleyan College
Cedar Crest College
Daily Newspaper - The Chronicle, 6th &
Linden Streets
Chamber of Commerce - PO Box 1229
Community Events -
Colonial Craft Day, Annual, June
Festival of the Colonies Bands Competition,
Annual, June

•**ALLISON**, Village; Fayette County; Pop. 1,040; Area Code 412; Zip Code 15413; Elev. 1,060'; SW Pennsylvania.

•**ALLISON HEIGHTS**, Village; Fayette County; Pop. 100; Area Code 412; Zip Code 15413; Elev. 1,060'; SW Pennsylvania; suburb of Allison.

•**ALLISON PARK**, Borough; Allegheny County; Pop. 5,600; Area Code 412; Zip Code 15101; Elev. 861'; W Pennsylvania; suburb of Pittsburgh.

•**ALMEDIA**, Village; Columbia County; Pop. 945; Area Code 717; Zip Code 17815; E central Pennsylvania.

•**ALMONT**, Village; Bucks County; Pop. 100; Area Code 215; Zip Code 18960; SE Pennsylvania.

•**ALSACE MANOR**, Village; Berks County; Pop. 300; Area Code 215; Zip Code 19560; near Reading in SE Pennsylvania.

•**ALTAMONT**, Village; Schuylkill County; Pop. 450; Area Code 717; Zip Code 17931; near Mahoney City in E central Pennsylvania.

•**ALTOONA**, City; Blair County; Pop. 57,078; Area Code 814; Zip Code 166 plus zone; Elev. 1,171'; S central Pennsylvania.

9

POINTS OF INTEREST

BAKER MANSION MUSEUM- Mid-19th century Greek Revival home of ironmaster; now houses Blair County Historical society. Historical exhibits.
MISHLER THEATER- Built in 1906 for *I.E. Mishler*, who presented many star performers, including *W.C. Fields, Sarah Bernhardt, Anna Pavlova* and *Rachmaninoff*. Example of extravagance in early-20th C. theater design. Beaux Arts Classicism.

•**ALUM BANK (alt. PLEASANTVILLE)**, Village; Bedford County; Pop. 280; Area Code 814; Elev. 1,240'; on Juniata River in S Pennsylvania; named for pure alum deposits found here.

•**ALUTA**, Village; Northampton County; Pop. 700; Area Code 717; Zip Code 18064; E Pennsylvania.

•**ALVERDA**, Village; Indiana County; Pop. 700; Area Code 814; Zip Code 15710; Elev. 1,917'; 25 m. N of Johnstown in W central Pennsylvania; name means "all green."

•**ALVERTON**, Village; Westmoreland County; Pop. 400; Area Code 814; Zip Code 15612; Elev. 1,100'; W central Pennsylvania.

•**AMBLER**, Borough; Montgomery County; Pop. 6,628; Area Code 215; Zip Code 19002; SE Pennsylvania.

Named for a prominent family of early settlers one of which (*Joseph Amber*) settled here in 1723. *William Harmer* established a mill here in 1728 and the town achieved a reputation as a grain and milling center. During *General Washington's* Valley Forge encampment, a road was built to Ambler in order to connect it with Philadelphia.

The Ambler Homestead still stands here, the main part was constructed eight years before *Joseph Ambler* arrived here.

Higher Education - Temple University
Chamber of Commerce - 12 Cavalier Dr.

•**AMBRIDGE**, Borough; Beaver County; Pop. 9,575; Area Code 412; Zip Code 15003; Elev. 775'; W Pennsylvania.

Ambridge was named for the American Bridge Company, which bought the community called Harmony Society here in 1901. In 1903, the company opened a railroad station here to deal with its increasing freight, and it was named Ambridge at the suggestion of railroad traffic manager *Charles S. Besterling.* The city now encompasses the old village Economy, where the old rail station had been, and the town bought by the Ambridge Land Company, a corporation independent of the bridge manufacturers.

Economy had been the earlier settlement on this site. The Harmony Society, a Christian communal group from Germany, established the village in 1825 under the leadership of *Frederick Reichert.* Throughout the Harmony Society's e xistence (1805-1906), members retained Old World dress and practiced celibacy, which eventually restricted numerical growth and later resulted in a breakup of the sect. However, several reminders of this group remain here, including the great House, Church and Music Hall as well as several individual houses.

Today, the city is not the major industrial center it was during the early 20th century.

POINT OF INTEREST

OLD ECONOMY- 19th century 17-building disitrict, original buildings of third village constructed for members of the *Harmony Society*, a communitarian theocracy organized in 1805. Musuem.

Chamber of Commerce - 292 Fifth St.
Community Events -
    Kunstfest, Annual, June
    Nationality Days, Annual, May

•**AMBRIDGE HEIGHTS**, Village; Beaver County; Pop. 2,000; Area Code 412; Zip Code 15003; Elev. 751'; suburb of Ambridge in Pittsburgh area, in W Pennsylvania.

•**AMEND**, Village; Fayette County; Pop. 300; Area Code 412; Zip Code 15401; near Uniontown in SW Pennsylvania.

•**AMESVILLE**, Village; Clearfield County; Pop. 50; Area Code 814; Zip Code 16651; near Phillipsburg in central Pennsylvania.

•**AMITY**, Village; Washington County; Pop. 170; Area Code 412; Zip Code 15311; Elev. 1,204'; 10 m. S of Washington in SW Pennsylvania.

Laid out in 1797, the village grew up around Amity Presbyterian Church; named for "the religious and social amity which the people decided to foster."

Amity was founded in 1797, and grew up around the Amity Presbyterian Church. In the Amity Cemetery is the grave of *Solomon Spaulding*, wandering evangelist and antiquary who spent his declining years writing *The Manuscript Found*, which many have declared to be the basis of the *Book of Mormon*, published in 1830, on which the Mormon faith is founded. *Spaulding* died in Amity in 1816. *Spaulding* advanced the theory that the American Indians were descended from the Lost Tribes of Israel, supporting his contention with Biblical and mythological evidence. The *Book of Mormom* similarly accounts for the Indians, duplicating names and historical matter contained in *The Manuscript Found*. *Sidney Rigdon*, a one-time Baptist minister, and *Joseph Smith*, the mystic, collaborated in the formulation of Mormonism. *Rigdon* was a part-time employee of a Pittsburgh printer to whom *Spaulding* submitted his manuscript. The printer held it for some time before deciding against publication, and it is possible that *Rigdon* copied the manuscript. After *Spaulding's* death his manuscript found its way to his brother-in-law, *W.H. Sabine*, of Onondaga Valley, New York, where *Smith* worked for a time. Some contend that *Smith* saw the manuscript there, but *Smith* himself declared that an angel in a vision directed him to the Hill Cumorah and there he found gold plates bearing hieroglyphics. Translated, these became the *Book of Mormon*.

Community Event - Agricultural Americana Folk Festival, Annual, August

•**AMSBRY**, Village; Cambria County; Pop. 100; Area Code 814; Zip Code 16641; W central Pennsylvania.

•**AMWELL**, Township; Washington County; Pop. 3,401; Area Code 412; SW Pennsylvania.

•**ANALOMINK**, Village; Monroe County; Pop. 150; Area Code 717; Zip Code 18320; Elev. 530'; E Pennsylvania.

•**ANCIENT OAKS**, Village; Lehigh County; Pop. 1,800; Area Code 717; Zip Code 18062; E central Pennsylvania; suburb of Allentown.

•**ANDALUSIA**, City; Bucks County; Pop. 4,500; Area Code 215; Zip Code 19020; Elev. 37'; near Philadelphia in SE Pennsylvania; on Delaware River; named for 95 acre estate of *Charles T. Biddle* which he named for Southern region of Spain. *John Craig*, a Philadelphia merchant, bought land and built the older part of this house in 1794, *Biddle* was a descendant of *Craig*. Formerly, this was the site of a Neshaminy Indian village. Nearby is the Red Lion Inn (1730), one of the few Colonial inns left in the state.

•**ANDREAS**, Village; Schuylkill County; Pop. 110; Area Code 717; Zip Code 18211; Elev. 591'; E central Pennsylvania.

•**ANDREWS PLAN**, Village; Beaver County; Pop. 350; Area Code 412; Zip Code 15001; W Pennsylvania.

•**ANGELS**, Village; Wayne County; Pop. 100; Area Code 717; Zip Code 18445; NE Pennsylvania.

•**ANITA**, Village; Jefferson County; Pop. 600; Area Code 814; Zip Code 15711; Elev. 1,500'; near Punsatavney in mountainous region in W central Pennsylvania.

•**ANNVILLE**, Elev. 420'; on Quitapahilla Creek, was formerly called Millerstown for *Abraham Miller*, who laid it out in 1762; but the name was changed, at Miller's suggestion, to honor his wife *Ann*.

Agriculture - Varied farming
Industry/Mfg. - Clothing, grain milling, quarrying
Higher Education - Lebanon Valley College

•**APOLLO**, Borough; Armstrong County; Pop. 2,212; Area Code 412; Zip Code 15613; Elev. 809'; W Pennsylvania; once known as Warren for an Indian trader who often stopped here, it was renamed in 1848 by *Dr. Robert McKisson*, physician, poet, and student of the classics.

> *Agriculture* - Varied farming
> *Industry/Mfg.* - Steel products, coal, gas

•**APPALACHIAN MOUNTAINS**, Mountain range, Eastern United States; extends from NE New York to central Alabama; includes several mountain ranges in Tennessee, Georgia, North Carolina, Virginia, West Virginia, Maryland, Pennsylvania, New York, and Vermont. Highest point is Mount Mitchell in W North Carolina.

•**APPLEWOLD**, Borough; Armstrong County; Pop. 395; Area Code 412; W Pennsylvania.

•**ARCHBALD**, Borough; Lackawanna County; Pop. 6,295; Area Code 717; Zip Code 18403; Elev. 919'; NE Pennsylvania.
    Archbald was called White Oak Run until 1846 when the Delaware and Hudson Canal Company began exploiting its coal deposits and named it for *James Archbald*, a company engineer. The coal-black Lackawanna River flows through the town between high artificial banks, and periodic floods add silt to heavy layers of grime.

> *Chamber of Commerce* - 522 Main St.

•**ARCHBALD POTHOLE**, a great glacial pothole, 38 feet deep and 42 feet at its greatest diameter, in a deserted spot amid ugly mining debris. In 1884 a blast set off by a miner filled his working chamber with rock. Each effort to remove the debris precipitated a new slide. Investigation at the surface revealed the pothole, which was then excavated. Glacial waterfalls cascading through crevices from the top of the ice sheet hollowed it out of solid rock. A thousand feet to the northeast is another pothole, believed to be larger, but never excavated.

•**ARCOLA**, Village; Montgomery County; Pop. 190; Area Code 215; Zip Code 19420; near Norristown in SE Pennsylvania.

•**ARDARA**, Village; Westmoreland County; Pop. 500; Area Code 412; Zip Code 15615; Elev. 900'; SW central Pennsylvania.

•**ARDMORE**, Village; Delaware and Montgomery Counties; Pop. 13,600; Area Code 215; Zip Code 19003; Elev. 360'; SE Pennsylvania; unincorporated suburb of Philadelphia.
   Originally called the Welsh Barony for settlers who arrived here shortly before *William Penn*. Today it is a wealthy residential section of the Philadelphia metropolitan area. Nearby is the old Merion Meetinghouse, built in the early days of Quaker settlement.

•**ARDSLEY**, Borough; Montgomery County; Pop. 4,800; Area Code 215; Zip Code 19038; SE Pennsylvania; suburb north of Philadelphia.

•**ARENDTSVILLE**, Borough; Adams County; Pop. 600; Area Code 717; Zip Code 17303; Elev. 711'; S Pennsylvania.

•**ARGENTINE**, Village; Butler County; Pop. 100; Area Code 814; Zip Code 16040; 50 m. N of Pittsburgh in W Pennsylvania.

•**ARISTES**, Village; Columbia County; Pop. 325; Area Code 717; Zip Code 17920; Elev. 1,640'; NE central Pennsylvania; near Shamokin in highland area.

•**ARMAGH**, Borough; Indiana County; Pop. 133; Area Code 412; Zip Code 15920; Elev. 1,520'; W central Pennsylvania; named for area in Ireland by Irish immigrants who settled here in 1792; name means "field on a hill" in Gaelic. Armagh was one of the first settlements in this section, was settled in 1792.

•**ARMBRUST**, Village; Westmoreland County; Pop. 300; Area Code 412; Zip Code 15616; Elev. 960'; W central Pennsylvania.

•**ARMSTRONG**, County; W Pennsylvania; Area 658 sq. m.; Pop. 75,590; Seat Kittanning; Established March 12, 1800; named for Revolutionary War *General John Armstrong* (1758-1843), whose army had destroyed a hostile Indian village at Kittanning in 1756, and later led forces at the battles of Brandywine and Germantown. County is cut through by Allegheny River and is mountainous.

•**ARMSTRONG**, Township, Indiana County; Pop. 1,867; Area Code 814; Zip Code 15774; W central Pennsylvania.

•**ARNOLD**, City; Westmoreland County; Pop. 6,853; Area Code 417; Zip Code 15068; SW Pennsylvania; surrounded by New Kinsington, this independent borough was named for *Andrew Arnold*, who originally owned the town. First settled in 1852, the borough was incorporated in 1896.

> *Industry/Mfg.* - Glass
> *Chamber of Commerce* - 1701 Ridge Ave.

•**ARNOLD CITY**, Village; Fayette County; Pop. 700; Area Code 412; Zip Code 15012; near Belle Vernon in SW Pennsylvania.

•**ARNOT**, Village; Tioga County; Pop. 300; Area Code 717; Zip Code 16911; Elev. 1,687'; near Tioga River in N Pennsylvania.

•**ARONA**, Borough; Westmoreland County; Pop. 446; Area Code 417; Zip Code 15617; Elev. 1,000'; SW Pennsylvania.

•**ASHFIELD**, Village; Carbon County; Pop. 200; Area Code 717; Zip Code 18212; Elev. 550'; E central Pennsylvania.

•**ASHLAND**, Village; Clearfield County; Pop. 100; Area Code 814; Zip Code 16666; Central Pennsylvania.

•**ASHLAND**, Borough; Schuylkill County; Pop. 4,737; Area Code 717; Zip Code 17921; Elev. 885'; E central Pennsylvania; in valley between Mahoney and Logan Mountains.

Named for *Henry Clay's* estate in Lexington, Kentucky by *Samuel Lewis* in 1847. *Clay*, the American statesman, was enjoying the height of his popularity at that time. Industries include mines, metals and clothing. The first land purchase was made in 1845, and two years later the town was laid out and mining began.

•**ASHLEY**, Borough; Luzerne County; Pop. 3,512; Area Code 717; Zip Code 18706; Elev. 643'; E Pennsylvania.

Town was known as Scrabbletown, Coalville, Skunktown, Peestone, Hightown, Newton, Hendricksburg, Nanticoke Junction and Alberts since it was settled in 1810. Current name was adopted in 1871 for a prominent family of coal operators including *Herfert Henry Ashley* of Wilkes-Barre. Railroad repair and coal mining center which has declined in business in recent years.

•**ASHVILLE**, Borough; Cambria County; Pop. 383; Area Code 814; Zip Code 16613; Elev. 1,680'; SW central Pennsylvania.

•**ASPERS**, Village; Adams County; Pop. 275; Area Code 717; Zip Code 17304; Elev. 651'; S Pennsylvania.

•**ASPINWALL**, Borough; Allegheny County; Pop. 3,284; Area Code 412; Zip Code 15215; Elev. 800'; SW Pennsylvania; founded in 1796 and named for the *Aspinwall* family, early landowners; on Allegheny River.

•**ASTON**, Borough & Township; Delaware County; Pop. 6,900 (Township 13,704); Area Code 215; Zip Code 19014; Elev. 200'; suburb of Philadelphia near Delaware state line and Delaware River.

•**ASYLUM**, Township; Bradford County; Pop. 843; Area Code 717; Towanda area.

Colony was originally established in 1794 for refugees of the French Revolution, promoted by *Robert Morris* and *John Nicholson*. The settlement failed, however after the city-bred Frenchmen were unable to live in the wilderness outpost. *Louis Phillipe*, later King of France, was an early visitor.

•**ATGLEN**, Borough; Chester County; Pop. 669; Area Code 215; Zip Code 19310; Elev. 504'; SE Pennsylvania.

•**ATHENS**, Borough; Bradford County; Pop. 3,662; Area Code 717; Zip Code 18810; Elev. 772'; N Pennsylvania.
Athens took the name of the township, founded in 1786, and named for the capital of Greece; probably because the ring of hills surrounding the city resembles the Greek metropolis. The site was originally a large Indian town called Tiogo, "meeting of the waters." Tioga Park Museum is nearby, where many Indian burial sites were found. *Col. Thomas Hartley* destroyed the town in 1778 in retaliation for Battle at Wyoming.

Chamber of Commerce - PO Box 255
Community Event - Stephen Foster Ice Cream
Social and Music Festival, Annual, July

•**ATHOL**, Village; Berks County; Zip Code 200; Area Code 215; Zip Code 19502; Elev. 280'; 45 m. N of Philadelphia in SE Pennsylvania.

•**ATLANTIC**, Village; Clearfield County; Pop. 100; Area Code 814; Zip Code 16651; Central Pennsylvania.

•**ATLANTIC**, Village; Crawford County; Pop. 175; Area Code 717; Zip Code 16111; Elev. 1,150'; NW Pennsylvania.

•**ATLAS**, Village; Northumberland County; Pop. 1,527; Area Code 717; Zip Code 17851; Elev. 1,160'; near Mt. Carmel and Kulpmont in E central Pennsylvania.

•**ATLASBURG**, Village; Washington County; Pop. 550; Area Code 412; Zip Code 15004; Elev. 1,120'; SW Pennsylvania.

•**ATWOOD**, Borough; Armstrong County; Pop. 107; Area Code 412; Elev. 1,240'; W Pennsylvania.

•**AUBURN**, Borough; Schuylkill County; Pop. 999; Area Code 717; Zip Code 17922; Elev. 500'; E central Pennsylvania.

•**AUDENREID**, Village; Carbon County; Pop. 180; Area Code 717; Zip Code 18201; near Hazleton in E central Pennsylvania.

•**AUDUBON**, Montgomery County; Pop. 4,400; Area Code 215; Zip Code 19407; Elev. 200'; SE Pennsylvania; unincorporated suburb of Norristown and Philadelphia.
　　Located on the Perkiomer Creek, this borough is nearby the former estate of *John James Audubon*, the ornithologist for whom it was named. Audubon inherited the estate from his father.

> **MILL GROVE**- Colonial house built in 1762, the home of *John James Audubon*, where he studied area wildlife. Located on 120-acre wildlife sancturary. Museum.

•**AULTMAN**, Village; Indiana County; Pop. 300; Area Code 814; Zip Code 15713; Elev. 1,120'; N central Pennsylvania.

•**AUSTIN**, Borough; Potter County; Pop. 740; Area Code 814; Zip Code 16720; Elev. 1,340'; N Pennsylvania; founded in 1886 by a lumber company.

•**AUSTINBURG**, Village; Tioga County; Pop. 100; Area Code 717; Zip Code 16928; N Pennsylvania.

•**AUSTINVILLE**, Village; Bradford County; Pop. 100; Area Code 717; Zip Code 16914; N Pennsylvania.

•**AVALON**, Borough; Allegheny County; Pop. 6,240; Area Code 412; Elev. 727'; SW Pennsylvania.
　　First settled in late 1700s by Irish trader *James Taylor*. Originally known as Birmingham for *Captain John Birmingham* who purchased land from *Taylor*. In 1874, it was incorporated as West Bellevue, and in 1894 the name was changed to Avalon, a Celtic word meaning "orchard," or "land of apples."

•**AVELLA**, Village; Washington County; Pop. 1,109; Area Code 412; Zip Code 15312; Elev. 960'; approx. 25 m. SW of Pittsburgh in W Pennsylvania.

Community Event - Nature Day, Annual, May

•**AVIS**, Borough; Clinton County; Pop. 1,718; Area Code 717; Zip Code 17721; Elev. 600'; Central Pennsylvania; named for *Avis Cochran*, daughter of one of the chief promoters of the town in the early 20th century.

•**AVOCA**, Borough; Luzerne County; Pop. 3,536; Area Code 717; Zip Code 18641; Elev. 660'; E Pennsylvania; at the junction of the Lackawanna and Wyoming Valleys, was originally named Pleasant Valley.

•**AVON**, Village; Lebanon County; Pop. 1,271; Area Code 717; Zip Code 17042; SE central Pennsylvania; suburb of Lebanon.

•**AVONDALE**, Borough; Chester County; Pop. 891; Area Code 215; Zip Code 19311; Elev. 227'; on White Clay Creek in SE Pennsylvania; in agricultural area; mainly producing mushrooms.

•**AVONMORE**, Borough; Westmoreland County; Pop. 1,234; Area Code 417; Zip Code 15618; Elev. 880'; SW Pennsylvania.

•**AXEMANN**, Village; Center County; Pop. 150; Area Code 814; Zip Code 16823; Elev. 900'; near Bellefonte in central Pennsylvania; named for *William and Harvey Mann*, axe manufacturers who settled here in 1828; site of Mann axe factory is at Logan Branch Creek where it empties into Spring Creek.

B

•**BACHMANVILLE**, Village; Dauphin County; Pop. 100; Area Code 717; Zip Code 17033; near Hershey in SE central Pennsylvania.

•**BADEN**, Borough; Beaver County; Pop. 5,318; Area Code 412; Zip Code 15005; Elev. 673'; on Ohio River, just N of Ambridge in W Pennsylvania; residential; incorporated as a borough 1868.

•**BAEDERWOOD**, Borough; Montgomery County; Pop. 1,300; Area Code 215; Zip Code 19046; residential suburb of Philadelphia.

•**BAGDAD**, Village; Westmoreland County; Pop. 80; Area Code 814; Zip Code 15656; W Pennsylvania.

•**BAGGALEY**, Village; Westmoreland County; Pop. 450; Area Code 814; Zip Code 15063; near Latrobe in W Pennsylvania.

•**BAIDLAND**, Village; Washington County; Pop. 800; Area Code 412; Zip Code 15063; W Pennsylvania.

•**BAINBRIDGE**, Village; Lancaster County; Pop. 650; Area Code 717; Zip Code 17502; Elev. 320'; on Susquehanna River in SE Pennsylvania; named for *Cmdr. William Bainbridge* in 1817.

•**BAIR**, Village; York County; Pop. 200; Area Code 717; Zip Code 17405; 10 m. W of York in S Pennsylvania.

•**BAIRDFORD**, Village; Allegheny County; Pop. 950; Area Code 412; Zip Code 15006; Elev. 900'; 15 m. NE of Pittsburgh in SE Pennsylvania.

•**BAKERS SUMMIT**, Village; Bedford County; Pop. 125; Area Code 814; Zip Code 16614; Elev. 1,440'; 20 m. S of Altoona in S Pennsylvania.

•**BAKERSTOWN**, Village; Allegheny County; Pop. 1,000; Area Code 412; Zip Code 15007; Elev. 1,107'; 20 m. NE of Pittsburgh in W Pennsylvania.

•**BAKERSVILLE**, Village; Somerset County; Pop. 200; Area Code 814; Zip Code 15501; 10 m. NW of Somerset in S Pennsylvania; Laurel Hill; near ski and camping areas.

•**BALA-CYNWYD**, Borough; Montgomery County; Pop. 8,600; Area Code 215; Zip Code 19004; Elev. 304'; SE Pennsylvania; NW suburb of Philadelphia.

•**BALD EAGLE**, Township; Clinton County; Pop. 1,282; named for Indian Chief who once lived here.

•**BALDWIN**, Borough; Allegheny County; Pop. 24,598; Area Code 412; SW Pennsylvania; S suburb of Pittsburgh; named for locomotive originator *Mathias Bladwin.*

•**BALLIETTSVILLE**, Town; Lehigh County; Pop. 320; Area Code 717; Zip Code 18037; near Allentown in E Pennsylvania.

•**BALLY**, Borough; Berks County; Pop. 1,051; Area Code 215; Zip Code 19503; Elev. 480'; SE Pennsylvania.
    Bally was laid out in 1742 on ground owned by the Society of Jesus, was later named for the *Reverend Augustin Bally, S.J.,* who ministered to the Roman Catholics in the surrounding territory between 1837 and 1882. Here in 1743 the *Reverend Theodore Schneider, S.J.,* built the Chapel of St. Paul, third Catholic church in Pennsylvania. The Church of the Blessed Sacrament, erected in 1827, stands on the site of the chapel.

PHILIP CHRISTMAN HOUSE- Mid-18th century house, typical of early German structures built into mound slopes.

•**BALSINGER**, Village; Fayette County; Pop. 100; Area Code 412; Zip Code 15484; near Uniontown in S Pennsylvania.

•**BAMFORD**, Village; Lancaster County; Pop. 80; Area Code 717; Zip Code 17538; SE Pennsylvania.

•**BANETOWN**, Village; Washington County; Pop. 80; Area Code 412; Zip Code 15301; SW Pennsylvania.

•**BANGOR**, Borough; Northampton County; Pop. 5,006; Area Code 215; Zip Code 18013; Elev. 514'; E Pennsylvania.

Bangor was founded in 1773 and named for a slate producing city in Wales, is the center of Pennsylvania's slate quarrying area. Huge slate piles mar the landscape throughout this area, which is said to have produced two thirds of all roof slate used in the United States.

Agriculture - Varied farming
Industry/Mfg. - Clothing, boxes, quarrying
Daily Newspaper - The News, 13-15 S. Main
Community Event - Plainfield Farmers Fair,
Annual, July

•**BANNERVILLE**, Village; Snyder County; Pop. 75; Area Code 717; Zip Code 17841; Central Pennsylvania.

•**BANNING**, Village; Fayette County; Pop. 200; Area Code 814; Zip Code 15428; 35 m. SE of Pittsburgh in SW Pennsylvania.

•**BARBOURS**, Village; Lycoming County; Pop. 100; Area Code 717; Zip Code 17701; N central suburb of Williamsport.

•**BARD**, Village; Bedford County; Pop. 60; Area Code 813; Zip Code 15534; S Pennsylvania.

•**BARESVILLE**, Village; York County; Pop. 1,700; Area Code 717; Zip Code 17331; near Hanover in S Pennsylvania.

•**BAREVILLE**, Village; Lancaster County; Pop. 800; Area Code 717; Zip Code 17540; NE of Lancaster in SE Pennsylvania.

•**BARKEYVILLE**, Borough; Venango County; Pop. 266; Area Code 814; Elev. 1,479'; NW Pennsylvania.

•**BARNES**, Village; Warren County; Pop. 200; Area Code 814; Zip Code 16347; near Sheffield in N Pennsylvania.

•**BARNESBORO**, Borough; Cambria County; Pop. 2,741; Area Code 814; Zip Code 15714; Elev. 1,446'; SW central Pennsylvania.

Thomas Barnes, a coal mine operator, laid out the town in 1891 after first coal was discovered. Shopping and business center for the surrounding countryside.

>*Agriculture* - Truck farming
>*Industry/Mfg.* - Clothing, soft drinks, dairy products, coal

•**BARNESVILLE**, Village; Schuylkill County; Pop. 200; Area Code 717; Zip Code 18214; Elev. 1,064'; E central Pennsylvania.

>*Community Events* -
>Bavarion Summer Festival, Annual, June-July
>International Wine and Cheese Festival, Annual, July-August

•**BARNSLEY**, Village; Chester County; Pop. 125; Area Code 215; Zip Code 19363; near Oxford in SE Pennsylvania.

•**BARREE**, Village; Huntingdon County; Pop. 150; Area Code 814; Zip Code 16615; Elev. 720'; S central Pennsylvania.

•**BARRET PLAN**, Village; Beaver County; Pop. 300; Area Code 412; Zip Code 15001; W Pennsylvania; suburb of Alliquippa.

•**BARRVILLE**, Village; Mifflin County; Pop. 100; Area Code 717; Zip Code 17084; in Stone Mountain range in central Pennsylvania.

•**BART**, Village and Township; Lancaster County; Pop. 250 (township, 1,838); Area Code 717; Zip Code 17503; Elev. 678'; 15 m. SE of Lancaster in SE Pennsylvania; named for the abbreviation of the title Baronet, for *Sir William Keith, Bart.*, provincial governor of Pennsylvania (1717-26).

•**BARTO**, Village; Berks County; Pop. 70; Area Code 215; Zip Code 19504; Elev. 460'; SE Pennsylvania.

•**BATH**, Borough; Northampton County; Pop. 1,952; Area Code 215; Zip Code 18014; E Pennsylvania.

Industry/Mfg. - Clothing, concrete products

•**BATH ADDITION**, Village; Bucks County; Pop. 800; Area Code 215; Zip Code 19007; SE Pennsylvania; suburb of Philadelphia included with Bristol.

•**BAUERSTOWN**, Village; Allegheny County; Pop. 2,700; Area Code 412; Zip Code 15209; W Pennsylvania; suburb of Pittsburgh.

•**BAUMGARTNER**, Village; Lancaster County; Pop. 75; Area Code 717; Zip Code 17584; SE Pennsylvania.

•**BAUMSTOWN**, Village; Berks County; Pop. 400; Area Code 215; Zip Code 19508; Elev. 206'; 48 m. NW of Philadelphia in SE central Pennsylvania; across Schuylkill River from Birdsboro; steel industry is important.

Community Event - Patriot Days, Annual, June

•**BAUSMAN**, Village; Lancaster County; Pop. 450; Area Code 717; Zip Code 17504; SE Pennsylvania.

•**BAXTER**, Village; Jefferson County; Pop. 75; Area Code 814; Zip Code 15829; W central Pennsylvania.

•**BEACH HAVEN**, Village; Luzerne County; Pop. 450; Area Code 717; Zip Code 18601; NE Pennsylvania.

•**BEACH LAKE**, Village; Wayne County; Pop. 240; Zip Code 18405; Elev. 1,300'; near Honesdale in NE Pennsylvania; resort town on Beach Lake.

•**BEALSVILLE**, Borough; Washington County; Pop. 588; Area Code 412; Zip Code 15313; Elev. 1,136'; SW Pennsylvania.

•**BEAR CREEK**, Village and Township; Luzerne County; Pop. 200 (township, 2,450); Area Code 717; Zip Code 18602; Elev. 1,670'; near Wilkes-Barre in NE Pennsylvania; on W bank of Bear Creek. Named for numerous bears in region when it was first settled; Bear Creek became a lumbering center after a sawmill was built in 1800. The creek forms the western boundary of the best Pocono hunting territory; deer is the biggest game.

•**BEAR LAKE**, Borough; Warren County; Pop. 249; Area Code 814; Zip Code 16402; Elev. 1,550'; NW Pennsylvania.

•**BEAR ROCKS**, Village; Fayette County; Pop. 500; Area Code 412; Zip Code 15610; in Chestnut Ridge region in SW Pennsylvania.

•**BEAR VALLEY**, Village; Northumberland County; Pop. 100; Area Code 717; Zip Code 17872; near Shamokin in central Pennsylvania.

•**BEARTOWN**, Village; Franklin County; Pop. 165; Area Code 717; Zip Code 17268; S Pennsylvania.

•**BEATTY**, Village; Westmoreland County; Pop. 100; Area Code 412; Zip Code 15650; SW Pennsylvania.

•**BEAUFORT FARMS**, Village; Dauphin County; Pop. 75; Area Code 717; Zip Code 17110; SE central Pennsylvania.

•**BEAVER**, Borough; Seat of Beaver County; Pop. 5,441; Area Code 412; Zip Code 15009; Elev. 723'; 25 m. NW of Pittsburgh in W Pennsylvania.
    Beaver was founded in 1778, occupies a high plateau along the Ohio River and is primarily residential, with broad streets, stately trees, and lawn-fronted houses.

26

The Quay House was the home of *Matthew S. Quay* (1833-1904). At and prior to the turn of the century the powerful Pennsylvania Repbulican machine was controlled by *Quay*, who got his start as a local politician after being admitted to the bar in 1854. He became one of the most powerful politicians of that era; in 1885 he was elected State treasurer by the largest vote ever given a candidate for the office up to that time. He died in Beaver during his 17th year as United States senator.

> *Industry/Mfg.* - Household appliances, electronics
> *Daily Newspaper* - The Beaver County Times, PO Box 400

•**BEAVER ACRES**, Village; Allegheny County; Pop. 400; Area Code 412; Zip Code 15136; W Pennsylvania; suburb of Pittsburgh-McKeesport.

•**BEAVER BROOK**, Village; Luzerne County; Pop. 375; Area Code 717; Zip Code 18201; NE Pennsylvania; incorporated with Hazleton.

•**BEAVER COUNTY**, One month after Centre County was created, eight new counties were formed in the western part of the state by the Act of March 12, 1800. One of these was Beaver County, taken from Washington and Allegheny, and named for the Big Beaver, or Creek, which was so called because of the great number of beavers once found on its banks and in its waters.

Beaver County, in its modern aspect, has been celebrated by no less a writer than *Rudyard Kipling*, who asks his reader to "imagine a rolling, wooded English landscape, with the softest of blue skies, dotted at three mile intervals with fat little, quiet little villages, or aggressive little manufacturing towns."

•**BEAVERDALE**, Village; Cambria County; Pop. 1,579; Area Code 814; Zip Code 15921; Elev. 1,929'; 80 m. W of Pittsburgh in W central Pennsylvania.

•**BEAVERDALE**, Village; Northumberland County; Pop. 60; Area Code 717; Zip Code 17851; E central Pennsylvania; incorporated with Mount Carmel.

•**BEAVER DAM**, Village; Erie County; Pop. 100; Area Code 814; Zip Code 16407; NW Pennsylvania.

•**BEAVER FALLS**, City; Beaver County; Pop. 12,525; Area Code 412; Zip Code 15010; Elev. 758'; 30 m. NW of Pittsburgh in W Pennsylvania; on W bank of Beaver River where it forms falls.

Laid out in 1806, the town was called Brighton by the *Constable brothers* of Brighton, England. However, after New Brighton was founded, the name was changed to Beaver Falls in 1866 by members of the Harmony Society. Incorporated, borough in 1868, city in 1930.

Seat of Geneva College (1880), founded by the Presbyterian Church, which had moved it here from Northwood, Ohio.

> *Agriculture* - Truck, cattle farming
> *Industry/Mfg.* - Chinaware, electronics,
>   cloth, coal, dairy products
> *Higher Education* - Geneva College
> *Daily Newspaper* - The News-Tribune, 715
>   Thirteenth Street
> *Chamber of Commerce* -1008 Seventh Ave., Room
>   106

•**BEAVER MEADOWS**, Borough; Carbon County; Pop. 1,078; Area Code 717; Zip Code 18216; Elev. 1,355'; near Hazelton in E Pennsylvania; named for nearby Beaver Creek; mining and silk industries important.

•**BEAVERSPRINGS**, Village; Snyder County; Pop. 725; Area Code 717; Zip Code 17812; Elev. 591'; near Beavertown in central Pennsylvania; settled in 1806, when iron ore mines began operations; Highland area.

•**BEAVER RIVER**, River, NW Pennsylvania; Flows S approx. 25 m. through industrial towns from its source at the confluence of the Shenango and Mahoning Rivers in Lawrence County to the Ohio River bend at Rochester. Falls at the city of Beaver Falls. Named for the large number of beavers once found on its banks and in its waters.

•**BEAVERTOWN**, Borough; Snyder County; Pop. 853; Area Code 717; Zip Code 17813; Elev. 651'; 8 m. W of Middleburg in central Pennsylvania; clothing is important industry; named for beaver colonies once numerous here.

Community Event - Folk Frolic Days, Annual, July

•**BEAVERTOWN**, Village; York County; Pop. 100; Area Code 717; Zip Code 17019; S Pennsylvania.

•**BECCARIA**, Village and Township; Clearfield County; Pop. 200, (township, 1,877); Area Code 814; Zip Code 16616; Central Pennsylvania; named for Italian publicist and philosopher *Cesare the Marquis of Beccaria* (1735-94).

•**BECHTELSVILLE**, Borough; Berks County; Pop. 832; Area Code 215; Zip Code 19505; Elev. 420'; SE Pennsylvania.

•**BEDFORD**, Borough; Seat of Bedford County; Pop. 3,326; Area Code 814; Zip Code 15522; Elev. 1,060'; S Pennsylvania; was settled about 1750 and first named Raystown for a Scottish trader named *John Wray* who had a post here.

In 1757 *Lieutenant Colonel John Armstrong* urged *Governor Denny* to erect a fort at Raystown, as "a visible, large, and direct stride" toward Fort Duquesne. The next year *Brigadier General John Forbes*, in command of 7,500 soldiers and almost 1,000 wagons, reached Raystown in his advance on Fort Duquesne. The army, which had assembled at Lancaster, set about making a wagon road west of Bedford. Known as Forbes Road, it later became an important highway for western emigration. *Forbes's* men built Fort Raystown, which was renamed Fort Bedford the following year for the Duke of Bedford. The site of Fort Bedford is marked by a tablet on Pitt Street, east of Juliana. Built of 18-foot logs and surrounded by water defenses - the river and deep moats - the fort was, for those days, virtually impregnable.

In 1769 *Captain James Smith* of the Sideling Hill Volunteers, the same Smith who had forced the British to evacuate Fort London in 1765 learned that several pioneers had been imprisoned at Fort Bedford for destroying arms and other goods destined for the Indian trade around the

29

Ohio Forks. Announcing that he would free the prisoners, Smith marched toward the fort with a force of 18 men. Making certain that the British were aware of his movements, he encamped at Juniata Crossing, supposedly for the night, but he resumed his march before midnight. The Fort Bedford garrison did not expect him until noon, but he lay concealed only 100 yards away long before daybreak, at which time the gate was regularly opened. The guards were lounging about, their guns stacked nearby, when Smith and his men charged the entrance, captured the arms, overpowered the guards, and freed the prisoners. In his memoirs *Smith* wrote: "This was the first British fort in America that was taken by what they called "American rebels." Fort Bedford was in ruins by the time of the Revolution.

Agriculture - Cattle, poultry farming
Industry/Mfg. - Grain milling, electronics, animal feed. Resort area.
Daily Newspaper - The Gazette, PO Box 671
Chamber of Commerce - PO Box 1771
Community Events -
  Fall Foliage Festival, Annual, October
  North Appalachian Crafts Festival, Annual, May

•**BEDFORD COUNTY**, In 1768 the great township of Bedford was organized as a part of Cumberland County. The increasing number of settlers in this western region now began to complain about the hardship of traveling all the way to Carlisle for the transaction of public business, and to clamor for the erection of a new county. In March, 1771, their petition was granted by the formation of Bedford County, which was doubtless so called for the town and township of Bedford. Within five weeks after the county was established the first Pennsylvania court for the benefit of the scatered settlers in the western part of the province was convened at Bedford, the county-seat. *Arthur St. Clair* was the first prothonotary of the new county.

•**BEDFORD SPRINGS**, Elev. 992'; is the site of nationally known springs, whose medicinal properties were reputedly known to the Indians, and were revealed to the whites when a fisherman's disability was relieved after he waded into a spring here. Before the Civil War the magnesia, limestone, iron, sweet water, and sulphur springs attracted wealthy Southerners.

In pioneer days a cave near here is said to have been the haunt of *Davy Lewis*, a bandit who reputedly robbed the rich and gave to the poor. Jailed for counterfeiting in 1815, *Lewis* burrowed under a wall, stopped long enough to release all the prisoners except "a common fellow who had robbed a poor widow," and made his escape.

•**BEDMINSTER**, Village and Township; Bucks County; Pop. 350 (township, 3,252); Area Code 215; Zip Code 18910; Elev. 440'; approx. 35 m. N of Philadelphia in SE Pennsylvania.

•**BEECH CREEK**, Borough; Clinton County; Pop. 760; Area Code 717; Zip Code 16822; Elev. 617'; on E bank of Beech Creek in central Pennsylvania; near Lock Haven.

•**BEECHMONT**, Village; Allegheny County; Pop. 100; Area Code 412; Zip Code 15071; 15 m. W of Pittsburgh in W Pennsylvania.

•**BEERSVILLE**, Village; Northampton County; Pop. 175; Area Code 215; Zip Code 18067; near Northampton in E Pennsylvania.

•**BEESONS**, Village; Fayette County; Pop. 60; Area Code 412; Zip Code 15445; SW Pennsylvania.

•**BELAIR PARK**, Village; Lancaster County; Pop. 300; Area Code 717; Zip Code 17601; suburb of Lancaster.

•**BELFAST**, Village; Northampton County; Pop. 275; Area Code 717; Zip Code 18064; Elev. 520'; 10 m. NW of Easton in E Pennsylvania; agricultural; nearby is Henry's Gun Factory, where firearms were made for the War of 1812.

•**BELFAST JUNCTION**, Village; Northampton County; Pop. 100; Area Code 717; Zip Code 18042; near Belfast and incorporated with Easton.

•**BELL ACRES**, Borough; Allegheny County; Pop. 1,307; Area Code 412; Zip Code 15143; Elev. 1,200'; SW Pennsylvania.

•**BELLA VISTA**, Village; Lycoming County; Pop. 150; Area Code 717; Zip Code 17754; NE central Pennsylvania.

•**BELLEFONTE**, Borough; Seat of Centre County; Pop. 6,300; Area Code 814; Zip Code 16823; Elev. 749'; Central Pennsylvania.
Bellefonte (French, beautiful fountain), was surveyed in 1769 and settled shortly afterward, occupies seven hills at the southeastern base of Bald Eagle Mountain. The name is attributed, in story, to *Talleyrand's* exclamation of pleasure upon seeing the Big Spring here during his exile from France in 1794-5.
George Grey Barnard (1863-1938), the noted sculptor, was born in Bellefonte. Through struggle and privation he was able to study at the Art Institute of Chicago and the Ecole des Beaux Arts, Paris. His *The Two Natures*, in the Metropolitan Museum of Art, New York, and *Norway* have been called masterpieces by critics. Barnard considered his symbolic group of figures, *The Apotheosis of Labor*, which adorns the entrance to the State Capitol at Harrisburg, his best work. *Boucher*, noted French sculptor said this group would rank with the great sculpture of all time.

>*Agriculture* - Wheat, poultry, dairy farming
>*Industry/Mfg.* - Heavy machinery, quarrying, animal feed. Resort Area.
>*Chamber of Commerce* - Train Station

•**BELLEGROVE**, Village; Lebanon County; Pop. 300; Area Code 717; Zip Code 17003; SE central Pennsylvania.

•**BELLE VERNON**, Borough; Fayette County; Pop. 1,489; Area Code 412; Zip Code 15012; Elev. 903'; on Monongahela River in SW Pennsylvania.

•**BELLEVILLE**, Village; Mifflin County; Pop. 1,817; Area Code 814; Zip Code 17004; Elev. 800'; approx. 10 m. NW of Lewiston in central Pennsylvania.

•**BELLEVUE**, Borough; Allegheny County; Pop. 10,128; Area Code 412; Zip Code 15202; Elev. 727'; SW Pennsylvania; suburb of Pittsburgh; on Ohio River. Name means "beautiful view" in French, given for the sight obtained from a nearby hill. In colonial times Bellevue was a Delaware Indian hunting ground under *Chief Killbuck*. White settlement began in 1802. Incorporated, 1867.

•**BELLPOINT**, Village; Westmoreland County; Pop. 200; Area Code 814; Zip Code 15613; near Conemaugh River in SW Pennsylvania.

•**BELLS LANDING**, Village; Clearfield County; Pop. 150; Area Code 814; Zip Code 15757; Central Pennsylvania.

•**BELLWOOD**, Borough; Blair County; Pop. 2,114; Area Code 814; Zip Code 16617; Elev. 1,060'; 10 m. N of Altoona in S central Pennsylvania; named for prominent pioneer family, especially *Edward Bell*, who settled here in 1800. Town surveyed by *Dr. A.K. Bell* in 1877.

•**BELMONT**, Borough; Cambria County; Pop. 1,800; Area Code 814; Zip Code 15904; W central Pennsylvania; suburb of Johnstown.

•**BELMONT HILLS**, Borough; Bucks County; Pop. 1,300; Area Code 215; Zip Code 19020; unincorporated suburb of Philadelphia near Trevoze in SE Pennsylvania.

•**BELMONT HOMES**, Village; Cambria County; Pop. 350; Area Code 814; Zip Code 15904; unincorporated suburb of Johnstown in W central Pennsylvania; residential.

•**BELSANO**, Village; Cambria County; Pop. 350; Area Code 814; Zip Code 15922; Elev. 1,187'; 10 m. W of Ebensburg in S central Pennsylvania; founded in 1830 and named for a town in Italy.

•**BEN AVON**, Borough; Allegheny County; Pop. 2,134; Area Code 412; Elev. 727'; suburb to NW of Pittsburgh in SW Pennsylvania; incorporated borough in 1891; name is Scottish for "hill by the waters."

•**BEN AVON HEIGHTS**, Borough; Allegheny County; Pop. 398; Area Code 412; SW Pennsylvania.

•**BENDERSVILLE**, Borough; Adams County; Pop. 533; Area Code 717; Zip Code 17306; Elev. 740'; S Pennsylvania.

•**BENEZETT**, Village and Township; Elk County; Pop. 175 (township 353); Area Code 814; Zip Code 15821; Elev. 1,020'; N central Pennsylvania; on the Trout Run and Bennett branch of the Sinnemahoning River.

•**BENFER**, Village; Snyder County; Pop. 75; Area Code 717; Zip Code 17812; Central Pennsylvania.

•**BENS CREEK**, Village; Cambria and Somerset Counties; Pop. 500; Area Code 814; Zip Code 15905; S central Pennsylvania.

•**BENSON**, Borough; Somerset County; Pop. 308; Area Code 814; Elev. 1,560'; S Pennsylvania.

•**BENTLEYCREEK**, Village; Bradford County; Pop. 130; Area Code 717; Zip Code 14894; just S of New York state line in N Pennsylvania.

•**BENTLEYVILLE**, Borough; Washington County; Pop. 2,525; Area Code 412; Zip Code 15314; Elev. 960'; approx. 25 m. S of Pittsburgh in SW Pennsylvania; named for *Sheshbazzar Bentley, Jr.*, who laid out the town in 1816.

> *Agriculture* - Grain and poultry farming
> *Industry/Mfg.* - Dairy products

•**BENTON**, Borough; Columbia County; Pop. 981; Area Code 717; Zip Code 17814; Elev. 760'; 15 m. N of Bloomsburg in E central Pennsylvania; named in honor of *Col. Thomas H. Benton*, popular U.S. Senator from Missouri; incorporated in 1850.

•**BENVENUE**, Village; Dauphin County; Pop. 70; Area Code 717; Zip Code 17020; SE central Pennsylvania.

•**BERKELEY HILLS,** Borough; Allegheny County; Pop. 3,700; Area Code 412; Zip Code 15237; unincorporated suburb of Pittsburgh in W Pennsylvania.

•**BERKLEY,** Village; Berks County; Pop. 200; Area Code 215; Zip Code 19605; suburb of Reading in SE Pennsylvania.

•**BERLIN,** Borough; Somerset County; Pop. 1,999; Area Code 814; Zip Code 15530; Elev. 1,163'; 40 m. S of Johnstown in S Pennsylvania; on a ridge in Brothers Valley; named by Germans who settled here in 1769; coal mining and farming region.

•**BERLINSVILLE,** Village; Northampton County; Pop. 300; Area Code 717; Zip Code 18088; 15 m. NE of Bethlehem in E Pennsylvania.

•**BERNE,** Village; Berks County; Pop. 65; Area Code 251; Zip Code 19506; SE Pennsylvania; settled in early 1700s by emigrants from the Berne region in Switzerland.

•**BERNVILLE,** Borough; Berks County; Pop. 798; Area Code 215; Zip Code 19506; Elev. 322'; SE Pennsylvania.

•**BERRYSBURG,** Borough; Dauphin County; Pop. 447; Area Code 717; Zip Code 17005; Elev. 700'; SE central Pennsylvania.

•**BERWICK,** Borough; Columbia County; Pop. 12,189; Area Code 717; Zip Code 18603; Elev. 505'; E central Pennsylvania.

Berwick was founded in 1786 y *Evan Owen,* a Quaker, as a place of refuge for his co-religionists. It is named for Berwick upon Tweed, an English town on the Scottish border.

The site of Fort Jenkins was part of a defense line that ran in Revolutionary times along the North and west Branches of the Susquehanna. This fort, not to be confused with Jenkins' Fort in West Pittston, was erected in 1777 and garrisoned by 30 men under *Colonel Thomas Hartley.*

Agriculture - Varied farming
Industry/Mfg. - Trucks, beverages, lumber,
　dairy products
Daily Newspaper - The Enterprise, 106 E.
Front Street
Chamber of Commerce - PO box 328

•**BERWINSDALE**, Village; Clearfield County; Pop. 60; Area Code 814; Zip Code 16656; Central Pennsylvania.

•**BERWYN**, Borough; Chester County; Pop. 9,300; Area Code 215; Zip Code 19312; Elev. 500'; residential suburb W of Philadelphia in SE Pennsylvania.

•**BESCO**, Village; Washington County; Pop. 100; Area Code 412; Zip Code 15322; SW Pennsylvania.

•**BESSEMER**, Borough; Lawrence County; Pop. 1,293; Area Code 412; Zip Code 16112; Elev. 1,100'; 10 m. W of New Castle in W Pennsylvania; named for *Sir Henry Bessermer*, inventor of an economical process to make steel that revolutionized the industry.

•**BETHANY**, Borough; Wayne County; Pop. 282; Area Code 717; Elev. 1,070'; near Honesdale in NE Pennsylvania; site of the David Wilmot House, the former home of the U.S. Senator (1845-51), author of the Wilmot Proviso.

•**BETHEL**, Village and Township; Berks County; Pop. 600 (township, 2,600); Area Code 215; Zip Code 19501; Elev. 525'; 40 m. E of Harrisburg in SE Pennsylvania; near Round Head Mountain (elev. 1,620); 3 m. N is site of Fort Henry, a stronghold of the French and Indian War. Bethel was founded in 1814.

•**BETHEL PARK**, Borough; Allegheny County; Pop. 34,755; Area Code 412; Zip Code 15102; Elev. 1,200'; SW Pennsylvania; suburb of Pittsburgh to S; residential.

•**BETHLEHEM**, City; Lehigh and Northampton Counties; Pop. 70,419; Area Code 215; Zip Code 180 + zone; Elev. 237'; borders on Allentown in E Pennsylvania; on the Lehigh River.

Founded in 1741 by the Moravian Brethren, Bethlehem was named on Christmas Eve that year when the congregation and their leader, *Count Nicholas Ludwig*, sang an old German hym meaning "Bethlehem gave us that which makes life rich." Soon afterward, the religious town grew into a missionary center for local Indians and settlers. It also became a music center as the Moravians established a music college and published *Bach* scores before they were even printed in Europe.

During the Revolution, wounded American soldiers were brought here to be cared for, as a hospital was established in what is now Colonial Hall. However, Bethlehem's growth was slow paced until the Lehigh Canal was opened in 1829 and coal traffic began. Shortly after the borough was incorporated in 1845, the first railroads passed by, easing the way for the great iron and steel industries of the latter nineteenth century. In 1920, after consolidation with all the surrounding boroughs, Bethlehem was incorporated as a city.

Despite its peaceful and religious beginnings, the city became a large munitions manufacturing center during the world wars.

City is the seat of Lehigh University (1865), founded by *Asa Packer*. Many old German-style homes and churches reflect the Moravian influence here.

POINTS OF INTEREST

ANNIE S. KEMERER MUSEUM- Art, glassware, china, furniture and early kitchen displays.

BETHLEHEM HISTORIC DISTRICT, SUB-DISTRICT A-Founded in 1741 by Moravian immigrants, the downtown district includes numerous 18th-19th century commercial, residential and industrial structures in a variety of styles.

GRISTMILLER'S HOUSE- Built in 1782 for miller's family near community gristmill. Illustrates adoption of exogenous building techniques and styles in Moravian community.

MORAVIAN MUSEUM OF BETHLEHEM- 5-story log structure, oldest building in the city.

OLD WATERWORKS- Constructed in 1762 and considered the first pumped or forced water system in the U.S.

SUN INN- Restored Moravian Inn from 1758; once hosted the Continental Congress.

Industry/Mfg. - Iron mills, auto parts,
cloth, varied manufacturing, trade and
services.
Higher Education -
Lehigh University
Moravian College
Northampton County Area Community College
Daily Newspaper - The Globe-Times, 202 W.
Fourth Street
Chamber of Commerce - 11 W. Market Street
Community Events -
Art Festival Week, Annual, April
Bethlehem Bach Festival, Annual, May

•**BETHLEHEM ANNEX**, Borough; Northampton County; Pop. 1,200; Area Code 717; Zip Code 18017; unincorporated suburb of Bethlehem-Allentown.

•**BETHTON**, Village; Bucks County; Pop. 75; Area Code 215; Zip Code 18964; Elev. 460'; SE Pennsylvania.

•**BEULAH**, Village; Clearfield County; Pop. 80; Area Code 814; Zip Code 16671; W central Pennsylvania.

•**BEVERLY ESTATES**, Borough; Lancaster County; Pop. 500; Area Code 717; Zip Code 17601; suburb of Lancaster in SE central Pennsylvania.

•**BEVERLY HEIGHTS**, Village; Lebanon County; Pop. 100; Area Code 717; Zip Code 17042; SE central Pennsylvania.

•**BEVERLY HILLS**, Village; Blair County; Pop. 100; Area Code 814; Zip Code 16601; S central Pennsylvania.

•**BEYER**, Village; Indiana County; Pop. 180; Area Code 717; Zip Code 16211; Elev. 1,200'; W central Pennsylvania.

•**BIESECKER GAP**, Village; Franklin County; Pop. 150; Area Code 717; Zip Code 17268; S Pennsylvania.

•**BIG BEAVER**, Borough; Beaver County; Pop. 2,815; Area Code 412; suburb of Beaver Falls in W Pennsylvania; residential.

•**BIGLER**, Village; Clearfield County; Pop. 400; Area Code 814; Zip Code 16825; Elev. 1,669'; W central Pennsylvania; named for *Governor William Bigler* (1852-55), former resident of the area.

•**BIGLERVILLE**, Borough; Adams County; Pop. 991; Area Code 717; Zip Code 17307; Elev. 649'; 7 m. N of Gettysburg in S Pennsylvania; surveyed in 1817, the town is the center of a fruit growing region.

•**BIG MINE RUN JUNCTION**, Village; Schuylkill County; Pop. 125; Area Code 717; Zip Code 17921; near Ashland in E central Pennsylvania.

•**BIGMOUNT**, Village; York County; Pop. 100; Area Code 717; Zip Code 17315; S Pennsylvania.

•**BIG POND**, Village; Bradford County; Pop. 90; Area Code 717; Zip Code 16914; N Pennsylvania.

•**BIG RUN**, Borough; Jefferson County; Pop. 822; Area Code 814; Zip Code 15715; Elev. 1,286'; 7 m. N of Punxsutawney in W central Pennsylvania; founded in 1822 and named for a stream that flows into Stump Creek here; coal mining and farming area.

•**BINGEN**, Village; Northampton County; Pop. 250; Area Code 717; Zip Code 18015; near Bethlehem in E Pennsylvania; named for Bingen region in Germany.

•**BIRCHRUNVILLE**, Village; Chester County; Pop. 300; Area Code 215; Zip Code 19321; Elev. 390'; SE Pennsylvania.

•**BIRD IN HAND**, Village; Lancaster County; Pop. 700; Area Code 717; Zip Code 17505; Elev. 355'; 30 m. SW of Reading in SE Pennsylvania; named for an early inn that displayed a sign reading "a bird in the hand is worth two in the bush;" Tavern was rebuilt three times over original 18th century site.

•**BIRDSBORO**, Borough; Berks County; Pop. 3,481; Area Code 215; Zip Code 19508; Elev. 190'; 11 m. W of Pottstown in SE Pennsylvania; on Schuylkill River; founded in 1740; named for ironmaster *William Bird*, whose mansion was built here in 1751. Nearby is Bird's Hopewell Forge, erected in 1744, and a reconstructed Hopewell Village recreational area.

POINT OF INTEREST

DANIEL BOONE HOMESITE AND BERTOLET CABIN- 18th century fieldstone house built on the site of the Boone family log cabin. Site of birthplace of *Daniel Boone.*

•BIRMINGHAM, Borough; Huntingdon County; Pop. 121; Area Code 814; Zip Code 16686; Elev. 960'; S central Pennsylvania; laid out in 1797 by iron manufacturer *John Cadwallader*, who named it for the English industrial city.

•BISHOP, Village; Washington County; Pop. 400; Area Code 412; Zip Code 15057; 20 m. SW of Pittsburgh in SW Pennsylvania.

•BITNER, Village; Fayette County; Pop. 150; Area Code 412; Zip Code 15431; SW Pennsylvania.

•BITTERSVILLE, Village; York County; Pop. 275; Area Code 215; Zip Code 17366; S Pennsylvania.

•BLACK GAP, Village; Franklin County; Pop. 175; Area Code 717; Zip Code 17222; S Pennsylvania.

•BLACK HORSE, Village; Delaware County; Pop. 150; Area Code 215; Zip Code 19063; suburb of Chester in SE Pennsylvania; incorporated with Media.

•BLACK HORSE, Village; Montgomery County; Pop. 370; Area Code 215; Zip Code 19401; suburb of Norristown in SE Pennsylvania.

•BLACK LICK, Village; Indiana County; Pop. 1,074; Area Code 814; Zip Code 15716; Elev. 967'; near Blainsville on Conemaugh River Reservoir in W central Pennsylvania.
    Settled in 1807 and laid out in 1860, this town was named for a nearby coal-black creek, which once contained a salt lick. Coal mining is important.

•**BLAIN**, Borough; Perry County; Pop. 274; Area Code 717; Zip Code 17006; Elev. 720'; 40 m. W of Harrisburg in S central Pennsylvania; on Sherman Creek.

•**BLAIN CITY**, Village; Clearfield County; Pop. 400; Area Code 814; Zip Code 16627; W central Pennsylvania.

•**BLAINE HILL**, Village; Allegheny County; Pop. 1,300; Area Code 412; Zip Code 15037; SE suburb of Pittsburgh in W Pennsylvania.

•**BLAINSPORT**, Village; Lancaster County; Pop. 65; Area Code 717; Zip Code 17569; SE Pennsylvania.

•**BLAIR COUNTY**, In 1846 Blair County was formed from Huntingdon and Bedford. It was named for the Honorable *John Blair* of Blair's Gap, and is the only county in the state named for a purely local celebrity. His father, *Captain Thomas Blair*, a native of Scotland, was instrumental during the Revolutionary period in clearing the upper Juniata valley of Indians and Tories. After the war *Captain Blair* settled in Blair's Gap, built the old Blair homestead, which is still standing, and became a man of considerable property and influence. Here *John Blair* was born and lived all his life.

He was elected to the Legislature, where he showed himself a warm friend of internal improvement. He was president of the Hollidaysburg and Pittsburgh Turnpike Company, which built the macadamized road through the gap in 1820, and ten years later he was active in promoting the Pennsylvania Canal and the Portage Railroad, which carried the canal-boats across the mountains. In his day he was known as one of the most prominent and public-spirited citizens in central Pennsylvania. Blair Township, in Blair County, and the borough of Blairsville, in Indiana County, were also named for him. He died fourteen years before Blair County was created.

•**BLAIRS MILLS**, Village; Huntingdon County; Pop. 80; Area Code 814; Zip Code 17213; Elev. 735'; S central Pennsylvania.

41

•**BLAIRSVILLE**, Borough; Indiana County; Pop. 4,166; Area Code 412; Zip Code 15717; Elev. 1,012'; W central Pennsylvania.

Located on the Conemaugh River, Blairsville was settled in 1792 and named for *Captain John Blair*, of Blair's Gap, who was among the first promoters of the turnpike and canal-portage system. The late 1920's and early 1830's were lush days for this region. The canal's western division was completed to Blairsville in 1828, while the eastern section was still being constructed. Pending completion of the latter, the turnpike brought bustle and prosperity to Blairsville. Hotels and warehouses sprang up, five churches were built in three years, and speculators were active. When the canal and portage were opened in 1834, turnpike traffic declined sharply, and idle merchants and innkeepers of Blairsville watched the stream "pass by on the other side," but the natural resources of the district saved the town.

•**BLAIRTOWN**, Village; Greene County; Pop. 75; Area Code 412; Zip Code 15370; SW Pennsylvania.

•**BLAKELY**, Borough; Lackawana County; Pop. 7,438; Area Code 717; Zip Code 18447; Elev. 872'; NE Pennsylvania; suburb of Scranton; on Lackawana River; named for *Captain Johnston Blakely*, naval commander during the War of 1812.

•**BLAKESLEE**, Village; Monroe County; Pop. 225; Area Code 717; Zip Code 18610; Elev. 1,589'; 25 m. E of Wilkes-Barre.

•**BLAKESLEE CORNERS**, Elev. 1,589'; a crossroads settlement, was named for *Jacob Blakeslee*, the first postmaster.

•**BLANCHARD**, Village; Allegheny County; Pop. 120; Area Code 412; Zip Code 15084; W Pennsylvania.

•**BLANCHARD**, Village; Centre County; Pop. 750; Area Code 717; Zip Code 16826; Elev. 650'; Central Pennsylvania.

•**BLANCHARD LAKE**, Lake, 20 m. N of State College in Centre County, in central Pennsylvania; 10 m. long and approx. 1 m. wide at widest point. Bald Eagle state park and campground is at northern tip; recreational area.

•**BLANDBURG**, Village; Cambria County; Pop. 775; Area Code 814; Zip Code 16619; Elev. 2,047'; in Allegheny Mountain Range in W central Pennsylvania.

•**BLANDON**, Village; Berks County; Pop. 1,113; Area Code 215; Zip Code 19510; Elev. 400'; suburb of Reading in SE central Pennsylvania.

•**BLAWNOX**, Borough; Allegheny County; Pop. 1,653; Area Code 412; Zip Code 15238; Elev. 740'; SW Pennsylvania.
    Blawnox, named for a local steel company, occupies a site taken over by a land development enterprise in 1867. The earliest known inhabitants in the vicinity were the Allegiwi Indians. After them came the Shawnee and the Iroquois. Hatchets, darts, fish spears, skinning stones, amulets, and other relics of their occupancy have been unearthed.

•**BLOOMFIELD**, Borough; Seat of Perry County; Pop. 1,109; Area Code 717; Zip Code 152 + zone; S central Pennsylvania.

•**BLOOMINGDALE**, Village; Lancaster County; Pop. 1,200; Area Code 717; Zip Code 17601; suburb of Lancaster of SE Pennsylvania.

•**BLOOMING GLEN**, Village; Bucks County; Pop. 600; Area Code 215; Zip Code 18911; Elev. 420'; SE Pennsylvania.

•**BLOOMING GROVE**, Village and Township; Pike County; Pop. 250 (township, 548); Area Code 717; Zip Code 18428; NE Pennsylvania.

•**BLOOMING GROVE**, Village; York County; Pop. 100; Area Code 717; Zip Code 17331; near Hanover in S Pennsylvania.

•**BLOOMINGTON**, Village; Clearfield County; Pop. 75; Area Code 814; Zip Code 16833; W central Pennsylvania.

•**BLOOMING VALLEY**, Borough; Crawford County; Pop. 374; Area Code 814; NW Pennsylvania.

•**BLOOMSBURG**, Town; Seat of Columbia County; Pop. 11,717; Area Code 717; Zip Code 17815; Elev. 482'; E central Pennsylvania.

The only community in the state to be incorporated as a town, Bloomsburg lies at the foot of Spectator Bluff, and on Fishing Creek. *Ludwig Eyer* laid it out in 1802, and the name was chosen in honor of *Samuel Bloom*, who had been a county commissioner when the old Bloom Township was organized in 1797. During the Civil War, Bloomsburg was the supposed site of a colony of draft evaders who had formed a "confederacy" and built a fort on Fishing Creek. However, when 1,000 Union soldiers were dispatched to break up the colony, they "found not a man, nor evidence that a man had ever been there."

> *Agriculture* - Livestock, grain and varied
> farming
> *Industry/Mfg.* - Dairy products, cement, food
> processing, clothing
> *Higher Education* - Bloomsburg State College
> *Daily Newspaper* - The Press, 3185 Lackawana
> Ave.
> *Chamber of Commerce* - 233 Market St.

•**BLOOMSDALE GARDENS**, Village; Bucks County; Pop. 550; Area Code 215; Zip Code 19057; near Levittown in SE Pennsylvania.

•**BLOSERVILLE**, Village; Cumberland County; Pop. 160; Area Code 717; Zip Code 17241; S central Pennsylvania.

•**BLOSSBURG**, Borough; Tioga County; Pop. 1,757; Area Code 717; Zip Code 16912; Elev. 1,348'; N Pennsylvania.

First known as Peters Camp; Renamed for *Aaron Bloss*, who opened a tavern here in 1802; early coal veins were exhausted here; near Bloss Mountain.

•**BLOSSER HILL**, Village; Fayette County; Pop. 150; Area Code 412; Zip Code 15451; SW Pennsylvania.

•**BLOSSOM HILL**, Village; Lancaster County; Pop. 1,300; Area Code 717; Zip Code 17601; suburb of Lancaster in SE Pennsylvania.

•**BLOUGH**, Village; Somerset County; Pop. 150; Area Code 814; Zip Code 15936; SW Pennsylvania.

•**BLUE BALL**, Village; Lancaster County; Pop. 700; Area Code 717; Zip Code 17506; Elev. 469'; 45 m. W of Chester in SE Pennsylvania; founded in 1766 by *Robert Wallace* who opened an inn and tavern here called the "Blue Ball," which was a favorite stopping place for marketing farmers.

•**BLUE BELL**, Village; Montgomery County; Pop. 1,600; Area Code 215; Zip Code 19422; Elev. 360'; northern suburb of Philadelphia in SE Pennsylvania.

•**BLUE MARSH**, Village; Berks County; Pop. 150; Area Code 215; Zip Code 19608; SE Pennsylvania.

•**BLUE KNOB**, Mountain, Bedford County, Pennsylvania; Elev. 3,136'; 25 m. N of Bedford in the Blue Ridge mountain region of S Pennsylvania. Ski facilities.

•**BLUE MOUNTAINS**, Mountain range, NE Pennsylvania; extends approx. 50 m. from Lebanon County, NE to W Lehigh County; considered part of the Kittatinny Range.

•**BLUE RIDGE SUMMIT**, Village; Franklin County; Pop. 800; Area Code 717; Zip Code 17214; Elev. 1,400'; near Waynesboro in S Pennsylvania.

•**BLYTHEBURN**, Village; Luzerne County; Pop. 200; Area Code 717; Zip Code 18707; NE central Pennsylvania.

•**BLYTHEDALE**, Village; Allegheny County; Pop. 450; Area Code 412; Zip Code 15018; suburb of Pittsburgh, near Buena Vista in W Pennsylvania.

•**BLYTHEWOOD**, Village; Bucks County; Pop. 60; Area Code 215; Zip Code 18901; SE Pennsylvania.

•**BOALSBURG**, Village; Centre County; Pop. 950; Area Code 717; Zip Code 16827; Elev. 1,100'; near State College in central Pennsylvania.

Laid out in 1810, this village was named for *Capt. David Boal*, a native Irishman who settled here in 1798; nearby is old iron works of the *Carnegie Brothers*.

Community Event - Ole Town Days, Annual, May

•**BOARDMAN**, Village; Clearfield County; Pop. 75; Area Code 814; Zip Code 16863; W central Pennsylvania.

•**BOBTOWN**, Village; Greene County; Pop. 1,055; Area Code 412; Zip Code 15315; near Dunkard Creek in SW Pennsylvania.

•**BODINES**, Village; Lycoming County; Pop. 60; Area Code 717; Zip Code 17722; Elev. 761'; 30 m. S of Troy in N central Pennsylvania; hunting region near Trout Run.

•**BOILING SPRINGS**, Village; Cumberland County; Pop. 1,521; Area Code 717; Zip Code 17007; 15 m. SW of Harrisburg; rural.

Agriculture - Corn, grain and varied farming

•**BOLIVAR**, Borough; Westmoreland County; Pop. 706; Area Code 417; Zip Code 15923; Elev. 1,060'; SW Pennsylvania.

•**BOLIVAR RUN**, Village; McKean County; Pop. 400; Area Code 814; Zip Code 16701; near Bradford in N Pennsylvania.

•**BOLTZ**, Village; Indiana County; Pop. 200; Area Code 814; Zip Code 15954; W central Pennsylvania.

•**BON AIR**, Village; Cambria County; Pop. 525; Area Code 814; Zip Code 15909; suburb of Johnstown in W central Pennsylvania.

•**BON AIRE**, Village; Butler County; Pop. 900; Area Code 814; Zip Code 16001; Elev. 1,160'; suburb of Butler in W Pennsylvania.

•**BON MEADE**, Village; Allegheny County; Pop. 300; Area Code 412; Zip Code 15108; near Ohio River and Coraopolis in W Pennsylvania.

•**BONNEAUVILLE**, Borough; Adams County; Pop. 920; Area Code 717; Elev. 560'; S Pennsylvania.

•**BOONEVILLE**, Village; Clinton County; Pop. 75; Area Code 717; Zip Code 17747; Central Pennsylvania.

•**BOON TERRACE**, Village; Washington County; Pop. 400; Area Code 412; Zip Code 15342; south suburb of Pittsburgh in SW Pennsylvania.

•**BOOTH CORNER**, Village; Delaware County; Pop. 250; Area Code 215; Zip Code 19061; near Chester in SE Pennsylvania; residential.

•**BOOTHWYN**, Borough; Delaware County; Pop. 7,100; Area Code 215; Zip Code 19061; Elev. 100'; suburb of Philadelphia in SE Pennsylvania; residential.

POINT OF INTEREST

CHICHESTER FRIENDS MEETING HOUSE- Typical 18th-19th century Quaker meetinghouse.

•**BORLAND MANOR**, Village; Washington County; Pop. 950; Area Code 412; Zip Code 15317; near Canonsburg, 10 m. SW of Pittsburgh in SW Pennsylvania.

•**BOSTON**, Borough; Allegheny County; Pop. 1,200; Area Code 412; Zip Code 15135; Elev. 760'; suburb of Pittsburgh to SE.

•**BOSTON RUN**, Village; Schuylkill County; Pop. 90; Area Code 717; Zip Code 17948; near Mahoney City in E central Pennsylvania.

•**BOSWELL**, Borough; Somerset County; Pop. 1,480; Area Code 814; Zip Code 15531; S Pennsylvania.

•**BOUQUET**, Village; Westmoreland County; Pop. 120; Area Code 814; Zip Code 15644; near Jeannette in W central Pennsylvania.

47

•**BOVARD**, Village; Westmoreland County; Pop. 900; Area Code 412; Zip Code 15619; Elev. 1,120'; near Greensburg in W central Pennsylvania.

•**BOWDERTON**, Village; Indian County; Pop. 60; Area Code 814; Zip Code 15724; W central Pennsylvania.

•**BOWER HILL**, Village; Washington County; Pop. 150; Area Code 412; Zip Code 15367; SW Pennsylvania.

•**BOWERS**, Village; Berks County; Pop. 200; Area Code 717; Zip Code 19611; Elev. 440'; SE central Pennsylvania.

•**BOWLING GREEN**, Village; Delaware County; Pop. 200; Area Code 215; Zip Code 19063; near Media in SE Pennsylvania.

•**BOWMAN ADDITION**, Village; York County; Pop. 160; Area Code 717; Zip Code 17331; near Hanover in S Pennsylvania.

•**BOWMANS**, Village; Schuylkill County; Pop. 60; Area Code 717; Zip Code 17948; E central Pennsylvania.

•**BOWMANSDALE**, Village; Cumberland County; Pop. 300; Area Code 717; Zip Code 17008; Elev. 440'; 10 m. SW of Harrisburg on Breeches Creek in S Pennsylvania.

•**BOWMANSTOWN**, Borough; Carbon County; Pop. 1,078; Area Code 717; Zip Code 18030; Elev. 437'; E Pennsylvania.
Bowmanstown was founded in 1796. It occupies the flat center of a large mountain-rimmed bowl.

•**BOWMANSTOWN**, Village; Carbon County; Pop. 864; Area Code 717; Zip Code 18030; Elev. 437'; 50 m. S of Wilkes-Barre in E central Pennsylvania; founded in 1796; on Lehigh Canal.

•**BOWMANSVILLE**, Village; Lancaster County; Pop. 500; Area Code 717; Zip Code 17507; Elev. 440'; SE Pennsylvania.

•**BOWOOD MINES NO. 1**, Village; Fayette County; Pop. 60; Area Code 814; Zip Code 15478; SW Pennsylvania.

•**BOYDS MILLS**, Village; Wayne County; Pop. 90; Area Code 717; Zip Code 18443; NE Pennsylvania.

•**BOYDSTOWN**, Village; Butler County; Pop. 75; Area Code 814; Zip Code 16025; W Pennsylvania.

•**BOYERS**, Village; Butler County; Pop. 300; Area Code 814; Zip Code 16020; Elev. 1,200'; W Pennsylvania.

•**BOYERS JUNCTION**, Village; Berks County; Pop. 75; Area Code 717; Zip Code 19522; SE Pennsylvania.

•**BOYERTOWN**, Borough; Berks County; Pop. 4,428; Area Code 717; Zip Code 19512; Elev. 386'; 25 m. S of Allentown in SE central Pennsylvania.

First settled in 1720 and founded in 1834, this town was named for *Henry Boyer*, early settler.

> *Agriculture* - Varied farming
> *Industry/Mfg.* - Campers, iron works, footwear, bottles and clothing, quarrying

•**BOYNTON**, Village; Somerset County; Pop. 330; Area Code 814; Zip Code 15532; Elev. 1,990'; SW Pennsylvania; once an active mining town.

•**BRACKENRIDGE**, Borough; Allegheny County; Pop. 4,297; Area Code 412; Zip Code 15014; Elev. 757'; N suburb of Pittsburgh in SW Pennsylvania; named for *Brackenridge* family, prominent in the area during the nineteenth century; incorporated as a borough, 1901; industries include coal, steel and beer; residential.

•**BRADDOCK**, Borough; Allegheny County; Pop. 5,634; Area Code 412; Zip Code 15104; Elev. 700'; 10 m. E of Pittsburgh in SW Pennsylvania; incorporated as a borough, 1867 and named for *Gen. Edward Braddock* who was fatally wounded nearby in a battle with the French and Indians in 1755; an important steel and coal manufacturing center around the turn of the century.

POINT OF INTEREST

CARNEGIE FREE LIBRARY OF BRADDOCK- Built 1888-1889, the first of many U.S. libraries built from funds supplied by *Andrew Carnegie*. Richardsonian Romanesque. *William Halsey Wood*, architect.

Industry/Mfg. - Steel, petroleum products, paper

•**BRADDOCK HILLS**, Borough; Allegheny County; Pop. 2,556; Area Code 412; Elev. 1,100'; SW Pennsylvania.

•**BRADEN PLAN**, Village; Greene County; Pop. 165; Area Code 412; Zip Code 15322; near Clarkesville in SW Pennsylvania.

•**BRADENVILLE**, Village; Westmoreland County; Pop. 1,200; Area Code 814; Zip Code 15620; Elev. 1,100'; near Latrobe in W central Pennsylvania.

•**BRADFORD**, City; McKean County; Pop. 11,211; Area Code 814; Zip Code 16701; Elev. 1,443'; 4 m. S of New York state line in N Pennsylvania.

First known as Littleton, for the county's first landowner *Col. L.C. Little* of Boston, the name was changed to honor *William Bradford* when *Daniel Kingsbury* purchased the land in 1850. *Kingsbury* also had ancestors from Bradford, England. Oil was discovered here before the Civil War, but no derricks were erected until 1875. City was incorporated in 1879 as an oil boom began.

Although the oil industry has declined in recent years here, the city still manufactures chemicals and explosives.

Industry/Mfg. - Oil drilling, brick, explosives, electronics
Higher Education - University of Pittsburgh
Daily Newspaper - The Era, 43 Main St.
Chamber of Commerce - PO Box 135

•**BRADFORD COUNTY**, On March 24, 1812, a new legislature changed the name of Ontario County to Bradford in honor of *William Bradford* of Philadelphia, the second attorney-general of the United States, whom *Washington*, in January, 1794, appointed to succeed *Edmund Randolph*. *William Bradford* was born in Philadelphia in 1755, and was the son of *Colonel William Bradford*, printer and patriot, and great-grandson of *William Bradford*, the first printer in Philadelphia and New York, who early put to the test the freedom of the press in his keenly contested legal controversy with the Quaker magistrates who had accused him of seditious libel.

•**BRADFORD HILLS**, Village; Chester County; Pop. 300; Area Code 215; Zip Code 19335; suburb of Philadelphia in SE Pennsylvania.

•**BRADFORDWOODS**, Borough; Allegheny County; Pop. 1,264; Area Code 412; Zip Code 15015; Elev. 1,200'; SW Pennsylvania.

•**BRADLEYTOWN**, Village; Venango County; Pop. 75; Area Code 814; Zip Code 16317.

•**BRADYS BEND**, Village and Township; Armstrong County; Pop. 150, (township, 1,095); Area Code 814; Zip Code 16041; on Brady Creek in W central Pennsylvania.

Brady's Bend is a village of varicolored frame houses strung along the highway, was also named for *Captain Brady*, who owned a tract here. Brady deeded this land to *Judge James Ross*, an attorney who had won him acquittal on a charge of murdering an Indian. With the opening of the Great Western Iron Works in 1839, this whole region experienced a 40-year boom that gave employment to thousands. At the height of activity, 40 blast furnaces roared in the wilderness of Clarion County, and Brady's Bend had 700 houses and a population of 3,500.

•**BRANCH DALE**, Village; Schuylkill County; Pop. 600; Area Code 717; Zip Code 17923; Elev. 840'; 10 m. W of Pottsville; former mining town.

51

•**BRANCHTON**, Village; Butler County; Pop. 90; Area Code 814; Zip Code 16021; Elev. 1,201'; W central Pennsylvania.

•**BRANCHVILLE**, Village; Erie County; Pop. 100; Area Code 814; Zip Code 16426; NW Pennsylvania.

•**BRANDAMORE**, Village; Chester County; Pop. 200; Area Code 215; Zip Code 19316; Elev. 618'; SE Pennsylvania; named for nearby Brandywine Creek.

•**BRANDONVILLE**, Village; Schuylkill County; Pop. 300; Area Code 717; Zip Code 17967; E central Pennsylvania.

•**BRANDY CAMP**, Village; Elk County; Pop. 300; Area Code 814; Zip Code 15822; N central Pennsylvania; on Little Toby Creek.

•**BRENTWOOD**, Borough; Allegheny County; Pop. 11,907; Area Code 412; Zip Code 15227; Elev. 884'; SW Pennsylvania.
    Brentwood was incorporated in 1915 with the merger of the villages of Brentwood, Whitehall, and Point View.

•**BRIAR CREEK**, Borough; Columbia County; Pop. 637; Area Code 717; E central Pennsylvania.

•**BRICKERVILLE**, Elev. 539'; Here *Baron Heinrich Wilhelm Stiegel* (1729-85), the outstanding glass and iron manufacturer of this area in the 1760's, spent part of his later years in comparative poverty, living in the parsonage of the Lutheran Church, teaching school, preaching, and giving music lessons. Before he went bankrupt, the Baron, so-called because of his wealth and manner of living, awed the entire region with his activities. He entertained lavishly in his castle at Schaefferstown; his visits to Manheim, site of his glass factory, were occasions for celebrations.

POINT OF INTEREST

STIEGEL-COLEMAN HOUSE- Built 1756-1758 as residences and offices for early industrialists *William Henry Stiegel* and *Robert Coleman.* Georgian.

•**BRIDGEPORT**, Borough; Montgomery County; Pop. 4,843; Area Code 215; Zip Code 19405; SE Pennsylvania.

•**BRIDGEVILLE**, Borough; Allegheny County; Pop. 6,154; Area Code 412; Zip Code 15017; SW Pennsylvania.

> *Agriculture -* Fruit and poultry farming
> *Industry/Mfg. -* Includes cement, soft drinks, chemicals, lumber and dairy products
> *Chamber of Commerce -* PO Box 396

•**BRIDGEWATER**, Borough; Beaver County; Pop. 879; Area Code 412; Elev. 710'; W Pennsylvania.
   Bridgewater, across the Beaver River from Rochester, was consolidated with Sharon in 1868, 70 years after *Major Robert Darragh* erected the first building and opened the first store. Because of its position on the river, a number of industrial plants flourished here in early years. In the 1840's silkworm culture was introduced, and most of the cocoons were sold to the Harmony Society. Stone's Harbor here was considered one of the safest and most commodious on the Ohio. *Aaron Burr* found suitable facilities at Sharon for construction of the famous "arks", also known as Orleans boats, which he planned to use in his scheme to divorce the Mississippi Valley from the republic.

•**BRILHART**, Village; York County; Pop. 75; Area Code 717; Zip Code 17402; S Pennsylvania.

•**BRIQUETTE**, Village; Allegheny County; Pop. 364; Area Code 412; Zip Code 15110; W Pennsylvania; incorporated with Suquesne, a suburb of Pittsburgh.

•**BRISBIN**, Borough; Clearfield County; Pop. 387; Area Code 814; Zip Code 16620; W central Pennsylvania.

•**BRISTOL**, Borough; Bucks County; Pop. 10,867; Area Code 215; Zip Code 19007; Elev. 21'; 20 m. NE of Philadelphia in SE Pennsylvania, on the Delaware River.

53

First settled in 1697 and designated as Bucks County Seat in 1705. Named for the western seaport in England, where some of *William Penn's* ancestors lived. Local progress began after the Easton and Bristol canal was opened in 1834, but today it is not used. A Friends Meetinghouse still stands here, built in 1710-14.

•**BRISTORIA**, Village; Greene County; Pop. 75; Area Code 412; Zip Code 15337; SW Pennsylvania.

•**BRITTANY FARMS**, Village; Bucks County; Pop. 900; Area Code 215; Zip Code 18914; SE Pennsylvania.

•**BROAD ACRES**, Village; Mercer County; Pop. 100; Area Code 814; Zip Code 16127; W Pennsylvania.

•**BROAD AXE**, Village; Montgomery County; Pop. 300; Area Code 215; Zip Code 19002; suburb of Philadelphia in SE Pennsylvania; named for an inn built about 1792.

•**BROAD TOP CITY**, Borough; Huntingdon County; Pop. 340; Area Code 717; Zip Code 16621; Elev. 1,978'; S central Pennsylvania; named for nearby Broad Top Mountains.

•**BROADVIEW**, Village; Allegheny County; Pop. 85; Area Code 412; Zip Code 15084; W Pennsylvania.

•**BROCKPORT**, Village; Elk County; Pop. 450; Area Code 814; Zip Code 15823; Elev. 1,479'; near Brockway in N central Pennsylvania, on Toby Creek; once a lumber and coal mining center.

•**BROCKTON**, Village; Schuylkill County; Pop. 550; Area Code 717; Zip Code 17925; Elev. 700'; 10 m. N of Pottsville in E central Pennsylvania.

•**BROCKWAY**, Borough; Jefferson County; Pop. 2,376; Area Code 814; Zip Code 15824; Elev. 1,445'; W central Pennsylvania.
First settled in 1822 by *Alonzo and Chauncey Brockway*, they named the town for themselves 14 years later while laying out the streets. At first, the town was a

lumbering center because of its proximity to the little Toby Creek and Clarion River. Today's industries include clay products, glass, and macaroni.

•**BRODHEAD**, Village; Northampton County; Pop. 100; Area Code 717; Zip Code 18017; near Bethlehem in E Pennsylvania.

•**BRODHEAD CREEK**, which divides East Stroudsburg form Stroudsburg, was named for *Daniel Broadhead*, who established a Moravian mission on the west bank in 1739.

•**BRODHEADSVILLE**, Village; Monroe County; Pop. 500; Area Code 717; Zip Code 18322; Elev. 675'; 20 m. NW of Easton in E Pennsylvania; near Weir Mountain range, near ski resorts; named for *David Brodhead*, who established a Moravian mission nearby in 11739.

•**BROGUE**, Village; York County; Pop. 200; Area Code 717; Zip Code 17309; S Pennsylvania.

•**BROOKDALE**, Village; Cambria County; Pop. 90; Area Code 814; Zip Code 15942; SW central Pennsylvania.

•**BROOKDALE**, Village; Susquehanna County; Pop. 80; Area Code 717; Zip Code 18822; NW Pennsylvania.

•**BROOKES MILLS**, Village; Blair County; Pop. 200; Area Code 814; Zip Code 16648; near Hollidaysburg in SW central Pennsylvania.

•**BROOKHAVEN**, Borough; Delaware County; Pop. 7,912; Area Code 215; Zip Code 19015; Elev. 119'; SE Pennsylvania.

•**BROOKLYN**, Village and Township; Susquehanna County; Pop. 225; Area Code 717; Zip Code 18813; Elev. 1,176'; on Bottom Creek, approx. 30 m. N of Scranton; named for town in Connecticutt.

•**BROOKSIDE**, Village; Cumberland County; Pop. 80; Area Code 717; Zip Code 17257; near Shippensburg in S central Pennsylvania.

•**BROOKSIDE**, Borough; Erie County; Pop. 1,800; Area Code 814; Zip Code 16510; 2 m. W of Lake Erie shore and the city of Erie in NW Pennsylvania; residential.

•**BROOKSIDE**, Village; Schuylkill County; Pop. 100; Area Code 717; Zip Code 17963; W central Pennsylvania.

•**BROOKSIDE**, Village; York County; Pop. 190; Area Code 717; Zip Code 15241; S Pennsylvania.

•**BROOKVALE**, Village; Fayette County; Pop. 150; Area Code 412; Zip Code 15425; SW Pennsylvania.

•**BROOKVILLE**, Borough; Seat of Jefferson County; Pop. 4,568; Area Code 814; Zip Code 15825; Elev. 1,269'; approx. 80 m. NW of Pittsburgh in W central Pennsylvania; on Red Bank Creek and three of its tributaries.

First settled in 1801, but not laid out and named until 1830, when it became the county seat and was christened for the various brooks flowing in and around town. An early lumber industry town, Brookville became an important coal and railroad center as well during the 1800s.

> *Agriculture* - Dairy farming
> *Industry/Mfg.* - Cement, grain milling, oil, gas, coal
> *Chamber of Commerce* - 100 Frankin Ave.
> *Community Event* - West Penn Laurel Festival, Annual, June

•**BROOMALL**, Borough; Delaware County; Zip Code 25,040; Area Code 215; Zip Code 19008; Elev. 350'; 15 m. NW of Philadelphia in SE Pennsylvania; residential; incorporated as the township of Marple.

POINT OF INTEREST

> THOMAS MASSEY HOUSE- Begun in 1696, one of the state's earliest brick house. Home of *Thomas Massey*, township constable and official of the Friends Meeting.

•**BROUGHTON**, Borough; Allegheny County; Pop. 2,800; Area Code 412; Zip Code 15236; suburb of Pittsburgh in W Pennsylvania; in the South Park-Bethel Park area; residential.

•**BROWNBACKS**, Village; Chester County; Pop. 70; Area Code 215; Zip Code 19475; SE Pennsylvania.

•**BROWNDALE**, Village; Wayne County; Pop. 275; Area Code 717; Zip Code 18421; in Moosic Mountains, near Forest City and Union Dale Dam in NE Pennsylvania.

•**BROWNFIELD**, Village; Fayette County; Pop. 500; Area Code 412; Zip Code 15416; Elev. 1,120'; SW Pennsylvania.

•**BROWNSTOWN**, Village; Armstrong County; Pop. 150; Area Code 814; Zip Code 15630; on Black Lick Creek in W central Pennsylvania.

•**BROWNSTOWN**, Borough; Cambria County; Pop. 649; Area Code 814; Zip Code 17508; Elev. 1,443'; SW central Pennsylvania.

•**BROWNSTOWN**, Village; Fayette County; Pop. 365; Area Code 412; Zip Code 15438; near Fayette City in SW Pennsylvania.

•**BROWNSTOWN**, Village; Lancaster County; Pop. 800; Area Code 717; Zip Code 17508; Elev. 320'; NE suburb of Lancaster in S Pennsylvania; near airport.

•**BROWNSVILLE**, Village; Berks County; Pop. 80; Area Code 215; Zip Code 19565; SE central Pennsylvania.

> *Agriculture* - Cattle, poultry and varied
>   farming
> *Industry/Mfg.* - Dairy products, coal, boats
> *Daily Newspaper* - The Telegraph, 16-18 Bridge
>   Street
> *Chamber of Commerce* - Union Station Bldg.
> *Community Events* -
>   Arts and Crafts Festival, Annual, June
>   National Pike Festival, Annual, May

•**BROWNSVILLE**, Borough; Fayette County; Pop. 4,043; Area Code 412; Zip Code 15417; Elev. 900'; SW Pennsylvania.
    Brownsville, combined with South Brownsville borough since 1933, an industrial community on a slope above the Monongahela River, was an early boatbuilding

center. The *Comet*, built here in 1813, was the first steamer to navigate the Monongahela, Ohio, and Mississippi Rivers, making a successful trip to New Orleans early in 1814. The *Enterprise*, second boat built at Brownsville, was the first steam vessel to come up the rivers as far as Louisville.

The site of Redstone Old Fort, an early Indian fortification, was chosen in 1758 by *Colonel James Burd* for his stockade, and a town was founded in 1785 by *Thomas and Basil Brown*. To thousands of westward-bound emigrants the early settlement here marked the end of their journey's most toilsome stage, and the gleaming bosom of the Monongahela signified travel less hazardous and far less wearying than that over the mountains.

The Whiskey Rebellion began to simmer on July 27, 1791, when a group assembled here in Brownsville to protest the four pence per gallon impost laid on whiskey by the new Federal Government. Corn was only one sixth as valuable as whiskey of equivalent bulk, and farmers found it profitable to convert surplus corn into whiskey for shipment to the East; the excise ate up the profit. Trials and tax protest hearings were held in Philadelphia, and farmers refused to waste precious time in traveling. After the Brownsville meeting others were held in various places. The excise was not paid; there was talk of secession; revenue collectors were manhandled, and several persons were killed in riots. Matters ran along thus until the autumn of 1794 when *General Daniel Morgan* reached Uniontown at the head of 13,000 Federal troops under orders to collect the excise and quell resistance. The Rebellion soon subsided.

•**BROWNSVILLE**, Village; Franklin County; Pop. 60; Area Code 814; Zip Code 17222; S Pennsylvania.

•**BROWNSVILLE**, Village; Schuylkill County; Pop. 450; Area Code 717; Zip Code 17916; near Shenandoah in E central Pennsylvania.

•**BROWNTOWN**, Village; Luzerne County; Pop. 550; Area Code 717; Zip Code 18640; suburb of Wilkes-Barre-Pittston, near the Susquehanna River.

•**BRUIN**, Borough; Butler County; Pop. 722; Area Code 412; Zip Code 16022; Elev. 1,090'; approx. 60 m. NE of Pittsburgh in W Pennsylvania, on Bear Creek; named for the creek and the once-prevalent bears nearby.

•**BRUNNERVILLE**, Village; Lancaster County; Pop. 300; Area Code 717; Zip Code 17543; Elev. 520'; near Lititz in S Pennsylvania; site of a Ephrata Cloister.

•**BRUSHTOWN**, Village; Adams County; Pop. 200; Area Code 717; Zip Code 17331; S Pennsylvania.

•**BRUSHTOWN**, Village; Cumberland County; Pop. 60; Area Code 717; Zip Code 17241; S central Pennsylvania.

•**BRUSH VALLEY**, Village; Indiana County; Pop. 230; Area Code 814; Zip Code 15720; Elev. 1,488'; W central Pennsylvania.

•**BRYAN HILL**, Village; Indiana County; Pop. 150; Area Code 814; Zip Code 15701; W central Pennsylvania.

•**BRYN ATHYN**, Borough; Montgomery County; Pop. 947; Area Code 215; Zip Code 19009; Elev. 280'; N of Philadelphia in SW Pennsylvania; residential suburb; name is Welsh for "hill of cohesiveness," and on a hill overlooking the town is the Bryn Athyn cathedral, built in 1914-19. The cathedral is the seat of Swedeborgianism in the U.S.

Agriculture - Truck farming
Higher Education - Academy of the New Church

•**BRYN GWELED**, Village; Bucks County; Pop. 500; Area Code 215; Zip Code 18966; N of Philadelphia and near Southampton in SE Pennsylvania; residential suburb.

•**BRYN MAWR**, Unincorporated town; Montgomery and Delaware Counties; Pop. 9,500 (including college); Area Code 215; Zip Code 19010; Elev. 413'; NW suburb of Philadelphia in SE Pennsylvania; residential.

Name means "great hill" in Welsh. Town was a favorite summer resort spot in the early 1900s. It is the seat of Bryn Mawr College, founded in 1880 for women.

POINT OF INTEREST

BRYN MAWR (HARRITON)- Fieldstone house built in 1704. Operated by *Richard Harriton* as a tobacco plantation; later owned by *Charles Thomson,* secretary of the First Continental Congress and first person in North America to translate the Bible into English.

Higher Education - Bryn Mawr College
    Ellen Cushing Junior College
    Harcum Junior College
Community Event - May Day, Annual, May

•**BUCK**, Village; Lancaster County; Pop. 70; Area Code 717; Zip Code 17566; E Pennsylvania.

•**BUCKEYE**, Village; Westmoreland County; Pop. 75; Area Code 814; Zip Code 15666; SW central Pennsylvania.

•**BUCK HILL FALLS**, Village; Monroe County; Pop. 400; Area Code 717; Zip Code 18323; Elev. 1,360'; 32 m. SE of Scranton in E Pennsylvania; in Pocono Mountains and named for the natural falls nearby; resort and skiing area.

•**BUCKHORN**, Village; Cambia County; Pop. 80; Area Code 814; Zip Code 16613; SW central Pennsylvania.

•**BUCKHORN**, Village; Columbia County; Pop. 225; Area Code 717; Zip Code 17815; near Bloomsburg in E central Pennsylvania.

•**BUCKINGHAM**, Village and Township; Bucks County; Pop. 500; Area Code 215; Zip Code 18912; Elev. 217'; N suburb of Philadelphia in SE Pennsylvania; founded in 1702.

General Nathaniel Greene stayed at the white stucco inn, preserved here, during the Revolution.

•**BUCKINGHAM VALLEY**, Village; Bucks County; Pop. 200; Area Code 215; Zip Code 18938; near New Hope in SE Pennsylvania.

•**BUCK MOUNTAIN**, Village; Carbon County; Pop. 80; Area Code 717; Zip Code 18255; E central Pennsylvania.

•**BUCK MOUNTAIN**, Village; Schuylkill County; Pop. 150; Area Code 717; Zip Code 18214; E central Pennsylvania.

•**BUCK RUN**, Village; Chester County; Pop. 100; Area Code 215; Zip Code 19320; SE Pennsylvania.

•**BUCK RUN**, Village; Schuylkill County; Pop. 250; Area Code 717; Zip Code 17926; Elev. 1,200'; E central Pennsylvania.

•**BUCKS COUNTY**, Bucks County was named for the English shire or county of Buckingham, generally abbreviated Bucks. This name was appropriate for two reasons: the *Penns* were an old Buckinghamshire family and had been seated there for generations; and many of the Quakers who had come over with *Penn* on the *Welcome* had migrated from Buckinghamshire. At first the Pennsylvania county was called Buckingham, and twenty-five years after it was formed Oldmixon speaks of it as Buckingham County; but the abbreviated name Bucks was always the more usual and popular form, and its use gradually became general.

The name Buckingham is commonly explained as meaning "the home of the men of the beech forest." Certainly the beech was long the predominant tree in the forests of Buckinghamshire. Yet it seems more likely that the name signifies simply "the home of the Buccings," the progenitor of this family or clan either being called Bucca, or having the *buck* as his totem.

•**BUCKSTOWN**, Village; Somerset County; Pop. 120; Area Code 814; Zip Code 15564; S Pennsylvania.

•**BUENA VISTA**, Village; Allegheny County; Pop. 200; Area Code 412; Zip Code 15018; Elev. 700'; S suburb of Pittsburgh in W Pennsylvania.

•**BUENA VISTA**, Village; Butler County; Pop. 75; Area Code 814; Zip Code 16025; W Pennsylvania.

•**BUFFALO**, Village; Washington County; Pop. 150; Area Code 412; Zip Code 15301; SW Pennsylvania.

61

•**BUFFALO CROSS ROADS**, Village; Union County; Pop. 90; Area Code 717; Zip Code 17837; Central Pennsylvania.

•**BUFFALO MILLS**, Village; Bedford County; Pop. 100; Area Code 814; Zip Code 15534; S Pennsylvania.

•**BUFFALO SPRINGS**, Village; Lebanon County; Pop. 75; Area Code 717; Zip Code 17042; SE central Pennsylvania.

•**BUFFALO VALLEY (alt. Buffalo Creek)**, Village; Armstrong County; Pop. 150; Area Code 814; Zip Code 16262; W central Pennsylvania.

•**BUFINGTON**, Village; Fayette County; Pop. 530; Area Code 412; Zip Code 15468; near Uniontown in SW Pennsylvania.

•**BULGER**, Village; Washington County; Pop. 600; Area Code 412; Zip Code 15019; Elev. 1,200'; 20 m. W of Pittsburgh and 10 m. E of West Virginia state line in W Pennsylvania.

•**BULLY HILL**, Village; Venango County; Pop. 60; Area Code 814; Zip Code 16323; Just S of Franklin in NW Pennsylvania; site of Venango County Museum.

•**BUNGALOW PARK**, Village; Lehigh County; Pop. 140; Zip Code 18102; Suburb of Allentown in E Pennsylvania.

•**BUNKER HILL**, Village; Lebanon County; Pop. 350; N suburb of Lebanon in SE central Pennsylvania.

•**BUNOLA**, Village; Allegheny County; Pop. 450; Zip Code 15020; Elev. 780; 15 m. S of Pittsburgh in SW Pennsylvania; small port facilities on Monongahela River.

•**BURGETTSTOWN**, Borough; Washington County; Pop. 1,867; Area Code 412; Zip Code 15021; Elev. 989'; 20 m. W of Pittsburgh in SW Pennsylvania; named for Fort Burgett, which was erected here during the Revolutionary War by

Sebastian Burgett, a native of Germany. His son, *George Burgett,* laid out the town in 1795.

> *Agriculture* - Cattle, grain and varied
> farming
> *Industry/Mfg.* - Soft drinks, dairy products,
> steel milling, coal

•**BURLINGTON,** Borough; Bradford County; Pop. 162; Area Code 717; Zip Code 18814; Elev. 894'; on Sugar Creek in N Pennsylvania.

•**BURNHAM,** Borough; Mifflin County; Pop. 2,457; Area Code 717; Zip Code 17009; Elev. 520'; Central Pennsylvania.

Burnham sits in a bowl-shaped valley, has been an ironmaking community since Freedom Forge was established here in 1795. First known as Freedom Forge, and later as Logan, the town was renamed in 1911 for *William Burnham,* official of a local steel plant.

•**BURNSIDE,** Borough; Clearfield County; Pop. 347; Area Code 814; Zip Code 15721; Elev. 1,340; W central Pennsylvania.

On west branch of the Susquehanna River, 35 m. NW of Altoona.

•**BURNSTOWN,** Village; Lawrence County; Pop. 150; Zip Code 16117; near Ellwood City and Neshannock Creek.

•**BURNT CABINS,** Village; Fulton County; Pop. 125; Zip Code 17215; Elev. 900'.

Burnt Cabins is at the foot of Cove Mountain; was so named because the cabins of early squatters here were burned down by order of the provincial government after the Indians had complained against white encroachment on their lands.

•**BUSHKILL,** Pop. 500 (summer 1,000); Elev. 641'; name means "little river" in Dutch; was settled in 1812.

Today it is a quaint summer vacation town. Tourists enjoy visiting nearby "Niagara of Pennsylvania," the Bushkill Falls. Marked nature trails lead through scenic gorge to the majestic Main Falls.

•**BUSHKILL CENTER**, Village; Northampton County; Pop. 135; Zip Code 18064; E central Pennsylvania; named for the creek that flows nearby.

•**BUTLER**, City; Seat of Butler County; Pop. 17,026; Area Code 412; Zip Code 16001; Elev. 1,011'; 33 m. N of Pittsburgh in W Pennsylvania.

Butler, built on rolling hills originally owned by *Robert Morris* of Philadelphia, financier of the American Revolution, was laid out in 1803, and named for *Richard Butler* of York County, a lieutenant colonel with Morgan's Rifles in 1777, an Indian agent in Ohio in 1787, and a major general in the St. Clair expedition of 1791, in which he was killed. The city is bisected by Conoquenessing Creek.

Today it is the business and banking center for a large rural region.

> *Industry/Mfg.* - Rubber products, coal, concrete, oil, quarrying, clothing, dairy products
> *Higher Education* - Butler County Community College
> *Daily Newspaper* - The Eagle, 114 W. Diamond Street
> *Chamber of Commerce* - 100 N. Main Street

•**BUTLER COUNTY**, formed from Allegheny in 1800, was named for *General Richard Butler*, who served with distinction as a Revolutionary officer and perished in the bloody battle in the Miami in which *General Arthur St. Clair* was so disastrously defeated in November, 1791. *Richard Butler* was born in 1743 in Dublin, Ireland, whence his parents emigrated to Pennsylvania. He studied law and spent most of his life in the practice of his profession at Carlisle. At the age of twenty-one he received his first military experience as an ensign in the expedition that *Colonel Henry Bouquet* led westward for the relief of Fort Pitt.

He entered the American Revolution as major, served with distinction at Saratoga and Monmouth, and emerged as colonel. Both *Washington* and *Wayne*, under who he served, thought highly of his ability as an officer. He was especially familiar with Indian life, ways, and warfare, and knew several Indian dialects. The last three or four years of his life he spent in western Pennsylvania. He was prominent in urging the formation of Allegheny County, serving as one of its judges and representing it in the Legislature. He was popular in Pittsburgh, where one of the chief taverns bore his name, and where "many a partial parent called a son after him."

When *General St. Clair* and his little army were sent forth to punish the hostile Indians on the Miami and the Wabash, *Richard Butler* was made a major-general and was second in command. Wounded unto death in the dreadful battle, in which more than three-fifths of the American force were killed, injured, or missing, *General Butler* urged his comrades to leave him to his fate, and to make good their escape.

•**BUTTONWOOD**, Village; Luzerne County; Pop. 380; Zip Code 18702; near Wilkes-Barre in E central Pennsylvania; on the Penn Central and other major rail lines.

•**BUTTONWOOD MANOR**, Village; Bucks County; Pop. 200; Zip Code 18901; SE Pennsylvania; residential area near Doylestown.

•**BUTZTOWN**, Village; Northampton County; Pop. 900; Elev. 350; NE suburb of Bethlehem in E Pennsylvania.

•**BYRNEDALE**, Village; Elk County; Pop. 500; Zip Code 15827; Elev. 1,225'; 20 m. S of Johnsonburg; rural.

65

•CABOT, Village; Butler County; Pop. 400; Zip Code 16023; Elev. 1,200'; on Penn Central rail line SE of Butler.

•CADOGAN, Village; Armstrong County; Pop. 563; Zip Code 16212; Elev. 900'; on Allegheny River, approx. 10 m. S of Kittanning.

•CAIRNBROOK, Village; Somerset County; Pop. 800; Zip Code 15924; Elev. 2,200'; on Shade Creek and Penn Central rail line from Johnstown, approx. 20 m. N.

•CALIFORNIA, Borough; Washington County; Pop. 5,703; Area Code 412; Zip Code 15419; Elev. 800'; 40 m. S of Pittsburgh in SW Pennsylvania; annexed to E Pike Run Township in 1954; site of California State College.

The town was laid out in 1849, shortly after the discovery of gold in California, when this alluring name was in everyone's mouth.

POINT OF INTEREST

OLD MAIN, CALIFORNIA STATE COLLEGE- Main administration building of California State College from 1870-1971. *Barr* and *Moser*, architects. Romanesque Revival.

•CALLENSBURG, Borough; Clarion County; Pop. 248; Area Code 814; Zip Code 16213; Elev. 1100'; 45 m. NE of Pittsburgh on the Clarion River in W Pennsylvania.

•CALLERY, Borough; Butler County; Pop. 415; Area Code 412; Zip Code 16024; Elev. 974'; NW suburb of Pittsburgh in W Pennsylvania.

•CALLIMONT, Borough; Somerset County; Pop. 32; Area Code 814; S Pennsylvania.

•**CALUMET**, Village; Westmoreland County; Pop. 800; Zip Code 15621; Elev. 1,080'; E suburb of Pittsburgh in W central Pennsylvania.

•**CAMBELLTOWN**, Village; Lebanon County; Pop. 1,355; Zip Code 17010; Elev. 440; 20 m. E of Harrisburg and near Hershey in SE central Pennsylvania.

•**CAMBRIA HEIGHTS**, Village; Cambria County; Pop. 500; Zip Code 15906; in the hills near Johnstown in S Pennsylvania; name is derived from the old poetic word for Wales, "Cymry."

•**CAMBRIDGE SPRINGS**, Borough; Crawford County; Pop. 2,102; Area Code 814; Zip Code 16403; Elev. 1,181'; NW Pennsylvania.

Cambridge Springs is on French Creek. *Dr. John H. Gray* found a mineral spring here in 1884 while prospecting for oil; he advertised its therapeutic qualities widely at a time when people thought a little iron in the water would cure almost anything. Prosperous as a summer health resort, Cambridge Springs also has winter recreation facilities: a toboggan slide, a ski trail, and a skating rink at nearby Mount Pleasant. Alliance College is located here.

•**CAMERON**, Village; Cameron County; Pop. 75; Zip Code 15834; Elev. 960'; once a thriving lumbering and mining town.

The village and the county were named for *Simon Cameron* (1799-1889) of Lancaster County, who controlled the Republican Party in Pennsylvania for more than three decades. He was the first Secretary of War under *Lincoln* and several times a member of the United States Senate.

•**CAMERON COUNTY**, formed in 1860 out of parts of Clinton, Elk, McKean, and Potter, was named in honor of *Simon Cameron*, then United States Senator for Pennsylvania. *Simon Cameron*, of Lancaster County, began his career as printer and editor in Doylestown and Harrisburg, and later became wealthy as a banker and as a builder of railroads. Long the "Czar of Pennsylvania politics," he filled various important public offices. He was adjutant-general of Pennsylvania and served his state in the United States Senate for eighteen years. He was a prominent candidate for the presidential nomination at the Republican convention that selected *Abraham Lincoln*. He became *Lincoln's* first secretary of war, resigning the appointment in January, 1862, to become the Minister to Russia. The village of Cameron, in Cameron County, is also named for him. Cameron is a Scotch family name of personal characteristic, signifying in the Gaelic "the man with the crooked nose."

•**CAMP HILL**, Borough; Cumberland County; Pop. 8,422; Area Code 717; Zip Code 17011; Elev. 420'; SW suburb of Harrisburg in S Pennsylvania; south of town is a State Correctional Institution, with 1,300 inmates.

A Department of Defense supply depot is located in town.

POINT OF INTEREST

PEACE CHURCH- Built in 1798 and used by the county's early Reformed and Lutheran congregations; rare 1807 pipe organ.

Industry/Mfg. - Animal feed, paint

•**CANADENSIS**, Village; Monroe County; Pop. 800; Zip Code 18325; Elev. 1,002; E Pennsylvania; on Brodhead Creek at Buck Hill Falls; resort village near several ski facilities. Summer and vancation time population rises to approx. 2,000.

•**CANONSBURG**, Borough; Washington County; Pop. 10,459; Area Code 412; Zip Code 15317; Elev. 931'; 17 m. SW of Pittsburgh in SW Pennsylvania.

Canonsburg was settled about 1773 and laid out in 1787 by *Colonel John Canon*, militia officer and member of the State assembly.

According to a story told of *George Washington's* efforts to oust squatters from his property here, the local justice of the peace sided with the squatters and exasperated *Washington* by repeatedly post-poning the hearing. When it was held and *Washington* assertedly began his testimony with the words: "By God, I'll...", the justice banged his gavel and fined him for profanity in court.

In 1921 *Mme. Marie Curie*, co-discoverer of radium, visited the now defunct Standard Chemical Company, then one of the largest radium producers. A gram of the element produced here, worth $120,000 was presented to her in Washington, D.C., by *President Harding*, as a gift of "the people of Pittsburgh."

An old log Academy is in town. Built in 1780, it is the oldest school building west of the Alleghenies. Jefferson College was once situated here before it merged with Washington College in the town of Washington.

Electrical parts and structural steel are made in town today.

•**CANTON**, Borough; Bradford County; Pop. 1,959; Area Code 717; Zip Code 17724; Elev. 1,255'; 30 m. NE of Williamsport in N Pennsylvania.

Canton was founded in 1800 and named for the Connecticut town by early settlers.

> *Agriculture* - Varied farming
> *Industry/Mfg.* - Boxes, wood products,
> plastics, dairy products

•**CARBON**, Village; Westmoreland County; Pop. 350; Zip Code 15601; just S of Greensburg; named for coal mining activities in the region.

•**CARBON COUNTY**, formed from Northampton and Monroe in 1843 after twenty-seven years of agitation, received its name form the fact that it was known to be underlaid with rich deposits of anthracite coal, which has formed its chief source of wealth. The pioneers in the Lehigh coal industry of Carbon County were *Josiah White*, *Erskine Hazard* and *George F.A. Hauto*.

•**CARBONDALE**, City; Lackawanna County; Pop. 11,255; Area Code 717; Zip Code 18407; Elev. 1,078'; on Lackawanna River, 16 m. NE of Scranton in NE Pennsylvania.

Carbondale had been an anthracite town since 1814, when *William Wurts*, a Philadelphia merchant, owner of large tracts in the vicinity, and *David Nobles*, a hunter who knew the region, opened veins and obtained coal for exhibition and appraisal in New York and Philadelphia. In the winter of 1822, *Maurice Wurts*, Williams brother, mined 800 tons and sent part of it by sleigh to "the rafting place," probably White Mills. Within a few years the Delaware and Hudson Canal Company gained control of the mines and adjacent property. Tools and supplies were addressed to the "dale where carbon was found," hence the present name. The settlement grew rapidly; Irishmen and Welshmen predominated, and their crowded communities, resembling army encampments, were known as Irish Hill and Welsh Hill. The greater part of Carbondale was consumed by fire on December 15, 1850.

Today, the city is part of the vast Scranton metropolitan area, along the Lackawanna River.

Agriculture - Fruit, poultry and varied
    farming
Industry/Mfg. - Campers, cloth, coal, dairy
    products, electronics, chemicals

•CARLISLE, Borough; Seat of Cumberland County; Pop. 18,314; Area Code 717; Zip Code 17013; Elev. 478'; 15 m. W of Harrisburg in S Pennsylvania.

Molly Pritcher, the famous Revolutionary War fighter and nurse, died and was buried here. The Carlisle Barracks (Civil War), have been preserved nearby.

In 1735 *James Le Tort*, a French Protestant trader with the Indians, had built his cabin at a spring which took his name, where Carlisle now stands.

On this site *Nicholas Scull*, then surveyor-general of the province, following instructions from the proprietary government, laid out in 1751 a town which was called Carlisle from the capital of the English county of Cumberland. It became the permanent county-seat in the following year. In 1753 there were only five dwellings in the place. Thirty years later, Dickinson College, which is next to the oldest college in Pennsylvania, was chartered, and was named in honor of *John Dickinson*, then governor of Pennsylvania, in gratitude for his liberal gifts to the new college.

POINTS OF INTEREST

CARLISLE INDIAN SCHOOL- Indian Industrial School founded here, 1879, as semimilitary school which educated thousands of Indian students, including *Jim Thorpe*, famed Indian athlete.

HESSIAN POWDER MAGAZINE- Built in 1777 as one of powder magazines of Carlisle Barracks; later converted to guardhouse. Museum.

OLD WEST, DICKINSON COLLEGE- Original building of Dickinson College, inc. 1783. *Benjamin H. Latrobe*, architect. Federal and Greek Revival elements.

Agriculture - Grain, vegetable and varied
     farming
Industry/Mfg. - Clothing, footwear,
     electronics, boxes
Higher Education - Dickinson College
Daily Newspaper - The Sentinel, 457 E. North
     Street
Chamber of Commerce - PO Box 572

•**CATASAUQUA**, Borough; Lehigh County; Pop. 7,944; Area Code 215; Zip Code 18032; Elev. 320'; on Lehigh River, N of Allentown in E Pennsylvania. Site of Allentown-Bethlehem-Easton Airport.

The first settlement was called Cranesville, for the ironmaster, *George Crane*, of the Lehigh Crane Iron Company, which began operations here in 1839. About five years later the name was changed to Sideropolis, which is Greek for "iron city." This ponderous name was dropped after a few years, and in 1853 the growing town was incorporated as Catasauqua, for the creek flowing nearby, a name corrupted from the Delaware Indian phrase *gotto-shacki*, "burnt ground", "parched land," or "the earth thirsts". We can only guess why the Indians should have given so odd a name to this stream. Perhaps they wished to designate a spot or region which they had burnt over in successive years to destroy the undergrowth, in order that they might more freely follow the chase. The Indians were in the habit of clearing ground in this way.

Catasauqua was the home of *George Taylor*, one of the signers of the Declaration of Independence. His home, built in 1768, overlooking the Lehigh River, has been restored.

•**CARMICHAELS**, Borough; Greene County; Pop. 630; Area Code 412; Zip Code 15320; Elev. 1,000'; 40 m. S of Pittsburgh in SW Pennsylvania; on Muddy Creek.

•**CARNEGIE**, Borough; Allegheny County; Pop. 10,099; Area Code 412; Zip Code 15106; Elev. 769'; 6 m. W of Pittsburgh in SW Pennsylvania.

Carnegie is in the heart of the fertile Chartiers Valley, bears unmistakable marks of coal and steel.

Formed in 1894 by the consolidation of Chariters and Mansfield, the community was named for *Andrew Carnegie*. Five years later *Carnegie* gave the borough $200,000 for the Andrew Carnegie Free Library.

Today the borough is one of the out-lying suburbs of Pittsburgh, where many commute into the city each day for work.

> *Agriculture* - Fruit, vegetable, poultry and
> varied farming
> *Industry/Mfg.* - Steel, chemicals, coal, dairy
> products
> *Chamber of Commerce* - 150 E. Mall Plaza

•**CARNOT**, Village; Allegheny County; Pop. 4,000; Area Code 412; Zip Code 15108; NW suburb of Pittsburgh in SW Pennsylvania; near Coraopolis in a hilly area.

•**CARROLL PARK**, Village; Delawre and Montgomery Counties; Pop. 1,500; Area Code 215; Zip Code 19151; NW suburb of Philadelphia in SW Pennsylvania; in a low density, residential area with several golf courses nearby.

•**CARROLLTOWN**, Borough; Cambria County; Pop. 1,395; Area Code 814; Zip Code 15722; Elev. 2,140'; SW central Pennsylvania.

Carrolltown was laid out in 1840, was named by *Prince Demetrius Gallitzin* for *John Carroll* who, in 1788, became the first Roman Catholic Bishop in the United States and 20 years later was Archbishop of Baltimore. His cousin, *Charles Caroll*, signed the Declaration of Independence, and later resided here.

•**CARROLL VALLEY**, Borough; Adams County; Pop. 817; Area Code 717; near Gettysburg in S Pennsylvania.

•**CASHTOWN**, Village; Adams County; Pop. 250; Area Code 717; Zip Code 17310; Elev. 745'; 8 m. W of Gettysburg in S Pennsylvania.

This tiny agricultural village lies in the shadow of Rock Top, which once marked the western limit of pioneering German emigration. It is said to have been named for an early tavernkeeper's insistence that all patrons pay cash. An old tavern, possibly the legendary one, stands here, built in 1797. Nearby is the Conewago Mission, one of the first Jesuit outposts when it was built in 1817.

•**CASSANDRA**, Borough; Cambria County; Pop. 238; Area Code 814; Zip Code 15925; Elev. 1,800'; 15 m. SW of Altoona near Admiral Peary Park in SW central Pennsylvania; Conemaugh Creek flows through town.

•**CASSELMAN**, Borough; Somerset County; Pop. 114; Area Code 814; S Pennsylvania.

•**CASSVILLE**, Borough; Huntingdon County; Pop. 183; Area Code 717; Zip Code 16623; Elev. 1,241'; S central Pennsylvania.

Cassville took its name from Cass Township, which was named in 1843 for the statesman, *Lewis Cass* shortly after the public welcome he had received in Philadelphia upon his return from France, where he had served as United States ambassador.

•**CASTLE SHANNON**, Borough; Allegheny County; Pop. 10,164; Area Code 412; Zip Code 15234; Elev. 1,040'; 8 m. S of Pittsburgh in SW Pennsylvania; on Saw Mill Run; suburban area.

POINT OF INTEREST

GEORGE TAYLOR HOUSE- Home (1768-1776) of *George Taylor*, politician and signer of Declaration of Indepencence. Restored. Musuem.

•**CATAWISSA**, Borough; Columbia County; Pop. 1,568; Area Code 717; Zip Code 17820; E central Pennsylvania; on Susquehanna River near a group of mountains and a creek by the same name.

Catawissa is a corruption of *gattawisi*, "growing fat." The Indian hunters may have killed a deer along the stream in the season when deer fatten. Catawissa was laid out in 1787 by *William Hughes*, a Berks County Quaker.

•**CECIL**, Village; Washington County; Pop. 900; Area Code 412; Zip Code 15321; Elev. 980'; 10 m. SW of Pittsburgh in SW Pennsylvania; on a branch of Chartiers Creek.

•**CEDAR CLIFF MANOR**, Village; Cumberland County; Pop. 1,300; Area Code 717; Zip Code 17011; S Pennsylvania; large residential subdivision across the Susquehanna River from Harrisburg.

•**CEMENTON**, Village; Lehigh County; Pop. 1,200; Area Code 215; Zip Code 18052; 7 m. N of Allentown in E Pennsylvania; on Lehigh River; in a residential-industrial area.

•**CENTERPORT**, Borough; Berks County; Pop. 246; Area Code 215; Zip Code 19516; Elev. 340'; 10 m. NW of Reading in SE Pennsylvania; on Irish Creek.

POINT OF INTEREST

BELLMAN'S UNION CHURCH- Early-18th century example of sophisticated country church; Georgian.

•**CENTER SQUARE**, Village; Montgomery County; Pop. 600; Area Code 215; Zip Code 19422; Elev. 250'; 3 m. E of Blue Bell in SE Pennsylvania; residential village in a rural area; the county newspaper is published here.

•**CENTERVILLE**, Borough; Crawford County; Pop. 245; Area Code 814; Zip Code 16404; NW Pennsylvania; near Oil Creek in a farming area.

•**CENTERVILLE**, Borough; Washington County; Pop. 4,207; Area Code 412; Zip Code 16404; Elev. 1,160'; SW Pennsylvania.
    Centerville was laid out in 1821 as a pike town, was named for its position between Uniontown and Washington. The first settlement on the land now within the borough of Centerville was made in 1766.

•**CENTRAL CITY**, Borough; Somerset County; Pop. 1,496; Area Code 814; Zip Code 15926; 15 m. S of Johnstown on Shade Creek in S Pennsylvania; Terminal of Penn Central rail line is here.

•**CENTRAL HIGHLANDS**, Village; Allegheny County; Pop. 1,000; Area Code 412; Zip Code 15037; Elev. 1,100';

SW Pennsylvania; suburb of Pittsburgh in the hilly regions SE of the city.

•CENTRALIA, Borough; Columbia County; Pop. 1,017; Area Code 717; Zip Code 17927; Elev. 1,484'; 30 m. E of Sunbury in E central Pennsylvania; was founded in 1826 and named for its then strategic commercial situation.

•CENTRE HALL, Borough; Centre County; Pop. 1,233; Pop. 814; Zip Code 16828; Elev. 1,320'; Central Pennsylvania.

Centre Hall is a crossroads settlement on gently sloping ground, is named for its central position in Penn's Valley, one of the state's finest hunting and fishing sections.

This borough was first settled by *John Lyon*, an ironmaster of Scotch-Irish descent, who married *Jane Maclay*. The town was built on the *Lyon's* farm. *Henry Whitmen* named the place Centre Hall because it was midway between the eastern and western ends of Penn's Valley. "Hall" is said to have originated in imitation of the British practice of using Hall as the name of a manor house with an adjoining hamlet.

Community Event - Steam Engine Days, Annual, September

•CHADDS FORD, Village; Delaware County; Pop. 250; Area Code 215; Zip Code 19317; Elev. 168'; SE Pennsylvania.

Chadds Ford, center of the Battle of the Brandywine, occupies the east bank of Brandywine Creek. Here, on September 11, 1777, the American Revolutionary Army suffered a major defeat when *Washington*, in an effort to halt the British march on Philadelphia, hurled 12,000 troops against a force of 18,000 British and Hessian soldiers under *General Howe* and *General Knyphausen*. Maneuvering went on in a fog for hours. Finally, late in the afternoon, the British crossed the creek, flanked the Americans, forced them to retreat, and moved on to Philadelphia, as the Colonials withdrew to the northwest of the city and prepared for the Battle of Germantown.

The town was named for *John Chadds*, son of *Francis Chadds*, or *Chadsey*, who emigrated from Wiltshire in 1689, and settled on a tract that included all the present village of Chadds Ford. "As the tide of emigration moved westward, public travel increased, and as the Brandywine in rainy weather and in springtime was so swollen that it was almost impossible to cross it, *John Chadds* was solicited to establish a ferry at this place; and to aid him in that public work, the county of Chester lent him 30 pounds to meet the expense he was put to in building a flat or schowe." He entered upon his duties as ferryman at Chadds' Ford in 1737. He was also allowed to open an inn on the road from Philadelphia to Nottingham. *John Chadds* kept "the Chadds' Ford tavern" for 10 years, but he was apparently in charge of the ferry until his death in 1760. *Joseph Davis* was the innkeeper at the time of the battle of Brandywine.

Today, people come to the village to enjoy the nearby Chadd's Peak Ski area in winter.

POINTS OF INTEREST

BRANDYWINE BATTLEFIELD- Site of Battle of Brandywine, Sept. 11, 1777. 50-acre park includes *Lafayette's* headquarters (restored) and *Washington's* headquarters (reconstructed).

CHADD HOUSE- Uncoursed fieldstone house, built before 1725 by *John Wyeth, Jr.*, who was probably hired by landowner *John Chadd.*

CHADD'S FORD HISTORIC DISTRICT- 18th-19th century village containing predominantly stone structures; notable are the Chadd House and springhouse. Retains small town appearance.

GILPIN HOMESTEAD- 18th century house and outbuildings; served as *Maj. Gen. William Howe's* headquarters following the Battle of Brandywine in Sept. 1777.

WILLIAM PAINTER FARM- Built in 1808, the home of *William Painter*, abolitionist and Quaker instrumental in founding of the Concord Friends Meeting.

TWADDELL'S MILL AND HOUSE- Late-18th-early-19th Century stone house (restored). Home of *Henry Gordon*, engineer to generals *Braddock* and *Forbes* ; and of *William Twaddell*, prosperous grist, saw and powder miller.

•**CHALFANT**, Borough; Alegheny County; Pop. 1,140'; SW Pennsylvania; E suburb of Pittsburgh in a low density residential area.

•**CHALFONT**, Borough; Bucks County; Pop. 2,802; Area Code 215; Zip Code 18914; Elev. 225'; SE Pennsylvania.

Chalfont, originally Butlers Mill, was renamed for *Chalfont St. Giles*, an English parish where *William Penn* is buried.

In Chalfont, along Neshammy Creek, is the spot where, according to local tradition, the famed Delaware chief, *Tamenend*, better known as *Tammany*, was buried. Repeated investigations have failed to discover the grave. *Tammany*, an intelligent and peaceful Indian from whom *William Penn* bought the land between the Neshaminy and Pennypack Creeks in 1683, lived in what is now Bucks County. Admirers dubbed him *King Tammany*, and later *Saint Tammany*. A number of early patriotic societies took his name. The Sons of King Tammany was organized in Philadelphia in 1772; the Tammany Society of New York, known for its association with the New York Democratic organization, in 1786. In the Revolution some of the Pennsylvania troops adopted *Tammany* as their patron saint.

Chalfont was originally the name of a station on the Doylestown branch of the Philadelphia and Reading Railroad. The name was later adopted by the town.

Chalfont is a residential suburb of Pennsylvania today. It is the headquarters of the German Shepherd Dog Club of America.

•**CHAMBERSBURG**, Borough; Seat of Franklin County; Pop. 16,174; Area Code 717; Zip Code 17201; Elev. 620'; 50 m. SW of Harrisburg in S Pennsylvania.

Chambersburg lies in the midst of the vast peach and apple section of the Cumberland Valley. *Benjamin Chambers* settled on this tract as miller, sawyer, trader, physician, militia colonel, judge, and arbitrator and the town was formally laid out in 1764. Chambersburg was pillaged and burned by the Confederates under *General McCausland* and *General Johnson* on July 30, 1864, in retaliation for a Federal raid on the Shenandoan Valley. Perhaps the fact that *John Brown* lived in Chambersburg in 1859, prior to his attack on Harpers Ferry, contributed to the thoroughness of the destruction, which resulted in more than $2,000,000 property damage.

John Brown had his headquarters here. He came to be regarded in the North as a martyr and in the South as a

77

dangerous criminal, was born in 1800 at Torrington, Connecticut. His boyhood was spent in Ohio and was followed by years of business failures. Indeed, he was 50 before he attained any degree of prominence. Always an ardent abolitionist, he had conducted a station of the Undergound Railroad at Richmond, Ohio. In 1855, five of his sons took up land in Kansas, then torn by bitter civil warfare on the slavery question. Their avowed purpose was to give every aid thay could to the Free State cause. Soon they were followed by their father, who loaded his wagon with arms and journeyed to Osawatomie, Kansas. Here he became a surveyor and captain of militia, and was known as "Old Brown of Osawatomie."

The sack of Lawrence, Kansas, by pro-slavery men served to arouse *Brown* to a frenzy. With four of his sons and two other men, *Brown* attacked a small pro-slavery settlement on the Pottawatomie River on the night of May 24, 1856. Asserting that he was only an instrument in God's hands, *Brown* and his followers killed five of the pro-slavery men and subsequently conducted a fierce guerilla campaign.

Late in 1857 *Brown* began enlisting men in furtherance of a plan which took definite form at a meeting held at Chatham, Canada, in 1858. At this meeting a provisional constitution for a free mountain state to be established in Maryland or Virginia was drawn up, with *Brown* as commander-in-chief. From abolitionist sources he obtained money with which to buy arms. *Brown* came to Chambersburg in the summer of 1859, describing himself as a prospector. At his headquarters he received large boxes marked "tools," which really contained carbines. These were removed to a small farm in Maryland where *Brown* assembled his 21 followers. On October 16, 1859, the raiders seized the U.S. Marines and Virginia militia under the ocmmand of *Robert E. Lee*, then a colonel. Convicted of treason, *Brown* was hanged on December 2, 1859, and those of his followers who had survived the fight at the arsenal subsequently shared his fate.

Today, a U.S. Army depot stands near the site of Brown's Battle.

POINTS OF INTEREST

JOHN BROWN HOUSE- 19th century log construction; upstairs was occupied by abolitionist *John Brown* from June to October, 1859.

FRANKLIN COUNTY COURTHOUSE- The third courthouse on the site; built in 1865 to replace the structure burned by Confederates in 1864.

FRANKLIN COUNTY JAIL- One of the oldest continuously used penal institutions in the U.S.

Agriculture - Fruit, grain and varied farming
Industry/Mfg. - Varied manufacturing, trade
and services
Higher Education - Wilson College
Daily Newspaper - The Public Opinion, 77 N.
Third Street
Chamber of Commerce - PO Box 399

•**CHAPEL DOWNS**, Village; Allegheny County; Pop. 600; Area Code 412; Zip Code 15024; residential suburb of Pittsburgh in SW Pennsylvania.

•**CHAPMAN**, Borough; Northampton County; Pop. 255; Area Code 215; in Allentwon-Bethlehem metropolitan area, in E Pennsylvania.

•**CHARLEROI**, Borough; Washington County; Pop. 5,717; Area Code 412; Zip Code 15022; Elev. 761'; 2 m. S of Pittsburgh in SW Pennsylvania.

Charleroi is the trading center of this glass manufacturing region. It was laid out in 1890 as the site of a large glass plant, and named Charleroi for an industrial town of that name in Belgium, which has long been noted for its fine glassmaking.

Agriculture - Grain and varied farming
Industry/Mfg. - Clothing, dairy products,
boxes
Chamber of Commerce - PO Box 127

•**CHATHAM**, Village; Chester County; Pop. 300; Area Code 215; Zip Code 19318; Elev. 400'; suburb of Philadelphia in SE Pennsylvania; named for the English statesman *William Pitt*, the Earl of Chatham.

•**CHATWOOD**, Village; Chester County; Pop. 1000; Area Code 215; Zip Code 19380; NW suburb of Philadelphia in SW Pennsylvania; residential.

79

•**CHELTENHAM**, Village; Montgomery County; Pop. 6,500; Area Code 215; Zip Code 19012; Elev. 130'; N suburb of Philadelphia in SE Pennsylvania; seat of a large township by the same name.

•**CHERRY CITY**, Village (uninc.); Allegheny County; Pop. 4,000; Area Code 412; Zip Code 15223; NE suburb of Pittsburgh that grew substantially after World War II; on the Allegheny River.

•**CHERRY TREE**, Borough; Indiana County; Pop. 520; Area Code 412; Zip Code 15724; Elev. 1,365'; W central Pennsylvania.

Cherry Tree is at the junction of a small creek with the West Branch and was founded in 1822. Known to the Indians as Canoe Place, it was renamed for the cherry tree that was used to determine one of the boundaries of the territory conveyed to the Pennsylvania Proprietaries by the Fort Stanwix Treaty of 1768.

•**CHERRY VALLEY**, Borough; Butler County; Pop. 91; Area Code 412; W Pennsylvania.

•**CHERRYVILLE**, Village; Northampton County; Pop. 350; Area Code 215; Zip Code 18035; Elev. 760'; 10 m. N of Allentown in E Pennsylvania.

•**CHESTER**, City; Delaware County seat; Pop. 45,705; Area Code 215; Zip Code 19013; Elev. 23'; 15 m. SW of Philadelphia on the Delaware River.

Chester is the second oldest settlement in Pennsylvania. The city, center of an industrial area and the second port of Pennsylvania, was named by *William Penn* allegedly in honor of *Lord Chester*. Long before the coming of *Penn*, however, the Swedes had settled here and called it Upland, a name perpetuated in a small borough just outside the city.

The Chester of today is far removed in physical aspect and atmosphere from the gentle Quaker community of its founding days. Upon the river, which gave the little English village its importance, the city still depends for its vitality. Great industrial plants line the water front, their blackened piers reaching like giant fingers into the stream. Where once stretched "the Green" of the Swedish church lands and the peaceful farms of early settlers, now is heard the whir of machinery, the clang of metal, and the roar of furnaces as Chester goes about its business of building ships, assembling automobiles, refining oil, and manufacturing products of steel, glass, paper, textiles and hundreds of other commodities.

Up from the river the city spreads like a huge slipper, its heel outlined by Ridley and Chester Creeks, its toe abutting on Lower Chichester Township several miles west. The whole scene, however, is one of compactness, even of overcrowding. Streets are narrow and buildings are tightly packed in short blocks, as though the city were loath to depart from the plan of its founders. The business section clings for the most part to "Old Chester," that section bounded by Front, Welsh, and 6th Streets and Edgmont Avenue.

Settled by the Swedes in 1644, when the Swedish crown granted part of this area to *Joran Kyn*, one of the bodyguards of *Governor Printz*, Chester was the most important town in Pennsylvania until 1683. Until the coming of *William Penn* in 1682 the settlement of Upland, or "Oplandt," as it was called by the Dutch, was ruled by several governments. Swedish control ended in 1655 when *Peter Stuyvesant*, Dutch governor of New York, sailed up the Delaware with a fleet of seven vessels and captured the Swedish strongholds. In 1664 *Stuyvesant's* compatriots capitulated to the English, following a naval victory by the Duke of York. The colony was recaptured by the Dutch in 1673, but this later Dutch occupation lasted only six months, and then Upland again passed into the possession of the English.

With the English occupation, the government was reorganized, with the old magistrates continuing in office. Upon the arrival in 1681 of *William Markham*, *Penn's* cousin and deputy governor, the seat of the proprietary government was established here, and here also the first general assembly convened, in December 1682, with *Penn* presiding. Five years later one of the earliest juries of women to serve in any court in the United States was impaneled. In 1701 Chester was chartered as a borough.

Chester grew slowly despite its location on the Delaware, the rich land about it, and the fur trade with the Indians; by 1760 it still contained less than 150 houses.

Between 1761 and 1770, when *Francis Richardson* constructed extensive warehouses and two piers along the river, the town hoped to rival the rapidly growing Philadelphia as a port. *Richardson*, however, was ruined by the Revolution, and the expected growth of commerce and industry did not come until a much later period.

Chester's role in the War of Independence was a dramatic, though a minor one. It was from this port, before hostilities broke out, that *Benjamin Franklin* embarked on his journey to England to present the grievances of the Colonies to *George III*. From the town and its environs *"Mad Anthony" Wayne* mustered his command (the Fourth Battlalion of the Pennsylvania Line) in February 1776, making his headquarters in the courthouse and drilling his raw recruits in the city streets. Following the Battle of the Brandywine on September 11, 1777, the defeated Continental Army straggled into town. *Lafayette's* wounds were treated in a private house here, and *General Washington* spent the night at an inn, where he wrote the only official report of the battle. A part of the British forces meanwhile were encamped at Village Green three miles northwest of Chester.

After the Revolution the little town enjoyed a certain amount of importance, first as the county seat of Chester County and then as the seat of the newer Delaware County. In 1851 court records and county property were removed to Media. This, instead of proving a setback, marked the beginning of Chester's expansion in manufacture and trade. Since World War I when it became a center of the munitions industry, it has been a thriving port.

It is also important for those seeking education at Widener College, a private coeducational institution of 2,000 students, founded in 1821, or the Crozier Chester Medical Center.

One of the oldest places of worship in Pennsylvania is in Chester, the Friends Meetinghouse, which was built n 1736 in a Georgian Colonial design of red brick. The nearby Steamboat Hotel was erected in 1765, but has been much altered since that time.

POINTS OF INTEREST

FRIENDS MEETINGHOUSE- Built in 1736, one of the oldest places of worship in the state.

WILLIAM PENN LANDING SITE- Landing site of *Penn's* ship *Welcom*, Oct. 1682; also location of the log house where the first Quaker meeting was held.

1724 CHESTER COURTHOUSE- Built in 1724, among the earliest public buildings in the U.S.; county courthouse from 1789-1851.

Industry/Mfg. - Varied manufacturing, trade and services
Higher Education - Widener College
Daily Newspaper - The Delaware County Daily Times, 500 Mildred Ave.
Community Event - Newlife Folk Festival, Annual, November

•**CHESTER HEIGHTS**, Borough; Delaware County; Pop. 1,302; Area Code 215; Zip Code 19017; Elev. 340'; SE Pennsylvania.

•**CHESTER HILL**, Borough; Clearfield County; Pop. 1,054; Area Code 814; Zip Code 16866; Elev. 1,440'; on the Moshannon Creek near Phillipsburg in W Pennsylvania.

•**CHESTER SPRINGS**, Borough; Cambria County; Pop. 198; Area Code 814; Zip Code 16624; Elev. 260'; 9 m. NW of West Chester in SW central Pennsylvania.
    Set in the outskirts of the Philadelphia metropolitan area as well as a larger agricultural region, Chester Springs is a town that belies its number of inhabitants.

POINT OF INTEREST

HALL'S BRIDGE- The county's oldest covered bridge, built c. 1850.

•**CHESTNUT RIDGE**, Mountain ridge; W central Pennsylvania; extends approx. 130 m. from West Virginia state line NW to Indiana County. Considered part of the Allegheny and Appalachian Mountain ranges. Several ski resorts and coal mines lie along this thin line of hills.

•**CHESWICK**, Borough; Allegheny County; Pop. 2,336; Area Code 412; Zip Code 15024; 12 m. NE of Pittsburgh in an industrial-mining area in SW Pennsylvania; on Allegheny River.

•**CHICORA**, Borough; Butler County; Pop. 1,192; Area Code 412; Zip Code 16025; Elev. 1,247'; 10 m. NE of Butler in W Pennsylvania; on B&O Railroad line; name was changed from Millerstown in 1956.

•**CHRISTIANA**, Borough; Lancaster County; Pop. 1,183; Area Code 717; Zip Code 17509; Elev. 494'; SE Pennsylvania.

Christiana was not named, as has often been asserted, for *King Christian* and *Queen Christiana* of Sweden, but for *Christiana*, the first wife of *William Noble*, who built the first house and started a machine-shop here in 1833.

•**CHURCHILL**, Borough; Allegheny County; Pop. 4,285; Area Code 412; Zip Code 15221; Elev. 1,100'; E suburb of Pittsburgh in SW Pennsylvania; site of the Westinghouse Research and Development Center as well as a large golf course.

•**CHURCHVILLE**, Village; Bucks County; Pop. 2,600; Area Code 215; Zip Code 18966; near Southampton in SE Pennsylvania; N suburb of Philadelphia.

•**CLAIRTON**, City; Alegheny County; Pop. 12,188; Area Code 412; Zip Code 15025; Elev. 960'; SW Pennsylvania.

Clairton was almost entirely residential until the 1890s. A glass plant and a brickyard were established in 1892, and several years later steel works began operating. At the turn of the century the steel plants were amalgamated, and a by-product coke plant, occupying 175 acres along two miles of river front, was erected, the largest plant of its kind in the United States, with 1,134 ovens in 18 great batteries.

The origin of the city's name is not certain. One can be fairly sure the the name Clairton has been made by adding the locative suffix *ton* ("town") to *Clair* ("clear, bright, or illustrious"), the second syllable of the surname St. Clair or its variant form, Sinclair. The current traditional explanation is that the name Clairton is derived from the name of *Samuel Sinclair*, who once owned a tract of 215 acres of land on which part of the present city is built, and not from *General Arthur St. Clair*, who was a prominent figure in the early history of western Pennsylvania, and for whom the old township of Saint Clair and the former borough of Saint Clair, in Allegheny County, were named. Clairton was incorporated as a borugh in 1903 and received a city charter in 1922.

•**CLARENDON**, Borough; Warren County; Pop. 776; Area Code 814; Zip Code 16313; Elev. 1,399'; NW Pennsylvania.

Clarendon was named for *Thomas Clarendon.* who set up a tannery and sawmill in 1871. Oil was discoverd along Dutchman's Run nearby in 1868; prospectors swarmed in to fill rapidly built hotels and boarding houses.

•**CLARIDGE**, Village; Westmoreland County; Pop. 1,100; Area Code 412; Zip Code 15623; Elev. 1,060; 20 m. E of Pittsburgh, near Jeannette in SW Pennsylvania. Claridge is the site of the Battle of Bushy Run during the Civil War.

•**CLARION**, Borough; Seat of Clarion County; Pop. 6,664; Area Code 814; Zip Code 16214; Elev. 1,491'; 28 m. SE of Oil City in W Pennsylvania.

John Sloan laid out Clarion on a plateau along the Clarion River in 1840, after this site had been chosen as the Clarion County seat because of its central location on the Bellefonte-Meadville Turnpike.

The village, whose origin was purely political, grew so rapidly that within a year it had a population of 800 and in 1841 it was incorporated as a borough.

> *Agriculture* - Cattle, truck and varied farm
> ing
> *Higher Education* - Clarion State College
> *Chamber of Commerce* - 517 Main Street
> *Community Event* - Autumn Leaf Festival,
> Annual, October

•**CLARION COUNTY**, Clarion County, established in 1839, received its name from the Clarion River, which flows westward through this county into the Alegheny. Until 1817 this stream had been called Toby's Creek, and sometimes Stump Creek. In that year a survey was made for a state road extending from Bedford to Franklin and passing through the town of Indiana. The traditional explanation of the origin of the name of the Clarion River runs as follows:

The three viewers appointed to lay out the new state road encamped along Toby's Creek. As they lay in their tent in the evening, "they were struck by the cler sound of the distant ripples." The course of the stream was then lined by a dense forest of giant trees, which "condensed and reflected the murmur, giving it a silvery mellowness," which it no longer possesses since the timber has been cut down. One of the surveyors, *Danial Stanard*, remarked that the sound of the river was like the notes of a distant clarion. "Why not call it the Clarion River?" asked his assistant, *David Lawson.* "

The new name slowly but steadily gained in favor; the old pioneer names, Toby's Creek, dating from 1758, and Stump Creek, bestowed somewhat later, had nothing to commend them to a civilized community. In 1819, when the law known as the "Olean Road Act" was passed, the new name of the Clarion River received something like official sanction by being mentioned in the bill. Three years later another act of legislature designated the stream as "Toby's Creek, otherwise called Clarion River." Thenceforth, while pioneers and lumbermen naturally showed their partiality for the old names, the constantly growing number of new settlers evinced a preference for the more poetic designation, which eventually won its way to general acceptance.

•**CLARION RIVER**, River; W Pennsylvania; flows SW from source in Elk County to mouth at the Allegheny River in Clarion County. Fed by several smaller streams, popular with fishers. River is dammed S of the town of Clarion.

Until 1817 this river was known as Toby's Creek, and sometimes as Stump Creek. In that year, surveyors were struck "by the clear sound of the distant ripples" of the stream, and one of them, *Daniel Standard*, claimed that the sound was like a "distant clarion." In 1819, the name was made official under a land act.

•**CLARK**, Borough; Mercer County; Pop. 667; Area Code 412; Zip Code 16113; Elev. 900'; W Pennsylvania; near Sharon on Shenanto River Reservoir.

•**CLARKS GREEN**, Borough; Lackawanna County; Pop. 1,862; Area Code 717; Elev. 1,400'; near Clarks Summit, a N suburb of Scranton in NE Pennsylvania.

•**CLARKS SUMMIT**, Borough; Lackawanna County; Pop. 5,272; Area Code 717; Zip Code 18411; Elev. 1,240'; 5 m. NW of Scranton in NE Pennsylvania; residential.

Clarks Summit was lifted from rural status with the construction in 1906 of an electric railway to link it with Scranton. Clarks Summit has strong ties with Clarks Green, the adjacent borough. Both were named for *Deacon William Clark* who in 1799 cleared the triangular "Green"; the "Summit" was the peak of a grade on the Legett's Gap Railroad, northern division of the Lackawanna and Western.

Just outside of town is the Clarks Summit State Hospital.

•**CLARKSVILLE**, Borough; Greene County; Pop. 251; Area Code 412; Zip Code 15322; approx. 10 m. NE of Waynesburg in SW Pennsylvania; at fork of Tenmile and Wheeling Creeks.

•**CLAYSBURG**, Village (uninc.); Blair County; Pop. 1,516; Zip Code 16625; Elev. 1,148'.

Claysburg is a narrow town set on a mountain side, and threaded by the Frankstown branch of the Juniata River; the town was founded in 1804 by *John Ulrich Zeth.*

•**CLAYSVILLE**, Borough; Washington County; Pop. 1,029; Area Code 412; Zip Code 15323; Elev. 1,001'; 38 m. SW of Pittsburgh in SW Pennsylvania.

Claysville was named by its founder for *Henry Clay*, probably because he championed both the National Highway and a protective tariff on coal, once the comunity's chief support.

Early settler, *John Purviance*, had been keeping tavern in his large log house a number of years when the preliminary surveys were made for the great national road, and when it became certain that the road would pass through his place, he promptly surveyed and laid out a prospective town upon his land.

Beef and dairy farmers gather in town to do their shopping and to talk "shop."

Industry/Mfg. - Meat packing, dairy products

•**CLEARFIELD**, Borough; Seat of Clearfield County; Pop. 7,580; Area Code 814; Zip Code 16830; Elev. 1,112'; 50 m. N of Altoona in W central Pennsylvania.

Clearfield, on the West Branch of the Susquehanna River, at the southeastern edge of the Moshannon State Forest, is named for near-by Clearfield Creek, so called because buffalo are supposed to have cleared the undergrowth from large tracts along the creek "so as to give them the appearance of cleared fields." The town, a railroad and industrial center with wide, well-shaded streets and neat houses, was laid out in 1805 by *Abraham Witmer* of Lancaster. Drives, bordered in season with honeysuckle, rhododendron, and mountain laurel, crisscross adjacent hills. this was once the site of an Indian town called Chinklacamoose (Ind. no one tarries here willingly), said to have been so named because of the activities of an Indian hermit, who, garbled in terrifying costumes, used to confront well-laden huntsmen and gather up the skins and game they dropped in their flight. The latter part of his name still survives in that of Moose Creek, which flows into the Susquehanna near the northwestern boundary of the present borough of Clearfield. *Witmer* laid out the town of Clearfield and named it for the county, donating one building lot for the county courthouse, one for a jail, one for a market-house, and three for an academy, besides giving his bond for the payment of $3,000, "one-half therof to be applied for the use of an academy or public school in said town, and one-half for the purpose of erecting public buildings."

The founder of the town of Clearfield was the same *Abraham Witmer* who, in 1799, erected his own monument in the stone bridge that still spans the Conestoga Creek at Lancaster.

Industry/Mfg. - Stainless steel, bricks
Daily Newspaper - The Progress, 206 East Locust Street
Chamber of Commerce - PO Box 250.

•**CLEARFIELD COUNTY**, Clearfield County, one of the six new counties formed by the Act of March 26, 1804, was, according to Morse's *American Gazetteer* of 1810, "named from a stream running through the county into the western branch of the Susquehanna." This stream, the Clearfield Creek, which is mentioned on *Nicholas Scull's* map of 1770, empties into the Susquehanna about a mile and a half east of Clearfield. The first recorded literary reference to the name of Clearfield occurs in an entry that the *Reverend John Ettwein* made in his journal while he was removing a flock of 241 Christian Indians from Wyalusing to the region of the Beaver River in western Pennsylvania. Under date of July 14, 1772, *Ettwein* made this entry: "Reached Clearfield Creek, where the buffaloes formerly cleard large tracts of undergrowth, so as to give them the appearance of cleared fields. Hence the Indians called the creek Clearfield." Clearfield Township, in the adjoining county of Cambria, was also named for Clearfield Creek. *Sherman Day*, without discrimination between the creek and county, says that the name Clearfield had its origin in the fact that "clear fields, or open patches of parairie, apparently the site of some ancient cornfields, were found in this vicinity."

•**CLEARVIEW**, Village; Lancaster County; Pop. 1,200; Area Code 717; Zip Code 17601; 2 m. N of Lancaster in SE central Pennsylvania; residential.

•**CLEONA**, Borough; Lebanon County; Pop. 2,003; Area Code 717; Zip Code 17042; Elev. 460'; just W of Lebanon in SE central Pennsylvania; residential.

•**CLIFFORD**, Village; Susquehanna County; Pop. 350; Area Code 717; Zip Code 18413; Elev. 1,080'; NE Pennsylvania; a crossroads town on the East Branch of Tunkhannock Creek, settled in 1800 by *Adam Miller.*

•**CLIFTON HEIGHTS**, Borough; Delaware County; Pop. 7,320; Area Code 215; Zip Code 19018; Elev. 109'; SE Pennsylvania; settled in the last decade of the eighteenth century and incorporated as a borough in 1885.

•**CLINTON COUNTY**, The counties of Lycoming and Centre were divided to make a new county, to be called Clinton. *George Clinton*, who served seven terms, or twenty-one years, as governor of New York and was twice elected Vice-President of the United States, was the uncle of *DeWitt Clinton* ; but *George Clinton* died in 1812, and the founder of Clinton County was far more likely to be attracted by the fame of the great contemporary advocate of internal improvements, who, in 1826, inaugurated the opening of the Erie Canal with imposing ceremonies. In five other states, counties are named for *DeWitt Clinton*. *Clint* is an Old Norse word for "headland'; and Clinton was originally a place name signifying "the farmstead by the headland or crag."

Lock Haven was, of course, made the county seat of Clinton County. *Jerry Church's* dream had come true. He donated a suitable site for the court-house, and he immediately sold more than one hundred and fifty building lots in the new county town. Lock Haven began to grow rapidly; it became a borough in 1840, and thirty years later it received a city charter.

•**CLINTONVILLE**, Borough; Venango County; Pop. 512; Area Code 814; Zip Code 16372; Elev. 1,473'; NW Pennsylvania; near U.S. Highway 80, which travels 35 m. W to Youngstown, Ohio.

•**CLYMER**, Borough; Indiana County; Pop. 1,761; Area Code 412; Zip Code 15728; Elev. 1,218'; 10 m. NE of Indiana in W central Pennsylvania; on Two Lick Creek.

Clymer was laid out in 1905 by the Dixon Run Land Company, which chose this name in honor of *George Clymer*, a Pennsylvania signer of the Declaration of Independence and one of the framers of the Constitution of the United States.

•**COAL CENTER**, Borough; Washington County; Pop. 255; Area Code 412; Zip Code 15423; Elev. 780'; 35 m. S of Pittsburgh in SW Pennsylvania; on the Monongahela River.

•**COALDALE**, Borough; Bedford County; Pop. 233; Area Code 814; Zip Code 16679; S Pennsylvania.

•**COALDALE**, Borough; Schuylkill County; Pop. 2,762; Area Code 717; Zip Code 18218; Elev. 1,040'; 15 m. SE of Hazleton in E central Pennsylvania; on Highway 209.

Coaldale, incorporated in 1906, owes its existence and its name to a dale containing rich deposits of anthracite coal.

•**COALMONT**, Borough; Huntingdon County; Pop. 128; Area Code 717; Zip Code 16678; Elev. 1,126'; 30 m. SE of Altoona in S central Pennsylvania; on a branch of the Juniata River.

•**COALPORT**, Borough; Clearfield County; Pop. 739; Area Code 814; Zip Code 16627; Elev. 1,380'; 20 m. N of Altoona in W central Pennsylvania; on Clearfield Creek in an old mining region.

Chamber of Commerce - PO Box 393

•**COATESVILLE**, City; Chester County; Pop. 10,698; Area Code 215; Zip Code 19320; Elev. 381'; 38 m. W of Philadelphia in SE Pennsylvania.

Coatesville is in the shadow of South Mountain and divided by the west branch of the Brandywine River. It became a post-office in 1812; and its first postmaster was *Moses Coates*, who owned a large tract of land now occupied by the town. He planned the place and called it Coatesville, but it is not known whether he named the town for himself or for his grandfather, *Moses Coates*, an Irish Quaker, who had emigrated to Pennsylvania in 1717. The family, as the name indicates, was of English origin. The word *coate*, in the north of England, is the equivalent of the Anglo-Saxon, *cot*, signifying "thatched cottage." Coates would naturally become first a village name, and then a family name.

Agriculture - Grain, mushrooms and varied
farming
Industry/Mfg. - Steel products, dairy
products
Daily Newspaper - The Record, 204 E. Lincoln
Highway
Chamber of Commerce - 235 E. Lincoln Hwy.

•**COCHRANTON**, Borough; Crawford; County; Pop. 1,240; Area Code 814; Zip Code 16314; Elev. 582'; approx. 10 m. SE of Meadville in NW Pennsylvania; on French Creek; residential.

•**CODORUS CREEK**, Creek, S Pennsylvania; Flows N through York County; dammed to form Lake Marburg near the Maryland state line. Name is Indian for "rapid water."

•**COGAN STATION**, Village; Lycoming County; Pop. 100; Area Code 717; Zip Code 17728; Elev. 600'; N central Pennsylvania.

The town was named for the first settler, *David Cogan*, who came here about 1825, built a log house, and cleared the land. His place gradually fell into decay, and came to be known among hunters as Cogan's House.

•**COKEBURG**, Borough; Washington County; Pop. 796; Area Code 412; Zip Code 15324; Elev. 1,040'; 13 m. SE of Washington in SW Pennsylvania; named for the ore produced here.

•**COLLEGEVILLE**, Borough; Montgomery County; Pop. 3,406; Area Code 215; Zip Code 19426; Elev. 200'; 20 m. NW of Philadelphia in SE Pennsylvania.

The town was originally known as Perkiomen Bridge and then as Freeland. In 1869, the Reformed Church established Ursinus College here and that year the name was changed to Collegeville.

POINT OF INTEREST

KUSTER MILL- Built in 1702. Property purchased by *Hermanus Custer* (originally Kuster), and operated as the county's first fulling mill.

•**COLLINGDALE**, Borough; Delaware County; Pop. 9,539; Area Code 215; Zip Code 19023; Elev. 120'; 5 m. SW of downtown Philadelphia in SE Pennsylvania; residential.

•**COLONIAL PARK**, Village; Dauphin County; Pop. 9000; Area Code 717; Zip Code 17109; NE suburb of Harrisburg in SE central Pennsylvania; home of many city workers.

•**COLUMBIA**, Borough; Lancaster County; Pop. 10,466; Area Code 717; Zip Code 17512; Elev. 255'; 12 m. W of Lancaster in SE Pennsylvania.

Columbia, on the east bank of the Susquehanna River, received its name at the time it was being considered as one of many possible sites for the national capital. Originally known as Wright's Ferry, it had its beginning when *John Wright*, a Quaker "speaker", came from Chester in 1726 to preach to the Indian inhabitants and remained to become a ferryman, landowner, and judge. *Samuel Wright*, *John's* grandson, laid out the town. Traffic became too heavy for the ferry, and a bridge was constructed in 1812; a second span, built in 1834, was burned in 1863 to prevent Confederates from crossing the river. The present bridge, the fifth, is a mile-long, arched structure of concrete. The House voted in favor of Wright's Ferry "on the east bank of the River Susquehanna in the State of Pennsylvania" becoming the capital but the Senate refused to concur, sending the bill back to the House with amendments favoring either Philadelphia or the present location on the Potomac. *President Washington* is said to have preferred Wright's Ferry, now Columbia. If the Pennsylvania representatives had been a little more energetic and diplomatic, Columbia might have been chosen as the capital of the United States. The debate ended in an agreement that Philadelphia was to be the national capital for the next 10 years, and that in 1800 the permanent seat of government was to be located on the Potomac River near Georgetown. Thus Columbia missed its opportunity to become a great city; and a decade later its name was assumed by the District of Columbia.

In allusion to the English royal houses of Lancaster and York, which engaged in the War of the Roses, red roses have been grown at the eastern approach in Lancaster County and white roses at the western approach in York County.

During the mid-nineteenth century, activity in Columbia revolved about the "descending lumber of the Susquehanna." Early canal and railroad activity centered here; the Philadelphia-Columbia Railroad was completed in 1834.

Agriculture - Tobacco, grain and varied
   farming
Industry/Mfg. - Clothing, machinery, glass
Daily Newspaper - The News
Chamber of Commerce - 104 Lancaster Ave.

•**COLUMBIA COUNTY**, was separated from Northumberland in March 1813. Fifteen years before, on the evening of April 25, 1798, *Joseph Hopkinson's* song, *Hail Columbia*, was sung for the first time in the Chestnut Street Theater, Philadelphia, by the popular young actor, *Gilbert Fox.* This song at once attained wide currency as a patriotic protest against the undiplomatic and highly reprehensible conduct of *Citizen Adet,* the French minister, who had had the hardihood to issue an address to the citizens of the United States designed to incite them against their own government. As a result, the name Columbia became immensely popular as a poetic designation for America. Though this name had become generally current before *Hail Columbia* was written, there can be no doubt that the famous song helped to popularize it; and this great increase in its popularity may partly explain the fact that seven counties and twenty-three towns in the United States are now called Columbia.

This name is derived from Columbus, the Latinized form of Columbo, the Italian name of the great explorer, believed to have had its origin, through the Irish monks in northern Italy, from St. Columba, "the dove."

•**COLUMBUS**, Village; Warren County; Pop. 500; Area Code 814; Zip Code 16405; Elev. 1,425'; NW Pennsylvania; named for the legendary discoverer of North America.

•**COLWYN**, Borough; Delaware County; Pop. 2,851; Area Code 215; Zip Code 19023; Elev. 50'; 10 m. SW of downtown Philadelphia on Cobbs Creek (the city boundary) in SE Pennsylvania.

•**COMPASS**, Village; Chester County; Pop. 80; Area Code 215; Zip Code 17527; SE Pennsylvania.

Compass took its name from an old tavern on the Lancaster Road, at the sign of the "Mariner's Compass."

•CONCORDVILLE, Village; Delaware County; Pop. 400; Area Code 215; Zip Code 19331; Elev. 380'; SE Pennsylvania.

Concordville lies secluded upon a wooded ridge overlooking the Brandywine Valley. Quakers who settled here in the seventeenth century named it for their central desire. Within a short time, however, they were petitioning *Penn* to punish the Indians for "ye Rapine and Destruction of Hoggs." This was a break from the generally "harmonious feelings which in early times prevailed among the settlers there."

POINTS OF INTEREST

CONCORDVILLE HISTORIC DISTRICT- 18th-19th century crossroad town district including two 18th Century meetinghouses.

NICHOLAS NEWLIN HOUSE- Built in 1742 by *Nicholas Newlin*, Irish immigrant active in regional political and business affairs.

Community Event - Brandywine Mountain Music Convention, Annual, July

•CONEMAUGH RIVER, River, SW Pennsylvania; flows W approx. 44 m. from source at the confluence of the Little Conemaugh River and Stony Creek in Cambria County, to join Loyalhanna Creek in Westmoreland County.

Conemach was an Indian word meaning "Otter Creek." The Conemaugh became famous when it overflowed in 1889, creating the disastrous Johnstown flood. Several less destructive floods have taken place since then.

•CONESTOGA, Village; Lancaster County; Pop. 225; Area Code 717; Zip Code 17516; Elev. 500'; on Beaver Creek in SE central Pennsylvania; named for the Indian tribe.

•CONEWAGO CREEK, Stream, S Pennsylvania; flows E approx. 80 m. from source in Fanklin County through several twisting paths until its mouth at the Susquehanna River, N of York. Name means "at the rapids," from an Indian phrase.

•CONFLUENCE, Borough; Somerset County; Pop. 968; Area Code 814; Zip Code 15424; Elev. 1,332'; S Penn-

95

sylvania; on N tip of Youghiogheny Lake, at the dam which formed it.
Confluence was laid out at the joining of three creeks in a "turkey foot" formation; hence the name.

•CONNEAUT LAKE, Borough; Crawford County; Pop. 767; Area Code 814; Zip Code 16316; Elev. 1,100'; 40 m. SW of Erie in NW Pennsylvania; on a lake by the same name, which is Indian for "a long time since they went," or "snow place."
Today, the town is a summer resort, with boat works and varied agriculture as other sources of income.

> *Agriculture* - Grain, truck and varied farming
> *Industry/Mfg.* - Dairy products. Resort area.
> *Community Event* - Snow Ball Festival, Annual,
> February

•CONNEAUTVILLE, Borough; Crawford County; Pop. 971; Area Code 814; Zip Code 16406; Elev. 935'; 30 m. SW of Erie in NW Pennsylvania.
Conneautville, the trading center for a rich agricultural district, was settled in 1815 on Conneaut Creek.
According to linguist *Heckewelder*, Conneaut means "it is a long time since they went"; according to *Boyd* it signifies "snow place," so called because the snow remained frozen on the ice of the lake long after it had melted from the land.

> *Agriculture* - Varied farming
> *Industry/Mfg.* - Food packing, furniture,
> dairy products

•CONNELLSVILLE, City; Fayette County; Pop. 10,319; Area Code 412; Zip Code 15425; Elev. 890'; 47 m. SE of Pittsburgh in SW Pennsylvania.
Connellsville, on the Youghiogheny River at the base of a ridge, occupies the site of an early Shawnee village. *Zachariah Connell* and several other pioneers came to this vicinity in 1770 about the time coal was discovered here, and 23 years later *Connell* laid out a village. In October 1770, during a stopover at *Captain William Crawford's* cabin across the river from the present town site, *George*

Washington wrote: "We went to see a coal mine ... on the banks of the Youghiogheny River. The coal seemed to be of the very best kind, burning freely, and abundance of it." *William McCormick*, a son-in-law of *Captain Crawford*, was one of the first settlers in the town. Westward-bound travelers and settlers reached the first navigable waters of the Youghiogheny here, and boatbuilding developed as early as 1788. Connellsville was incorporated as a borough in 1806, and chartered as a city in 1911.

> *Industry/Mfg.* - Construction materials, containers
> *Daily Newspaper* - The Courier, 127 N. Apple Street
> *Chamber of Commerce* - 107 S. Pittsburgh St.
> *Community Event* - Youghiogheny River Festival Annual, June-July

•**CONNOQUENESSING**, Borough; Butler County; Pop. 539; Area Code 412; Zip Code 16027; Elev. 1,200'; W Pennsylvania.

Connoquenessing is the white man's version of an Indian name meaning "for a long time straight," which describes the creek running through town. It was once named Petersville for *Peter McKinney*, who settled here in 1792.

The Washington Monument commemorates a near-tragedy involving *George Washington*. Accompanied by *Christopher Gist*, the noted frontiersman, and several others. *Washington*, a 21-year-old major, was returning from visits to Forts Le Boeuf and Machault. On December 27, 1753, the party came upon a lone Indian who, appearing friendly, was permitted to accompany them. After traveling with the party for some time, the Indian fired point-blank at Washington. Miraculously, for the distance was only 15 paces, the future President was not struck. *Gist* wanted to kill the attacker, but was prevailed upon by *Washington* merely to relieve the Indian of his gun, and send him on his way. The marker places the incident along the bank of Connoquenessing Creek, 500 yards from the monument.

•**CONNEQUENESSING CREEK**, Creek; W Pennsylvania; flows through Butler and Lawrence Counties; name is Indian for "for a long time straight."

•**CONSHOHOCKEN**, Borough; Montgomery County; Pop. 8,475; Area Code 215; Zip Code 19428; Elev. 220'; 11 m. NW of Philadelphia on the Schuylkill River in SE Pennsylvania; suburban.

"Conshohocken" is an Indian name meaning "pleasant valley."

POINT OF INTEREST

MOUNT JOY (PETER LEGAUX MANSION)- Built 1735, later became the home of *Peter Legaux*, French emigrant scientist and entrepreneur who was elected to the American Philosophical Society in Philadelphia based on his expertise in the field of meteorology.

Agriculture - Varied farming
Industry/Mfg. - Steel, glass, rubber
   products, plastics, concrete
Chamber of Commerce - 128 Fayette Street

•**CONWAY**, Borough; Beaver County; Pop. 2,747; Area Code 412; Zip Code 15027; Elev. 760'; 19 m. NW of Pittsburgh on E bank of the Ohio River in W Pennsylvania; suburban-industrial community.

•**CONYNGHAM**, Borough; Luzerne County; Pop. 2,242; Area Code 717; Zip Code 18219; Elev. 940'; 5 m. W of Hazleton in an old mining area in E Pennsylvania.

•**COOPERSBURG**, Borough; Lehigh County; Pop. 2,595; Area Code 215; Zip Code 18036; Elev. 539'; 10 m. S of Allentown in E Pennsylvania; founded in 1780.

Chamber of Commerce - 5 N. Main Street

•**COOPERSTOWN**, Borough; Venango County; Pop. 644; Area Code 814; Zip Code 16317; Elev. 1,146'; 15 m. NW of Oil City on Sugar Creek in NW Pennsylvania.

•**COPLAY**, Borough; Lehigh County; Pop. 3,130; Area Code 215; Zip Code 18037; Elev. 380'; on Lehigh River, N of Allentown in E Pennsylvania; suburban; name is Indian for "smooth running stream."

•**CORAOPOLIS**, Borough; Allegheny County; Pop. 7,308;

Area Code 412; Zip Code 15108; Elev. 730'; 10 m. NW of Pittsburgh in SW Pennsylvania.

Coraopolis on the Ohio River with a number of sturdily built houses, was settled about 1760. According to some, the name comes from the Greek *Koreopolis*, "maiden city," but others hold that it was named for *Cora Watson*, daughter of an influential citizen..

The site of Coraopolis, in Allegheny County, in 1769 came into possession of *Andrew (sometimes called Henry) Montour*, son of *Madame Catherine Montour*, for whom Montour County was named. During the American Revolution *Robert Vance* settled near Montour's tract, and in his honor the post-office was long called Vance Fort. Before 1886 the little village at this point was commonly known as Middletown because it was situated midway between Pittsburgh and Beaver. Since there was an older place in Pennsylvania called Middletown, in 1886 the village was incorporated as Coraopolis.

Today, Coraoplis is an important industrial suburb of Pittsburgh. It is the site of the Ohio-Coraopolis Seaplane Base.

> *Agriculture* - Truck, poultry and varied
>   farming
> *Industry/Mfg.* - Steel products, oil refining, dairy products
> *Higher Education* - Robert Morris College
> *Chamber of Commerce* - 912 Narrows Run Rd.

•**CORNWALL**, Borough; Lebanon County; Pop. 2,653; Area Code 717; Zip Code 17016; Elev. 680'; SE central Pennsylvania; served by major rail lines heading to and from Lebanon, 3 m. north. Site of the old Cornwall Blast Furnace. Named for a region in England.

POINT OF INTEREST

CORNWALL IRON FURNACE- Complex from 1742 containing foundry and furnace; complemented by Cornwall Mine, the oldest continuously used iron mine in U.S.; and "Miners Village," a group of houses constructed in the 1860's.

•**CORNWELLS HEIGHTS**, Village; Bucks County; Pop. 8,200; Area Code 215; Zip Code 19020; Elev. 60'; 12 m. NE of downtown Philadelphia in SE Pennsylvania; on the Delaware River.

> *Industry/Mfg.* - Steel, clothing, wood products, quarrying

•**CORRY**, City; Erie County; Pop. 7,149; Area Code 814; Zip Code 16407; Elev. 1,429'; 28 m. SE of Erie in NW Pennsylvania; on S branch of the French Creek.

Corry, born in 1861 when the rights of way of two railroads intersected on *Hiram Corry's* farm, was nursed on the oil discovered by *Drake* at Titusville, some 25 miles to the south. By 1862 the town had two hotels, an oil works, and several mills. The work of clearing went on so rapidly that the settlement became known as "the city of stumps"; by 1866 a city charter had been obtained.

> *Agriculture* - Varied farming
> *Industry/Mfg.* - Office furniture, aircraft, parts, plastics, dairy products
> *Daily Newspaper* - The Journal, 28 W. South Street
> *Chamber of Commerce* - 127 N. Center Street

•**CORSICA**, Borough; Jefferson County; Pop. 381; Area Code 814; Zip Code 15829; Elev. 1,600'; 80 m. NE of Pittsburgh in a hilly farming area in W central Pennsylvania; named for the French isle in the Mediterranean.

•**COUDERSPORT**, Borough; Seat of Potter County; Pop. 2,791; Area Code 814; Zip Code 16915; Elev. 1,650'; N Pennsylvania, near the New York state line.

Coudersport is on the west bank of the Allegheny. *John Keating*, Irish soldier of fortune, manager of the Ceres Land Company which had acquired 300,000 acres in this and an adjoining county, gave 50-acre homesteads to each of the first 50 settlers. At *Keating's* suggestion, Coudersport was named for *Jean Samuel Couderc*, of the Amsterdam banking firm that had managed the interests of those exiled Frenchmen of Asylum who had invested in the Ceres Land Company. The final letter in *M. Couderc's* name was dropped for the sake of euphony. The little town grew very slowly at first and still contained only about 50 people in 1835, when the first courthouse was built.

Today, it is the business center of a large resort region. A few light industries add to the town's economy.

> *Agriculture* - Dairy, truck and varied
> farming
> *Industry/Mfg.* - Toys, leathers. Resort
> area.
> *Community Events* -
> Woodmen's Carnival, Annual, August
> Palma Craft Festival and Birling Contest,
> Annual, July
> Potter-Tioga Maple Festival, Annual, May
> Sidewalk Festival Days, Annual, July

•**COURTDALE**, Borough; Luzerne County; Pop. 844; Area Code 717; Zip Code 18704; Elev. 740'; 3 m. NW of Wilkes-Barre in E Pennsylvania.

•**COVINGTON**, Village; Tioga County; Pop. 600; Area Code 717; Zip Code 16917; Elev. 1,187'; on Tioga River.

Covington, settled by *Aaron Bloss* in 1801, muddled along for 30 years as "The Corners", but was renamed when it became a center for land speculators attracted by a coal and iron boom. Factories and stores were established, but early in the 1840s the bubble burst. The town was formally laid out by *William Patten* in 1822. Both the village and the township of Covington were named in honor of the great Indian fighter and comrade of *Anthony Wayne*, *General Leonard Covington*.

•**COVODE**, Village; Indiana County; Pop. 100; Area Code 412; Zip Code 15767; 22 m. N of Indiana in W central Pennsylvania.

Covode bears the name of a distinguished Pennsylvanian, *John Covode*, who represented Indiana County in Congress from 1854 to 1870. "Honest John Covode," as he was commonly called, was the grandson of *Garret Covode*, a native of Holland, who had been kidnaped in childhood from the streets of Amsterdam by a sea captain, who brought him to Philadelphia and sold him as a bondservant or "redemptioner." *Garret Covode* is said to have been a domestic servant in the household of *Washington*. The name Covode was not the real name of the Dutch lad, but is supposed to have been given him by the sea captain.

•**COWANESQUE**, Village; Tioga County; Pop. 150; Area Code 717; Zip Code 16918; Elev. 1,320'; approx. 2 m. S of New York state line on Cowanesque River, in N Pennsylvania.

Cowanesque is an Indian name meaning "overrun with briars."

•**COWANESQUE RIVER**, River; N Pennsylvania; flows E from source in E Potter County through Tioga County to its mouth on the Tioga River; Name means "overrun with briars.

•**CRAFTON**, Borough; Allegheny County; Pop. 7,623; Area Code 412; Zip Code 15205; Elev. 880'; SE suburb of Pittsburgh in SW Pennsylvania; on Chartiers Creek; site of a public golf course.

This attractive residential borough was laid out about 1870 by *Charles C. Craft*, and named in honor of his father, *James S. Craft*, a prominent Pittsburgh lawyer, from whom he inherited the land on which the town is built. The founder of Crafton sold lots on easy terms, enabling many men of moderate means to build their own homes. The town was incorporated in 1890.

•**CRAMER**, Village; Jefferson County; Pop. Rural; Area Code 814; Zip Code 15863; Elev. 1,340'; once a lively lumbering settlement, it takes its name from Kramer's Mill, erected along Stump Creek prior to 1885. It has also been an important coal mining town.

•**CRANESVILLE**, Borough; Erie County; Pop. 703; Area Code 814; Zip Code 16410; Elev. 937'; NW Pennsylvania.

Cranesville was named for *Elisha Crane*, who settled here in the 1790s.

•**CREEKSIDE**, Borough; Indiana County; Pop. 383; Area Code 412; Zip Code 15732; Elev. 1,060'; 10 m. N of Indiana in W central Pennsylvania; on Crooked Creek.

•**CREIGHTON**, Village; Allegheny County; Pop. 2,081; Area Code 412; Zip Code 15030; Elev. 800'; suburb of Pittsburgh.

Creighton grew up about a tavern erected here in 1792.

•**CRESCO**, Village; Monroe County; Pop. 500; Area Code 717; Zip Code 18326; Elev. 1,207; E Pennsylvania; resort town, with about 2,000 seasonal residents. Cresco is a Latin verb meaning "am growing."

•**CRESSON**, Borough; Cambria County; Pop. 2,184; Area Code 814; Zip Code 16630; Elev. 2,100'; 15 m. SW of Altoona in SW central Pennsylvania; near old village of Sankertown.

Cresson is a major shipping center for a coal mining region. The town was once a quiet health resort, named for *Elliot Cresson,* a Philadelphia merchant.

> *Agriculture* - Varied farming
> *Industry/Mfg* - Steel, plastics, coal
> *Chamber of Commerce* - 323 Cathedral Ave.

•**CRESSONA**, Borough; Schuylkill County; Pop. 1,810; Area Code 717; Zip Code 17929; Elev. 600'; E central Pennsylvania.

Cressona was named for *John Chapman Cresson,* who laid out the town. He was a civil engineer in Philadelphia, manager of the Schuylkill Navigation Company, president of the Mine Hill and Schuylkill Haven Railroad Company, and chief engineer of Fairmount Park in Philadelphia.

•**CROSS ROADS**, Borough; York County; Pop. 267; Area Code 717; Zip Code 17322; Elev. 800'; 15 m. S of York in S Pennsylvania; hilly area.

•**CROYDON**, Village; Bucks County; Pop. 9,800; Area Code 215; Zip Code 19020; 10 m. NE of downtown Philadelphia in SE Pennsylvania; on Neshaminy Creek; named for a suburb of London, England.

•**CRUM LYNNE**, Village; Delaware County; Pop. 3,700; Area Code 215; Zip Code 19022; Elev. 20'; SW suburb of Philadelphia near Chester, in SE Pennsylvania.

•**CURWENSVILLE**, Borough; Clearfield County; Pop. 3,116; Area Code 814; Zip Code 16833; Elev. 1,167'; W central Pennsylvania.

Curwensville, at the junction of Anderson Creek and

the West Branch, and on the site of the old Bellefonte and Meadville Turnpike, is a well-built town. Surrounding woods and streams offer splendid hunting and fishing. The first settlement occurred in 1812, 14 years after *John Curwen* obtained title to the tract. *Curwen* never resided here, however. Curwensville State Park is nearby.

•**CUSTER CITY**, Village; McKean County; Pop. 500; Area Code 814; Zip Code 16725; Elev. 1,516'; N Pennsylvania.

Custer City was named for *General George A. Custer*, Civil War hero and tragic figure of the battle with the Indians on the Little Big Horn in 1876.

The town is 4 miles S of Bradford, near the New York state line. It is on the edge of the Allegheny National Forest.

•DAGUSCAHONDA, Village; Elk County; Pop. 190; Area Code 814; Zip Code 15853; Elev. 1,476'; N central Pennsylvania.

Daguscahonda (Ind. "wildcat run" or "pure water"), in a hollow on Wildcat Run, was founded in 1860 as an offshoot of the lumber industry. Today it is the center of a farming region, near the town of St. Mary's.

•DAISYTOWN, Borough; Cambria County; Pop. 421; Area Code 814; Zip Code 15427; Elev. 860'; suburb of Johnstown in SW central Pennsylvania.

•DALE, Borough; Cambria County; Pop. 1,906; Area Code 814; Zip Code 15902; Elev. 1,250'; suburb of Johnstown in SW central Pennsylvania; in a hilly area.

•DALLAS, Borough; Luzerne County; Pop. 2,679; Area Code 717; Zip Code 18612; Elev. 1,128'; 10 m. NW of Wilkes-Barre in E Pennsylvania.

The borough and the township of Dallas took their name from the Philadelphia author, lawyer, statesman, and financier, *Alexander James Dallas*, who won fame by his efficient administration as Secretary of the Treasury in 1814-17.

Dallas is the site of the Catholic College of Misericordia as well as a state Correctional Institution.

> *Agriculture* - Poultry, truck and varied farming
> *Industry/Mfg.* - Cloth, dairy products
> *Higher Education* - College Misericordia

•DALLASTOWN, Borough; York County; Pop. 3,949; Area Code 717; Zip Code 17313; Elev. 880'; 10 m. SE of York in S Pennsylvania.

Dallastown was founded in 1842, and was named two years later in honor of *George Mifflin Dallas* of Philadelphia, who served as United States Senator from Pennsylvania in 1831, as Vice-President of the United States during *Polk's* administration, and as minister to Great Britain from 1856 to 1861. *George M. Dallas* was the son of *Alexander J. Dallas.*

•**DALTON**, Borough; Lackawanna County; Pop. 1,383; Area Code 717; Zip Code 18414; NE Pennsylvania.

•**DANBORO**, Village; Bucks County; Pop. 800; Area Code 215; Zip Code 18916; Elev. 500; small farming community in SE Pennsylvania.

•**DANVILLE**, Borough; Seat of Montour County; Pop. 5,239; Area Code 717; Zip Code 17821; Elev. 490'; 12 m. N of Sunbury in E central Pennsylvania; on the Susquehanna River.

Danville, became the county-seat in 1850, and was named in honor of *General Daniel Montgomery*, who laid out the town in 1795. The little settlement that grew up about *Dan Montgomery's* store and his father's grist-mill was at first called Dan's-town, which later, by an easy transition became Danville. During his lifetime *Daniel Montgomery* was the most prominent man in that part of the state. He was a member of the legislature in 1800, and seven years later he was elected to Congress, declining a reelection. In 1809 he became major-general of the northern division of the Pennsylvania militia. Danville was the county-seat of Columbia County from 1813 to 1845.

A state hospital with 1,900 residents, is outside of town.

Agriculture - Fruit, cattle and varied
    farming
Industry/Mfg. - Heavy machinery, medicines,
    castings, dairy products
Daily Newspaper - The Danville News, 14 E.
    Mahoning Street
Chamber of Commerce - PO Box 263

•**DARBY**, Borough; Delaware County; Pop. 11,513; Area Code 215; Zip Code 19023; Elev. 50'; 7 m. SW of downtown

Philadelphia in SE Pennsylvania; in a residential area along Darby Creek.

Darby was so called for old pearing as "Derbytown" in 1698. Three centuries ago the form Darby was used quite as frequently as Derby. Site of Fitzgerald Mercy Hospital.

Chamber of Commerce - 824 Main Street

•DARLINGTON, Borough; Beaver County; Pop. 377; Area Code 412; Zip Code 16115; Elev. 912'; 5 m. NW of Beaver Falls in W Pennsylvania; rural area.

•DAUPHIN, Borough; Dauphin County; Pop. 901; Area Code 717; Zip Code 17018; Elev. 346'; SE central Pennsylvania.

Dauphin, at the narrows of majestic Second Mountain Gap, by the Juniata River, was the site of a gristmill as early as 1770. The borough was once called Greenburg for *General Innis Green*, who laid it out in 1825. It was later renamed for Dauphin County.

•DAUPHIN COUNTY, What is now Dauphin County was once Paxtang Township in Lancaster County. The petitioners who asked that a new county be formed from Lancaster in 1785 suggested the name of Dauphin in a desire to honor the friendly court of France by bestowing upon the new county the name of the hereditary title of the eldest son of the French king. *Louis XVI* was then king of France, and his eldest son, *Louis*, the Dauphin, who was born on October 22, 1781, was not yet four years of age. He died in 1789.

Our interest lies more in the name of Dauphin than in the youthful prince. This curious title has been the subject of considerable controversy. In all probability it originated in a personal name. Among the Norsemen and in the countries that they colonized the name Dolfin or Dolphin was not uncommon. From a personal name, the original meaning of which is now unknown, Dauphin, in the thirteenth century, became firmly established as a title of nobility. The usual explanation is that the French province of Dauphiny was "so called from the dolphin assumed by the Counts of the Viennois as a symbol of the mildness of

107

their rule." But, on the contrary, the armorial device was probably assumed from the name Dolphin.

In 1349 *Humbert II*, Count of the Viennois, and the last of his line, sold Dauphiny to *Charles of Valois* on condition that the heir to the French crown should assume the arms and bear the title of the Dauphin of the Viennois. When *Charles* became king of France in 1364, he transferred the title of Dauphin to his eldest son. After that time the eldest sons of the French kings always bore this title.

The borough of Dauphin, once called Greensburg for *General Innis Green*, who laid it out about 1825, was later named for Dauphin County.

•**DAVIDSON HEIGHTS**, Village; Beaver County; Pop. 2,000; Area Code 412; Zip Code 15001; Suburb of Aliquippa in W Pennsylvania.

•**DAVIDSVILLE**, Village; Somerset County; Pop. 900; Area Code 814; Zip Code 15928; Elev. 1,700'; 8 m. S of Johnstown in S Pennsylvania, by the Quamohoning Creek.

•**DAWSON**, Borough; Fayette County; Pop. 661; Area Code 412; Zip Code 15428; Elev. 850'; along the Youghigheny River in SW Pennsylvania.

The borough was named for *James Dawson*, who owned the land when the town was being plotted.

•**DAYTON**, Borough; Armstrong County; Pop. 648; Area Code 412; Zip Code 16222; Elev. 1,360'; 18 m. NW of Kittanning in W Pennsylvania, on the S fork of Pine Creek.

•**DEEMSTON**, Borough; Washington County; Pop. 829; Area Code 412; Zip Code 15333; Elev. 920'; 40 m. SE of Pittsburgh in SW Pennsylvania, near Monongahela River.

•**DEER LAKE**, Borough; Schuylkill County; Pop. 515; Area Code 717; Zip Code 17961; Elev. 500'; 15 m. SE of Pottsville in E central Pennsylvania.

•**DEFIANCE**, Village; Bedford County; Pop. 250; Area Code 814; Zip Code 16633; Elev. 1,010'; approx. 30 m. SE of Altoona in S Pennsylvania; on Juniata River; named for old Fort Defiance, erected in this region during the French and Indian War.

•DELAWARE COUNTY, was named directly for the Delaware River, which forms its southeastern boundary. This important stream, which the Dutch called the Zuydt (or South) River to distinguish it from the North River, was named in honor of *Thomas West*, twelfth Baron de la Warr, governor and first captain-general of Virginia, who spent his time, his energies, and his money in establishing the Virginia colony. *Lord de la Warr* "passed the capes" of the Delaware in 1610.

•DELAWARE RIVER, River, NE United States; flows 280 m. SE from source in S New York, along E border of Pennsylvania, and boundary between Delaware and New Jersey before emptying into the Delaware Bay, S of Philadelphia. Navigable from the mouth N to Trenton, New Jersey.

The river was named for the Delaware Indians, or the Lennis-Lenape people who lived in this region. The name "De la Warre" was given to the Indians by white settlers who had named the region for *Thomas West*, Lord de la Warr, a Virginia governor.

•DELAWARE WATER GAP, Borough; Monroe County; Pop. 597; Area Code 717; Zip Code 18327; Elev. 365'; E Pennsylvania.

Delaware Water Gap is a village named for the gap through which the Delaware flows between Mt. Minsi and Mt. Tammany of the Kittatinny range of the Blue Mountains. Since 1793, when *Antoine Dutot*, a Frenchman from Santo Domingo, settled here, it has been a much visited spot. All trace of the settlement called Dutotsburg has vanished; decline began before 1843 when *Sherman Day* described it as "once a merry place; but the lumber trade has decreased...and with it the glory of Dutotsburg has departed."

The town is now located along the Applachian Trail, where it traverses into New Jersey. Ten miles north of town is the Poconos Magic Valley Amusement Park.

•DELMONT, Borough; Westmoreland County; Pop. 2,159; Area Code 417; Zip Code 15626; Elev. 1,260'; approx. 10 m. N of Greenville in SW Pennsylvania, on Beaver Run.

Community Event - Bye-Gone Days, Annual, July

•**DELTA**, Borough; York County; Pop. 692; Area Code 717; Zip Code 17314; Elev. 440'; on Maryland state line near the Susquehanna River in S Pennsylvania.

Delta is the home of the Peach Bottom atomic energy information center.

> *Agriculture* - Varied farming
> *Industry/Mfg.* - Clothing, food packing,
> quarrying

•**DENVER**, Borough; Lancaster County; Pop. 2,018; Area Code 717; Zip Code 17517; Elev. 380'; 15 m. NE of Lancaster in SE Pennsylvania.

•**DERRY**, Borough; Westmoreland County; Pop. 3,072; Area Code 417; Zip Code 15627; 35 m. E of Pittsburgh in SW Pennsylvania.

Named for the Northern Irish town that was known as Derry before the British took control and renamed it Londonderry.

> *Chamber of Commerce* - 118 E. First Ave

•**DERRY CHURCH**, Village; Dauphin County; Pop. (included with Hershey); named for an old Scotch-Irish Presbyterian church, which was built in 1729.

•**DEVON**, Village; Chester County; Pop. 4,500; Area Code 215; Zip Code 19333; Elev. 495'; 10 m. NW of Philadelphia in SE Pennsylvania; Devereux Foundation is located here.

> *Community Event* - Delco Scottish Games,
> Annual, June

•**DICKSON CITY**, Borough; Lackawanna County; Pop. 6,699; Area Code 717; Zip Code 18519; Elev. 752'; NE Pennsylvania.

Dickson City was named for *Thomas Dickson*, president of the Delaware and Hudson Canal Company (1869-84), merges with Blakely on one side and Scranton on the other. *William H. Richmond*, of Scranton, opened coal drifts here in 1859; the following year the first breaker was erected.

At one time, Dickson was also an extensive coal operator in the neighborhood of Dickson City. The son of a Scotch machinist, he came to America in his boyhood with his father, who first settled in Canada, but later came to the region of Carbondale, where the lad had to go to work at the age of 13. Although he developed into a man of scholarly tastes and habits, he spent his youth in hard labor and was entirely self-taught. When 30 years old, he became interested in the manufacture of iron, and in 1856 he organized the Dickson Manufacturing Company, which soon became an important producer of locomotives and mining machinery. In 1860 he became identified with the Delaware and Hudson Company; four years later he was its general superintendent; and in 1867 he was made vice-president. As an officer or director in a score or more of industrial companies, he became a man of large wealth, influence, and usefulness in Scranton, where he lived, and in all the surrounding country. Dickson City was incorporated as a borough in 1875.

•**DILLSBURG**, Borough; York County; Pop. 1,733; Area Code 717; Zip Code 17019; Elev. 580'; 15 m. S of Harrisburg in S Pennsylvania; reached by U.S. Highway 15, where a roadside picnic area marks the outskirts of town.

> *Agriculture* - Truck, poultry, grain and
> varied farming
> *Industry/Mfg.* - Clothing, flour, lumber,
> dairy products

•**DINGMAN'S FERRY**, Village; Pike County; Pop. 300; Area Code 717; Zip Code 18328; Elev. 445'.
Dingman's Ferry, at the confluence of Dingman's Creek and the Delaware River, was founded in 1735. The small houses here are owned by summer vacationers, who bring the town's population to 2,000 at some periods of the year.

•**DIXONVILLE**, Village; Indiana County; Pop. 900; Area Code 412; Zip Code 15734; Elev. 1,292'; on Two Lick Creek in W central Pennsylvania; located in an agricultural area.

•**DONEGAL**, Borough; Westmoreland County; Pop. 212; Area Code 417; Zip Code 15628; Elev. 1,839'; 45 m. SE of

Pittsburgh in SW Pennsylvania, off Interstate Highway 70/76, the Pennsylvania Turnpike; on Indian Creek. Named for a county in Ireland.

•**DONORA**, Borough; Washington County; Pop. 7,524; Area Code 412; Zip Code 15033; Elev. 780'; SW Pennsylvania.

Donora, an important industrial town founded in 1900 on the west bank of the Monongahela River. It is named for *William H. Donner*, president of the town's developing company, and *Nora Mellon*, wife of *Andrew W. Mellon*.

Chamber of Commerce - 581-583 McKean Ave.

•**DORMONT**, Borough; Allegheny County; Pop. 11,275; Area Code 412; Zip Code 15216; Elev. 1,220'; S suburb of Pittsburgh in SW Pennsylvania; population declined in the 1970s.

Dormont, a residential borough, was incorporated in 1909, when it had a population of only three or four hundred. The ornate and somewhat pretentious name Dormont, from the French *d'or mont*, "mount of gold," was suggested by *Gilbert M. Brown*, who became the first burgess of Dormont. The name refers to the beautiful hills on which the town is built and to the wonderful opportunities that they offered.

•**DORRANCE**, (alt. Dorranceton), Village; Luzerne County; Pop. 30; Area Code 717; Zip Code 18707; approx. 15 m. SW of Wilkes-Barre in E Pennsylvania, near Wapwallopen Creek.

Dorance was named for the township it sits in, which in turn was christened for the patriot *Col George Dorrance* in 1840. It is now considered part of the borough of Kingston.

•**DOUBLING GAP**, Village; Cumberland County; Pop. (Rural); Area Code 717; Zip Code 17241; S Pennsylvania; named for the two mountain gaps that meet and double upon each other at this point, forming two great loops.

•**DOUGLASSVILLE**, Village; Berks County; Pop. 700; Area Code 215; Zip Code 19518; Elev. 163'; a neat farming village on the Schuylkill River, was settled by the Swedes in 1693 and originally called Molatten.

POINT OF INTEREST

OLD SWEDE'S HOUSE- Oldest house in Berk's County, built 1716; excellent example of few remaining Swedish settlers' houses.

•**DOVER**, Borough; York County; Pop. 1,910; Area Code 717; Zip Code 17315; Elev. 431'; S Pennsylvania; on Fox Run Creek at the foot of the Conewago Mountains; residential town named for the English port city.

•**DOWNINGTOWN**, Borough; Chester County; Pop. 7,650; Area Code 215; Zip Code 19335; Elev. 264'; SE Pennsylvania.

Downingtown, on the East Branch of Brandywine Creek, was settled by emigrants from Birmingham, England. First known as Milltown, it was renamed for *Thomas Downing*, who purchased a mill here in 1739, and was incorporated as a borough in 1859. Today the town is a quiet residential suburb of Philadelphia.

POINTS OF INTEREST

ROBERT ROOKE HOUSE- Built c. 1841 by prosperous meatpacker *Robert Rooke*. Significant example of the local practice of constructing large mid-19th century addition perpendicular to existing, smaller structure.

WHEELEN HOUSE- Stone house from mid-18th century, representative of regional interpretation of domestic Georgian architecture.

•**DOYLESTOWN**, Borough; Seat of Bucks County; Pop. 8,717; Area Code 215; Zip Code 18901; Elev. 355'; 25 m. N of Philadelphia in SE Pennsylvania.

Doylestown, settled in 1735 by *William Doyle*, was once an overnight stop of stage travelers between Easton and Philadelphia.

A Mercer Museum and Farm School are near the downtown area.

POINTS OF INTEREST

FONTHILL- Early 20th century complex of estate buildings, Romantic Eclectic. Home of archeologist

113

and anthropologist *Dr. Henry Chapman Mercer.* Museum.

FOUNTAIN HOUSE- Built 1758, oldest remaining town tavern and social center; site of town's first post office.

JAMES-LORAH HOUSE (JUDGE CHAPMAN HOUSE)-Constructed 1830's-1840's; Italianate. Home of *Henry Chapman,* state senator, U.S. Congressman and district judge. Museum.

MERCER MUSEUM- Museum complex consisting of late-18th century log cabin, 1904 Georgian Revival sturcture and a later concrete library.

MORAVIAN POTTERY AND TILE WORKS- Established in 1912 by archeologist *Dr. Henry Chapman Mercer.* Factory won gold medal from American Institute of Architects, 1921. Museum.

Agriculture - Fruit, poultry, truck and
    varied farming
Industry/Mfg. - Electronics, clothing, dairy
    products
Higher Education - Delaware Valley College
Daily Newspaper - Intelligencer, 333 N.
    Broad Street
Chamber of Commerce - 379 N. Main Street
Community Events -
    Music Festival, Annual, May
    Polish Festival, Annual, September

•**DRAVOSBURG,** Borough; Allegheny County; Pop. 2,511; Area Code 412; Zip Code 15034; Elev. 800'; SE suburb of Pittsburgh, on the Mongahela River in SW Pennsylvania; bordered by the Allegheny County Airport. The town was named for *John F. Drava,* pioneer coal operator. Many residents of Dravosburg today work at the nearby Westinghouse Electric Plant.

•**DREXEL HILL,** Village; Delaware County; Pop. 30,000; Area Code 215; Zip Code 19026; Elev. 210; 6 m. W of Philadelphia, along the Darby Creek in SE Pennsylvania; in a residential area.

•**DRIFTWOOD,** Borough; Cameron County; Pop. 163; Area Code 814; Zip Code 15832; Elev. 850'; on the Sinnemahoning Creek, and near the Bucktail State Historical Park; N central Pennsylvania. It was named for the nearby creek, which is often filled with fallen timber.

•**DRUMS,** Village; Luzerne County; Pop. 400; Area Code 717; Zip Code 18222; Elev. 1,100; on Nescopeck Creek, 25 m.

SW of Wilkes-Barre in E Pennsylvania.

Drums was christened for the tavern kept here in the 1790s by *Abram Drum*.

•**DRYVILLE**, Village; Berks County; Pop. 100; Area Code 215; Zip Code 19539; SE Pennsylvania; named in 1852 for its first postmaster, *Benjamin Dry*.

•**DUBLIN**, Borough; Bucks County; Pop. 1,565; Area Code 215; Zip Code 18917; SE Pennsylvania.

POINT OF INTEREST

GREEN HILLS FARM- Built in 1835, with later additions. Typical vernacular stone architecture. Home of author *Pearl S. Buck* for many years.

•**DUBOIS**, City; Clearfield County; Pop. 9,290; Area Code 814; Zip Code 15801; Elev. 1,339'; 100 m. N of Pittsburgh in W central Pennsylvania.

DuBois, bisected by Sandy Lick Creek, lies in a narrow basin at the lowest pass in the Alleghenies. The city was first called Rumberger for *John Rumberger*, who laid out a town and sold building lots in 1772. In the same year *John DuBois*, a famous lumberman, who owned large tracts of white pine timber in Clearfield County, and who had exhausted the supply that could conveniently be floated down the Susquehanna to his mills at Williamsport, came to the little cluster of three or four houses on the western slope of the Allegheny Mountains, and at the age of 63 began extensive lumbering operations on his Sandy Creek tract. In May, 1876, his great mills were completed. Owning land adjacent to the settlement already begun, he built 100 or more houses for his employees after his business was well established, and he devoted his declining years to clearing and improving his great farm of 1200 acres.

Shortly after his arrival the post-office of DuBois was established, and in 1880 the town was incorporated under the name of DuBois, given in honor of *John DuBois*, its most important citizen. *John DuBois* was a New

115

Yorker of Huguenot descent, his name being the French equivalent of the English surname Wood.

Dubois is a favorite mountain resort.

> *Agriculture* - Dairy, truck and varied
>   farming
> *Industry/Mfg.* - Rubber products, silk,
>   coal, luggage. Resort area.
> *Daily Newspaper* - The Courier Express, 50-58
>   W. Long Ave.
> *Chamber of Commerce* - 128 W. Long Ave.

•**DUBOISTOWN**, Borough; Lycoming County; Pop. 1,218; Area Code 717; Zip Code 17702; Elev. 526'; 1 m. S of Williamsport in N central Pennsylvania, on the Susquehanna River; the borough was named for *John DuBois*, who first began his lumbering operations here.

•**DUDLEY**, Borough; Huntingdon County; Pop. 282; Area Code 717; Zip Code 16634; Elev. 1,415'; 33 m. SE of Altoona in a hilly area along a scenic route in S central Pennsylvania.

•**DUNBAR**, Borough; Fayette County; Pop. 1,369; Area Code 412; Zip Code 15431; Elev. 1,000'; 7 m. NE of Uniontown in a farming area in SW Pennsylvania.

Col. Thomas Dunbar was defeated by a French and Indian army here in 1755. His name was given to the new town shortly afterwards.

•**DUNCANNON**, Borough; Perry County; Pop. 1,645; Area Code 717; Zip Code 17020; Elev. 260'; 15 m. N of Harrisburg on the Susquehanna River, in S central Pennsylvania.

> *Agriculture* - Varied farming
> *Industry/Mfg.* - Grain milling, clothing

•**DUNCANSVILLE**, Borough; Blair County; Pop. 1,355; Area Code 814; Zip Code 16635; Elev. 1,020'; 4 m. SW of Lakemont in S central Pennsylvania.

Duncansville was founded by *Samuel Duncan* ; at the same time *Jacob Walter* owned a site to the east called Walterstown; the two met on a bridge spanning Blair Creek and tossed a penny to decide what the common name should be. In the settlement's anonymous days, about 1800, the operations of Old Forge brought it the nickname of Iron Town. Today the town is mainly residential.

•**DUNKARD**, Village; Greene County; Pop. 135; Area Code 412; Zip Code 15328; Elev. 920; 1 m. N of West Virginia state line in SW Pennsylvania.

Dunkard was named for the large colony of "Dunkards," or German Baptists who moved here from eastern Pennsylvania in the early nineteenth century.

•**DUNLEVY**, Borough; Washington County; Pop. 463; Area Code 412; Zip Code 15432; Elev. 800'; 35 m. S of Pittsburgh along the Monongahela River in SW Pennsylvania.

•**DUNMORE**, Borough; Lackawanna County; Pop. 16,781; Area Code 717; Zip Code 18512; Elev. 939'; NE Pennsylvania.

Dunmore was settled in 1783 by *William Allsworth*, a convivial shoemaker. Called Buckstown until 1840, it was renamed for the second son of the fifth Earl of Dunmore. This young Englishman, after enjoying the excellent shooting in the Lackawanna Valley and Moosic Mountain area, promised local boosters to raise $1,500,000 in England for a railroad construction project, which never materialized. Dunmore's growth was slow until the Pennsylvania Coal Company opened machine shops in 1847.

•**DUPONT**, Borough; Luzerne County; Pop. 3,460; Area Code 717; Zip Code 18641; Elev. 701'; E Pennsylvania.

Dupont was founded in 1917 and named for the *duPonts*, operators of a nearby powder plant, is set in a hollow.

Birthplace of *Faustin Wirkus*. In 1915 *Wirkus* quit his job as a breaker boy to join the Marine Corps. Sent to Haiti, he was detailed eventually to La Gonave, a neighboring island, and shortly became "King" of 10,000 voodooistic, polygamous natives who dwelt in the interior. His easy accession to kingship was possible because a deposed ruler, *Faustin* by name, had foretold the coming of a second Faustin to rule the island. *Wirkus* was later recalled by Marine authorities.

•**DUQUESNE**, City; Allegheny County; Pop. 10,094; Area Code 412; Zip Code 15110; Elev. 841'; SW Pennsylvania.

Duquesne was a collection of farms until 1885, when the Duquesne Steel Company erected a plant here. In 1889 a strike halted operations, and Carnegie acquired control the following year.

The city of Duquesne was incorporated in 1891. The name came from old Fort Duquesne, which was built at the forks of the Ohio in 1754, and named in honor of the *Marquis Duquesne de Menneville*, then governor of New France. The present town includes an earlier settlement long known as Germantown, which is supposed to have received its name from the first German colony in America, planted near Philadelphia in 1683. The name Duquesne, always very popular in the region of Pittsburgh, has been applied to many institutions and business concerns. Probably the city took its name directly from these steel works; but in the last analysis its origin must be traced to the historic old French fort.

•**DURYEA**, Borough; Luzerne County; Pop. 5,415; Area Code 717; Zip Code 18642; Elev. 589'; E Pennsylvania.

Duryea was named for *Abram Duryea*, who opened coal mines here in 1845. For a time the settlement was known as Babyton because of the mixture of tongues occasioned by the influx of immigrant miners. *Duryea* was a colonel in the Civil War of the fifth New York Infantry.

•**DUSHORE**, Borough; Sullivan County; Pop. 692; Area Code 717; Zip Code 18614; Elev. 1,593'; 45 m. NW of Wilkes-Barre in NE central Pennsylvania.

Dushore occupies ground cleared in 1794 by *Aristide Aubert Dupetit Thouars*, a refugee from the French Revolution. "Dushore" is the backwoodsmen's corrupted version of his name, adopted in 1859 when the settlement was incorporated. *Thouars* was known as a "genial, high-spirited" exile of the Asylum Company who bravely tried to make a new home in the wilderness although he had lived all his life in the comforts of a city.

Agriculture - Varied farming
Industry/Mfg. - Lumber, wood, metal products
   dairy products
Higher Education - Lafayette College
Chamber of Commerce - PO Box C

•EAGLES MERE, Borough; Sullivan County; Pop. 164; Area Code 717; Zip Code 17731; Elev. 2,000; NE central Pennsylvania.

Eagles Mere is on a small lake by the same name and near several snow skiing and all-season recreational areas.

Eagles Mere, or "the eagles lake," is the poetic designation given about 150 years ago to what had long been known as Lewis's Lake, which took its name from a wealthy Englishman named *Lewis*, who came there about 1810 and started extensive glass works. The isolated location and the lack of facilities for transportation made the enterprise unprofitable.

•EAGLEVILLE, Village; Montgomery County; Pop. 1,000; Area Code 215; Zip Code 19408; Elev. 380'; 6 m. NW of Norristown in SE Pennsylvania; in a rural-residential area.

•EAST BANGOR, Borough; Northampton County; Pop. 955; Area Code 215; Zip Code 18013; Elev. 572'; 1 m. NE of Bangor in E Pennsylvania; named for the old Welsh seaport by *R.M. Jones*, a Welsh expert in slate mining. See Also *Bangor*.

•EAST BERLIN, Borough; Adams County; Pop. 1,054; Area Code 717; Zip Code 17316; Elev. 430'; along the Conewago Creek in S Pennsylvania; named by German settlers.

•EAST BRADY, Borough; Clarion County; Pop. 1,153; Area Code 814; Zip Code 16028; Elev. 1,080'; on Brady's Bend of the Allegheny River in W Pennsylvania.

Easy Brady was laid out in 1866 and named for *Captain Brady*. During the Revolutionary War, *Captain*

Brady's father and brother were killed by Indians. The captain swore vengeance and for many years led expeditions against his enemies. To the settlers he was a glamourous figure whose perseverance was exceeded only by his bravery; to the Indians he was a demon. Brady's Bend was the scene of one of his famous exploits.

•**EAST BUTLER**, Borough; Butler County; Pop. 799; Area Code 412; Zip Code 16029; Elev. 1,080'; 2 m. NE of Butler on Thorn Creek in W Pennsylvania.

•**EAST CONEMAUGH**, Borough; Cambria County; Pop. 2,128; Area Code 814; Zip Code 15909; Elev. 1,240'; 1 m. N of Johnstown in SW central Pennsylvania.

East Conemaugh dates back to a time when it was necessary to use the prefix East to distinguish this town from the older borough of Conemaugh, which was consolidated with Johnstown about 130 years ago. The Conemaugh River, which became famous at the time of the Johnstown flood in 1889, has given its name to East Conemaugh. The name is derived from the Indian *Connemach*, which signifies "otter creek." Both Cambria and Somerset County have a Conemaugh Township.

•**EAST FAXON**, Village; Lycoming County; Pop. 4,000; Area Code 717; Zip Code 17706; 1 m. E of Williamsport along the Susquehanna River in E central Pennsylvania; residential suburb.

•**EAST GREENVILLE**, Borough; Montgomery County; Pop. 2,456; Area Code 215; Zip Code 18041; Elev. 415'; 20 m. S of Allentown on the main rail lines between that city and Philadelphia; SE Pennsylvania; also near Perkiomen Creek.

Community Event - Goschenoppen Folk Festival, Annual, August

•**EAST LANSDOWNE**, Borough; Delaware County; Pop. 2,806; Area Code 215; Zip Code 19050; Elev. 130'; 5 m. W of downtown Philadelphia along Cobbs Creek in SE Pennsylvania.

•**EAST LAWN**, Village; Northampton County; Pop. 18064; Area Code 717; Zip Code 18064; suburb of Easton and Allentown-Bethlehem in E Pennsylvania.

•**EASTLAWN GARDENS**, Village; Northampton County; Pop. 780; Area Code 717; Zip Code 18064; suburb of Easton in E Pennsylvania; considered part of Nazareth.

•**EAST MCKEESPORT**, Borough; Allegheny County; Pop. 2,940; Area Code 412; Zip Code 15035; Elev. 1,200'; near McKeesport in SW Pennsylvania; incorporated about 1895. Site of the Bliss Speedway, near State Highway 48.

•**EAST MAUCH CHUNK**, Village; Carbon County (annexed to Jim Thorpe in 1954).

•**EAST NORRITON**, Village; Montgomery County; Pop. 11,837; Area Code 215; Zip Code 19401; near Norristown in SE Pennsylvania; residential.

•**EASTON**, City; Northampton County seat; Pop. 26,069; Area Code 215; Zip Code 18042; Elev. 271'; on Delaware River, E of Allentown in E Pennsylvania; near Phillipsburg, New Jersey.

Like Allentown and Bethlehem, the city is bisected by the Lehigh River and much of its area looks down upon the valley floor from the heights of College Hill and Mount Ida.

Easton's older section, which includes College Hill, lies north of the river and retains much of the town's Colonial heritage; red brick houses with white marble steps and white doorways, shutters, and latticed blinds. South of the Lehigh, in the Mount Ida section, a more diversified style of architecture prevails. Both parts of the city have steep slopes into which steps have been cut to aid pedestrians.

Downtown Easton is dominated by a square locally called the "Circle." This traffic hub and center of civic activity is an open plot containing a Civil War monument; around the circle or near it are grouped the larger stores, movie theaters, and restaurants.

The city is a composite of a hurried commercial present and a sedate mercantile past, leavened by a college atmosphere. A familiar sight on market days is the trucks and wagons loaded with farm produce, drawn up to the curb at the Circle.

Under instructions from *Thomas Penn*, "ground at the forks of the Delaware" was surveyed for a town in 1750, and a more formal plan was outlined in 1752 by *William Parsons* and *Nicholas Scull* ; the town was named Easton, at the proprietor's wish, for the Northamptonshire estate (Easton-Weston) of *Lord Pomfret*, Penn's father-in-law.

The region around the Delaware Forks was long the seat of Delaware Indian influence. The Delaware called it *Lechauwitank*, or "Place at the Forks," and after they had lost their ancestral lands through the "Walking Purchase" of 1737, conferences between the proprietary government and the natives were conducted here. "I will treat with you nowhere but at the Forks," declared *Tedyuscung*, spokesman for the evicted Delaware, when Pennsylvania made belated overtures for conciliation during the opening years of the French and Indian War.

At one of these meetings in Easton, in 1756, the Delaware "King" stamped his foot angrily upon the ground and said: "This ground was my land and inheritance, and is taken from me by fraud!" During these conferences, too, agents of the province plied the chieftain with rum. The affair is thus recorded in a letter written at the time by *Charles Thompson*, *Tedyuscung's* clerk and later Secretary of the Continental Congress:

> The first two or three days were spent in deliberating whether the King should be allowed the privilege of a clerk. When he was resolute in asserting his right and would enter into no business without having a secretary of his own, they at last gave it up, and seem to have fallen on another scheme which is to unfit him to say anything worthy of being inscribed by his secretary. On Monday night the King was made drunk...He did not go to sleep last night...This morning he lay down under a shed about the break of day and slept a few hours, He is to speak this afternoon. He is to be sure in a fine capacity to do business...I for my part wish myself at home.

As early as 1752 Easton became a county seat, and by 1755 a combined church building and schoolhouse had been erected. It is said that a flag bearing stars and stripes was unfuled from Easton's courthouse steps when the Declaration of Independence was read there on July 8,

1776 - almost a year before the Continental Congress adopted the Flag Resolution in Philadelphia. The financial aid rendered to Washington's forces in the Revolutionary War was augmented by the formation of a company of militia and the donation of Durham boats, made at iron furnaces near the town, for the transport of troops. The First Reformed Church, still standing on North 3rd Street, served as a military hospital.

The town's location at a crossroads of traffic brought rapid development and growth. In 1789 it was incorporated as a borough, and in 1887 it became a city. From 1789 to 1853 the gristmills along Bushkill Creek were an important source of supply for eastern Pennsylvania and Philadelphia grain markets, and western migration of New Englanders through the town was a stimulus to trade. Passenger stagecoaches went into operation in 1796; a volunteer fire department was established in 1797; and in 1798 a bridge was thrown across the Lehigh. The Liberty Insurrection, or Fries' Rebellion, prompted by a house tax levied to finance a threatened war with France, called a civil posse into being in 1798-9 to quell the rioters. By the end of the eighteenth century Easton's population had increased to 1,100, and there were 200 dwellings.

The Lehigh Canal, from Mauch Chunk to Easton, was opened in 1829, and within three years the Delaware Division and the Morris Canal were opened. These, united with the discovery of anthracite in the upper Lehigh Valley, established Easton as a shipping center for coal. During this period South Easton began to develop, and the town, because of its situation in an area of iron ore, cement, and slate, grew steadily. In 1887, South Easton was merged with Easton.

Today, Easton is still an important mining and manufacturing center, and part of the sprawling Allentown-Bethlehem-Easton metropolitan area. Paper, pumps, compressors, other machinery, textiles, electronics, and chemicals are important products. Printing and publishing companies also employ many residents.

The city's cultural life centers around Lafayette College, founded in 1826 and opened in 1832 on the south side of the Lehigh River. It was named for the French Marquis who aided the American cause during the Revolution.

After coal investor Ario Pardee endowed the school with $200,000 in 1873, it began to grow into an important institution, emphasizing engineering.

Easton's population has declined by 5,000 since 1960, which may be due to the general nationwide decline in metal and coal mining-related industries.

POINTS OF INTEREST

CHAIN BRIDGE- Example of an early suspension bridge using stranded cables. Contstructed 1856-1857, *E.A. Douglas,* engineer.
NORTHAMPTON COUNTY HISTORICAL SOCIETY- Library and museum.

Industry/Mfg. - Varied manufacturing, trade and services
Higher Education - Lafayette College
Daily Newspaper - The Express, 30 North Fourth Street
Chamber of Commerce - 157 S. Fourth Street
Community Events -
Spring Festival, Annual, May-June
Water Carnival, Annual, August

•**EAST PETERSBURG,** Borough; Lancaster County; Pop. 3,600; Area Code 717; Zip Code 17520; Elev. 380'; 5 m. N of Lancaster in SE Pennsylvania.

•**EAST PITTSBURGH,** Borough; Allegheny County; Pop. 2,493; Area Code 412; Zip Code 15112; Elev. 1,000'; adjacent to Pittsburgh in SW Pennsylvania; near Monongahela River in a residential area.

•**EAST PROSPECT,** Borough; York County; Pop. 529; Area Code 717; Zip Code 17317; Elev. 493'; 10 m. E of York in S Pennsylvania; on the Susquehanna River. Samuel S. Lewis State Park is nearby.

•**EAST ROCHESTER,** Borough; Beaver County; Pop. 789; Area Code 412; Zip Code 15074; Elev. 800'; adjacent to Rochester in W Pennsylvania; located on the Ohio River.

•**EAST SIDE,** Borough; Carbon County; Pop. 302; Area Code 717; Zip Code 18661; Elev. 1,140'; 25 m. S of Wilkes-Barre off Interstate Highway 80.

East Side was named for its location on the east banks of the Lehigh River. Population here has increased 100 percent in the 1970s. Nearby are several snow skiiing facilities.

•**EAST STROUDSBURG**, Borough; Monroe County; Pop. 8,039; Area Code 717; Zip Code 18301; Elev. 430'; E Pennsylvania.

Adjacent to Stroudsburg near McMichaels Creek. East Stroudsburg is the site of a state college. Originally just an extension of Stroudsburg, it is almost as large and important today as the older town.

POINT OF INTEREST

ZION LUTHERAN CHURCH- Fine Greek Revival style church, with unusual scale; built 1851 for congregation established in 18th century.

•**EASTVALE**, Borough; Beaver County; Pop. 379; Area Code 412; Zip Code 15010; Elev. 895'; on E bank of the Shenango River, across from Beaver Falls in W Pennsylvania.

•**EAST VANDERGRIFT**, Borough; Westmoreland County; Pop. 955; Area Code 417; Zip Code 15629; Elev. 800'; SW Pennsylvania.

•**EAST WASHINGTON**, Borough; Washington County; Pop. 2,241; Area Code 412; Zip Code 15301; Elev. 1,220'; adjacent to Washington in SW Pennsylvania. The historic Lemoyne House is located here.

•**EAU CLAIRE**, Borough; Butler County; Pop. 420; Area Code 412; Zip Code 16030; Elev. 1,520'; Crossroads town approx. 40 m. N of Pittsburgh in W Pennsylvania. Name is French for "fresh water."

•**EBENSBURG**, Borough; Seat of Cambria County; Pop. 4,096; Area Code 814; Zip Code 15931; Elev. 2,022'; 18 m. NE of Johnstown in SW central Pennsylvania; on N branch of Conemaugh Creek.

Ebensburg was founded in the early 1800's by the *Reverend Rees Lloyd*, a religious dissenter and leader of

125

Welsh immigrants. Ebensburg was chosen as the county seat in 1805 when it was found to be at the geographical center of Cambria County. In 1842 it was still a rarity to have church services conducted in English rather than the ancient Cambrian tongue. *Rev. Lloyd* named the town for his son, *Eber*, who died in childhood. It was incorporated as a borough in 1825. Today it is a popular summer and health resort.

>*Agriculture* - Truck and varied farming
>*Industry/Mfg.* - Coal, lumber. Resort area.

•**ECHO**, Village; Armstrong County; Pop. 50; Area Code 412; Zip Code 16222; W Pennsylvania.
Echo took its name from the three ravines that meet here and cause sounds to echo.

•**ECONOMY**, Borough; Beaver County; Pop. 9,538; Area Code 412; Zip Code 15005; Elev. 1,180'; W Pennsylvania; incorporated in 1958.
In 1825 the Harmony Society moved into Pennsylvania, bought about three thousand acres of land, and founded the town and the township of Economy. Economy was no misnomer: for the society exercised an economy which supervised with the closest scrutiny all the operations of house, farm, and workshop. their business enterprises extended over most of western Pennsylvania. They opened coal mines and started salt works. They engaged in extensive lumbering operations. They established cotton, woolen, and silk mills. Finally, the discovery of oil on their lands made them immensely wealthy.
Meanwhile, the community suffered from frequent and prolonged litigation, from bitter internal dissensions, and from their unnatural state of celibacy. In 1903 *Susie C. Duss* became sole trustee of the society; and a few years later, when no heirs or successors claimed it, the Harmony Society property reverted to the state.
The old section of town is preserved as a historic site.

•**EDDYSTONE**, Borough; Delaware County; Pop. 2,555; Area Code 215; Zip Code 19013; Elev. 20'; 15 m. SW of Philadelphia in SW Pennsylvania, on the Delaware River; port facilities along the riverfront.

•**EDGEWOOD**, Borough; Allegheny County; Pop. 4,382; Area Code 412; Zip Code 15218; Elev. 920'; E suburb of Pittsburgh in SW Pennsylvania; in a residential area.

•**EDGEWORTH**, Borough; Allegheny County; Pop. 1,738; Area Code 412; Zip Code 15143; Elev. 723'; NW of Pittsburgh in SW Pennsylvania, on Ohio River.

Edgeworth was the first municipality in Pennsylvania to adopt the borough manager form of government. This is the birthplace of *Ethelbert Nevin* (1862-1901), composer of "The Rosary," "Narcissus," and other well-known works, spent many years of his life here.

•**EDINBORO**, Borough; Erie County; Pop. 6,324; Area Code 814; Zip Code 16412; Elev. 1,210'; 20 m. S of Lake Erie Shore in NW Pennsylvania; named for city in Scotland.

Edinboro State College is located in town, as is a small lake by the same name. A few light industrial plants add to the mainly retail aspects of the town's economy.

•**EDWARDSVILLE**, Borough; Luzerne County; Pop. 5,729; Area Code 717; Zip Code 18704; Elev. 760'; 3 m. NW of Wilkes-Barre in E Pennsylvania.

Edwardsville, incorporated in 1884, was named for *Daniel Edwards*, superintendent of the Kingston Coal Company, whose mining operations opened here soon after the borough was incorporated. *Edwards*, Welsh by birth, lived here until his death in 1901. Today Edwardsville is a large suburb in the Wilkes-Barre metropolitan area.

•**EHRENFELD**, Borough; Cambria County; Pop. 360; Area Code 814; Zip Code 15933; Elev. 1,520'; 10 m. E of Johnstown in SE central Pennsylvania. Incorporated in 1956 from Crayle Township.

•**EIDENAU**, Village; Butler County; Pop. 30; Area Code 412; Zip Code 16037; W Pennsylvania; small summer resort village.

The name is German for "the vale of Eden," and was so called by *George Rapp*, founder of the Harmony Society, when he purchased land here.

•**EIGHTY-FOUR**, Village; Washington County; Pop. 250; Area Code 412; Zip Code 15330; Elev. 1,020; 6 m. E of Washington in SW Pennsylvania, off Interstate Highway 70. Named because the post office was established here in 1884.

•**ELCO**, Borough; Washington County; Pop. 417; Area Code 412; Zip Code 15434; Elev. 765'; 30 m. S of Pittsburgh in SW Pennsylvania, on Monongahea River.

•**ELDERTON**, Borough; Armstrong County; Pop. 420; Area Code 312; Zip Code 15736; Elev. 1,265'; 15 m. SE of Kittanning in W Pennsylvania, on Plum Creek.

Elderton was founded in 1822 and named for *Sara Elder*, an early settler.

•**ELDRED**, Borough; McKean County; Pop. 965; Area Code 914; Zip Code 16731; Elev. 1,500'; 3 m. S of New York state line in N Pennsylvania, along the Allegheny River. Rural center.

•**ELGIN**, Borough; Erie County; Pop. 235; Area Code 814; Zip Code 16413; Elev. 1,440'; 30 m. SE of Erie in NW Pennsylvania, on S branch of the French Creek.

•**ELIZABETH**, Borough; Allegheny County; Pop. 1,892; Area Code 412; Zip Code 15037; Elev. 731'; SE suburb of Pittsburgh in SW Pennsylvania.

Elizabeth, on the east bank of the Monongahela, owes much of its early growth to the river. In 1778 flatboat construction began, and keels laid down here were used in the exploration and settlement of the Ohio and Mississippi Rivers. Keelboats and steamboats were constructed on its ways, and for a time Elizabeth was one of the most important boatbuilding centers in the country.

The town was laid out in 1787 by *Stephen Bayard* and named in honor of his bride, *Elizabeth Mackay Bayard*, daughter of *Colonel Aeneas Mackay*, once commandant at Fort Pitt.

•**ELIZABETHTOWN**, Borough; Lancaster County; Pop. 8,233; Area Code 717; Zip Code 17022; Elev. 462'; 15 m. SE of Harrisburg in SE Pennsylvania.

Elizabethtown had its beginning in 1732 as a trading post conducted by *Captain Thomas Harris*, whose brother founded Harrisburg. In 1735 the captain established a tavern here, expanding it after 10 years into an elaborate stone structure. Known as the Black Bear, and modernized in 1915, the tavern stands at the southwest corner of Market and Hummelstown Streets. Elizabethtown was named for the wife of *Captain Barnabas Hughes* who purchased the tavern and the original Harris tract in 1750.

> *Agriculture* - Tobacco, grain and varied
> farming
> *Industry/Mfg.* - Clothing, candy, dairy
> products, fertilizer
> *Higher Education* - Elizabethtown College

•**ELIZABETHVILLE**, Borough; Dauphin County; Pop. 1,531; Area Code 717; Zip Code 17023; Elev. 640'; SE central Pennsylvania, on Wisonisco Creek.

John Bender, a tavernkeeper on the old Harrisburg road, established a settlement here in 1817 and named it for his wife; the town is a shopping center for neighboring farmers.

•**ELK COUNTY**, In 1843 Elk County was created out of Clearfield, Jefferson, and McKean. In all probability it received its name from Elk Creek, which flows into the Clarion River at Ridgeway, though *Sherman Day* maintains that the county derived its name directly from Elk Mountain, in the southern part of the county. Though this mountain is also mentioned in Lippincott's *Gazetteer*, one can find no conclusive evidence of its existence. In the last analysis, of course, the origin of the name can be traced to the great heard of elks which once frequented these wilds. In 1832 *Judge Geddes*, in the report of a survey, noted that a "few elks still remain" in this region. As late as 1852 a drove of twelve or more elks were found near Ridgeway by two hunters, who killed seven. In the early days the county contained several favorite wintering places for elks, one of which was in the neighborhood of Portland Mills.

•**ELKINS PARK**, Village; Montgomery County; Pop. 10,000; Area Code 215; Zip Code 19117; Elev. 200'; N suburb of Philadelphia in SE Pennsylvania, near the Breyer Boy Scout Training Area.

•**ELKLAND**, Borough; Tioga County; Pop. 1,974; Area Code 717; Zip Code 16920; Elev. 1,130'; just S of New York state line in N Pennsylvania.

At this point, the valley of the Cowanesque River is only a half mile wide. Into this area, elk once trooped down to drink, and large numbers of them crossed from one range of hills to another.

Although this town is mainly a recreational center for hunters and mountain lovers, small industrial plants manufacture various goods.

> *Agriculture* - Poultry, fruit and varied
>   farming
> *Industry/Mfg.* - Electronics, lumber, dairy
>   products

•**ELLPORT**, Borough; Lawrence County; Pop. 1,290; Area Code 412; Zip Code 16117; Elev. 880'; 2 m. E of Ellwood City in W Pennsylvania, on Slippery Rock Creek.

•**ELLSWORTH**, Borough; Washington County; Pop. 1,228; Area Code 412; Zip Code 15331; Elev. 1,060'; 30 m. S of Pittsburgh in SW Pennsylvania, in an old coal mining region.

•**ELLWOOD CITY**, Borough; Beaver and Lawrence Counties; Pop. 9,998; Area Code 412; Zip Code 16117; Elev. 900'; 10 m. N of Beaver Falls in W Pennsylvania, on the Shenango River.

Ellwood City was laid out in 1890 by the Pittsburgh Company, and was named in honor of *Colonel I.L. Ellwood* of Indiana, who pioneered the manufacturing of wire fencing.

> *Agriculture* - Varied farming
> *Industry/Mfg.* - Steel products, clothing,
>   quarrying, dairy products
> *Daily Newspaper* - The Ledger, 835 Lawrence
>   Avenue
> *Chamber of Commerce* - 314 Fifth Street

•**ELVERSON**, Borough; Chester County; Pop. 530; Area Code 215; Zip Code 19520; Elev. 660'; 2 m. S of French Creek State Park in SE Pennsylvania; rural crossroads town.

POINT OF INTEREST

WARWICK MILLS- Late-18th-early-19th century mill complex, includes stone gristmill and manor house. Mill operated until 1968.

•**EMLENTON**, Borough; Clarion and Venango Counties; Pop. 807; Area Code 814; Zip Code 16373; Elev. 902'; 50 m. NE of Pittsburgh in NW Pennsylvania, on Allegheny River.

Named for *Hannah Emlen*, the maiden name of the town founder's wife. Oil refining is the main activity here, as there are many oil wells nearby.

Agriculture - Varied farming
Industry/Mfg. - Oil, coal, cables

•**EMMAUS**, Borough; Lehigh County; Pop. 11,001; Area Code 215; Zip Code 18049; Elev. 433'; 5 m. S of Allentown in E Pennsylvania.

Emmaus,, founded shortly after 1740 by the Moravians, was called successively Maguntchi (Ind. "place of the bears") and Salzburg. Not until 1761, when *Bishop August Spangenberg*, founder of the Moravian Church in America, conducted a feast here, was it named for the biblical town of Emmaus. In the succeeding years one "m" was dropped from the name, but in 1939 the earlier spelling was officially restored. The Moravian economy, wherein none but members of the church could own property or have a voice in the government, persisted until 1835.

The national magazines, *Organic Gardening* and *Prevention* are published here. The Lehigh Valley Velodrome is the site of championship cycling events here.

Agriculture - Varied farming
Industry/Mfg. - Lumber, cement, cloth, chemicals
Chamber of Commerce - 408 Chestnut St.

131

•**EMPORIUM**, Borough; Seat of Cameron County; Pop. 2,837; Area Code 814; Zip Code 15834; Elev. 1,031'; on Bucktail Trail, near New York state line in N central Pennsylvania.

Emporium was settled in 1810, it grew with the lumber boom in the middle of the nineteenth century. The borough became the seat of Cameron County in 1861. Emporium is the Latinized form of the Greek word for "market, or centre of trade." For several years the place was called Shippen because it was located in Shippen Township, which was named for *Edward Shippen*, one of the early settlers, who came into this locality in 1819. The name Emporium, which was assumed by the county-seat at the time of its incorporation in 1864, is said to date back as far as 1785. In that year, according to tradition, an agent ½&Ethe Holland Land Company, coming up the Driftwood branch of the Sinnemahoning Creek by boat, camped with his companions at its confluence with Portage Creek, now in the eastern end of the town. Here he shaved off the bark from the side of a large tree and carved on it the word *Emporium* in prophetic anticipation of the future inportance of the place.

> *Agriculture* - Poultry farming
> *Industry/Mfg.* - Lumber, electronics, coal,
>   explosives. Resort area.
> *Chamber of Commerce* - 33 E. 4th Street

•**EMSWORTH**, Borough; Lawrence County; Pop. 408; Area Code 412; Zip Code 15202; Elev. 723'; 5 m. NW of Pittsburgh in W Pennsylvania, on the Ohio River.

Emsworth was named for an English duke who held an early land patent. Prior to 1872 the community was called Courtneyville for *James and William Courtney*, who settled here in 1803.

•**ENDEAVOR**, Village; Forest County; Pop. 300; Area Code 814; Zip Code 16322; Elev. 1,113'; NW Pennsylvania.

Endeavor took its name from the fact that about 100 years ago the *Reverend J.V. McAnich* organized a Christian Endeavor Society here, which ripened into a Presbyterian church and gave its name to the village.

•**ENOLA**, Village; Cumberland County; Pop. 7,000; Area Code 717; Zip Code 17025; Elev. 400'; across the Susquehanna River from Harrisburg in S Pennsylvania; a residential and industrial suburb.

The town was originally a tiny hamlet until the Pennsylvania Railroad built its large freight-classification yards here. The erroneous popular explanation of this peculiar name is that the call for the lonely telegraph tower which once stood across the river from Harrisburg was the word *alone*, and that the name Enola was suggested by spelling this word backward.

In point of fact, the name Enola has been traced to *Amanda Gingrich Underwood* who once lived in Mechanicsburg, Pennsylvania. In 1861 *Mrs. Underwood* read a novel entitled *The Dangers of Darkness*. Both she and her husband were so much attracted by the name of Enola, one of the characters in the story, that they christened their baby girl *Enola Underwood*. *Wesley G. Miller*, living near Harrisburg, married a cousin of *Mrs. Underwood*, *Fannie Longsdorf*, and they named their first daughter *Enola Miller*. *Mr. Miller* purchased the Longsdorf place, the homestead of his wife's parents. When the residents of this region petitioned the Pennsylvania Railroad Company for a station, a site was purchased from *Mr. Miller*, who proposed the name of Longsdorf for the new station. but the Pennsylvania Railroad already had a station with this name, and at the suggestion of *Mr. Miller* the new station was called Enola in honor of his four-year-old daughter, *Enola*.

•**EPHRATA**, Borough; Lancaster County; Pop. 11,095; Area Code 717; Zip Code 17522; Elev. 380'; 12 m. NE of Lancaster in SE Pennsylvania; site of the historic Ephrata Clioster along a scenic route.

The German Seventh-Day Adventists established a monastic community here in 1735. The old convent and the "Gebruderhaus" each housed 35 devotees. *Johann Beissel* was the founder of this colony.

POINT OF INTEREST

EPHRATA CLOISTER- From 1740-1746, one of America's earliest communal societies. Complex includes extensively restored *Saal* (Community House), *Saron* (Sister's House) and other houses, cottages and cabins.

Agriculture - Tobacco, grain, truck and
varied farming
Industry/Mfg. - Clothing, footwear. Resort
area
Chamber of Commerce - 104-1/2 E. Main Street

•**EQUINUNK**, Village; Wayne County; Pop. 185; Area Code 717; Zip Code 18417; Elev. 800; NE Pennsylvania; name is Indian for "where clothing was distributed."

POINT OF INTEREST

HILL'S SAWMILL- The area's only remaining water-powered sawmill was built in 1873, operated until 1973, and is still in operating condition.

•**ERDENHEIM**, Village; Montgomery County; Pop. 3,700; Area Code 215; Zip Code 19118; just outside N Philadelphia border in SE Pennsylvania; All Saints Hospital is located in this residential community.

•**ERIE**, City; Erie County seat; Pop. 118,964; Area Code 814; Zip Code 165 + zone; Elev. 709'; on Lake Erie, 90 m. W of Buffalo, New York in NW Pennsylvania.

Erie, Pennsylvania's only port on the Great Lakes and its northernmost city, lies on a plain 113 feet above the level of Lake Erie. At its front door is a landlocked harbor formed by a curved peninsula seven miles long; from its back door extend miles of gently rolling farmland.

Laid out on a modification of the plan of the nations capital, Erie gives the impression of the spaciousness that characterized early Washington, especially with its wide tree-lined streets, broad lawns, and pleasing architecture.

Generally the city has the restful quiet of a resort center, but the water front presents a scene of activity when the lake, ice-locked several months of the year, is open to navigation. Here thousands of vessels annually warp into and away from the piers, carrying heavy cargoes of lumber, coal, petroleum, grain, iron ore, and fish; until 1925 more fresh-water fish were shipped from Erie than from any other port in the world. To the Public Steamboat Landing, where the Coast Guard, Naval Reserve, and fishing craft tie up, Erie citizens come to see sunset on the bay and to patronize the seafood restaurants at the pier's approach.

Another function of the lake is to provide transportation facilities and water for Erie and its industries. Thus the lake indirectly determined the make-up of the population, for Germans, Poles, Russians, Italians, and other national groups were drawn to Erie in the late nineteenth century, not only by the mills and factories, but by fishing and shipping.

Lake Erie tempers the climate of the city and its environs, prolonging the normal growing season and providing a constant cooling breeze in summer. While somewhat dreary in winter, Erie becomes a lively resort as warm weather approaches. During the hot days of summer, thousands of bathers and picnickers line the sandy beaches of Presque Isle Peninsula.

Erie's first known inhabitants were Indians of the Eriez nation, from which the lake and later the city received their names. They were exterminated by the Seneca about 1654, and for decades thereafter the region remained under control of the Iroquois Confederacy. In the summer of 1753 a French force under *Sieur Marin* from Montreal, recognizing the strategic possibilities afforded by the sheltering arm of the peninsula, established a fort at Presque Isle (Fr.:peninsula). By 1760, however, French claims to the rich Ohio Valley had been shattered and Fort Presque Isle was abandoned to the conquering English who soon garisoned the post. No permanent settlement was established until 1795.

The Seneca, who had camped and hunted along Lake Erie's shores and had allied themselves at various times with both the French and English, now began to fear continued encroachment on the part of the white man. In 1763, at the start of the *Pontiac* uprising, they captured Fort Presque Isle, which *Colonel Henry Bouquet* had built near the site of the old French stronghold, and burned it to the ground.

In 1784 Pennsylvania aquired by treaty with the Six Nations all land in the northwestern part of the state, but this did not include the triangular tract fronting on Lake Erie. Congress, taking up Pennsylvania's plea for adequate frontage on that body of water, requested New York, Massachusetts, and Connecticut to relinquish their claims to the territory. It was therefore deeded to the United States Government, and in 1792 was sold to Pennsylvania for 75 cents an acre.

The Indians on Lake Erie and in western Pennsylvania resisted colonization on and near the Triangle, even after accepting payment from Pennsylvania and the Federal Government for it. *Joseph Brant*, the Mohawk chief, tried repeatedly to emulate *Pontiac* in resisting the northward and westward spread of the white man's domain. There were continued outbursts of violence in western Pennsylvania and Ohio until *General Anthony Wayne* launched a vigorous campaign and won the Battle of Fallen Timbers, after which the spirit of the western Indians was broken. *Wayne* made a treaty with the western tribes in August 1795, and with the Six Nations the following November.

That same year the town of Erie was laid out by *Major Andrew Ellicott* and *General William Irvine*. It grew slowly; by 1805, when it was incorporated as a borough, the little lake settlement boasted only 100 houses inhabited by New Yorkers, New Englanders, and a scattering of Scotch-Irish and German pioneers from southern Pennsylvania. Then came sawmills, gristmills, brickyards, foundries, and a number of other enterprises to stimulate growth.

When the War of 1812 was declared, Great Britain had a series of military posts stretching along the Canadian border and a provincial navy that gave her mastery of the Great Lakes. Early in the war the British captured America's only armed vessel in inland waters and were in a position to strike a fatal blow upon Lake Erie's south shore. On March 27, 1813, *Lieutenant Oliver Hazard Perry* was sent to Lake Erie to take command of a small fleet then being hurriedly constructed for defense against the British squadron. The enemy tried to bottle him up in Presque Isle Bay, but on July 19 *Perry* nosed part of his squadron out of the bay to engage briefly with the British until they withdrew. Later he conquered the fleet in a battle off Sandusky, Ohio.

Prior to the War of 1812 there were about a dozen merchant ships on Lake Erie, with salt and furs the principal commodities shipped through the city's port. Roads were extremely poor, and crude wagons of the time were drawn mainly by oxen. By 1826, however, three steamboats and from two to ten schooners cleared from the port every week, and by 1846 daily steamboat service had been established between Erie and Buffalo.

With the opening of the Erie and Pittsburgh Cana in 1844 and the advent of the railroads in the 1850s, Erie made rapid strides. Incorporated as a city in 1851, it enjoyed a brief boom when a difference in the gauge of tracks made it necessary for trains to stop here to transfer passengers and freight. It lost its dreams of becoming the great lake terminus of the railroads when a standard gauge was adopted.

Still, Erie is Pennsylvania's third largest city. Its port is one of the best in the Great Lakes, and despite a recent decline in the economy, it remains a major manufacturing center. The city's metropolitan area, with such suburbs as Lawrence Park, Mill Creek, Harborcreek and Fairview, boasts of a growing population of 279,290.

Despite its industrial appearances, Erie is also an educational center, with four colleges and several museums.

Visitors to Erie usually see the restored flagship, *Niagara*, on which *Oliver Perry* sailed, at the Public Dock. A large monument also honors *Perry* on Presque Isle. A public beach lines the seven mile-long peninsula.

POINTS OF INTEREST

CASHIER'S HOUSE- Built c. 1839 for Peter Benson, first cashier of Erie branch of United States Bank. Ornate Egyptian Revival interior.

ERIE HISTORICAL MUSEUM- Art and history exhibits.

ERIE PUBLIC MUSEUM AND PLANETARIUM

GLENWOOD PARK AND ERIE ZOO- More than 300 animals; childrens zoo; golf course; indoor ice rink.

OLD CUSTOM HOUSE- Built as Erie branch of United States Bank in 1839; later served as post office and custom house. Greek Revival.

PRESQUE ISLE- 3,000-acre state park, including 7 miles of beach.

U.S.S. NIAGARA- One of six ships built at Erie to challenge the British on the lake during the War of 1812. Museum.

Industry/Mfg. - Varied manufacturing, trade
    and services
Higher Education -
    Gannon College
    Mercyhurst College
    Pennsylvania State University
    Villa Maria College

Daily Newspaper - The Times, 205 West 12th
Street
Chamber of Commerce - 1006 State Street
Community Events -
Polka Festival, Annual, August
Spring Arts Festival, Annual, April

•**ERIE COUNTY**, Erie was one of the eight new counties created on March 12, 1800. Erie County was named for the great lake that forms its northwestern boundary. The original northern boundary of the state ran due west, and Pennsylvania had only about four miles of frontage on Lake Erie. The "Erie triangle" was disputed territory, the contending claimants being New York, Massachusetts, and Connecticut. Just eight years before Erie County came into existence, the United States, apparently acting on the assumption that none of the claimants had a sound title to the "Erie triangle," sold it to Pennsylvania for $150,000. By this purchase the state secured fifty miles of lake shore, and 202,187 acres of land.

The word Erie, according to the French, means *chat sauvage*, or "wild cat," which was their name for the raccoon. The earliest reference to this name is in a French map of 1651, on which Lake Erie is styled Lac du Chat, "Lake of the Cat." *Charlevoix* said of Lake Erie: "The name it bears is that of an Indian nation of the Huron language, which was formerly seated on its banks, and which has been entirely destroyed by the Iroquois. Erie in that language signifies ¢at," and in some accounts this nation is called the Cat Nation. This name probably comes from the large number of these animals found in this country." Some have thought that the name was descriptive of the character of the tribe; others suppose, apparently with more reason, that the *chat sauvage*, or raccoon, was the tribal totem.

The Eries are said to have been utterly annihilated by the Iroquois in 1654. It is more reasonable to suppose that the Eries ceased to exist as a distinct tribe, - that some were captured and others dispersed, and that those who thus escaped destruction joined themselves to other tribes. New York and Ohio have also named counties for Lake Erie.

•**ERNEST**, Borough; Indiana County; Pop. 584; Area Code 412; Zip Code 15739; Elev. 1,160'; 5 m. N of Indiana, near Crooked Creek in W central Pennsylvania.

•ESSINGTON, Village; Delaware County; Pop. 2,900; Area Code 215; Zip Code 19029; Elev. 20'; 8 m. SW of central Philadelphia in SE Pennsylvania; along the Delaware River across from the Little Tinicum Island and the Philadelphia Seaplane Base.

Community Event - Seafaring Days, Annual, August

•ETNA, Borough; Allegheny County; Pop. 4,534; Area Code 412; Zip Code 15223; Elev. 750'; SW Pennsylvania.

Etna, appropriately named for Sicily's famed volcano, is a town of flaming furnaces, iron works, and steel mills. Etna's history as an industrial town dates form 1832 when an ironmaking establishment was set up here. It became a borough in 1868.

General William Wilkins once owned the town site, and the large frame house that he occupied was the first building within the present borough. *David Anderson* bought the land from him and laid out a town, which early received the name of Stewartstown in honor of *David Stewart*, a prominent citizen. About 1832 two iron manufacturers, *H.S. Spang* and his son, came to Stewartstown from the region that is now Catharine Township, in Blair County, where they had operated an old charcoal furnace known as the "Etna Furnace." It is highly probable - but not certain - that they brought with them the name of Etna.

Today, Etna's industry benefits from its location on the Allegheny River, just across the Robert Fleming Bridge from central Pittsburgh.

•EUCLID, Village; Butler County; Pop. 90; Area Code 412; Zip Code 16001; W Pennsylvania; considered part of the city of Butler.

Euclid was named by its first postmaster for Euclid Street in Cleveland.

•EVANS CITY, Borough; Butler County; Pop. 2,299; Area Code 412; Zip Code 16033; Elev. 940'; W Pennsylvania.

Evans City was settled in 1796 by *Robert Boggs*, who exchanged a mare for a 400-acre tract on which he built a cabin and a mill. In 1836, *Thomas B. Evans* laid out the village, after buying half of *Boggs'* land.

139

•**EVERETT**, Borough; Bedford County; Pop. 1,828; Area Code 814; Zip Code 15537; Elev. 1,106'; 42 m. S of Altoona in S Pennsylvania; in the Tussey Mountains.

Everett, laid out in 1795 by *Michael Barndollar* and originally called Waynesboro, grew slowly until the railroad came in 1862.

> *Agriculture* - Poultry, grain, fruit and
> varied farming
> *Industry/Mfg.* - Lumber, clothing, animal
> feed, dairy products, quarrying
> *Community Event* - American Indian Revisited,
> Annual, August

•**EVERSON**, Borough; Fayette County; Pop. 1,032; Area Code 412; Zip Code f15631; Elev. 1,053'; SW Pennsylvania.

Everson, was laid out in 1874 at the time when *W.H.Everson* opened a sheet iron mill in Scottdale.

•**EXCHANGE**, Village; Montour County; Pop. 45; Area Code 717; Zip Code 17821; E central Pennsylvania; considered part of Danville.

Exchange is situated on an old mail route at a point where it was necessary to exchange horses in the old stage-coaching days.

•**EXETER**, Borough; Luzerne County; Pop. 5,493; Area Code 717; Zip Code 18643; Elev. 591'; E Pennsylvania.

Exeter was named for Exeter Township, organized in 1790 by settlers from Exeter, Rhode Island. This long narrow town, peopled by Italian and Polish stock, escaped the worst effects of the anthracite depression because its rich coal deposits can be mined at comparatively small cost.

•**EXPORT**, Borough; Westmoreland County; Pop. 1,143; Area Code 417; Zip Code 15632; Elev. 982'; 20 m. E of Pittsburgh in SW Pennsylvania.

Export, incorporated in 1911, was the first town in this area to mine coal for more than local markets which is transported along Penn Central rail lines that reach Pittsburgh.

> *Industry/Mfg.* - Cement, coal, dairy products

•**EXTON**, Village; Chester County; Pop. 2,000; Area Code 215; Zip Code 19341; Elev. 370'; 25 m. NW of Philadelphia in SE Pennsylvania; in a suburban area.

•FACTORYVILLE, Borough; Wyoming County; Pop. 924; Area Code 717; Zip Code 18419; Elev. 840'; NE Pennsylvania.

Factoryville was the site of an old woolen mill about 200 years ago. The New England settlers came here from miles around to have their homespun wool woven into cloth. The old woolen factory gave its name to the town.

•FAIRCHANCE, Borough; Fayette County; Pop. 2,106; Area Code 412; Zip Code 15436; 6 m. S of Uniontown in a rural area of SW Pennsylvania.

•FAIRFIELD, Borough; Adams County; Pop. 591; Area Code 717; Zip Code 17320; Elev. 608'; 8 m. SW of Gettysburg in S Pennsylvania; in a hilly, densely forested area.

POINT OF INTEREST

FAIRFIELD INN- Originally farmhouse, built in 1757 with later additions; contains much original hardware; used as quarters for Civil War general *J.E.B. Stuart* during his occupation of Gettysburg.

•FAIRHOPE, Village; Fayette County; Pop. 2,500; Area Code 412; Zip Code 15012; 2 m. E of Belle Vernon along the Monongahela River in SW Pennsylvania.

•FAIRLESS HILLS, Village; Bucks County; Pop. 12,500; Area Code 215; Zip Code 19030; Elev. 100'; NE suburb of Philadelphia in SE Pennsylvania; a residential area extending from Levittown.

Chamber of Commerce - 409 Hood Blvd.

•**FAIRMOUNT CITY**, Village; Clarion County; Pop. 350; Area Code 814; Zip Code 16224; Elev. 1,069'; was laid out on Red Bank Creek in the early 1870s as a bituminous coal mining town.

•**FAIRVIEW**, Borough; Butler County; Pop. 226; Area Code 412; W Pennsylvania; along Bear Creek in a farming region.

•**FAIRVIEW**, Borough; Erie County; Pop. 1,855; Area Code 814; Zip Code 16415; Elev. 717'; suburb of Erie in NW Pennsylvania; incorporated in 1868.

•**FALLENTIMBER**, Village; Campria County; Pop. 150; Area Code 814; Zip Code f16639; Elev. 1,432'; SW central Pennsylvania; so named because of the large windfall created by a huge storm that once swept the primeval forest in this region.

•**FALLS**, Village; Wyoming County; Pop. 150; Area Code 717; Zip Code 18615; Elev. 585'; NE Pennsylvania; was founded in 1824; lies in a deep valley surrounded by 2,000 foot mountains.

•**FALLS CREEK**, Borough; Clearfield and Jefferson Counties; Pop. 1,208; Area Code 814; Zip Code 15840; Elev. 1,440'; 4 m. NW of Dubois in W central Pennsylvania; in an old lumbering area.

•**FALLSTON**, Borough; Beaver County; Pop. 312; Area Code 412; Zip Code 15066; Elev. 760'; 2 m. S of Beaver Falls in W Pennsylvania, along the Shenango River.

•**FANNETSBURG**, Village; Franklin County; Pop. 300; Area Code 717; Zip Code 17221; Elev. 860'; S Pennsylvania; amid the Kittatinny and Tuscarora Mountains. Scotch-Irish settlers named this town for Fannett Point in County Donegal, Ireland.

•**FARMINGTON**, Village; Fayette County; Pop. 100; Area Code 412; Zip Code 15437; Elev. 1,831; 12 m. SE of Uniontown, along U.S. Highway 40 in SW Pennsylvania; nearby are the Fort Necessity Battlefield and General Braddock's grave historic sites. Named for a Connecticut town by settlers from the east.

•**FARRELL**, City; Mercer County; Pop. 8,645; Area Code 412; Zip Code 16121; Elev. 853'; W Pennsylvania.

Farrell was incorporated as South Sharon in 1901, it was renamed in 1911 to honor *James A. Farrell*, president of the United States Steel Corporation, which has since dominated the economy here. *Farrell* was born at New Haven, Connecticut, in 1863, and began active life at the age of 15 as an unskilled laborer in the New Haven wire mills. When 19 years old, he was a wire-drawer for the Oliver Wire Company in Pittsburgh. At the age of 26 he had become general manager of the Pittsburgh Wire Company. In 1901 he took charge of the export department of the United States Steel Corporation, of which he became president 10 years later.

Today, the city of Farrell is the central market for a large industrial area, and is the last stop in Pennsylvania for many traveling west to Ohio.

•**FASSETT**, Village; Bradford County; Pop. 100; Area Code 717; Zip Code 16925; Elev. 1,123'; Incorporated with Gillett. Fassett was formerly called State Line and renamed for early settler *Philo Fassett.*

•**FAWN GROVE**, Borough; York County; Pop. 516; Area Code 717; Zip Code 17321; Elev. 735'; 30 m. SE of York, and just N of Maryland state line in S Pennsylvania.

•**FAYETTE CITY**, Borough; Fayette County; Pop. 788; Area Code 412; Zip Code 15438; Elev. 620'; 8 m. S of Monessen in SW Pennsylvania, along the Monongahela River; named for the French *General de la Fayette*, who helped the Americans during the Revolution.

•**FAYETTE COUNTY**, once claimed by Virginia as a part of Monogalia County, was erected in 1783 out of Westmoreland County, and was named in honor of *Roche Yves Gilbert Motier, Marquis de la Fayette*, whose influence and bravery had been of inestimable value to the American colonies in the war just ended. No country has ever had a more disinterested friend than this enthusiastic young French nobleman, who was not yet twenty years of age when congress commissioned him a major-general. Though he won no victories, and though he seems never to have exercised any important, independent command, or to have been in charge of any considerable number of troops, the value of his example, his personal sympathy, and his moral support was priceless. Not only did he serve without pay throughout the Revolutionary War, but he actually expended $140,000 of his own money in promoting the American cause. On his return to France Congress commended him to his king as "wise in council, brave in battle, and patient under the fatigues of war."

On May 26, 1825, by special invitation, *General de la Fayette*, accompanied by his only son, *George Washington de la Fayette*, visited Uniontown, the county-seat of Fayette County. The people turned out *en masse* to greet their distinguished guest. The address of welcome on behalf of the citizens of Fayette County was delivered by *Albert Gallatin*, who had been United States Senator from Pennsylvania in 1793 and Secretary of the Treasury from 1801 to 1814.

•**FAYETTEVILLE**, Village; Franklin County; Pop. 2,400; Area Code 717; Zip Code f17222; Elev. 800'; 7 m. SE of Chambersburg in S Pennsylvania; named for *General la Fayette.*

•**FEARNOT**, Village; Schuylkill County; Pop. (Rural); Area Code 717; Zip Code 17938; E central Pennsylvania; name indicates the optimism of early settlers.

•**FELTON**, Borough; York County; Pop. 483; Area Code 717; Zip Code 17322; Elev. 560'; 10 m. SE of York in S Pennsylvania; in a rural area.

•**FERNDALE**, Borough; Cambria County; Pop. 2,204; Area Code 814; Zip Code 18921; S suburb of Johnstown in SW central Pennsylvania; residential.

•**FINLEYVILLE**, Borough; Washington County; Pop. 402; Area Code 412; Zip Code 15332 Elev. 960'; 20 m. S of Pittsburgh in SW Pennsylvania.

•**FISHING CREEK**, (alt. Drumore), Village; Lancaster County; Pop. 30; Area Code 717; Zip Code 11518; Elev.

140; on the Susquehanna River in SE Pennsylvania; near the Susquehannock State Park. Named for the creek flowing nearby.

•**FISHING CREEK**, Creek, NE Pennsylvania; flows E and S from source in S Sullivan County to mouth on the Susquehanna River.

This little stream was made famous by the so-called "Fishing Creek Confederacy," a small company of men who refused to be drafted into the army during the Civil War. They retreated into the wilderness of the Fishing Creek Valley to escape the law, but were eventually caught without force.

•**FLEETWOOD**, Borough; Berks County; Pop. 3,422; Area Code 215; Zip Code 19522; Elev. 440';15 m. NE of Reading in SE Pennsylvania.

Fleetwood bore the name of Coxtown after a pioneer settler for 60 years or more, until the establishment of the railroad in 1859, when the growing settlement took the name of Fleetwood after a prominent English capitalist, who encouraged the construction of the railroad.

•**FLEMINGTON**, Borough; Clinton County; Pop. 1,416; Area Code 717; Zip Code 19522; Elev. 440'; Central Pennsylvania; named for *John Fleming*, an associate justice in Lycoming County (1798), who once owned this site.

•**FLOURTOWN**, Village; Montgomery County; Pop. 5,000; Area Code 215; Zip Code 19031; Elev. 169'; SE Pennsylvania.

Flourtown, founded in 1743, was once noted for its flour trade; farmers came to buy supplies and have their wheat ground by the millers along the Wissahickon River.

•**FOLCROFT**, Borough; Delaware County; Pop. 8,231; Area Code 215; Zip Code 19032; Elev. 70'; SW suburb of Philadelphia in SE Pennsylvania.

•**FORD CITY**, Borough; Armstrong County; Pop. 3,923; Area Code 412; Zip Code 16226; Elev. 785'; W Pennsylvania.

Ford City, off U.S. Highway 422 on the Allegheny River, was named for *Captain John B. Ford*, "father of the plate glass industry in America," who erected a factory here in 1887. The first American glass furnace, built near Jamestown, Virginia, soon after its settlement in 1607, operated but briefly. The industry was more substantially established late in the eighteenth century in Boston, New Hampshire, and Pittsburgh, where plate glass was first made in 1853.

•**FORD CLIFF**, Borough; Armstrong County; Pop. 516; Area Code 412; Zip Code f16228; Elev. 840'; just S of Ford City along the Allegheny River in W Pennsylvania.

•**FOREST CITY**, Borough; Susquehanna County; Pop. 1,924; Area Code 717; Zip Code 18421; Elev. 1,480'; 20 m. NE of Scranton in NE Pennsylvania.

Forest City, a coal mining town situated on the slope of a hill on the west side of the Lackawanna River, at the extreme northern tip of the anthracite fields. Economic emphasis was shifted from lumbering to mining when coal was discovered on a nearby farm in 1873.

Today the area is important to winter sports enthusiasts, especially at nearby Elk Mountain. The river is dammed nearby, forming a small lake. As late as 1885, however, the town was a mere lumber camp known as Pentecost, for one of its owners, *William Pentecost*. The lumbermen frequently went from their camp to the neighboring town of Carbondale. In one of these visits a young woodsman, *John D. Blake*, in answer to some bantering remarks about the name of the place, is said to have replied, "We come from Forest City." This impromtu name seemed to strike the popular fancy; and in 1888, when the lumbering town was incorporated, it was suitably christened Forest City.

Agriculture - Poultry and truck farming
Industry/Mfg. - Dairy products, clothing

•**FOREST COUNTY**, Forest County was created out of Jefferson on April 11, 1848, by a joint resolution of the two houses of the legislature. No other county in the state has been established this way. In this instance the joint resolution was a parliamentary safety device designed to prevent defeat. *Cyrus Blood*, born in New Hampshire in 1795, educated in Boston, principal of the Chambersburg

Academy and a professor in Dickinson College, migrated into this wilderness region with his family in 1833, bought a large tract of land, started the hamlet long known as Blood's Settlement, and became obsessed with the idea of establishing a new county. He was the pioneer settler and founder of Forest County. He chose the name Forest because the whole county was then one vast, unbroken, primeval forest. Wisconsin is the only other state that has a Forest County named for the forests within its territory.

•**FOREST HILLS**, Borough; Allegheny County; Pop. 8,198; Area Code 412; Zip Code 15221; Elev. 1,080'; E suburb of Pittsburgh, off U.S. Highway 30 in SW Pennsylvania.

•**FORKSVILLE**, Borough; Sullivan County; Pop. 137; Area Code 717; Zip Code 18616; Elev. 1,019; NE central Pennsylvania.

Forkesville was named because it is at the forks of the Loyalsock, Little Loyalsock, and Lick Creeks, just E of Bear Mountain. South of town is the World's End State Park, with camping facilities.

•**FORT BEDFORD**, was one of the most important military posts during the French and Indian War. It served as a rendezvous and a depot of supplies for colonial troops recruited from the east and the south for the relief and defense of the exposed western frontier. In 1757-8 *General John Forbes* had a wagon road cut from Bedford westward toward Fort Duquesne for the convenient movement of his expeditionary army of 7850 men, with its artillery and its hundreds of wagons. "Forbes Trail" soon afterwards became a great highway over which a peaceful army of sturdy settlers invaded the western wilderness. At Bedford, in 1794, *President Washington* reviewed the army that he had brought together to quell the Whiskey Insurrection in western Pennsylvania.

Fort Bedford may be taken as a type of the pioneer fort, which was not only a defense, but a fortified or protected enclosure for the residence of settlers. In the colonial period and particularly during the Indian wars, these pioneer forts, of which there were nearly two hundred in Pennsylvania, were absolutely necessary as a means of protecting the lives, homes, and property of the settlers against treacherous and savage foes, who spared neither old men nor women nor children.

•**FORT HUNTER**, Village; Dauphin County; Pop. 150; Area Code 717; Zip Code 17110; SE central Pennsylvania; in Harrisburg metropolitan area. The town received its name from an important pioneer fort built about 1755 "where the Blue Hills cross the Susquehanna," six miles north of Fort Harris (now Harrisburg), on the land of a miller named *Hunter*, a son-in-law of *Thomas Chambers*, whose brother *Benjamin* built Fort Chambers and founded Chambersburg.

•**FORT LITTLETON**, Village; Fulton County; Pop. 130; Area Code 814; Zip Code 17223; Elev. 785'; S Pennsylvania; a collection of frame houses at the foot of a slope, was founded in 1756, the year the fort was built.

•**FORT LOUDON**, Village; Franklin County; Pop. 900; Area Code 717; Zip Code 17224; Elev. 641'.
    Fort Loudon, founded in 1795, is a farming community on the west branch of Conococheague (Ind. "it is a long way") Creek, in the foothills of Tuscarora Mountain. Settlement in the vicinity occurred before 1756, when a crude fort was erected by *Colonel John Armstrong* a mile southeast of the present village and named for the Earl of Loudon, who for a brief period commanded the British forces in the Colonies.
    The Conococheague Valley served as a buffer area between Indian country and the more densely settled sections; during uprisings the full force of Indian anger directed itself against remote settlements here; pioneers erected houses, cleared land, and tilled their acres under constant threat of Indian attacks which, when they came, had to be repulsed with little or no aid from the king's forces. Philadelphia merchants aggravated matters by sending westward train after train of pack horses laden with trinkets, knives, guns, ammunition, and rum - to be traded to the Indians for furs.

•**FORTY FORT**, Borough; Luzerne County; Pop. 5,590; Area Code 717; Zip Code 18704; Elev. 554'; E Pennsylvania; named for the first 40 settlers who came to the valley.

Wyoming Valley was a center of events in the long and bitter Pennamite-Yankee War waged between Connecticut and Pennsylvania settlers for control of the fertile area. (see *Wilkes-Barre*).

Today, Forty Fort is a large residential suburb of Wilkes-Barre. The site of Forty-Fort settlement is marked.

POINT OF INTEREST

DENISON HOUSE- Built in 1790 by Revolutionary soldier *Col. Nathan Denison*, one of the few American survivors of the 1778 Battle of Wyoming.

OLD MEETINGHOUSE- Restored Quaker meetinghouse dating back to 1807.

•**FORT WASHINGTON**, Village; Montgomery County; Pop. 4,000; Area Code 215; Zip Code 19034; Elev. 174'; 18 m. N of Philadelphia.

Fort Washington was named for *Washington's* encampment. The Clifton House, known as Sandy Tavern in Colonial days, is a three-story, gray stone structure with a slag-paved porch. Adjacent is a one-and-a-half-story mill, erected in 1714, which furnished flour for *Washington's* army.

Low density housing and light industry make this an attractive community.

POINTS OF INTEREST

FARMAR MILL (MATHER MILL)- Built c. 1690 for *Edward Farmar*, who served as interpreter at peace councils held on property between Indians and *William Penn*.

HOPE LODGE- Well-preserved Georgian house from mid-18th century. Headquarters for *Gen. Nathanael Greene* after defeat at Battle of Germantown, 1777. Museum.

Industry/Mfg. - Machine shop

•**FOUNTAIN HILLj**, Borough; Lehigh County; Pop. 4,805; Area Code 215; Zip Code 18015; Elev. 360'; 1 m. W of Bethlehem in E Pennsylvania; in a residential area.

•**FOUNTAIN SPRINGS**, Village; Schuylkill County; Pop. 250; Area Code 717; Zip Code 17921; Elev. 1,050'; E central Pennsylvania; founded in 1795.

•**FOXBURG**, Borough; Clarion County; Pop. 289; Area Code 814; Zip Code 16036; Elev. 890'; on Allegheny River, just S of Interstate Hwy. 80 in W Pennsylvania; rural.

•**FOX CHAPEL**, Borough; Allegheny County; Pop. 5,049; Area Code 412; Zip Code 15238; Elev. 980'; NE suburb of Pittsburgh in SW Pennsylvania; in a residential area with two golf courses and a large, private school the Shady Side Academy.

•**FRACKVILLE**, Borough; Schuylkill County; Pop. 5,308; Area Code 717; Zip Code 17931; Elev. 1,476'; 20 m. SW of Hazleton in E central Pennsylvania.

•**FRANKFORT SPRINGS**, Borough; Beaver County; Pop. 187; Area Code 412; Zip Code 15050; Elev. 1,180'; 25 m. W of Pittsburgh in W Pennsylvania; near the West Virginia state line and Raccoon Creek State Park.

•**FRANKLIN**, Borough; Cambria County; Pop. 559; Area Code 814; SW central Pennsylvania.

•**FRANKLIN**, City; Seat of Venango County; Pop. 8,146; Area Code 814; Zip Code 16323; Elev. 1,017'; 70 m. N of Pittsburgh in NW Pennsylvania.

Franklin, once the Indian town of Venango, is at the junction of French Creek and the Allegheny River. The town was laid out for the county seat in 1795 on a tract of 1,000 acres belonging to the state and took its name from Fort Franklin. The new town site was situated on level, sandy ground in a pleasant, sheltered valley, surrounded by lofty hills; and yet, five years later, there were only five families living in Franklin. Venango County was annexed to Crawford County for judicial purposes until 1805, when Franklin formally became the county-seat.

The town's modern history began in 1860, when Pennsylvania's third great oil gusher was brought in at Franklin by *James Evans*, a blacksmith, who had dug a well in an effort to obtain water. Today, the great oil town is the home of the Venango County museum as well as a small airport. Many other industries besides oil refining and drilling give the town a broad economic base.

Agriculture - Varied farming
Industry/Mfg. - Oil drilling and refining
    equipment, engines, soft drinks and coal
Daily Newspaper - The News-Herald, 631 12th
    Street
Chamber Commerce - 1411 Liberty Street

•**FRANKLIN PARK**, Borough; Allegheny County; Pop. 6,135; Area Code 412; SW Pennsylvania.

•**FRANKLINTOWN**, Borough; York County; Pop. 280; Area Code 717; Zip Code 17323; Elev. 700'; 18 m. SW of Harrisburg, off U.S. Hwy. 15 in S Pennsylvania.

The city council in 1982 voted to support the right to bear arms, in protest of gun control laws considered by the state. *Mayor Richard Harbold* said, "We passed our law to protect that right."

•**FRANKLINVILLE**, Village; Huntingdon County; Pop. 30; Area Code 717; Zip Code 16683; Elev. 900'; on Spruce Creek, was an early iron manufacturing center.

The ruins of the David Rittenhouse Porter House are visible from the highway. *Porter* (1788-1867), an early ironmaster, was the first governor of Pennsylvania under the constitution of 1838. Further south along state highway 45 are Indian Caverns and a small picnic area.

•**FRANKSTOWN**, Village; Blair County; Pop. 150; Area Code 814; Zip Code 16648; Elev. 940'; 6 m. SE of Altoona in S central Pennsylvania.

Frankstown was named for *Frank Stevens*, who is generally but erroneously called *Stephen Franks*, an important Indian trader operating in central and western Pennsylvania as early as 1734. Frank's Town was the name that the Indian traders gave to the old Delaware and Shawnee Indian town at this place. *Frank Stevens* may have set up a trading cabin at this point.

Conrad Weiser reports that in 1748 he "came to Frank's Town, but saw no houses or cabins." Hotels sprang up with the construction of the canal and the Portage Railroad; property values boomed as promoters crowded into Frankstown with their get-rich-quick schemes. One promoter, overreaching himself, demanded an exorbitant price for a canal basin site, and as a result, Hollidaysburg was chosen as the terminus of both the canal and railroad.

•**FREDERICKSBURG**, Village; Lebanon County; Pop. 700; Area Code 717; Zip Code 17026; Elev. 460'; in the blue Mountains, N of Lebanon in SE central Pennsylvania.

Fredericksburg was laid out about 1755 by *Frederick Stump* and named for him. The founder of Fredericksburg, who was peace-loving, should not be confused with the notorious Indian-killer, *Frederick Stump*, who, shortly after the French and Indian War, murdered 10 inoffensive Indians near the site of Selinsgrove, in Snyder County.

•**FREDERICKTOWN**, Village; Washington County; Pop. 1,000; Area Code 412; Zip Code 15333; Elev. 790'; SW Pennsylvania.

The town was named for its founder, *Frederick Wise*, in 1790.

•**FREDONIA**, Borough; Mercer County; Pop. 712; Area Code 412; Zip Code 16124; Elev. 1,175'; on Otter Creek, approx. 60 m. N of Pittsburgh in W Pennsylvania.

•**FREEBURG**, Borough; Snyder County; Pop. 643; Area Code 717; Zip Code 17827; 40 m. N of Harrisburg, near the Susquehanna River in central Pennsylvania.

•**FREEDOM**, Borough; Beaver County; Pop. 2,272; Area Code 412; Zip Code 15042; Elev. 703'; on bend of Ohio River in W Pennsylvania; was founded in 1832 when *Stephen Phillips* and *Jonathan Betz* moved their boatyard here after selling the land where Monaca now stands to *Bernhart Mueller* (Count de Leon) and a group of followers.

•**FREELAND**, Borough; Luzerne County; Pop. 4,285; Area Code 717; Zip Code 18224; Elev. 1,880'; 10 m. NE of Hazelton in E Pennsylvania.

Freeland is surrounded almost exclusively by coal-mining operations. Before discovery of coal, the land upon which the town was built was the farm of *Joseph Birkbeck*. This particular tract was not, like those surrounding it, underlaid with coal. In 1868 *A. Donop* bought most of the Birkbeck farm, laid out streets, and divided the tract into town lots, for which he found a ready sale. The Donop plot became generally known as "free land"; that is, land that

153

could be purchased, as distinguished from the coal companies' land, which was not for sale. *Mr. Donop* preferred to name his new town Freehold, a name that it retained until the establishment of a post-office in 1874. The postal authorities objected to this name because of the nearness and importance of Freehold in New Jersey; and the townspeople then adopted the nickname, Freeland.

•**FREEMANSBURG**, Borough; Northampton County; Pop. 1,879; Area Code 215; Zip Code 18017; Elev. 300'; 2 m. W of central Bethlehem in E Pennsylvania; named for its first settler, *Richard Freeman.*

•**FREEPORT**, Borough; Armstrong County; Pop. 2,381; Area Code 412; Zip Code 16229; Elev. 775'; W Pennsylvania.

Freeport, at the confluence of the Allegheny and Kiskiminetas Rivers and Buffalo Creek, in a fertile farming country with valuable orchard and dairy interests, was laid out in 1796 by *William and David Todd* as a free port for river craft. Construction of the Pennsylvania Canal here (1827-8) brought expansion, but the town's growth slowed down after the canal was abandoned in 1864. The town was incorporated in 1833.

•**FRENCH CREEK**, River, New York and Pennsylvania; flows SW and SE 140 m. from source in S New York to the Allegheny River in central Venango County. Named for the first European settlers in this region. A dam in Erie County once overflowed to create Union City Reservoir, but it is now dry.

•**FRENCHVILLE**, Village; Clearfield County; Pop. 80; Area Code 814; Zip Code 16836; Elev. 1,400'; W central Pennsylvania.

The village was settled by French pioneers from Normandy and Picardy, who gave the settlement its name.

•**FRIEDENSVILLE**, Village; Lehigh County; Pop. 300; Area Code 215; Zip Code 18017; E Pennsylvania; suburb of Allentown-Bethlehem; name is derived from *Fiedenskirche,* German for "church of peace."

•**FRIENDSVILLE**, Borough; Susquehanna County; Pop. 72; Area Code 717; Zip Code 18818; Elev. 1,460'; NE Pennsylvania.

Friendsville was laid out in 1819 by *Dr. R.H. Rose,* the Quaker physician for whom the town of Montrose was named. He named this village Friendsville because he had induced a colony of Friends to settle here.

•**FULTON COUNTY**, was separated from Bedford in 1850. The petition presented to the legislature proposed the name of Liberty for the new county. When the bill to establish the county had been approved by the House, it was discovered that it could not pass the Senate unless at least two of its opponents could be prevailed upon to favor it. *Senator William F. Packer* of Lycoming County, and *Senator Charles Frailery* of Schuylkill County, out of personal friendship for *John Pott* and Representitive *Samuel Robinson* of Bedford County, both active in advocating the passage of the bill, consented to vote for it, provided that they might have the privilege of naming the new county. *Senator Packer* made a motion to amend the act by substituting the name of Fulton for Liberty, and this amendment was seconded by *Senator Frailey.*

The the new county was voted into existence, and named in honor of *Robert Fulton,* one of the most distinguished citizens of Pennsylvania, whose fame and genuine service to humanity should not be minimized because others before him had made more or less successful attempts to apply steam to navigation. There can be no doubt that *Fulton's Clermont,* rude and imperfect though it was, was the first successful modern steamboat, and that *Robert Fulton* made navigation by steam practicable. In view of the fact that Fulton County was settled almost wholly by Scotch-Irish, it seems appropriate that it should bear the name of an illustrious Pennsylvanian of Scotch-Irish descent. The surname Fulton is variously explained as meaning "the fowls' enclosure" or "Fula's estate," or as a contraction of Fullerton, "the fowler's place."

G

•**GALETON**, Borough; Potter County; Pop. 1,462; Area Code 814; Zip Code 16922; Elev. 1,315'; at the forks of Pine Creek, near Lyman Run State Park in N Pennsylvania.

•**GALLATIN**, Village; Allegheny County; Pop. 200; Area Code 412; Zip Code 15063; near Monongahela River in SW Pennsylvania.

Gallatin, a coal town, received its name from *Albert Gallatin*, who was born at Geneva, Switzerland, in 1761, and who became famous as an American financier, statesman and diplomat. He was Secretary of the Treasury from 1801 to 1814.

•**GALLITZIN**, Borough; Cambria County; Pop. 2,315; Area Code 814; Zip Code 16641; Elev. 2,167'; 10 m. W of Altoona in SW central Pennsylvania; on a scenic route.

Gallitzin bears the name of the priest, *Prince Demetrius Augustine Gallitzin*, one of the pioneers of Cambria County. *Prince Gallitzin*, the son of a Russian diplomat and the scion of an ancient and noble family, moved to Baltimore on his *wanderjahr* in 1792 at the age of 22. Shortly after his arrival he decided to study for the Roman Catholic priesthood. He was ordained in 1795. Five years later the Russian prince was hard at work as the leader and the parish priest of the Roman Catholic colony that had bought 20,000 acres of land in the wilds of Cambria County. The settlement prospered for 40 years.

POINT OF INTEREST

FANTASY FOREST AMUSEMENT PARK- Storybook buildings and exhibits; petting zoo.

Community Event - Huckleberry Fair, Annual. July

•**GANISTER**, Village; Blair County; Pop. 200; Area Code 814; Zip Code 16642; Elev. 880'; 15 m. E of Altoona in S central Pennsylvania; on Clover Creek; named for the siliceous, clay-like rock, ganister, found in the hills here.

•**GAP**, Village; Lancaster County; Pop. 1,000; Area Code 717; Zip Code 17527; Elev. 559'; 20 m. E of Lancaster in an Amish farming region.

Popularly known for 200 years as "the Gap", this town lies in a notch or opening in the hills, the highest point on the old road leading from Philadelphia to the Susquehanna. This locality was once a favorite resort of the notorious "Gap gang," a body of thieves and kidnapers of free and escaped slaves.

•**GARRETT**, Borough; Somerset County; Pop. 563; Area Code 814; Zip Code 15542; Elev. 1,937'; 80 m. SE of Pittsburgh on Casselman River in S Pennsylvania.

•**GEISTOWN**, Borough; Cambria County; Pop. 3,304; Area Code 814; Zip Code 15904; Elev. 1,900'; 6 m. SE of Johnstown in SW central Pennsylvania.

•**GENESSEE RIVER**, River; Pennsylvania and New York; flows N approx. 140 m. from source in N Pennsylvania (Potter County) through central New York to its mouth at Lake Ontario in W New York. Name is derived from an Indian phrase meaning "beautiful valley."

•**GEORGETOWN**, Borough; Beaver County; Pop. 231; Area Code 412; Zip Code 15043; Elev. 760'; W Pennsylvania.

One of the oldest settlements in the county. Georgetown was named for founder *Benoni Dawson's* son *George* when he settled here in 1790.

•**GERMAINIA**, Village; Potter County; Pop. 80; Area Code 814; Zip Code 16922; Elev. 1,940'; on Kettle Creek in N Pennsylvania; summer population increases three times.

Germainia was founded in 1854 by Germans determined to keep the language and customs of the Fatherland intact.

•**GERMANTOWN**, Village; Philadelphia County; Pop. (incl. with City of Philadelphia); Area Code 215; Zip Code 19144; SE Pennsylvania.

Germantown is the oldest German settlement in the United States. Soon after *Penn* received his grant of Pennsylvania there appeared in London a little pamphlet entitled *Some Account of the Province of Pennsylvania in America.* Almost simultaneously a German translation was published in Amsterdam. Copies of this and other pamphlets were distributed in Holland, southern Germany, and Switzerland. Shortly before the Quaker colony was planted in Pennsylvania, *George Fox*, revered as the founder of the Society of Friends, *William Penn, Robert Barclay*, and *George Keith* had all made missionary journeys into Germany. The Quakers tried to attract the persecuted German sects to their colony in the new world. Their efforts soon bore fruit. A company of German Mennonites and Quakers from Frankfort, Kriegsheim, and Crefeld, the places visited by the Quaker missionaries, organized the "Frankfort Company," bought 25,000 acres of land six miles northwest of the Philadelphia settlement, and arrived at Philadelphia on board the *Concord* on October 6, 1683.

Their settlement at Germantown under the leadership of the learned *Dr. Francis Daniel Pastorius* was the beginning of a mighty Teutonic migration that brought 100,000 Swiss and German settlers to Pennsylvania before the outbreak of the American Revolution. Philadelphia then had only 80 houses - "such as they were," to use *Penn's* apologetic phrase. The Quakers and the Mennonites were kindred spirits, and it is noteworthy that the persecuted Germans came into their heritage in Pennsylvania almost as soon as their Quaker brethren. They were destined to play an important part in the development of the new commonwealth. The German settlements in Pennsylvania, from the very beginning, were an essential part of *Penn's* "holy experiment."

•**GETTYSBURG**, Borough; Seat of Adams County; Pop. 7,194; Area Code 717; Zip Code 17325; S Pennsylvania.

About ten years before Adams County was organized, *James Gettys*, who has been described as "a man of brains, force of character, and resources," scenting the certainty of a new county and the possibility of securing an eligible site for the county-seat, bought a tract of land and laid out a village, which he called Gettys-town. On the erection of Adams County this little settlement was chosen as the seat of justice; and the act of legislature authorizing the levy of a tax for the construction of the county buildings designated the place for the first time as Gettysburg. *James Gettys*, for whom Gettysburg was named, never dreamed that the name of the little town which he planned and plotted was destined to become famous throughout the world and memorable in history as the name of a bloody battlefield, on which the great Rebellion was to be checked and the fate of the Union decided.

POINTS OF INTEREST

ADAMS COUNTY COURTHOUSE- Mid-19th century, Italianate; *Stephen D. Button*, architect. Served as hospital during Civil War.

DOBBIN HOUSE- Built by *Rev. Alexander Dobbin*, an Irish missionary, in 1776; served as his home, a classical academy, a theological seminary and a church. One of Gettysburg's oldest structures.

GETTYSBURG NATIONAL MILITARY PARK- Site of the Battle of Gettysburg, 1863; includes Gettysburg National Cemetery, the site of Lincoln's Gettysburg Address.

LUTHERAN THEOLOGICAL SEMINARY-OLD DORM- First U.S. building erected (1832) to house Lutheran Theological Seminary. Served as Confederates' chief signal station and as a hospital during the Battle of Gettysburg, July 1863.

PENNSYLVANIA HALL, GETTYSBURG COLLEGE- Greek Revival. The first structure of Gettysburg College, America's oldest Lutheran college; built in 1837. Served as hospital during Civil War.

Agriculture - Cattle, grain, fruit farming
Industry/Mfg. - Clothing, dairy products,
    Resort area.
Higher Education - Gettysburg College
Daily Newspaper - The Times, 18 Carlisle St.
Chamber of Commerce - 33 York St.
Community Events -
    Apple Blossom Festival, Annual, May
    Apple Harvest Festival, Annual, October
    Square Dance Round-up, Annual, May
    State Craft Fair, Annual, July

•**GILBERTON**, Borough; Schuylkill County; Pop. 1,096; Area Code 717; Zip Code 17934; Elev. 1,140'; 25 m. SW of Hazleton in E central Pennsylvania; incorporated in 1873; named for *John Gilbert*, a wealthy coal operator.

•**GIRARD**, Borough; Erie County; Pop. 2,615; Area Code 814; Zip Code 16417; Elev. 831'; 10 m. SW of Erie on Elk Creek in NW Pennsylvania.

Settlement occurred prior to 1800; named for *Stephen Girard*, a Philadelphia merchant who owned land in the vicinity, it was incorporated as a borough in 1846.

In early 1982, some of Girard's working-class townspeople ordered a censoring of the *Studs Terkel* book *Working* from the high school library. *Terkel* subsequently went to the town to defend his 1973 collection of interviews with American workers about their jobs. Some of the interviews had taken place in Girard, and profanity appeared in some sections.

> *Agriculture* - Grain, fruit and varied
> farming
> *Industry/Mfg.* - Food storage, wood products

•**GIRARDVILLE**, Borough; Schuylkill County; Pop. 2,268; Area Code 717; Zip Code 17935; Elev. 1,020'; 25 m. SE of Hazleton in a rural area in E central Pennsylvania. Named for the Philadelphia merchant, *Stephen Girard*, who owned a large tract of land here.

•**GLADWYNE**, Village; Montgomery County; Pop. 3,400; Area Code 215; Zip Code 19035; Elev. 350'; just W of Philadelphia city border, along the Schuylkill River in SE Pennsylvania.

•**GLASGOW**, Borough; Beaver County; Pop. 106; Area Code 412; Zip Code 16644; Elev. 162'; W Pennsylvania.

Glasgow was laid out in 1836 and became a boat-building center. The keel of the *Silver Wave*, the first steamboat to run the Confederate batteries at the siege of Vicksburg in 1863, was laid here in 1854.

The town was named for the great industrial city and port in Scotland.

•**GLASSPORT**, Borough; Allegheny County; Pop. 6,242; Area Code 412; Zip Code 15045; Elev. 755'; SW Pennsylvania; on the east bank of the Monongahela, named in 1888 when the United States Glass Company established a plant here. The borough was incorporated in 1902.

•**GLEN CAMPBELL**, Borough; Indiana County; Pop. 352; Area Code 412; Zip Code 15742; Elev. 1,344'; 50 m. N of Johnstown in W central Pennsylvania; named for a Scottish glen.

•**GLENDON**, Borough; Northampton County; Pop. 354; Area Code 215; Zip Code 18042; Elev. 205'; just S of Easton and W of the Delaware River in E Pennsylvania; in an industrial area.

•**GLENFIELD**, Borough; Allegheny County; Pop. 246; Area Code 412; Zip Code 15143; Elev. 720'; 11 m. NW of Pittsburgh along the Ohio River in SW Pennsylvania; nearby is the Dixmont State Hospital.

•**GLEN HOPE**, Borough; Clearfield County; Pop. 206; Area Code 814; Zip Code 16645; Elev. 1,360'; 30 m. N of Altoona along a small creek in W central Pennsylvania.

•**GLENOLDEN**, Borough; Delaware County; Pop. 7,633; Area Code 215; Zip Code 19036; Elev. 90'; 5 m. SW of central Philadelphia in SE Pennsylvania; residential.

•**GLEN ROCK**, Borough; York County; Pop. 1,662; Area Code 717; Zip Code 17327; Elev. 560'; 15 m. S of York in a farming region in S Pennsylvania.

•**GLENSHAW**, Village; Allegheny County; Pop. 18,000; Area Code 412; Zip Code 15116; Elev. 1,060; NW suburb of Pittsburgh in SW Pennsylvania; Pine Creek flows through this hilly residential community.

•**GLENSIDE**, Village; Montgomery County; Pop. 17,000; Area Code 215; Zip Code 19038; Elev. 260'; one of the largest suburbs N of Philadelphia in SE Pennsylvania.
    Beaver College for Women is located in this residential community.

Industry/Mfg. - Quarrying
Higher Education - Beaver College
Chamber of Commerce - PO Box 22

•GOLDSBORO, Borough; York County; Pop. 477; Area Code 717; Zip Code 17319; Elev. 305'; along the Susquehanna River, 11 m. SE of Harrisburg in S Pennsylvania.

•GORDON, Borough; Schuylkill County; Pop. 892; Area Code 717; Zip Code 17936; Elev. 860'; E central Pennsylvania.
Gordon stands on a tract of land that originally belonged to *David and James McKnight*, whose descendants laid out the town and named it in honor of *Judge David Gordon* of Reading.

•GRACETON, Village; Indiana County; Pop. 300; Area Code 412; Zip Code 15743; Elev. 1,060'; W central Pennsylvania; founded in 1886, is named for the daughter of *Harry McCreary*, former owner of the coal mine and of most of the settlement.

•GRAMPIAN, Borough; Clearfield County; Pop. 464; Area Code 814; Zip Code 16838; Elev. 1,450'; W central Pennsylvania; was named by *Samuel Coleman*, pioneer physician, for the Grampian Hills of Scotland, from which he emigrated.

•GRANVILLE, Village; Mifflin County; Pop. 150; Area Code 717; Zip Code 17029; Elev. 500'; Central Pennsylvania; on the Juniata River; named for Fort Granville, built in 1756 near Lewsiton. The fort took its name from the English nobleman *John Carteret*, Earl of Branville.

•GRATERFORD, Village; Montgomery County; Pop. 800; Area Code 215; Zip Code 19426; Elev. 140'; 10 m. E of Pottstown; founded in 1756 and named for *Jacob Kreater*.
Today it is the site of a state correctional institution, with about 1,800 inmates.

•GRATZ, Borough; Dauphin County; Pop. 678; Area Code 717; Zip Code 17030; Elev. 800'; 35 m. NE of Harrisburg SE central Pennsylvania; amid the Mahantango and Berry Mountains.

162

•**GREAT BEND**, Borough; Susquehanna County; Pop. 740; Area Code 717; Zip Code 18821; Elev. 880'; NE Pennsylvania; founded in 1787 on the site of a Tuscarora Indian village, and was so named for its proximity to the deep curve in the Susquehanna's North Branch, which flows north into New York from here.

•**GREELEY**, Village; Pike County; Pop. 400 (summer 1,000); Area Code 717; Zip Code 18425; Elev. 1,100'.
Greeley, where in 1842 *Horace Greeley*, publisher of the New York *Tribune* (1841-72), founded a colony based on the Utopian Socialist ideas of *Francois Marie Charles Fourier* (1772-1837). *Fourier's* plan proposed the organization of society into self-sufficient groups of 1,600, called phalanxes, each inhabiting a phalanstery.
The colony, Sylvania, modeled on Brook Farm and organized on the principle of "common ownership of property and the equal division of labor," started with a capital of $10,000; membership shares sold for $25 each, most of which were bought by *Greeley*. The Sylvania Society bought several thousand acres of wild land, erecting a large common building and communal shops. The directing board, however, experienced difficulty in assigning tasks to everyone's satisfaction. *Greeley* decreed that a woman should rule the colony. Many of the three or four hundred colonists, among them wayward scions of affluent New York families, fled the regors of a place which, as *Greeley* later complained, could raise only snakes and stones. The experiment did not survive the crop failure of 1845, brought on by a late frost (July 4).

•**GREENE COUNTY**, Greene County, in the extreme southwestern corner of the State, was formed from Washington in 1796, and was named in honor of *General Nathaniel Greene*, the ablest of Washington's officers.

•**GREENCASTLE**, Borough; Franklin County; Pop. 3,679; Area Code 717; Zip Code 17225; Elev. 580'; S of Chambersburg in S Pennsylvania; on a scenic route (181); laid out in 1782 by *Colonel John Allison* and named for his native town, a tiny seaport in County Conegal, Ireland.

POINT OF INTEREST

MARTIN'S MILL COVERED BRIDGE- Built in 1849 as an approach to early grist and sawmill along the river. Reconstructed.

Agriculture - Varied farming
Industry/Mfg. - Steel, clothing, dairy
products
Chamber of Commerce - PO box 175

•**GREEN HILLS**, Borough; Washington County; Pop. 18; Area Code 412; Zip Code 19079; SW Pennsylvania; a village of six houses, incorporated as a borough in the 1970s.

•**GREEN LANE**, Borough; Montgomery County; Pop. 542; Area Code 215; Zip Code 18054; Elev. 240'; 30 m. N of Philadelphia in SE Pennsylvania; in a recreational, summer vacation area, with large suburban homes mixed in with the motels.

•**GREENSBORO**, Borough; Greene County; Pop. 377; Area Code 412; Zip Code 15338; Elev. 805'; 8 m. N of West Virginia state line in SW Pennsylvania; on Monongahela River.

•**GREENSBURG**, City; Seat of Westmoreland County; Pop. 17,558; Area Code 417; Zip Code 15601; Elev. 1,110'; 30 m. E of Pittsburgh in SE Pennsylvania.
    In 1784 what was known as the "Pennsylvania State Road" was opened up along the old Forbes Trail. About this time a town was laid out on the land of *Christopher Truby*, and named Greensburg in honor of *General Nathaniel Greene* (1742-86), under whom had fought many a Scotch-Irish soldier from Westmoreland. Greensburg became the second county-seat of Westmoreland County. The old inn at Greensburg, which furnished entertainment to Federal commissioners and to Pennsylvania officials who had met to settle the trouble known as the Whiskey Insurrection, had for its sign a full-length portrait of *General Greene*.
    Today the town spreads north and south along rolling crests, and east and west through the many valleys of Pittsburgh.

POINT OF INTEREST

SITE OF OLD HANNASTOWN- Site of colonial frontier town founded about 1768; town was burned by the British and Seneca in 1782 and never rebuilt. Excavated by Westmoreland County Historical Society.

Agriculture - Dairy, grain and varied farming
Industry/Mfg. - Metal products, soft drinks,
    clothing, oil, coal
Higher Education -
    Seton Hill College
    University of Pittsburgh
    Thiel College
Daily Newspaper - The Tribune-Review, Cabin
    Hill Drive, Review Bldg.
Chamber of Commerce - 662 N. Main Street
Community Events -
    Colonial Festival, Annual, July
    Festival Days, Annual, May-June

•**GREEN TREE**, Borough; Allegheny County; Pop. 5,722; Area Code 412; Zip Code 15242; Elev. 1,100'; S suburb of Pittsburgh which includes Mann Oak and Parkway Center; SW Pennsylvania.

•**GREEN VILLAGE**, Village; Franklin County; Pop. 150; Area Code 717; Zip Code 17201; 3 m. N of Chambersburg in S Pennsylvania. Green Village is the site of the Letterkenny Army Depot.

•**GREENVILLE**, Borough; Mercer County; Pop. 7,730; Area Code 412; Zip Code 16125; Elev. 963'; 70 m. N of Pittsburgh in W Pennsylvania.

Greenville, at the confluence of the Shenango and Little Shenango Rivers, was settled in 1796 by several German families. The town was laid out in 1819 by *Thomas Bean* and *William Scott* on the west bank of the Shenango, though the principal art of the village later grew up on the east side of the stream. The town, which was long called West Greenville, is generally believed to have been named for *General Nathaniel Greene.* No other plausible or authoritative explanation has ever been given. The dropping of the final *e* in the spelling of the name was probably due to carelessness in spelling. In 1844 Greene Township, which lies a little to the northwest of Greenville, was also named in honor of *General Greene.* In 1837 West Greenville was incorporated; and in 1865 its name was changed to Greenville.

POINTS OF INTEREST

KIDD'S MILLS COVERED BRIDGE HISTORIC DISTRICT-Example of typical 19th century riverside developments, including the only extant of Smith cross truss in eastern U.S.

NEW HAMBURG HISTORICAL AREA- Site of New Hamburg, a 19th century (1834-1871) industrial town on Erie Canal, and the Hamburg Furnace, an early pig-iron furnace; structures of historical significance now in ruins. Unexcavated.

Agriculture - Dairy, Fruit and varied farming
Industry/Mfg. - Boxes, railroad cars, aluminum products
Higher Education - Thiel College
Daily Newspaper - The Record-Argus, 10 Penn Ave.
Chamber of Commerce - 206 Main Street, Suite B

•**GROVE CITY**, Borough; Mercer County; Pop. 8,162; Area Code 412; Zip Code 16127; Elev. 1,246'; 55 m. N of Pittsburgh in W Pennsylvania; site of Grove City College.

Industry/Mfg. - Concrete, coal, dairy products, engines, iron castings
Chamber of Commerce - 220-B S. Broad St.

H

•**HALIFAX**, Borough; Dauphin County; Pop. 909; Area Code 717; Zip Code 17032; Elev. 380'; SE central Pennsylvania.

The town was named for Fort Halifax, which was built in 1756 by *Colonel William Clapham* about half a mile north of the present town, and which at the suggestion of Deputy Governor *Robert H. Morris*, was named in honor of *George Montagu*, second Earl of Halifax, who was once styled "father of the colonies" because as head of the Board of Trade he greatly increased British commerce in America. Halifax in Nova Scotia was also named for him. The Pennsylvania town was laid out in 1784.

•**HALLAM**, Borough; York County; Pop. 1,428; Area Code 717; Zip Code 17406; Elev. 380'; 5 m. NE of York along a scenic route; named by early settler *Samuel Blunston* for his native town of Upper Hallam in Yorkshire, England.

•**HALLSTEAD**, Borough; Susquehanna County; Pop. 1,280; Area Code 717; Zip Code 18822; Elev. 884'; on N branch of Susquehanna River in NE Pennsylvania; was named for *William F. Hallstead*, an official of the Lackawanna Railroad.

•**HAMBURG**, Borough; Berks County; Pop. 4,011; Area Code 215; Zip Code 19526; Elev. 387'; 17 m. N of Reading in SE Pennsylvania; founded in 1779, is on the east bank of the Schuyklill.

The Hamburg State School and Hospital, with a capacity of 800, is located here.

> *Agriculture* - Varied farming
> *Industry/Mfg.* - Furniture, clothing, dairy
> products

•**HANOVER**, Borough; York County; Pop. 14,890; Area Code 717; Zip Code 17331; Elev. 599'; 8 m. N of Massachusetts state line in S Pennsylvania.

Many early settlers were German, though the founder, *Colonel Richard McAllister*, was Scotch-Irish; during his life the settlement frequently went by his name, sometimes with the word "Folly" added. Among the many German settlers, the most influential was *Michael Danner* or *Tanner*, who had been appointed one of the commissioners to lay out York County in 1749, and was made one of his Majesty's justices of the peace in 1755. To please the German settlers, but without any thought of complimenting the reigning house of Hanover, the town was, at the suggestion of *Michael Danner*, who owned a large tract of land southeast of the site, formally christened Hanover for his native Hanover in Germany.

The new town lay so close to the Maryland line that it long remained a region of disputed jurisdiction; and as a result so many fugitives from justice resorted thither that the place was long known as "Rogues' Resort," or "Rogues' Harbor." Hanover was incorporated in 1815.

The first Civil War battle north of the Mason-Dixon line was fought here on June 30, 1863, when *General James E.B. Stuart's* cavalry rode into town just as a Union cavalry division was leaving. The Union generals, *Kilpatrick and Custer*, were at the head of the column three miles northeast of Hanover when they heard the noise of battle in the town behind them. *Kilpatrick* wheeled his horse and led a mad charge back across fields and over fences. *Custer* set up batteries on the hills north of town to answer to the Confederate cannon booming from the hills to the south and southwest. Horesmen charged and counter-charged along the town's streets. Some 11,000 soldiers were engaged in this conflict, which ended at nightfall when *Stuart* withdrew, leaving more than 100 dead, wounded, or missing; the Northern forces suffered approximately 200 casualties. The battle prevented *Stuart* from reaching Gettysburg until the day after the major engagement had begun there, thus depriving *Lee* of the "eyes of his army".

POINT OF INTEREST

GEORGE NACE (NEAS) HOUSE- Among the best Federal houses in the area, built c. 1795 for the town's first mayor, *George Nace.*

168

Agriculture - Varied farming
Industry/Mfg. - Footwear, clothing, clay
 products, furniture
Daily Newspaper - Sun, 135 Baltimore
Chamber of Commerce - 146 Broadway

•**HARBORCREEK**, Village; Erie County; Pop. 800; Area Code 814; Zip Code 16421; Elev. 730'; NW Pennsylvania; was the scene of violent activity during the "railroad war" of 1853.

•**HARLANSBURG**, Village; Lawrence County; Pop. 300; Area Code 412; Zip Code 16101; Elev. 1,143'; 9 m. E of New Castle in W Pennsylvania; settled in 1797 by *Jonathan Harlan*.

•**HARMONY**, Borough; Butler County; Pop. 1,334; Area Code 412; Zip Code 16037; Elev. 913'; W Pennsylvania.
   Harmony is the site of the first settlement of the Harmony Society, organized in 1805 by *George Rapp*, for more than 40 years the religious and industrial leader of the Harmony Society, was born in Wurtemberg in 1757. Although he came from peasant stock and had a meager education, he was a man of extraordinary energy and great natural ability. When about 30 years old he began to advocate religious ideas at variance with the established faith. A few years later he and his followers became obsessed with a desire to return to what they conceived to be primitive Christianity. In 1803, because of bitter persecution, *Rapp* came to Pennsylvania and bought from the eccentric *Dettmar W.F. Basse* about 5000 acres of land in the fertile valley of the Conoquenessing. In 1804, he brought from Germany about 600 of his adherents.
   In the first year members of the society cleared 150 acres and built 50 log houses, a church, a barn, a gristmill, and several shops. The Harmonists sold their holdings here in 1814. Many of Harmony's brick and frame houses have remained nearly undisturbed since *Father Rapp* sat in meditation on a thronelike rock formation, known as *Father Rapp's Seat*, on a hill overlooking the town. More than 100 members of *Rapp's* band were buried in the Harmonists Cemetery, a half-mile southeast of town. Over the gate of the walled graveyard is a German inscription promising redemption after death; within is a well-kept grass

plot, but no mounds, no headstones, no monuments. In the fifteenth canto of *Don Juan,* *Lord Byron* makes reference to *Rapp's* approval of celibacy.

POINT OF INTEREST

HARMONY HISTORIC DISTRICT- The first communistic settlement (1805-1814) of the Harmony Society, a group of German Pietists. Museum.

Community Event - Dankfest, Annual, August

•**HARRISBURG**, City, Dauphin County seat and capital of Pennsylvania; Pop. 53,113; Area Code 717; Zip Code 171 + zone; Elev. 374'; 100 m. W of Philadelphia on the Susquehanna River in S central Pennsylvania.

Lying on the east bank of the Susquehanna River at the head of the Cumberland and Lebanon Valleys, Harrisburg is the capital of Pennsylvania and seat of Dauphin County. The city is entered from the west by six bridges, one of which is for pedestrians only. Located halfway between Philadelphia and Pittsburgh along major air, rail and motor routes, Harrisburg has become a major transportation and distribution center as well as a seat of government.

Over 23,000 of the area residents work for the Commonwealth of Pennsylvania, and the Capitol building dominates the scene in this otherwise low-lying city. Many of the city's businesses cater to the people in government; printers, restauranteurs, and auto leasing agents all fare well in Harrisburg. The complex of Italianate structures that house the government of the Commonwealth has become the focus for Harrisburg's downtown redevelopment project, Harristown, with room for both state and business offices.

Although the city has experienced an 11 percent unemployment rate during the recent recession, the area's economy is one of the fastest growing in Pennsylvania, with retail sales higher than the national average. In the metropolitan area, metal products, electronic parst, ship parst, aircraft engines, processed food, and transportation-related goods are made. Nearby Hershey is well-known for its large cocoa and candy making plants. The Patriot-News Corporation has been publishing the local daily newspaper for a number of years, and today it distributes over 170,000 Sunday papers to Harrisburg-area residents.

Promoters of the city like to draw it in the center of the great metropolitan areas of the industrial Northeast, with all roads leading outward as the spokes of a wheel. Indeed, many major interstate highways do pass through Harrisburg, including the Pennsylvania Turnpike (U.S. 76).

All incoming roads lead to the capitol or Market Square, center of the downtown area, busy with the traffic of thousands of state workers who make Harrisburg their weekday home. The weekends, however, return the city to its permanent residents and visitors. When the assembly is in session it brings an influx of state senators and representatives, delegations, attorneys, lobbyists, and news correspondents. Hotels do a rushing business, and the street corners about Capitol Hill become outdoor caucus chambers.

On Market Street east of the Square the department and chain stores join forces with the nationwide five-and-tens to supply the needs of Saturday crowds from the neighboring countryside. A few blocks north of the Square is the capitol group. North of Maclay Street lies an attractive residential section of detached houses and terraced lawns. Abutting the city on the southeast is the suburb of Steelton, considered by many as industrial Harrisburg.

In the beginning Harrisburg's population was mainly Scotch-Irish and German. The Scotch-Irish stayed to engage in trades, but many of the Germans gravitated toward the surrounding countryside, establishing themselves on farms. Development of industry brought immigrants from almost every country in Europe, but their numbers are small.

The area around Harrisburg was originally called *Peshtank* or *Piestan* (swampy) by the Indians, later corrupted to Paxtang. The discovery of arrowheads, stone hatchets, pieces of crockery, beads, and numerous skeletons indicates that a large Indian village once existed here. *John Harris*, a Yorkshireman, licensed in 1705 as an Indian trader, settled at Paxtang about 1712 and established a trading post and ferry. Here a son and namesake was born in 1727.

171

In October 1736 the *Penn* heirs through treaty with the Indians acquired a deed "for all the said river Susquehanna with the land lying on both sides thereof," thereby validating a provincial government grant made to *Harris* in 1733. The settlement was early known as Harris' Ferry after the ferry across the river had become an important link in travel to the West. The son continued to operate the ferry after the elder Harris died.

In 1785 *John Harris, Jr.*, and his son-in-law, *William Maclay*, laid out a town at this frontier outpost. Believing that the capital of the Commonwealth might sometime be located here, *Harris* conveyed "four acres and thirteen perches to be held in trust until the legislature sees fit to use it," and named the village Harrisburg. But some state officials held that since the county was named for the Dauphin of France, the city might more properly be called Louisbourg, in honor of *Louis XVI*. In 1791, when the town became a borough, it was still known as Louisbourg, but the name was dropped when *Harris* declared: "You may Louisbourg all you please, but I'll not sell an inch more of land except in Harrisburg."

The Enabling Act of 1791 developed Harrisburg first as a canal and then as a railroad center. Proponents of the act demonstrated to the legislature that more than 150,000 bushels of grain had been brought down the Susquehanna River to Middletown, much of it on the Juniata River from the territory beyond the mountains. The committee then pointed out how much more could be transported if the western end of the state could be connected with the Susquehanna and Delaware Rivers by a system of canals. The Pennsylvania Canal was projected in 1826 and, with the railroad from Columbia to Philadelphia, was completed in 1834.

Meantime, in 1812, Harisburg had become the state capital; this stimulated trade; and the accessibility of coal and the proximity of iron deposits in Dauphin and Cumberland Counties led to new industrial development. Railroads followed the course of the old canals and eventually replaced them as common carriers. A car-building shop and large reclassification yards were established to meet the growing needs of the Pennsylvania and the Reading Railroads.

Harrisburg, with a population of 13,000, was incorporated as a city in 1860. During the Civil War the first concentration camp for Union forces was established here and named Camp Curtin in honor of the governor. In the summer of 1863 an advance guard of *Lee's* army approached within sight of the city, only to turn back at the last moment when the Confederates decided not to invade the Susquehanna Valley. The economic depression that followed the war had its ill effects on industry, but by the later 1870s the city was again in stride industrially, with a population of more than 25,000.

In February 1897 a fire of uncertain origin destroyed the capitol. Fire also leveled, in 1907, the Grand Opera House where Harrisburg theater goers had enjoyed the performances of such noted artists as *Edwin Booth, Joseph Jefferson, Mary Anderson,* and *Mrs. John Drew,* and where notable state political conventions had been held.

The twentieth century ushered in an era of civic and municipal improvements. Millions were spent on sewers, street paving, parks, and bridges. State office buildings were and still are being erected; apartment houses sprang up to relieve the housing problem; and new residential sections were developed in the suburbs.

The suburbs are still being developed around Harrisburg (the metropolitan area population is a substantial 435,000), but within the city it has declined by nearly 30,000 people since 1940. Many of those left during the 1970s, when the nationwide downturn in the industrial economy affected Harrisburg as much as other Northeastern cities. Some of the suburbs around the capital city continue to do well, and those who are lucky enough to have good jobs in state or federal government do not feel the effects of the recesion so much as workers in the steel and transportation-related industries.

Suburbanites go into town for cultural events, information about the outside world, and education. A large art association sponsors auctions and displays of local artists. A community theater group, youth symphony orchestra, and a choral society have entertained in Harrisburg since the turn of the century. Many events take place atop Mount Gretna, since there were two 600-seat auditoriums built in the hillside there in 1892. The new

William Penn museum functions as the main museum of the commonwealth, and there are many other museums in town.

Over 50 colleges serve the Harrisburg metropolitan area. The most important are the Capital Campus of the Pennsylvania State University, the Milton S. Hershey Medical Center (also part of PSU), and the University Center, a cooperative effort of five institutions-- Elizabethtown College, Lebanon Valley College, Temple University, Pennsylvania State University, and the University of Pennsylvania to provide education for working people in Harrisburg. A large community college also enrolls many area students.

Visitors to Harrisburg often see the home of the city's founder, *John Harris*, which was built in 1766. *Harris'* grave is in Harris Park, opposite Washington Street.

POINTS OF INTEREST

BROAD STREET MARKET-One of the oldest farmers' markets in the state, dating from the mid-19th century. Still in use.

JOHN HARRIS MANSION- Georgian house with outbuildings, built 1746-1766 by *John Harris*, founder of Harrisburg. A later resident was *Simon Cameron*, state senator, secretary of war under *Lincoln* and ambassador to Russia.

MUSEUM OF SCIENTIFIC DISCOVERY- Participatory displays of scientific principles.

STATE CAPITOL BUILDINGS- The capital group includes the main capitol, the Pennsylvania State Museum and 7 other major buildings. The main capital, with a dome patterned after St. Peter's in Rome, was completed in 1906; it was built to replace an earlier building which had been destroyed by fire.

WALNUT STREET BRIDGE- Late-19th century multispan bridge, one of the last remaining bridges of its type.

WILLIAM PENN MEMORIAL MUSEUM- Art, history, natural history exhibits. Planetarium.

Industry/Mfg. - Dairy products, varied
    manufacturing, trade and services
Higher Education -
    University Center at Harrisburg
    Thompson Institute
    Harrisburg Area Community College
Daily Newspaper - The News, 812 Market St.
Chamber of Commerce - PO Box 969

•HARRISONVILLE, Village; Fulton County; Pop. 40; Area Code 814; Zip Code 17228; Elev. 782'; S Pennsylvania; named for *William Henry Harrison* during his 1840 presidential campaign.

•HARRISVILLE, Borough; Butler County; Pop. 1,033; Area Code 412; Zip Code 16038; Elev. 1,340'; 25 m. NE of Newcastle in W Pennsylvania.

•HARTLETON, Borough; Union County; Pop. 220; Area Code 717; Zip Code 17829; Elev. 548'; Central Pennsylvania; was incorporated in 1858 and named for *Colonel Thomas Hartley*, who received the surrounding land for his services during the Revolutionary War. At the foot of the Big Mountains.

•HARVEYS LAKE, Borough; Luzerne County; Pop. 2,318; Area Code 717; Zip Code 18618; Elev. 1,287'; N of Wilkes-Barre in E Pennsylvania.

Borough was incorporated in 1968. Many city dwellers have summer homes here, on the small lake by the same name.

•HASTINGS, Borough; Cambria County; Pop. 1,574; Area Code 814; Zip Code 16646; Elev. 1,840'; SW central Pennsylvania.

The town was named for *Daniel Hartman Hastings* of Bellefonte, who was interested in coal mines at this place, and who happened to be at Hastings at the time of the memorable Johnstown flood. Being then Adjutant-General of Pennsylvania, he assumed the duty of directing the relief, and won general approval for his efforts. He then became a candidate for the governorship, to which he was elected five years later, serving from 1895 to 1899. The borough of Hastings was incorporated in 1894.

Near town is the Seldom Seen Valley Mine historic site, where tourists can actually descend 2,200 feet into an old coal mine.

•HATBORO, Borough; Montgomery County; Pop. 7,579; Area Code 215; Zip Code 19040; Elev. 250'; N suburb of Philadelphia in SE Pennsylvania; residential.

Hatboro, situated on the old York Road, took its name from the labors of *John Dawson*, a hatter, who plied his trade here in the 1700s in an old stone house, which later became the "Crooked Billet Tavern," a name borrowed from the famous old Philadelphia inn on Water Street, at which *Benjamin Franklin* breakfasted on his first arrival in the Quaker city. The name Hatborough was used as early as 1749.

Daily Newspaper - Today's Spirit, 101 N. York Road

•**HATFIELD**, Borough; Montgomery County; Pop. 2,533; Area Code 215; Zip Code 19440; Elev. 340'; N suburb of Philadelphia, 10 m. W of Dylestown in SE Pennsylvania.

Agriculture - Varied farming
Industry/Mfg. - Machine shop, dairy products, clothing

•**HAUTO**, Village; Carbon County; Pop. (incl. with Nesquehoning); Area Code 717; Zip Code 18240; E Pennsylvania; named for *George Hauto*, an organizer of the Lehigh Coal and Navigation Company which operated in the vicinity during the late nineteenth century.

•**HAVERFORD**, Village (Unincorporated); Montgomery & Delaware Counties; Pop. 6,500; Area Code 215; Zip Code 19041; Elev. 383'; NW suburb of Philadelphia in SE Pennsylvania.

Haverford was settled by Welshmen in the 1680s and is a residential community which merges imperceptibly with Ardmore.

The early settlers named the town for their native Haverford-West in Pembrokeshire, Wales. The township surrounding it existed as early as 1722. Today, Haverford College is an important part of the community, which is largely residential.

POINTS OF INTEREST

FEDERAL SCHOOL- Served as school 1797-1872; oldest school building in township.

NITRE HALL- Remaining elements of gunpowder mill company constructed shortly after 1800; one of the largest gunpowder producers until operations ceased c. 1840.

Higher Education - Haverford College
Chamber of Commerce - 551 W. Lancaster Ave.

•**HAVERTOWN**, Village; Delaware County; Pop. 35,000; Area Code 215; Zip Code 19083; NW suburb of Philadelphia in SE Pennsylvania; a large bedroom community for city commuters.

Industry/Mfg. - Machine shop, plastics

•**HAWLEY**, Borough; Wayne County; Pop. 1,181; Area Code 717; Zip Code 18428; Elev. 896'; 25 m. E of Scranton in NE Pennsylvania.
    Hawley was brought into existence in 1827 by the lumber industry. Today is a popular resort village at the Northern tip of Lake Wallenpaupack, which was formed by a damming of the Lackawaxen River.

Agriculture - Varied farming
Industry/Mfg. - Clothing, dairy products,
    Resort Area.
Chamber of Commerce - PO Box 150

•**HAWTHORN**, Borough; Clarion County; Pop. 547; Area Code 814; Zip Code 16230; Elev. 1,000'; on Red Bank Creek in W Pennsylvania; in a rural area.

•**HAYSVILLE**, Borough; Allegheny County; Pop. 117; Area Code 412; Zip Code 15143; NW suburb of Pittsburgh in SW Pennsylvania; is a residential subdivision.

•**HAZEL CREEK**, Creek; NE central Pennsylvania; flows through town of Hazleton, to which it gave its name. The creek itself was named for the abundance of hazel bushes growing along its banks.

•**HAZLETON**, City; Luzerne County; Pop. 27,318; Area Code 717; Zip Code 18201; Elev. 1,624'; E Pennsylvania.
    Hazleton, named for Hazel Creek, is underlaid with wide anthracite veins said to have been uncovered in 1818 by a deer pawing the earth. The town was laid out on Buck Mountain Plateau in 1837, but mining was carried on only sporadically until after the Civil War. In 1856, when

177

the borough was incorporated, the attorney who drew up the legal papers erroneously spelled the name Hazelton, and so Hazleton became the fixed name of the place.

Industry/Mfg. - Coal, steel, clothing, varied
manufacturing, trade and services
Daily Newspaper - The Standard Speaker, 21 W.
Wyoming Street
Chamber of Commerce - Northeastern Bldg.

•**HEIDELBERG**, Borough; Allegheny County; Pop. 1,606; Area Code 412; Zip Code 15106; Elev. 820'; 4 m. S of Central Pittsburgh in SW Pennsylvania; named by German founders for the medieval city in their native land. A large race track is located here.

•**HELEN FURNACE**, Village; Clarion County; Pop. (Rural); Area Code 814; Zip Code 15433; near Millsboro in W Pennsylvania.

Helen Furnace did not receive its name from the wife or the daughter of its owner, but seems to be a corruption of Hieland (i.e., Highland) Furnace, so named in honor of *Alexander McNaughton*, an early settler at this place, who boasted of his being a Hielander. Highland Township, in Clarion County, also took its name from this settler. (see *Hallam*).

•**HELLERTOWN**, Borough; Northampton County; Pop. 6,025; Area Code 215; Zip Code 18055; Elev. 310'; 2 m. S of Bethlehem in E Pennsylvania. The town was christened for *Christopher and Simon Heller*, who arrived from Germany in 1738 and settled here several years later.

Crystalline formations that took eons to fashion dazzle the eye at nearby Lost River Caverns. The Gillman Museum of Natural History is located here.

POINTS OF INTEREST

GILLMAN MUSEUM OF NATURAL HISTORY
LOST RIVER CAVERNS- Dazzling crystalline formations.

Chamber of Commerce - PO Box 33

•**HEREFORD**, Village; Berks County; Pop. 100; Area Code 215; Zip Code 18056; Elev. 460'; SE Pennsylvania.

Although settled by German Schwenkfelders in 1732, it was named for Herefordshire in England, the home of ironmasters who later came to the district. It is situated in a long, narrow valley, 10 m. S of Allentown.

•**HERNDON**, Borough; Northumberland County; Pop. 483; Area Code 717; Zip Code 17830; Elev. 428'; E central Pennsylvania; was settled in 1854.

The town was named at the suggestion of the postal authorities in honor of Commander *William Herndon* of the United States Navy, who lost his life in the Gulf of Mexico in 1857, while heroically rescuing as many passengers as possible from his sinking steamer, the *Central America*. A daughter of *Commander Herndon* became the wife of *Chester A. Arthur*, who was afterward President of the United States.

•**HERSHEY**, Village (Unincorporated); Area Code 717; Zip Code 17033; Elev. 400'; 15 m. E of Harrisburg.

Hershey is the privately owned and planned community of *M.S. Hershey*, (see Biographies) a former Lancaster caramel manufacturer, who bought a cornfield here in 1903 and created a chocolate manufacturing center.

The Hershey Chocolate Corporation was disturbed in April 1837 by a sitdown strike when a group of CIO workers demanded the dissolution of the Loyal Workers Club, which they termed a company union. After the strikers had occupied the plant for about a week, they were ejected, and in a subsequent NLRB election the CIO group was defeated.

Today, the town's economy still revolves around the chocolate factory and its related sweets industries. An Amusement Park as well as the chocolate factory tours attract visitors year round.

POINTS OF INTEREST

HERSHEYPARK AMUSEMENT PARK- Rides, Dutch crafts, family entertainment. ZooAmerica environmental zoo.

HERSHEY'S CHOCOLATE WORLD- Tour shows steps of chocolate production.

Agriculture - Varied farming
Industry/Mfg. - Chocolate and confectionary
  products
Higher Education - Pennsylvania State Univ.
Community Event - Pennsylvania Dutch Days,
  Annual, July

•**HICKORY**, Village; Washington County; Pop. 800; Area Code 412; Zip Code 15342; Elev. 1,089'; a crossroads town which is named for Hickory Tavern, a fanciful name given by a part of early road builders to a hickory tree at one of their temporary campsites.

•**HIGHSPIRE**, Borough; Dauphin County; Pop. 2,959; Area Code 717; Zip Code 17034; Elev. 299'; 5 m. SE of Harrisburg in SE central Pennsylvania.

Highspire, along the Susquehanna River, settled in 1775 and laid out in 1814, marks the boundary between an agricultural area and an industrial district; its frame houses are mostly frail and unpainted. It is said to have been named for the old church spire here that served as a landmark for Susquehanna River boatmen.

•**HOLLIDAYSBURG**, Borough; Seat of Blair County; Pop. 5,897; Area Code 814; Zip Code 16648; Elev. 953'; 5 m. S of Altoona in W central Pennsylvania.

The settlement was founded in 1768 by *Adam and William Holliday*, Irish immigrants, at a time when Indians were still fighting white encroachment. Its population leaped from 72 to 1,896 between 1830 and 1840, when the first unified transportation system was completed across the state, with the Portage Railroad between Johnstown and Hollidaysburg as the key link.

Spurred by the completion of the Erie Canal in 1825, the Pennsylvania legislature in 1826-authorized construction between Philadelphia and Pittsburgh of a complete system of rail-water transportation; it was completed in 1834. The Portage Railroad was an ingenious system of levels and inclined planes over the mountains between Hollidaysburg and Johnstown, connecting the eastern and western canal terminals.

Agriculture - Grain, corn and varied farming
Industry/Mfg. - Quarrying
Community Event - Ethnic Days, Annual, June

180

•**HOKENDAUQUA**, Village; Lehigh County; Pop. 2,000; Area Code 717; Zip Code 18052; N suburb of Allentown along the Lehigh River in E Pennsylvania; name is Indian for "searching for land," which probably came about as tribesmen observed the first white land surveyors here.

•**HOLLSOPPLE**, Village; Somerset County; Pop. 900; Area Code 814; Zip Code 15935; Elev. 1,600'; 10 m. S of Johnstown in S Pennsylvania.

The town took its name from the family who owned the land upon which the first buildings were built.

•**HOMER CITY**, Borough; Indiana County; Pop. 2,248; Area Code 412; Zip Code 15748; Elev. 1,023'; 7 m. S of town Indiana in W central Pennsylvania; founded in 1854.

•**HOMESTEAD**, Borough; Allegheny County; Pop. 5,092; Area Code 412; Zip Code 15120; Elev. 852'; adjoining Pittsburgh in SW Pennsylvania.

Homestead, originally Amity Homestead, and renamed when incorporated as a borough in 1880. The settlement was laid out in 1871 by a Pittsburgh corporation called the Homestead Bank and Life Insurance Company. The town took its name from this company. It happened, however, that one of the farms which the company bought belonged to *Abdiel McClure*, who lived in a fine old farmhouse locally known as "the McClure homestead," embowered in a clump of trees. Many believe that this stately old homestead suggested the name of the town.

Homestead is probably the best known of Pennsylvania's steel towns because of the 1892 strike. The strike, which occurred in the Homestead Works, now in the borough of Munhall, was an important factor in checking unionism in steel for more than four decades, except for a brief period after World War I.

The plant of the Pittsburgh-Bessemer Steel Company, today one of the largest units of the United States Steel Corporation, was opened in Homestead by *Andrew Carnegie* in 1881. In 1892, at the expiration of a three year contract, *Carnegie's* managers, chief of whom was *H.C. Frick*, offered a new contract, which contained provisions unacceptable to the skilled workers, backbone of the

Amalgamated Association of Iron and Steel Workers. On May 30 the men, including unaffected employees, went on strike.

The pitched battle of Homestead began on the evening of July 5 when the tugboat *Little Bill* steamed up the Monongahela towing two barges loaded with 300 Pinkerton men. News of their coming preceded them, and the shores were black with strikers and their sympathizers. The first shot, its source disputed, set off volleys from both sides; the barges continued upstream to the plant entrance. After a short halt for parley, hostilities were resumed. Soon the Pinkerton men, stranded on the barges because the *Little Bill* had left for Pittsburgh with the dead and wounded, became targets for burning oil, gas, and dynamite, and cannon and pistol fire. The strikers, themselves under rifle fire, accepted a truce, under the terms of which the Pinkertons were escorted to City Hall and allowed to depart by special train for Pittsburgh. For several days an advisory committee of strikers assumed governmental functions. On July 10, *Governor Robert E. Pattison* sent 8,000 National Guardsmen to Homestead, and the plants reopened on the company's terms. A U.S. Senate investigating committee later declared that the use of the Pinkerton men by the company was an "assumption of state authority," and that "there is no evidence damage was done...to property...by strikers."

> *Industry/Mfg.* - Steel, cement and dairy
> products
> *Daily Newspaper* - The Messenger, 139 E.
> Eighth Avenue
> *Chamber of Commerce* - 305 E. 8th Avenue

•**HOMEWOOD**, Borough; Beaver County; Pop. 188; Area Code 412; Zip Code 152 + zone; Elev. 956'; 5 m. N of Beaver Falls along the Shenango River in W Pennsylvania; in a rural area.

•**HONESDALE**, Borough; Seat of Wayne County; Pop. 5,128; Area Code 717; Zip Code 18431; Elev. 982'; 24 m. NE of Scranton in NE Pennsylvania.

All types of clothing are made in this resort town that was once an important coal storage and shipping point. In 1826, *Philip Hone*, mayor of New York City, later president of the Delaware & Hudson Canal Company, came to the settlement to push construction of a canal that would divert the flow of coal to his city.

In 1827, as soon as it was definitely known that "the forks of the Dyberry" were to be the terminus of the canal, the town was planned and laid out. Honesdale very properly received its name from *Hone*, the chief patron and the first president of the Delaware and Hudson Canal company. He was a wealthy merchant, and "the courtliest mayor New York ever saw." The family name *Hone* was first used to designate a "dweller by a large stone or rock." Honesdale was incorporated in 1831, and 11 years later it became the county seat of Wayne County.

One of the first locomotive engines introduced and worked in America, called the *Stourbridge Lion* and built in England, of the best workmanship and material, and the most approved pattern of that date - was run in 1828 for a while on a little railroad at "Hone's Dale."

Honesdale is in a hollow formed by low hills.

Agriculture - Fruit and varied farming
Industry/Mfg. - Lumber, clothing, dairy
 products. Resort area.
Chamber of Commerce - 865 Main Street

•**HONEY BROOK**, Borough; Chester County; Pop. 1,164; Area Code 215; Zip Code 19344; Elev. 740'; near Coatesville in SE Pennsylvania.

A garment factory and machine shop employ most of the town's workers. Honey Brook is an English translation of a Welsh word *Nantmel* meaning "sweet water." Welsh settlers had come here from Nantmel in Radnorshire.

Agriculture - Grain and varied farming,
 tobacco
Industry/Mfg. - Clothing, quarrying

•**HOOKSTOWN**, Borough; Beaver County; Pop. 228; Area Code 412; Zip Code 15050; Elev. 1,000'; just E of West Virginia and Ohio state lines in W Pennsylvania; coal mining district.

•**HOOVERSVILLE**, Borough; Somerset County; Pop. 863; Area Code 814; Zip Code 15936; Elev. 1,750'; 15 m. S of Johnstown on Stony Creek in S Pennsylvania; rural.

•**HOP BOTTOM**, Borough; Susquehanna County; Pop. 405; Area Code 717; Zip Code 18824; Elev. 880'; NE Pennsylvania; named for the creek nearby which once had an abundance of wild hops along its banks.

•**HOPEWEL**, Borough; Bedford County; Pop. 256; Area Code 814; Zip Code 16650; Elev. 900'; 50 m. SE of Altoona along the Juniata River in S Pennsylvania.

Community Event - Establishment Day, Annual, August

•**HOSENSACK**, Village; Lehigh County; Pop. (Rural); Area Code 717; Zip Code 18092; 12 m. S of Allentown in E Pennsylvania.

Hosensack, the name of a creek and the village, is German for "breeches pocket," a designation said to have been bestowed by a German hunter who once lost his way in this valley.

•**HOUSTON**, Borough; Washington County; Pop. 1,568; Area Code 412; Zip Code 15342; Elev. 960'; 18 m. SW of Pittsburgh in SW Pennsylvania.

•**HOUTZDALE**, Borough; Clearfield County; Pop. 1,222; Area Code 814; Zip Code 16651; Elev. 1,518'; 30 m. NE of Altoona in W central Pennsylvania.

Town was named for *Dr. Daniel Houtz*, who owned the land upon which it was built in 1870.

•**HOWARD**, Borough; Centre County; Pop. 838; Area Code 814; Zip Code 16841; Elev. 664'; Central Pennsylvania.

The borough and the township of Howard received their name in honor of the great English philanthropist, *John Howard* (1726-1790), who devoted his life to improvement of the condition of prisoners and captives.

•**HUDSONDALE**, Village; Carbon County; Pop. 100; Area Code 717; Zip Code 18255; Elev. 1,230'; was founded in 1800.

•**HUGHESTOWN**, Borough; Luzerne County; Pop. 1,783; Area Code 717; Elev. 760'; residential suburb of Wilkes-Barre in E Pennsylvania, just NE of Pittston.

•**HUGHESVILLE**, Borough; Lycoming County; Pop. 2,174; Area Code 717; Zip Code 17737; Elev. 483'; 15 m. E of Williamsport in N central Pennsylvania.

Hughesville was laid out in 1816 by *Jeptha Hughes*, who called it Hughesburg. In 1827, when the post office was established, the name was changed to Hughesville.

Industry/Mfg. - Campers, grain milling, dairy products

•**HULMEVILLE**, Borough; Bucks County; Pop. 1,014; Area Code 215; Zip Code 19047; Elev. 40'; NE suburb of Philadelphia in SE Pennsylvania.

•**HUMMELSTOWN**, Borough; Dauphin County; Pop. 4,267; Area Code 717; Zip Code 17036; Elev. 370'; SE central Pennsylvania.

Hummelstown, founded about 1740 by *Frederick Hummel* and known as Frederickstown until his death in 1780. During the Revolution Hummelstown was an important depot of arms and munitions for garrisons and forts situated to the west and the north.

Today it is a large suburb to the east of Harrisburg. Nearby is the Indian Echo Cave.

Agriculture - Varied farming
Industry/Mfg. - Clothing, quarrying

•**HUNKER**, Borough; Westmoreland County; Pop. 359; Area Code 417; Zip Code 15639; Elev. 980'; E suburb of Pittsburgh in SW Pennsylvania.

•**HUNTINGDON**, Borough; Seat of Huntingdon County; Pop. 7,042; Area Code 717; Zip Code 16652; Elev. 630'; 35 m. E of Altoona in S central Pennsylvania.

Huntingdon was originally called standing stone. The settlement was laid out in 1767 by *Dr. William Smith*, first Provost of the University of Pennsylvania, and named for *Selina Hastings*, Countess of Huntingdon, who had responded liberally to *Smith's* appeal for funds to aid the university. The earliest traders found here a camp of the Oneida (Ind. "standing stone"), whose wigwams, according to tribal practice, formed a circle around a 14-foot high, six-inch square stone pilar etched with petroglyphs.

Conrad Weiser and *John Harris* in their travel accounts described this stone as large, conspicuous, and highly venerated by the Indians. When the Treaty of Albany in 1754 gave the proprietaries the entire Juniata Valley, the Indians departed, taking the stone with them. The settlers, who referred to the settlement as Standing Stone, erected a similar one, replaced in 1896 by the Standing Stone Monument.

> *Agriculture* - Dairy, grain and varied farming
> *Industry/Mfg.* - Electronics, coal, clothing
> *Higher Education* - Juanita College
> *Daily Newspaper* - The News, 325 Penn St.
> *Chamber of Commerce* - 408 Penn Street
> *Community Event* - Old-Fashioned Fair, Annual, August.

•**HUNTINGDON COUNTY**, In 1787, when a new county was formed from Bedford, with Huntingdon centrally located as its chief settlement, the county naturally took the name of the town that had been laid out twenty years before, and Huntingdon became the county-seat of Huntingdon County. The borough seal of Huntingdon very appropriately bears a slender stone pillar, "the standing stone," as its central figure.

•**HYDE PARK**, Borough; Westmoreland County; Pop. 633; Area Code 417; Zip Code 15641; Elev. 793'; on Conemaugh Creek in SW Pennsylvania.

•**HYDETOWN**, Borough; Crawford County; Pop. 760; Area Code 814; Zip Code 16328; Elev. 1,245'; 30 m. E of Meadville in a rural area along Oil Creek in NW Pennsylvania.

•**HYNDMAN**, Borough; Bedford County; Pop. 1,106; Area Code 814; Zip Code 15545; Elev. 934'; On Wills Creek, 50 m. SW of Altoona in S Pennsylvania.

Hyndman was first called Bridgeport, for which, at the time of its incorporation in 1877, the name Hyndman was substituted, in honor of *E.K. Hyndman*, president of the Pittsurgh and Western Railroad.

I

•**IMPERIAL**, Village; Allegheny County; Pop. 2,000; Area Code 412; Zip Code 15126; Elev. 940'; NW suburb of Pittsburgh in SW Pennsylvania.

The town was laid out by the Imperial Coal Company in 1879, and was named for their Imperial Mine.

•**INDIANA**, Borough; Seat of Indiana County; Pop. 16,051; Area Code 412; Zip Code 15701; Elev. 1,310'; 46 m. NE of Pittsburgh in W central Pennsylvania.

Indiana, founded in 1805, when *George Clymer* of Philadelphia, one of the signers of the Declaration of Independence, donated 250 acres for county buildings, it was probably named for the Territory of Indiana, which Congress formed from the Northwest Territory in 1800. Before the Civil War, Indiana was an important station on the Underground Railroad.

POINT OF INTEREST

OLD INDIANA COUNTY COURTHOUSE- Clock tower and Corinthian columns; interior contains marble detailing, excellent woodwork and frescoes; built in 1870. Second Empire. Restored.

Agriculture - Varied farming
Industry/Mfg. - Soft drinks, bricks, clothing, coal
Higher Education - Indiana University of Pennsylvania
Daily Newspaper - The Gazette, 899 Water St.
Chamber of Commerce - 31 S. Carpeter Ave.

•**INDIANA COUNTY**, Indiana County is commonly said to have derived its name "from its first denizens." This explanation is not very enlightening. It is a little more accurate and definite to point out that in all likelihood the name of the county was suggested by that of the Territory of Indian, which Congress formed from the Northwestern

187

Territory on May 7, 1800, almost three years before the Pennsylvania county was established, and which received its name "from one of the old anti-Revolutionary land companies." *Captain William Trent* was one of the organizers of the Indiana Land Company, and it was he who gave the name of Indiana to the territory comprised in this grant, which appears as "Indiana" in Hutchins's map of 1778.

As to the ultimate source of the name, *Dr. Isaac Taylor* points out that "it is one of the curiosities of the nomenclature that the name of one of the United States should have to be explained by the Greek corruption of the Persian form of a Sanskrit word meaning a river." India received its name from the Indus River, and the American Indians were so called because Columbus thought that he had reached India.

•**INDIAN HEAD**, Village; Fayette County; Pop. 300; Area Code 412; Zip Code 15446; Elev. 1,392'; SW Pennsylvania; so named because it lies near the head of Indian Creek.

•**INDIAN LAKE**, Borough; Somerset County; Pop. 306; Area Code 814; Zip Code 15926; 20 m. S of Johnstown in S Pennsylvania; incorporated in 1966.

•**INDUSTRY**, Borough; Beaver County; Pop. 2,417; Area Code 412; Zip Code 15052; Elev. 695'; W Pennsylvania.
Industry was laid out in 1836. Lumbering, coal mining, and the building of keelboats were the mainstays of its more prosperous days. The borough was incorporated in 1958.

•**INGRAM**, Borough; Allegheny County; Pop. 4,346; Area Code 412; Zip Code 15205; Elev. 880'; S suburb of Pittsburgh in SW Pennsylvania.

•**IRVINE**, Village; Warren County; Pop. 300; Elev. 1,167'; laid out in the 1840s by *Dr. William A. Irvine* on the donation lands inherited from his grandfather, *William Irvine*, a brigadier general in the Revolutionary War. The quaint town is located on the Allegheny River, and is on the borders of the Allegheny National Forest.

•**IRVONA**, Borough; Clearfield County; Pop. 644; Area Code 814; Zip Code 16656; Elev. 1,380'; on Clearfield Creek in W central Pennsylvania.

Colonel E.A. Irvin of Curwensville founded this town, which was eventually named for him.

•**IRWIN**, Borough; Westmoreland County; Pop. 4,995; Area Code 417; Zip Code 15642; Elev. 879'; 20 m. SE of Pittsburgh in SW Pennsylvania.

Irwin was laid out on Brush Run in 1853. Today it lies near the Pennsylvania Turnpike. *John Irwin* founded the village within a forest of white oaks. It quickly became a bustling coal town. *John Scull*, father-in-law of Irwin, established the Pittsburgh *Gazette*, first newspaper in the region. *Scull's* homestead (1794) here has been restored.

> *Daily Newspaper* - The Standard-Observer, PO Box 280
> *Chamber of Commerce* - 8850 Route 30

•**IVYLAND**, Borough; Bucks County; Pop. 581; Area Code 215; Zip Code 18972; Elev. 300'; N suburb of Philadelphia in SE Pennsylvania.

J

•**JACKSON CENTER**, Borough; Mercer County; Pop. 265; Area Code 412; Zip Code 16133; Elev. 1,164'; W Pennsylvania; settled in 1835, and until the 1930s was supported by a bituminous coal mine.

•**JACKSONVILLE**, Borough; Indiana County; Pop. 121; Area Code 412; Zip Code 15752; Elev. 1,063'; W central Pennsylvania.

•**JACOBUS**, Borough; York County; Pop. 1,396; Area Code 717; Zip Code 17407; 10 m. S of York in S Pennsylvania.

•**JAMESTOWN**, Borough; Mercer County; Pop. 854; Area Code 412; Zip Code 16134; Elev. 990'; W Pennsylvania; founded by *James Campbell* in 1798, although the streets were not formally laid out until 1832, by *John Keck*.

•**JEANNETTE**, City; Westmoreland County; Pop. 13,106; Area Code 417; Zip Code 15644; Elev. 1,040'; 23 m. SE of Pittsburgh in SW Pennsylvania; named for the wife of *H. Sellers McKee*, who in 1889 helped to establish a glass works that led to the transformation of a farm site into an industrial city. Because of its glass manufactories, Jeannette is known as "the Glass City." All manner of fine glass and novelty glass figures are made here.

Agriculture - Varied farming
Industry/Mfg. - Glass, soft drinks, coal, clothing
Daily Newspaper - The News-Dispatch, 227 S. 4th Street

•**JEDDO**, Borough; Luzerne County; Pop. 128; Area Code 717; Zip Code 18224; Elev. 1,063'; 7 m. NE of Hazleton in E Pennsylvania.

•**JEFFERSON**, Borough; Allegheny County; Pop. 8,643; Area Code 412; Zip Code 15025; Elev. 780'; SE suburb of Pittsburgh in SW Pennsylvania; incorporated in 1950 as a residential subdivision; named for *Thomas Jefferson*.

•**JEFFERSON**, Borough; Greene County; Pop. 413; Area Code 412; Zip Code 15344; Elev. 960'; 10 m. E of Waynesburg along Tenmile Creek; named for *Thomas Jefferson*.

•**JEFFERSON**, Borough; York County; Pop. 685; Area Code 717; Zip Code 17311; Elev. 660'; S Pennsylvania.
The town was originally known as Codorus, or "swift water." Codorus State Park is located nearby.

•**JEFFERSON COUNTY**, On March 26, 1804, five new counties were formed out of Lycoming, and were named Clearfield, Jefferson, McKean, Potter, and Tioga. One of the counties carved out of the vast Lycoming County wilderness received the name of Jefferson in honor of *Thomas Jefferson*, then serving as the third President of the United States, and famous as the author of the Declaration of Independence and the founder of the Democratic Party, which was at that time dominant in Pennsylvania politics and destined to remain in power during the greater part of the next half-century. The borough of Jefferson, in Greene County, was also named for our third President. *Jefferson's* popularity is attested by the fact that at least a score of counties in the United States and nearly two score of towns are named in his honor.

•**JEFFERSONVILLE**, Village; Montgomery County; Area Code 215; Zip Code 19401; Elev. 225'; named for *Thomas Jefferson*. The Jeffersonville Inn, so named in 1804 was once a favorite resort of drovers and farmers. An inn erected on the site in 1776 was set afire by British soldiers searching for the patriot proprietor, *Colonel Archibald Thompson*. Participants in *John Fries* (Hot Water) Rebellion of 1799 were tried in the rebuilt tavern. Today it is a residential suburb.

•**JENKINTOWN**, Borough; Montgomery County; Pop. 4,942; Area Code 215; Zip Code 19046; Elev. 250'; in suburb

191

of Philadelphia in SE Pennsylvania; low density houses and country clubs are in vicinity.

Jenkintown was named for the Welsh pioneer, *William Jenkins,* who settled here before 1697. The place was called Jenkins'-town as early as 1759.

Chamber of Commerce - Box 172

•JENNERSTOWN, Borough; Somerset County; Pop. 656; Area Code 814; Zip Code 15547; Elev. 1,950'; S Pennsylvania.

Jennerstown, a village of two-story frame houses, was laid out in 1822 and named for *Edward Jenner,* the English physician who developed vaccination for smallpox. Picturesque Laurel Mountain, with skiing facilities is nearby.

•JERMYN, Borough; Lackawanna County; Pop. 2,411; Area Code 717; Zip Code 18433; Elev. 952'; NE Pennsylvania.

Jermyn, which with Mayfield forms the so-called "twin boroughs," was named by the Delaware and Hudson Canal Company for *John Jermyn,* a wealthy English merchant, and much of the subsequent immigration was from Great Britain. Before *Jermyn* arrived in 1874, the settlement was known as Gibsonburg, for *John Gibson* of Philadelphia, who had owned land here.

•JERSEY SHORE, Borough; Lycoming County; Pop. 4,631; Area Code 717; Zip Code 17740; Elev. 603'; 16 m. W of Williamsport on Susquehanna River in N central Pennsylvania.

Jersey Shore, settled in 1785 by several families from New Jersey, was named by settlers on the opposite shore of the river. The first settlers, *Reuben Manning* and his nephew, *Thomas Forster,* had migrated from Essex County, New Jersey. At first the term Jersey Shore was merely a derisive nickname given by the Irish settlers dwelling in the Nippenose bottom across the river. The traditional explanation of the origin of the name is that these Irishmen usually referred to the shore on which the Jerseymen had settled as "the Jersey Shore."

About 1805 the name was changed to Waynesburg, but the old name was readopted at the time of incorporation. In the 1820s Jersey Shore was a sporting center; fast horses found their way to the race track, shad were plentiful in nearby streams, and wild pigeons were shot down by the thousands (these brought as little as 6 cents a dozen).

Removal of the New York Central Railroad shops, which had employed 1,200, to West Albany, New York, in the early 1930s impoverished the town; the spring flood of 1936 was another damaging blow.

Chamber of Commerce - PO Box 231

•**JESSUP** (alt. Winton), Borough; Lackawanna County; Pop. 4,974; Area Code 717; Zip Code 18434; Elev. 872'; NE Pennsylvania.

This community, settled in 1849, was successively calley Saymour, and Mount Vernon; when *William W. Winton* established a coal breaker and laid out some semblance of a town in 1874, the townsmen named it for him. In 1877 it was incorporated as a borough.

•**JIM THORPE**, Borough; Seat of Carbon County; Pop. 5,263; Area Code 717; Zip Code 18229; Elev. 916'; 14 m. SE of Hazleton in E Pennsylvania, along the Lehigh River; in 1954, Mauch Chunk and East Mauch Chunk were consolidated and renamed Jim Thorpe.

The town of Mauch Chunk, which became the county seat only after keen competition with Lehighton, took its name from the curiously-shaped and imposing hill on the opposite side of the Lehigh River, called by the Indians *Machk Tschunk*, or "Bear Mountain." In 1824 the population was 734. In 1850, when Mauch Chunk was incorporated, the new town of East Mauch Chunk was laid out on the opposite bank of the Lehigh. It grew to be larger than the overcrowded parent town, by the time of reincorporation. The area has been called the "Switzerland of America" because of its immigrant population. The first gravity-powered railroad in America was laid between this town and the Summit Hill mine (nine miles away) in 1827.

Swift-moving water in the nearby Lehigh River gorge allows for white water rafting for several miles.

POINTS OF INTEREST

CARBON COUNTY JAIL- Mid-19th century stone jail; *John Haviland*, architect. Held numerous suspected members of "Molly Maguires," a secret organization of miners associated with state labor violence, prior to their trials (1875-1876).

ASA PACKER MANSION- Built in 1860 for *Asa Packer*, millionaire industrialist, politician and founder of Lehigh University. Italianate with Gothic Revival elements. Museum.

Chamber of Commerce - Box 267

•**JOHNSONBURG**, Borough; Elk County; Pop. 3,938; Area Code 814; Zip Code 15845; Elev. 1,453'; 100 m. NE of Pittsburgh in NW central Pennsylvania.

Johnsonburg, at the forks of the Clarion River, was laid out in 1888. It is said to have received its name from *John Johnson*, the traditional pioneer settler in that region, who about 50 years before the towns was laid out, occupied a small cabin at the junction of the east and west branches of the Clarion River, near the center of the present town. Johnsonburg has had extensive paper mills, but today tourism is as important as industry, since it is near both Bendigo State Park and the Allegheny National Forest.

Agriculture - Grain, potatoes and varied farming
Industry/Mfg. - Paper, dairy products
Chamber of Commerce - PO Box 237

•**JOHNSTOWN**, City; Cambria County; Pop. 35,496; Area Code 814; Zip Code 159 + zone; Elev. 1,184'; 75 m. E of Pittsburgh in SW central Pennsylvania.

Johnstown is squeezed firmly between narrow valley walls. The city was named for *Joseph Johns, Jahns, or Yahns* (as the name was variously spelled), a native Switzerland, who came to America in 1769, at the age of 19. He first settled in Berks County, whence he soon migrated to the neighborhood of Meyersdale in Somerset County. In 1793 *Joseph Johns* bought "the Campbell tract" of 249 acres, on which a large part of Johnstown is now built. The town that he laid out was christened by him Conemaugh, for the Conemaugh River. When he died in 1813, his son, *Joseph Johns, Jr.* inherited his real estate. The town was incorporated as the borough of Conemaugh in 1831, and three years later the legislature formally changed its name to Johnstown.

More than its steel or coal, the flood of 1889 has made its name known. First inundated in 1808, Johnstown has since been flooded 21 times. In May 1889 a week of heavy rainfall raised the Conemaugh River and Stoney Creek River, still swollen by spring thaws. The waters inched up the steep hills in a manner familiar to residents, who expected no greater damage than that which they had frequently experienced, and to which they had long since resigned themselves. On the afternoon of May 31 the South Fork Dam gave way; erected to form a feeder basin for the Pennsylvania Canal, it had been neglected since 1862. A wall of water, 75 feet high and half a mile wide, rushed upon the city. The torrent, carrying all sorts of debris, smashed and flung everything aside, exacting a toll of more than 2,200 lives and about $10,000,000 in property damage. Bodies were carried as far down-river as Pittsburgh. All parts of the nation contributed to the rescue and rehabilitation work. A national monument marks the tragic site. One precaution against a recurrence was subsequently taken, the widening of the Conemaugh River in 1891. The latest flood was in 1977.

The city today has its own airport, served by Allegheny Airlines. A campus of the University of Pittsburgh is also located here.

POINTS OF INTEREST

CAMBRIA PUBLIC LIBRARY BUILDING- Built 1890-1891 with funds provided by *Andrew Carnegie* after the 1889 Johnstown Flood. Chateauesque elements.

JOHNSTOWN INCLINED RAILWAY- Cablecar systen, completed 1891, one of the longest and steepest of its type in the world.

JOHNSTOWN FLOOD NATIONAL MEMORIAL- Site of 1889 flood caused by break in South Fork Dam, one the nation's worst disasters; victims were cared for by newly organized American Red Cross, under direction of *Clara Barton.*

Industry/Mfg. - Iron and steel, varied manufacturing, trade and services
Higher Education - University of Pittsburgh
Daily Newspaper - Tribune Democrat, 425 Locust Street

Chamber of Commerce - 219 Franklin Street
Community Event - Arts Festival, Annual,
September

•**JOLLYTOWN**, Village; Greene County; Pop. 30; Area Code 412; Zip Code 16229; SE Pennsylvania; named for *Titus Jolly*, who once owned land on this spot.

•**JONESTOWN**, Borough; Lebanon County; Pop. 814; Area Code 717; Zip Code 17038; Elev. 475'; 8 m. N of Lebanon in SE central Pennsylvania; in a rural area.

•**JOSEPHINE**, Village; Indiana County; Pop. 500; Area Code 412; Zip Code 15750; Elev. 1,020'; founded in 1905 and named for the wife of a partner in a local steel company. An exodus occured after this plant suspended operations about 1926.

•**JUNIATA COUNTY**, seperated from Mifflin in 1831, the county was named for the beautiful Juniata River, which flows through it from the west on its way to the Susquehanna. The old song entitled "The Blue Juniata" has made the name of this river famous. Juniata is an Iroquois word, and there can be little doubt that it is a variant of the more common form Oneida. In various documents written before 1765 the name Juniata was spelled in more than twenty different ways. One of these forms was Choniata. The initial gutteral sound is the only thing that really differentiates this form from Oneida, when the latter is divided, as it should be, into four syllables. *A.L. Guss* declares that an educated Wyandot, who spoke a dialect of the Iroquois tongue, is very positive in his assertion that Juniata means "standing-stone people," or "the people of the standing rock." This is the usual explanation of the name of the Oneidas, who were in the habit of setting up in each of their villages a standing stone as a national or tribal emblem.

•**JUNIATA CROSSING**, Village; Bedford County; Pop. Rural; Area Code 814; Elev. 1,000'; is on the shore of the Raystown Branch of the Juniata River, the beauty of which inspired *M.D. Sullivan's* "Blue Juniata," a popular ballad in the nineteenth century.

•**JUNIATA RIVER**, River; S Pennsylvania; flows N and E approx. 150 m. from source in Huntingdon County through central Pennsylvania to its mouth on the Susquehanna River, N of Harrisburg.

Juniata is an Iroquois word meaning "standing-stone people," and may be a variant of the word "Oneida," the name of a New York Indian tribe. the old song "Blue Juniata" has made the river somewhat famous.

•**JUNIATA TERRACE**, Borough; Mifflin County; Pop. 631; Area Code 717; Zip Code 17044; Elev. 560'; just S of Lewistown in central Pennsylvania, on a cliff over the Juniata River.

K

•KANE, Borough; McKean County; Pop. 4,916; Area Code 814; Zip Code 16735; Elev. 2,000'; on E border of the Allegheny National Forest in N Pennsylvania.

Agriculture - Varied farming
Industry/Mfg. - Oil, electronics, dairy
products. Resort area.
Daily Newspaper - Republican, 200 N. Fraley
Street
Chamber of Commerce - 14 Greeves Street

•KAOLIN, Village; Chester County; Pop. 100; Area Code 215; Zip Code 19374; near Toughkenamon in SE Pennsylvania; named because of the large deposits of the clay-like mineral kaolin in the area.

•KARNS CITY, Borough; Butler County; Pop. 354; Area Code 412; Zip Code 16041; Elev. 1,220'; W Pennsylvania.
Karns City, once an important town in Butler County, was named for *S.D. Karns,* who, shortly after the discovery of oil in 1871, leased more than 400 acres of land here. Five years later Karns City had a population of over 2,000. Now the village has diminished considerably, since the oil has dwindled.

•KARTHAUS, Village; Clearfield County; Pop. 300; Area Code 814; Zip Code 16845; Elev. 960; W central Pennsylvania.
The village derived its name from *Peter A. Karthaus* of Baltimore, who built an iron furnace here about 1820. Karthaus is the German equivalent of Carthusian, the name of a monastic order.

•KELAYRES, Village; Schuylkill County; Area Code Pop. 700; Area Code 717; Zip Code 18231; Elev. 651'.
At the height of the 1934 gubernatorial campaign,

marchers in a Democratic parade through Kelayres' streets were mowed down by a crossfire of bullets from the darkened windows of two houses; the volley killed five and wounded fourteen. *Joseph J. Bruno*, who had held several important county offices and five of his relatives were tried and convicted.

•**KENHORST**, Borough; Berks County; Pop. 3,187; Area Code 215; Zip Code 19607; Elev. 310'; residential suburb of Reading in SE Pennsylvania.

•**KENNETT SQUARE**, Borough; Chester County; Pop. 4,715; Area Code 215; Zip Code 19348; Elev. 268'; 12 m. NW of Wilmington, Delaware in SE Pennsylvania.

Kennett Square, settled in 1686 by *Francis Smith*, who had come from Kennett, a village in Wiltshire, England, the major shipping center for fresh mushrooms, it also has a large mushroom cannery.

The Site of *Bayard Taylor's* birthplace is marked by a plaque. *Taylor* (1825-78), novelist, journalist, poet, and diplomat, was one of the first of America's poor but adventurous young men to seek knowledge and experience in the old cities of Europe; his *Vies Afoot, or Europe Seen with Knapsack and Staff* was a best seller in 1846. He wrote other travel books, several novels and volumes of poetry, but is best known for his translation of *Goethe's Faust,* one of the best in our language. He died in Berlin while serving as American Minister to Germany.

Fresh cut roses are shipped from nurseries in this quiet town.

Chamber of Commerce - PO Box 395

•**KENSINGTON**, Residential village; Philadelphia County; Pop. (incl. with Philadelphia); Area Code 215; Zip Code 19125; SE Pennsylvania.

The founder of Kensington, which was incorporated as a separate municipal district in 1820, was *Anthony Palmer*, a rich ship captain and merchant, who came to Philadelphia from Barbados in 1709, bought extensive tracts of land north of the city, became prominent in the colony, lived in style, and was a conspicuous figure as he drove through the city with his coach and four, or sailed down the Delaware in his handsome pleasure barge. About 25 years after buying his land he laid out a town, which he called Kensington, after the English village which is now a part of London.

•**KENT**, See Jacksonville.

•**KERRMOOR**, Village; Clearfield County; Pop. 60; Area Code 814; Zip Code 16833; near Curwensville in W central Pennsylvania.

Kerrmoor was named for the two families which founded it, the *James Kerr* family and the *Robert Moore* family.

•**KING OF PRUSSIA (BRANDYWINE VILLAGE)**, Village; Montgomery County; Pop. 11,000; Area Code 215; Zip Code 19406; Elev. 190'.

King of Prussia had its nucleus in the King of Prussia Inn, which the first proprietor, a native of Prussia, named for the Brandenburg prince, who in 1701 transformed Prussia from a duchy into a kingdom, taking the title of *King Frederick I.*

Today the town is a residential suburb of Philadelphia and Norristown.

> *Industry/Mfg.* - Machine shop
> *Daily Newspaper* - Today's Post, 750 Moore Rd.

•**KINGSTON**, Borough; Luzerne County; Pop. 15,681; Area Code 717; Zip Code 18704; E Pennsylvania.

The name of Kingston was borrowed from Kingston in Rhode Island, from which some of the "first 40" of the early settlers had migrated. "Forty Township" was one of the five original Connecticut townships; it received its name from the famous Forty Fort, which was situated within its limits. In 1771 Forty Township was named Kingstown Township; and three years later occures, for the first time, the present form, Kingston. The town of Kingston in Rhode Island, which is now divided into North and South Kingston, was originally called King's Town or Kingstown, a name which was first used about 1665, and which had its origin in "the King's Province."

•**KINTNERSVILLE**, Village; Buck County; Pop. 100; Area Code 215; Zip Code 18920; Elev. 124'; settled in 1789 by *George Gintner*, of Wurttemberg.

•**KISTLER**, Borough; Mifflin County; Pop. 364; Area Code 717; Zip Code 17066; 45 m. E of Altoona near Mount Union in central Pennsylvania.

•**KITTANNING**, Borough; Set of Armstrong County; Pop. 5,432; Area Code 412; Zip Code 16201; Elev. 807'; 43 m. NE of Pittsburgh in W Pennsylvania; on Allegheny River.

Kittanning stretches along the eastern bank of the Allegheny. The town occupies the site of an Indian town of the same name, the largest in western Pennsylvania. On September 8, 1745, *Colonel Armstrong* destroyed the town, killing *Chief Jacob* and 42 of his braves, and releasing 11 captives.

Kittanning was laid out in 1803 by *Judge George Rose*. From this place a famous Indian trail known as "the Kittanning Path" led across the mountains to Standing Stone, now Huntingdon. It was this trail that *Colonel Armstrong* and his little army followed in their expedition against Kittanning. Made a borough in 1821.

> *Agriculture* - Varied farming
> *Industry/Mfg.* - Cement products, soft drinks,
>   coal, gas, oil and dairy products
> *Higher Education* - Indiana University of
>   Pennsylvania
> *Daily Newspaper* - Leader-Times, 115-121 N.
>   Grant Avenue
> *Chamber of Commerce* - Colwell-Arnold Bldg.
>   N. McKean Street
> *Community Event* - Fort Armstrong Folk
>   Festival, Annual, August

•**KITTATINNY MOUNTAINS**, Mountain Range; E Pennsylvania; part of the Appalachian Mountains; extends approx. 170 m. SW, forming the border of many E and SE counties; average elev. 2,000'; traversed by the Appalachian Trail. See also *Blue Mountains*.

•**KNOX**, Borough; Clarion County; Pop. 1,364; Area Code 814; Zip Code 16232; Elev. 1,400'; 20 m. SE of Oil City in W Pennsylvania.

•**KNOXVILLE**, Borough; Tioga County; Pop. 650; Area Code 717; Zip Code 16928; Elev. 1,241'; at the foot of 2,200' Fork Hill in N Pennsylvania.

•**KOPPEL**, Borough; Beaver County; Pop. 1,146; Area Code 412; Zip Code f16136; Elev. 890'; W Pennsylvania.
Koppel was named for *Arthur Koppel* of Germany, who established a freight car factory here a few years before World War I.

•**KOSSUTH**, Village; Clarino County; Pop. 50; Area Code 814; Zip Code 16331; Elev. 1,540'; 12 m. NW of Clarion in W Pennsylvania.
Kossuth received its name from the Hungarian patriot and revolutionary leader, *Louis Kossuth*, who was a political exile in the United States in 1852. He was very popular in the United States during his prime.

•**KREAMER**, Village; Snyder County; Pop. 400; Area Code 717; Zip Code 17833; Elev. 500'; includes the site of Hendrich's Fort, a refuge for settlers during Indian raids form 1770 to 1783.

Community Event - Pioneer Days, Annual, July

•**KULPMONT**, Borough; Northumberland County; Pop. 3,675; Area Code 717; Zip Code 17834; Elev. 900'; E central Pennsylvania; founded in 1875 and incorporated as a borough in 1914.

•**KUTZTOWN**, Borough; Berks County; Pop. 4,040; Area Code 215; Zip Code 19530; Elev. 450'; 18 m. N of Reading in SE Pennsylvania.
Kutztown was founded in 1771 and named for *George Kutz*, who laid it out. In 1866 the Manxatawny Seminary at Kutztown became the Keystone State Normal School, which in turn has become Kutztown State College, with 4,500 students. The town is important for its computer technology research and business centers. An eight day Folk Festival featuring the crafts and traditions of the Pennsylvania Dutch, is held here each July.

POINTS OF INTEREST

CRYSTAL CAVE- Oldest cave in the state.
HOTTENSTEIN MANSION- Late-18th century Georgian; excellent interior woodwork amd examples of *Fraktur* painting.

Agriculture - Varied farming
Industry/Mfg. - Clothing, quarrying, dairy
    products
Higher Education - Kutztown State College
Community Event - Pennsylvania Dutch
    Kutztown Folk Festival, Annual, June-July

•LACEYVILLE, Borough; Wyoming County; Pop. 498; Area Code 717; Zip Code 18623; Elev. 656'; NE Pennsylvania.

Laceyville, the twin of Skinners Eddy. The socalled 1790 House, a story-and-a-half log cabin built by *Ebenezer Skinner*. Held together with wooden pegs, it is now weatherboarded and has never known a coat of paint.

•LACKAWANNA COUNTY, is the youngest county in Pennsylvania, having been established in August 13, 1878. It was named for the Lackawanna River and valley. Lackawannock seems to have been the form at first generally used. The Delaware Indian name from which Lackawanna is derived is *Lechauhanne*, and signifies "the stream that forks." Obviously the name is meant to designate the confluence of two rivers. The streams that thus come together are the Lackawanna River and the North Branch of the Susquehanna.

•LACKAWANNA RIVER, River; NE Pennsylvania; flows S approx. 50 m. from source in the mountainous, lake-strewn area of E Susquehanna County through Scranton to its mouth on the Susquehanna River, N of Wilkes-Barre.

The name is Indian, meaning "the stream that forks."

•LACKAWAXEN, Village; Pike County; Pop. 500; Area Code 717; Elev. 647'.

Lackawaxen (Ind. "swift waters" or "where the way forks"), founded in 1770, lies on the Delaware at the mouth of Lackawaxen Creek, which *Zane Grey* described as "a little river hidden away...dashing white sheeted over ferny cliffs, wine-brown where the whirling pools suck the stain from the hemlock roots... (and) harbor the speckled trout."

The Battle of the Minisink occurred nearby on July 22, 1779. *Chief Joseph Brant*, a Mohawk, had led 300 Tories and Indians against Minisink (now Port Jervis) and burned it. Homeward-bound and booty-laden, *Brant's* men were attacked by 175 settlers under *Major Wood*. Most of the settlers were killed, and Wood and 25 men escaped only because of Wood's unintentional use of the Masonic distress signal. Seeing it, Brant is said to have allowed him and his men to escape across the creek into the forest. *Horace Greeley's* famous Sylvania Association made its settlement in Lackawaxen Township.

•**LAFAYETTE HILL**, Village; Montgomery County; Pop. 5,500; Area Code 215; suburb of Philadelphia; also known as Barren Hill.

•**LAFLIN**, Borough; Luzerne County; Pop. 1,650; Area Code 717; Elev. 727'; 4 m. N of Wilkes-Barre in E Pennsylvania, on Gardner's Creek.

•**LAHASKA**, Village; Bucks County; Pop. 200; Area Code 215; Elev. 300'; was founded in 1725.

•**LAKE ARTHUR**, Lake; 15 m. E of New Castle in Butler County, in W Pennsylvania; formed by a glacial moraine; 10 m. long and 3 m. wide at largest points.

•**LAKE CITY**, Borough; Erie County; Pop. 2,384; Area Code 814; Zip Code 16423; Elev. 721'; NW Pennsylvania. Name changed from North Girard in 1954. Located on Lake Erie shore, 15 m. SE of Erie.

•**LAKE WALLENPAUPACK**, (Ind. "deep, dead water"), Lake; NE Pennsylvania; was formed in 1926 when a public utility company dammed Wallenpaupack Creek. It is the largest body of water wholly within Pennsylvania, covering nine square miles and having an irregular 52-mile shoreline.

•**LAKE WILHELM**, Reservoir, W Pennsylvania; Extends approx. 15 m. long and 1 m. wide in N Mercer County; formed by a damming of Sandy Creek to prevent flooding.

•**LAKE WINOLA** (Ind. "water lily"), Lake; NE Pennsylvania; circled with gaily painted cottages, dreams placidly of the sad fate of *Winola,* daughter of *Chief Capoose,* who loved a white captive. The man eventually escaped, and the languishing girl was drawn to their trysting place by the lakeside; the clear water mirrored a face whiter than the water lilies. One day, while staring raptly into the depths, she saw in the rippling water the reflection of her father in his war paint. From his waist hung several fresh scalps, one of them unmistakably her lover's. *Winola* threw herself at the gruesome reflection and sank into the blue waters.

•**LAMAR**, Village; Clinton County; Pop. 650; Area Code 717; Zip Code 16848; Elev. 817'.

Lamar, formerly Yankeetown, and renamed for an early landowner, *Major James Lamar,* is a trading point for farmers in the Nittany (Ind. "single mountain") Valley. *Major Lamar* was killed at the Battle of Paoli in 1777.

•**LANCASTER**, City; Lancaster County Seat; Pop. 54,632; Area Code 717; Zip Code 176 + zone; 64 m. W of Philadelphia in SE Pennsylvania; near the Susquehanna River.

One of the top 20 farm markets in the U.S. and the most important farm market in Pennsylvania, Lancaster is also the business and financial hub of a wide area.

Here three distinct Lancasters meet: the city of trade and industry, of hustling workers and prosperous business people; the city of Colonial traditions and influence; the trading post for somber-clad Mennonite and Amish farmers, who bring to town their produce, laden in wagons, or come in horse and buggy to shop.

In all sections of the city, on the streets, behind shop counters, are seen the "plain" folks, the men distinguished by black beards and black clothes, the women by small white caps or bonnets.

The first settler of record was an Englishman named *George Gibson,* who in 1721 kept an inn and ran a brewery near what is now Penn Square, although it is believed that Palatine (German) squatters had occupied the site as early as 1709. *Gibson,* too, was a squatter, without patent to his land. In front of his tavern was a large hickory tree, said to have been the center pole of a wigwam where Indian councils met, in 1683, to choose a deputation to confer with *William Penn* at Shackamaxon. Tradition has it that Jesuits had visited these Indians, the Susquehannock, or Conestoga, as early as 1670.

The town that grew up around the inn was called Gibson's Pasture, or Hickory Town. When *James Hamilton* laid out the present town in 1730, a year after it was designated the seat of Lancaster County, 40 or 50 houses in the settlement sheltered a population of about 200. Both county and town were named by *John Wright*, chief magistrate, for his home shire of Lancaster, England.

The town was incorporated as a borough in 1742. Meanwhile, the provincial government had laid out the King's Highway from Penn (then Center) Square to the Chester county line at Compassville, where it connected with another road to Philadelphia. For more than 60 years this was the greatest factor in Lancaster's growth and influence. By 1752 the town was known for the manufacture of farm implements and guns, which found a ready market in the surrounding areas. It early became known as the largest and most attractive inland city in America.

Lancaster played a decisive part in the French and Indian War and, later, in the Revolution. Here *Benjamin Franklin* obtained horses, wagons, and provender for *General Braddock* on his march against the French at Fort Duquesne in 1755. At this time the town was a gunmaking center, its chief product an astoundingly accurate weapon called a rifle, far more deadly than the musket and fowling piece. This so-called "Kentucky rifle," with its long light barrel and small bullets, had its origin in the art and ingenuity of the early Swiss and Germans. One of the masters was *Matthew Roeser*, whose most successful apprentice, *William Henry*, later established a gun factory on the square and served as armorer to the Pennsylvania forces with *Braddock*. So vital was the town's gunmaking industry that in 1776 it was summarily taken over by the Continental Congress. Today only two small gunsmiths remain of this once flourishing business.

Lancaster was the "arsenal of the Colonies"; yet tradition relates that on one occasion during the French and Indian War, when the town feared attack, only 50 rifles could be found in it, and no ammunition. Fears of

207

attack increased after *Braddock's* defeat, and a blockhouse was built. In 1759, 500 men were stationed here. The Indian wars ended locally in December 1763 when the "Paxton Boys," determined to avenge a massacre in the outlands, invaded the Lancaster jail and murdered 14 Conestogas harbored there for safety.

Lancaster rallied early to the cause of independence. Citizens assembled at the courthouse on June 15, 1774, to demand repeal of the bill closing the port of boston; on July 9 they issued a call to resist the oppression of British Parliament, and on December 15, with *George Ross* presiding, they formed a Committee of Observation to enforce a boycott on British goods. On May 1, 1775, they organized military companies called the "Associators," some of whom went to Cambridge, Massachusetts, to join Washington's Continentals.

On the same day that *General Howe's* forces entered Philadelphia, September 27, 1777, the continental congress paused in its westward flight to hold a session here in the courthouse on Penn Square before continuing to York. The Supreme Executive Council of Pennsylvania also fled to Lancaster for safety, holding its first session at the Sign of the Grape Inn on October 1 and remaining in the city nine months. *Thomas Wharton, Jr.*, its president and commander of the forces of the province, died in office while the council was meeting here. *George Washington* was first referred to as "the Father of his Country" in a German pamphlet printed in 1779 by *Francis Bailey* in Lancaster.

With war at an end, normal growth began again. By 1786 there were many iron furnaces and mills in and around the town. when if offered itself as a "suitable place for the United States Capital," the appraisal of assets which accompanied the invitation stated: "We venture to assert that there is no part of the United States which can boast of more wagons and good teams than ourselves...We have five public buildings, including an elegant courthouse fifty by forty-eight feet. There are within the Borough 678 dwellings and about 4,200 souls. Many of the houses are large and elegant, and would in our idea, accomodate Congress and their Suite at this period without inconvenience..." Unfortunately for Lancaster, the invitation was not accepted.

The first macadamized road in the country, the 60-mile Philadelphia and Lancaster Turnpike, was completed in 1794 and improved in 1799 with construction of a nine-arch bridge over the Conestoga. Stagecoaches traveled on regular schedules to Harrisburg, Carlisle, Chambersburg, and Philadelphia. In 1818 Lancaster became a city, with 6,000 to 7,000 inhabitants, including numerous carpenters, shoemakers, blacksmiths, tailors, weavers, and other artisans and tradesmen; there were three printing presses and three breweries. It was a gay city, with about 40 places of entertainment.

During the 1820s a series of clashes occurred as a result of church controversies over the use of the German language, and there were several church schisms. The controversy projected itself into civic affairs, and in 1846 the city council passed a resolution to abandon the English street names, but no further action was taken. Meanwhile, advances in transportation were facilitating trade. In 1829 Conestoga Creek was made navigable to the Susquehanna, but the era of water transportation was short-lived. In March 1834 the Lancaster-Columbia Railroad was completed, and within a year the line had been extended to Mount Joy and Harrisburg.

Following the Civil War, industrial expansion continued apace, and by 1880 Lancaster had more than 200 industrial plants. From 1919 to 1929 industrial wage payments increased 76 percent as against a national average of 11 percent. The city adopted the commission form of government in 1926, and in 1929 celebrated its bicentennial.

Lancaster turns out a variety of products, chief of which are machinery and electronic equipment, fabricated metal products, clothing, furniture and food products. This diversification has allowed the city to continue to thrive despite a crippling recession in the Northeastern U.S. its population is not declining as much as other Pennsylvania cities, and Lancaster households substantially have more buying income than the national average.

Stock raising has also been important to the Lancaster economy since the Union Stockyards were opened in 1896 by the Pennsylvania Railroad as an outlet for the growing industry. A 1980 inventory of cattle numbered 231,500, and of hogs, 253,600 for the county. Dairying and poultry production is also important.

Farmers of grains, tobacco, potatoes, vegetables and fruits bring some of their products into town on certain days of the week to one of four farmers markets. The central market in Penn Square is the largest.

Lancaster has many points of interest, as well as popular factories and stores featuring local "Dutch food specialties such as pretzels and chocolate. Over 2.5 million people visited the Lancaster area in 1979, making it one of the largest tourist areas in Pennsylvania.

POINTS OF INTEREST

CENTRAL MARKET- City market constructed 1889 for town on site where first market was established, 1742.

THE FULTON OPERA HOUSE- Built in 1852, and the oldest theater in continuous use. It was designated as a national historic landmark in 1969.

HANS HERR HOUSE- Built in 1719, the county's oldest house and oldest Mennonite meeting place in U.S.

THE HERITAGE CENTER OF LANCASTER COUNTY-Displays local folk craft.

OLD CITY HALL- Built in 1797, the oldest building on downtown Penn Square; has served as city, county and state buildings at various times.

ROCK FORD PLANTATION- Once the home of Revolutionary War *General Edward Hand.*

SOLDIERS AND SAILORS MONUMENT- Monument with sculpture and statues on plaza in heart of city; 1874.

WHEATLAND- The mansion residence of *President James Buchanan.*

Agriculture - Tobacco and varied farming
Industry/Mfg. - Varied manufacturing, trade
    and services
Higher Education -
    Franklin & Marshall College
    Lancaster Bible College
Daily Newspaper - The New Era, 8 W. King St.
Chamber of Commerce - Box 1558
Community Events -
    Pennsylvania Guild of Craftsmen State Fair,
       Annual, August
    Craft Days, Annual, June
    Dutch Family Festival, Annual, June-August
    Harvest Days, Annual, October

•**LANCASTER COUNTY**, Among the early settlers, *John Wright*, who had come from Chester to the Susquehanna in 1726 and established Wright's Ferry where Columbia now stands, was undoubtedly the leading spirit, and one of the prime movers in the formation of the new county. For twenty years he was a justice of the peace for Chester and Lancaster Counties, and for many years a member of the Provincial Assembly. it was natural and proper that he should name the county of which he was perhaps the foremost citizen. Through his influence it was called Lancaster County from his native shire of Lancaster, now the most populous county in England. At the time of its formation Lancaster County covered a vast territory: the counties of York, Cumberland, Berks, Lebanon, Dauphin, and Northumberland have all been taken from Lancaster County. Virtually all the counties to the west were once a part of Lancaster County.

There were three contestants for the county seat, - Postlethwait's, the Indian Field or "Gibson's Pasture" (the present site of Lancaster), and Wright's Ferry. The last-named place seemed at first to be the strongest competitor: *Robert Barber*, the first sheriff, a neighbor of *John Wright*, felt so sure of this location that he had built, near his residence, a strong wooden building intended for the county jail. *John Postlethwait's* tavern near the Conestoga Creek, in what is now Manor Township, became the temporary seat of justice; and Gibson's Pasture was finally selected as the site of the permanent county seat. When this location was chosen, probably the only building standing in what is now the city of Lancaster was "a log tavern, with the sign of a hickory tree, kept by *George Gibson.* "

•LANDINGVILLE, Borough; Schuylkill County; Pop. 170; Area Code 717; Zip Code 17942; Elev. 500'; E central Pennsylvania.

•LANDISBURG, Borough; Perry County; Pop. 227; Area Code 717; Zip Code 17040; Elev. 600'; S central Pennsylvania.

Until the new county buildings were completed at New Bloomfield in 1827, Landisburg was the temporary seat of justice. The borough was founded in 1793 by *Abraham Landis.*

•**LANDISVILLE**, Village; Lancaster County; Pop. 2,000; Area Code 717; Zip Code 17538; Elev. 403'; German residential town, was laid out in 1808.

•**LANESBORO**, Borough; Susquehanna County; Pop. 465; Area Code 717; Zip Code 18827; Elev. 820'; 3 m. S of New York state line in NE Pennsylvania.

•**LANGHORNE**, Borough; Bucks County; Pop. 1,697; Area Code 215; Zip Code 19047; Elev. 220'; SE Pennsylvania.

Named for early settler *Jeremiah Langhorne*, chief justice of the province in 1739-43. Today it is a suburb of Philadelphia, mainly residential.

•**LANGHORNE MANOR**, Borough; Bucks County; Pop. 1,103; Area Code 215; Zip Code 19047; Elev. 200'; 1 m. N of Langhorne in SE Pennsylvania; also a suburb of Philadelphia.

•**LANDSDALE**, Borough; Montgomery County; Pop. 16,526; Area Code 215; Zip Code 19446 24 m. NW of Philadelphia in a suburban area in SE Pennsylvania.

> *Agriculture* - Varied farming
> *Industry/Mfg.* - Clothing, electronics,
>   medicines, dairy products
> *Daily Newspaper* - The Reporter
> *Chamber of Commerce* - 30 W. Vine Street
> *Community Event* - Festival Sunday, Annual,
>   June

•**LANSDOWNE**, Borough; Delaware County; Pop. 11,891; Area Code 215; Zip Code 19050; Elev. 205'; SE Pennsylvania; was probably named for *Lord Lansdowne*.

•**LANDSFORD**, Borough; Carbon County; Pop. 4,466; Area Code 717; Zip Code 18232; Elev. 1,100'; E Pennsylvania; founded in 1846 and named for *Asa Lansford Foster*, mining engineer, coal operator, and early champion of the public school system.

The town, situated on a plateau which forms the first terrace above the Panther Creek Valley, was originally composed of two distinct settlements, one called Ashton for *Mr. Ashton*, an early resident, and the other known as

Storm Hill because on this hill a violent storm had over-turned the house of *Peter Fisher*. In 1877 Ashton and Storm Hill were consolidated and incorporated under the name of Lansford.

Industry/Mfg. - Clothing
Chamber of Commerce - 6 Coal Street

•**LAPORTE**, Borough; Seat of Sullivan County; Pop. 230; Area Code 717; Zip Code 18626; Elev. 1,966'; NE central Pennsylvania.

Laporte, the smallest county seat in Pennsylvania, was laid out in 1850 by *Michael Meylert*, who named both the township and the village for his friend, *John Laporte*, who was speaker of the General Assembly in 1832, a member of Congress from 1832 to 1836 and the last surveyor-general of Pennsylvania, serving from 1845-1851. *John Laporte* was a descendant of one of the old exiled French families that settled in the region of Asylum, now in Bradford County, at the time of the French Revolution. The surname Laporte signifies "a dweller at the gateway" of a city.

Today, Laporte is a favorite warm-up place for snow skiers using the various slopes nearby.

•**LARKSVILLE**, Borough; Luzerne County; Pop. 4,410; Area Code 717; Elev. 940'; E suburb of Wilkes-Barre in E Pennsylvania; a mining borough originally called Blid-town, was renamed in 1895 in honor of *Peggy Lark*, who had owned the village site and died here at the reputed age of 106.

•**LATROBE**, Borough; Westmoreland County; Pop. 10,799; Area Code 417; Zip Code 15650; Elev. 1,006'; 41 m. SE of Pittsburgh in SW Pennsylvania.

Latrobe, on Loyalhanna Creek, was named for *Benjamin Henry Latrobe, Jr.*, son of the father of architecture in the United States. The land, purchased by *Oliver Barnes*, a friend of *Latrobe*, was laid out in building lots in 1851. The town was incorporated in 1854.

Outside the western limits of Latrobe is St. Vincent College, founded in 1846 by the Benedictine Fathers.

Arnold Palmer, the well known golfer, was born and learned his skills here.

Industry/Mfg. - Boxes, electronics, plastics
Higher Education - St. Vincent College
Daily Newspaper - The Bulletin, 1214 Ligonier
  Street
Chamber of Commerce - 511 Mellon Bank Bldg.

•**LAUGHLINTOWN**, Village; Westmoreland County; Pop. 750; Area Code 412; Zip Code 15655; Elev. 1,274'; at the base of Laurel Hill, was founded in 1797 by *Robert Laughlin.*

•**LAURELDALE**, Borough; Berks County; Pop. 4,047; Area Code 215; Zip Code 19605; Elev. 380'; N suburb of Reading in SE Pennsylvania.

•**LAUREL HILL**, Mountain Ridge; SW Pennsylvania; extends approx. 70 m. from border of Somerset and Fayette Counties NE to Indiana and Cambria Counties. Elev. ranges from 2,500 to 3,000 along this ridge, dotted with ski resorts and coal mining activities.

•**LAUREL RUN**, Borough; Luzerne County; Pop. 715; Area Code 717; Elev. 900'; Suburb of Wilkes-Barre in E Pennsylvania.

•**LAWRENCE COUNTY**, about 1820 the thriving town of New Castle, situated on the boundary line between the counties of Beaver and Mercer, conceived the ambitious scheme of becoming the civil center of a new county. Twenty-nine years later this ambition was realized in the creation of Lawrence County out of parts of Mercer and Beaver. Though this county bears the name of the naval hero, *Captain James Lawrence*, who died on June 6, 1813, at the age of thirty-one, from wounds received in the gallant defense that his frigate *Chesapeake* made against the British frigate *Shannon* off Boston harbor, Lawrence County was named directly for the *Lawrence*, *Perry's* flagship in his victorious battle with the British squadron on Lake Erie.

•**LAWRENCEVILLE**, Borough; Tioga County; Pop. 327; Area Code 717; Zip Code 16929; Elev. 903'; on New York state line in N Pennsylvania.
    Lawrenceville, at the confluence of the Cowanesque and Tioga Rivers was once a lively lumbering town. In

214

1816, 29 years after settlement, the village was christened for *Captain James Lawrence*, naval hero of the War of 1812, who is famous for admonishing his crews, "Don't give up the ship!"

•**LEBANON**, City; Seat of Lebanon County; Pop. 25,711; Area Code 717; Zip Code 17042; Elev. 468'; 80 m. NW of Philadelphia in SE central Pennsylvania.

Lebanon lies on a branch of Quitapahilla (Ind. "spring which flows from among pines") Creek between the South and Blue Mountains. Laid out in 1756 by *George Steitz*, the settlement was first known as Steitztown. Cedar trees growing in the vicinity may have reminded the Moravian settlers of the Biblical "cedars of Lebanon," and thus inspired its name. After the Battle of Trenton many Hessian prisoners were brought here and confined in the old Lutheran, Reformed, and Moravian churches. The community was incorporated as a borough in 1821 and chartered as a city in 1868. Situated in the center of the state's iron ore fields, much of Lebanons's industrial wealth is derived form its extensive iron works and rolling mills. The Bethlehem Steel Company plant stretches almost the whole length of the city.

POINTS OF INTEREST

CORNWALL AND LEBANON RAILROAD STATION- *George Watson Hewitt*, architect. Built in 1885 for *Robert Coleman*, iron ore millionaire. Victorian eclectic.

ST. LUKE'S EPISCOPAL CHURCH- High Victorian Gothic church with tower and gargoyles, built in 1800.

UNION CANAL TUNNEL- Oldest existing transportation tunnel in U.S., built 1825-1825; goes through solid rock 80' below summit of hill.

Agriculture - Fruit and varied farming
Industry/Mfg. - Campers, clothes, chemicals, dairy products
Daily Newspaper - The News, PO Box 600
Chamber of Commerce - PO Box 899

•**LEBANON COUNTY**, formed out of Dauphin and Lancaster in February, 1813, after two decades of agitation, is one of two Pennsylvania counties that have a Biblical name. Most of its territory was comprised in old Lebanon Township, organized in 1729 as one of the seventeen

215

original townships of Lancaster County. The new county took its name from this township.

Just why the name Lebanon was given to the township which eventually became Lebanon County is not positively known. It is reasonable to suppose, however, that the abundance of cedars which clothed the ridge of hills lying between Lancaster and Lebanon Counties may have suggested the "cedars of Lebanon" to the pious German settlers in this region. The Hebrew word *Lebanon*, "white mountain," probably refers to the white chalk cliffs or to the snow on the mountains of Palestine.

At the time of the erection of the new county, Lebanon which was and still is the chief town, became the seat of justice. About 1750 *George Steitz* laid out the village of Lebanon, which long bore the nickname of Steitztown in honor of its founder.

•**LEECHBURG**, Borough; Armstrong County; Pop. 2,682; Area Code 412; Zip Code 15656; Elev. 789' W Pennsylvania.

Leechburg, on the Kiskiminetas, was laid out in 1828 by *David Leech*, a native of Meicer County.

This flourishing industrial community produces steel products, liquors, and materials needed for nuclear energy.

•**LEESPORT**, Borough; Berks County; Pop. 1,258; Area Code 215; Zip Code 19533; Elev. 340'; SE Pennsylvania; name changed from West Leesport in 1950.

•**LEETSDALE**, Borough; Allegheny County; Pop. 1,604; Area Code 412; Zip Code 15056; Elev. 714'; suburb of Pittsburgh in SE Pennsylvania; settled by *William Leet* in 1796.

•**LEHIGH COUNTY**, organized in 1812, took its name from the Lehigh River, which separates it from Northampton, its mother county. The explanation that *Heckewelder* gives of this interesting name is the one generally accepted.

He informs us that the Delawares called this river *Lechauwekink*, "where there are forks," because, at the point where their main trail or throughfare from the lower parts of the Delaware Indian country crossed the river, numerous trails forked off in various directions to the north and the west. The Indian name Lechauwekink was

216

shortened by the early German settlers into *Lecha*, a name still used by their descendants. The form finally adopted by the English-speaking inhabitants was *Lehigh*. The name in its present form is unfortunately a corruption or an abbreviation of the original Indian name and conveys no special meaning.

•**LEHIGH GAP**, Village; Carbon County; Pop. Rural; Area Code 717; Elev. 391'.

Lehigh Gap is named for the spectacular breach in the Blue Mountain through which the Lehigh River flows. The gap, spanned by an iron suspension bridge, was called *Buchka-buchka* (two mountains butting against each other) by the Indians. The Devil's Pulpit, on the mountain side, is a looming pile of rocks fringed with pines. The Appalachian Trail passes nearby.

•**LEHIGH RIVER**, River, E Pennsylvania; flows SW and SE approx. 100 m. from source in S Wayne County through the Pocono Mountains to Lehighton, and then empties into the Delaware River at Easton. Dammed to form the Francis Walter Reservoir in E Luzerne County.

Delaware Indians called this river *Lechauwekink*, or "where the forks are," because numerous trails forked off from the main path in various directions at the river. The Indian name was shortened by German settlers into *Lecha*, and was finally adopted by the English settlers in its present form.

•**LEHIGHTON**, Borough; Carbon County; Pop. 5,826; Area Code 717; Zip Code 18235; Elev. 478'; 26 m. NW of Allentown in E Pennsylvania.

Lehighton is on a plateau overlooking river and valley. This site was settled by Moravians in 1746, but one of the series of Indian raids loosed by *Braddock's* defeat in 1755 engulfed and destroyed Gnadenhutten, as the Moravians called their village. The town was laid out in 1794 by *Colonel Jacob Weiss* and *William Henry*, and took its name from the Lehigh River, on which it is situated. The name Lehighton is a barbarous combination of the Indian form *Lehigh* with the early English *tun* or *ton*, meaning "town." In 1866 it was incorporated as a borough.

Agriculture - Grain, fruit and varied
  farming
Industry/Mfg. - Clothing, soft drinks, dairy
  products
Daily Newspaper - The Times-News, First and
  Iron Streets
Chamber of Commerce - 139 S. First Street

•**LEMOYNE**, Borough; Cumberland County; Pop. 4,178; Area Code 717; Zip Code 17043; Elev. 390'; 2 m. S of Harrisburg in S Pennsylvania.

The site of Fort Washington marks the northernmost point of Confederate invasion during the Civil War. In 1863 *Lee's* advancing army created panic, and embankments were thrown up along the western and southern sides of the eminence known as Washington Heights. Here, on June 29, 1863, Confederate cavalry under *Colonel A.G. Jenkins*, were reconnoitering the southwestern approach to the state capital, exchanged shots with Union defenders. Before and during the Gettysburg engagement all of the Harrisburg district was in a fever of apprehension. A scout risked his life to report the concentration of the two armies at Gettysburg, but even the assurance that the city was in no immediate danger failed to allay the universal feeling of dread..

Today the borough is a comfortable red brick suburb of Harrisburg, along the Susquehanna River.

Chamber of Commerce - PO Box 96

•**LENHARTSVILLE**, Borough; Berks County; Pop. 200; Area Code 215; Zip Code 19534; Elev. 384'; SE Pennsylvania.

Farming community, off Interstate Highway 78. Nearby are the Blue Rocks, a mile-long bed of sandstone boulders formed 550 million years ago. The Pennsylvania Dutch Folk Culture Center is here.

•**LENAPE**, Village; Chester County; Pop. 50; named for the Lenni-Lennape, or Delaware Indians who were "the native, genuine men," or "the first, or original people." The name may also mean "Indians of the same nation."

EAST BRADFORD BOARDING SCHOOL FOR BOYS-
Served as school 1816-1857, providing education for
boys until establishement of area free school.

•**LE RAYSVILLE**, Borough; Bradford County; Pop. 356;
Area Code 717; Zip Code 18829; Elev. 1,423'; N
Pennsylvania.

Le Raysville was named for *Vincent Le Ray de
Chaumont*, son of *James Le Ray de Chaumont*, who
bought 7,600 acres of wilderness land in this region from
Robert Morris, the Revolutionary War patriot and
financier.

•**LEVITT**, Unincorporated village; Bucks County; Pop.
7,200; Area Code 215; Zip Code 19053; Elev. 60'; 25 m. NE
of Philadelphia in SE Pennsylvania.

Levitt is a large residential area. Community was
planned by the *Levitt brothers* in the 1950s, who also
developed a Levittown on Long Island, N.Y. The town
boasts of five shopping centers and a nearby municipal
airport.

•**LEWISBERRY**, Borough; York County; Pop. 309; Area
Code 717; Zip Code 17339; Elev. 422'; 11 m. S of Harrisburg
in S Pennsylvania, near Round Top ski area.

•**LEWISBURG**, Borough; Seat of Union County; Pop.
5,407; Area Code 717; Zip Code 17837; Elev. 461'; 10 m. NW
of Sunbury in central Pennsylvania, on Susquehanna
River.

Laid out in 1785, the settlement was named for *Ludwig (Lewis) Doerr*, storekeeper and early settler. The
town lies in the center of a large dairy and grain farming
region. Furniture and textiles have long been the principal
manufactured products, but paper goods and lumber are
also important today.

Bucknell University, one of the state's leading
educational institutions, occupies a 200-acre campus in the
southern section of the town. The University of Lewisburg
was founded in 1846 as the result of a movement started in
1832 by the Northumberland Baptist Association. The college became coeducational in 1883. It was renamed for
William Bucknell, a long-time trustee.

Agriculture - Grain and varied farming
Industry/Mfg. - Paper goods, animal feed,
    lumber, dairy products
Higher Education - Bucknell University
Chamber of Commerce - 418 Market Street
Community Event - Arts Festival, Annual,
    May

•**LEWIS RUN**, Borough; McKean County; Pop. 677; Area Code 814; Zip Code 16738; Elev. 1,551'; N Pennsylvania.

Lewis Run is on a plain at the southern edge of the Bradford oil field, and bisected by the stream for which it is named. It also lies near the boundaries of the Allegheny National Forest.

South of Lewis Run the route traverses a forest region once included in a tract presented to *Lafayette* for his services during the Revolution.

•**LEWISTOWN**, Borough; Seat of Mifflin County; Pop. 9,830; Area Code 717; Zip Code 17044; Elev. 495'; 45 m. NW of Harrisburg in central Pennsylvania.

Lewistown, near the western end of Lewistown Narrows, was laid out in 1790, 60 years after trappers *James LeTort* and *Jonah Davenport*, paddling upstream in their canoes, saw here the Sahwnee village of Ohesson. *Samuel Edmiston*, who had but recently secured possession of 300 acres of land comprising the site finally chosen for the county seat, laid out the village, which he named Lewistown in honor of his friend, *William Lewis*, an ironmaster, who then owned and operated Hope Furnace, which was situated in old Derry Township, a few miles west of the new town.

POINT OF INTEREST

McCOY HOUSE- Birthplace (1874) of *Frank Ross McCoy* who commanded the "Fighting" 69th Regiment of the Rainbow Division in W.W.I. Musuem.

Agriculture - Varied farming
Industry/Mfg. - Plastics, clothing, soft
    drinks, electronics
Daily Newspaper - The Sentinel, Sixth &
    Summit Drive
Chamber of Commerce - 13 S. Dorcas Street

•**LIBERTY**, Borough; Allegheny County; Pop. 3,112; Area Code 412; Elev. 1,648'; SW Pennsylvania.

Liberty began its history as a blockhouse. In the village center is the site of the Liberty Blockhouse erected as a provision station and refuge in 1792 during construction of Blockhouse or Williamson Road, between Northumberland and Canoe Camp.

In 1792 *Charles Williamson*, land agent for a company that owned more than 1,000,000 acres in Pennsylvania and New York, was assigned to guide a group of settlers from Northumberland, then a frontier outpost, to the company's holdings near the present town of Bath, New York. As for routes, he had a choice between the long and hazardous journey up the North Branch of the Susquehanna and then overland, and the shorter but equally hazardous trek due north through the trackless forests. He chose the latter. On arrival of the immigrants, chiefly German redemptioners, *Williamson* set them to work felling trees and building a road. At intervals they erected blockhouses. The Williamson Road reduced travel distance between Northumberland and Painted Post, New York, by 100 miles, and opened a wide territory to settlement; for 30 years it served as the highway for settlers bound for north central Pennsylvania and southern New York.

Today it is a residential suburb of Pittsburgh.

•**LIBERTY**, Borough; Tioga County; Pop. 220; Area Code 717; Zip Code 16930; N Pennsylvania.

•**LIGONIER**, Borough; Westmoreland County; Pop. 1,917; Area Code 417; Zip Code 15658; Elev. 1,200'; SW Pennsylvania.

Ligonier was laid out in 1816 and named for Fort Ligonier, erected in 1758 by *Colonel Henry Bouquet* and named for a noted English soldier of French extraction, Field Marshal *Sir John Louis Ligonier*, who was raised to an earldom in 1766. In the woods surrounding Fort Ligonier, on October 12, 1758, the French and their Indian allies met defeat in their last battle with the English in the contest for the headwaters of the Ohio. The present town of Ligonier was laid out by *James Ramsey* in 1817.

It is both a summer and winter resort; children enjoy the story book forest nearby. Cattle, dairy and poultry farmers also do their shopping in town.

> *Agriculture* - Dairy, grain, poultry
> *Industry/Mfg.* - Resort area
> *Chamber of Commerce* - 120 E. Main Street
> *Community Events* -
>   Fort Ligonier Days, Annual, October
>   Ligonier Highland Games, Annual, September

•**LILY**, Borough; Cambria County; Pop. 1,462; Area Code 814; Zip Code 15938; Elev. 1,904'; in a hilly area, 20 m. SW of Altoona in SW central Pennsylvania.

•**LINCOLN**, Borough; Allegheny County; Pop. 1,428; Area Code 412; Elev. 1,100'; incorporated in 1958 from Lincoln Township; suburb of Pittsburgh in SW Pennsylvania.

•**LINDEN**, Village; Lycoming County; Pop. 200; Area Code 717; Zip Code 17744; Elev. 534'; village sprang up with the construction of the Pennsylvania Canal in 1832. Its earliest name, Shantytown, applied to the canal laborers' homes.

•**LINESVILLE**, Borough; Area Code 814; Zip Code 16424; Elev. 1,050'; NW Pennsylvania.

The town received its name from *Amos Line*, who was employed as a surveyor by the Pennsylvania Population Company, and who laid out the town about 1825.

The borough lies on the northern shore of the Pymatuning Reservoir, which brings tourists into town during the summer.

> *Agriculture* - Grain, poultry and varied
>   farming
> *Industry/Mfg.* - Machine shop, dairy products.
>   Resort area

•**LITITZ**, Borough; Lancaster County; Pop. 7,590; Area Code 717; Zip Code 17543; Elev. 360'; 8 m. N of Lancaster in SE Pennsylvania.

Lititz was laid out in 1757 by Moravian missionaries from Bethlehem, and named for a barony in Moravia. *John Reuter* and the *Reverend Nathaniel Seidel* formally laid out the town. The property was owned entirely by the Moravian Brethren, and for a long time all its interests were controlled by them. The old English name of Warwick was retained by the township in which Lititz is situated. For more than two centuries, Lititz, one of the most interesting and attractive villages in Pennsylvania, has exercised a religious and educational influence that is out of proportion to its size.

The manufacture of organs and pianos was started here in 1765. One of the first hard pretzel bakeries in the United States was established here in 1861 and for a while Lititz was known as the "Pretzel" town. Pretzels are still baked here, but shoes, chocolate and animal traps have become more important to this Pennsylvania "Dutch" community. *Lancaster Farming* magazine is published here.

POINT OF INTEREST

JULIUS STURGIS PRETZEL HOUSE- First commercial pretzel factory, started by *Julius Sturgis* in 1861; original factory equipment intact. Museum.

Agriculture - Varied farming
Industry/Mfg. - Clothing, footwear, candy, medicine
Community Event - Serendipity Saturday, Annual, June

•**LITTLE MEADOWS**, Borough; Susquehanna County; Pop. 375; Area Code 717; Zip Code 18830; Elev. 1,050'; 1 m. S of New York state line in NE Pennsylvania.

•**LITTLESTOWN**, Borough; Adams County; Pop. 2,870; Area Code 717; Zip Code 17340; Elev. 640'; S Pennsylvania.

Adam Klein, a German immigrant, began this settlement in 1765. Early on, the village was known both as Petersburg and Kleine-staedtel. Finally the latter name stuck, and was translated into "Littlestown."

•**LIVERPOOL**, Borough; Perry County; Pop. 809; Area Code 717; Zip Code 17045; Elev. 400'; S central Pennsylvania; named for the English port city.

Community Event - Apple Butter Boiling, Annual, October

•**LOCK HAVEN**, City; Seat of Clinton County; Pop. 9,617; Area Code 717; Zip Code 17745; Elev. 579'; on the Sus-

223

Loganton

quehanna River in the Bald Eagle Mountains in central Pennsylvania.

Lock Haven was a rude frontier settlement in 1834 and a lumber center in the 1890s. Both Clinton County and its county seat, Lock Haven, owe their existence to *Jeremiah Church*, an enterprising and eccentric speculator from New York. In 1833, *Jerry Church* as he was generally called, bought a large cornfield along the Pennsylvania Canal and the West Branch of the Susquehanna, and in the following year he laid out a town, which was christened Lock Haven because the canal had a *lock* here, and the river furnished an excellent harbor, or *haven*, for rafts. After Lock Haven was started, the proprietor, feeling the need of a stimulus that would make his town grow into a place of some size and consequence, conceived the scheme of making it the seat of a new county, which it did a few years later.

Today fine residences overlook the river, and small brick houses predominate in the rest of the city.

A large Indian mound near Jay and Water Streets was split in two during construction of the Bald Eagle Canal, and human bones and stone implements were unearthed.

POINTS OF INTEREST

HEISEY HOUSE- Built in 1833 as one of the town's earliest taverns. Museum.

WATER STREET DISTRICT- 19th century homes and commercial buildings associated with local lumber industry.

Agriculture - Grain and varied farming
Industry/Mfg. - Electronics, paper, aircraft
Higher Education - Lock Haven State College
Daily Newspaper - The Express, 9-11 W. Main Street
Chamber of Commerce - 138 E. Water Street

•**LOGANTON**, Borough; Clinton County; Pop. 474; Area Code 717; Zip Code 17747; on Fishing Creek, 15 m. SE of Lock Haven.

•**LOGANVILLE**, Borough; Area Code 717; Zip Code 17342; Elev. 782'; 10 m. S of York in S Pennsylvania.

Loganville was laid out about 1820 and named for *Colonel Henry Logan*, York County representative in Congress. The houses here are built on terraces above the main streets.

•**LONDON GROVE**, Village; Chester County; Pop. 75; Area Code 215; Zip Code 19348; named for the London Company, which once owned 17,000 acres of land in the county.

•**LONG BRANCH**, Borough; Washington County; Pop. 610; Area Code 412; Elev. 1,095'; SW Pennsylvania.

•**LORAINE**, Borough; Cambria County; Pop. 989; Area Code 814; Elev. 1,320'; SE suburb of Johnstown in SE central Pennsylvania.

•**LORETTO**, Borough; Cambria County; Pop. 1,395; Area Code 814; Zip Code 15940; Elev. 2,102'; 14 m. SW of Altoona in SW central Pennsylvania.
Loretto was named for the celebrated religious shrine in Italy near the Adriatic Sea by the priest *Demetrius Gallatzin.*

•**LOWER BURRELL**, City; Westmoreland County; Pop. 13,200; Area Code 417; Zip Code 15068; Elev. 760'; N suburb of Pittsburgh in SE Pennsylvania.

Chamber of Commerce - PO Box 2114

•**LOWVILLE**, Village; Erie County; Pop. 200; Area Code 814; Elev. 1,300'; founded in 1822 by *Samuel Low.*

•**LOYALHANNA RIVER**, River; SW Pennsylvania; flows NW approx. 40 m. from source in Westmoreland County to dam at Loyalhanna Lake and out to its mouth at the Conemaugh River in SW Indiana County. Name means "middle river," and comes from an Indian word.

•**LOYALSOCK**, Village; Lycoming County; Pop. 150; the name is a translation of an Indian word meaning "middle creek," which indicates the stream flowing by town.

•**LOYALSOCK CREEK**, Creek, NE central Pennsylvania; flows SW approx. 45 m. from source in NE Sullivan Coun-

225

ty; through a rural mountainous area to its mouth on the Susquehanna River E of Williamsport. name is taken from the Indian word for "middle creek."

•**LUCINDA**, Village; Clarion County; Pop. 250; Area Code 814; Zip Code 16235; Elev. 1,594'; was originally known as Vogelbacher for a native of the German Black Forest who settled here in 1820 when the region was an Indian hunting ground. Ammunition was scarce, and *Vogelbacher* made a practice of stalking deer until he got his quarry in front of a tree. Thus, when his bullet passed through the deer, it lodged in the tree trunk, enabling him to remold the lead and use it again. The Lucinda Furnace was built in 1833.

•**LUMBER CITY**, Borough; Clearfield County; Pop. 117; Area Code 814; Elev. 1,183'; W central Pennsylvania. So named because this has been a timbering center along the West Branch of the Susquehanna River.

•**LUTHERSBURG**, Village; Clearfield County; Pop. 400; Area Code 814; Zip Code 15848; Elev. 1,662'; a crossroads village, founded in 1820 by *Lebbeus Luther* of Massachusetts, was settled by Germans.

•**LUZERNE**, Borough; Luzerne County; Pop. 3,703; Area Code 717; Zip Code 18709; Elev. 570'; N suburb of Wilkes-Barre in E Pennsylvania.

•**LUZERNE COUNTY**, In 1783, when he returned to France, Luzerne Township in Fayette County was named in honor; and three years later, when a new county was erected out of Northumberland, it was called Luzerne County in token of the high regard in which the people of Pennsylvania held this distinguished foreigner. It is said that in the darkest hour of the Revolution, when the Continental army was almost destitute and the government practically without funds, the *Chevalier de la Luzerne* "raised money on his own responsibility to relieve the general distress."

Many years later, the borough of Luzerne, which was once known as Hartseph in honor of *Zachariah Hartseph*, an early settler who lived there a century ago, also took its name from that of the beloved *Chevalier*.

Luzerne was originally a Swiss place name. According to an old etymology the name of the Swiss lake and of the ancient city on its shore was derived from a certain watch-tower which served as a *lucerna*, or light-house, for vessels navigating the lake.

Wilkes-Barre was chosen as the county seat of Luzerne County in preference to old Forty Fort, or Kingston, its only formidable competitor.

•**LYCOMING COUNTY,** When Lycoming County was formed in 1795, it was as large as Connecticut and New Jersey combined, with an area of about 12,000 square miles. Four different names were proposed for the new county - Jefferson, Lycoming, Muncy, and Susquehanna. After much debate the legislature decided to call the great northwestern county Lycoming, after the Lycoming Creek, which had for so many years separated the settled part of Northumberland County from the disputed Indian lands. From the original area of Lycoming County have since been organized, in whole or in part, no less than seventeen counties. *Lycaumick* and *Lycomin* are earlier spellings of the name. Lycoming is corrupted from a Delaware Indian word meaning "sandy or gravelly creek."

•**LYCOMING CREEK,** River, N central Pennsylvania; flows S and SW approx. 33 m. from source in N Lycoming County into W. branch of the Susquehanna River at Williamsport.

For many years, Lycoming Creek separated Northumberland County from disputed Indian lands. The name is a corruption of a Delaware Indian term for "sandy or gravelly creek."

•**LYKENS,** Borough; Dauphin County; Pop. 2,181; Area Code 717; Zip Code 17048; Elev. 677'; SE central Pennsylvania; founded in 1826, one year after the discovery of anthracite at the lower end of Short Mountain. It is named for *Andrew Lycan*, or *Lykens*, who had settled here in 1732.

•**LYONS,** Borough; Berks County; Pop. 579; Area Code 215; Elev. 460'; 15 m. NE of Reading in SE Pennsylvania; important as a rail station.

M

•**MACUNGIE**, Borough; Lehigh County; Pop. 1,899; Area Code 215; Zip Code 18062; Elev. 380'; 5 m. SW of Allentown on Swope Creek, in E Pennsylvania; Indian name means "feeding place of the bears."

Community Event - Das Awkscht Fescht, Annual, August or October

•**MADISON**, Borough; Westmoreland County; Pop. 531; Area Code 417; Zip Code 15663; Elev. 1,130'; E suburb of Pittsburgh in SW Pennsylvania.

•**MAHAFFEY**, Borough; Clearfield County; Pop. 513; Area Code 814; Zip Code 15757; Elev. 1,323'; on west branch of the Susquehanna River in W central Pennsylvania.

•**MAHANOY CITY**, Borough; Schuylkill County; Pop. 6,167; Area Code 717; Zip Code 17948; Elev. 1,256'; E central Pennsylvania.

One of the larger coal towns in the county, Mahanoy City became a post office in 1839. The name Mahanoy, which is usually pronounced with a primary accent on the first syllable, and a secondary accent on the last, was derived from the language of the Delawares, the word mahoni meaning a "lick", a term used in pioneer days to denote saline deposits where deer congregate.

Chamber of Commerce - PO Box 248

•**MAHATANGO MOUNTAIN**, Mountain Ridge; E central Pennsylvania; considered part of the Appalachian Mountains; extends approx. 50 m. from Mahantango Creek's source in Schuylkill County, SW to the creek's source at the Susquehanna River. Coal mining important.

•**MAHONING**, Village; Armstrong County; Pop. 60; Area Code 412; name is a Delaware Indian translation for "where there is a salt lick," or saline deposit.

•**MAHONING CREEK**, River; NE Ohio and W Pennsylvania; flows NE and SE approx. 100 m. from source in Columbiana County, Ohio through Youngstown, and into Beaver County, Pennsylvania where it joins the Shenango River SW of New Castle.

The Delaware Indians called this creek *Mahonink*, or "where there is a salt lick."

•**MAIDEN CREEK**, Village; Berks County; Area Code 215; Zip Code 19606; Elev. 352'.

Formerly called Halfway House for an early inn, Maiden Creek took its present name from a stream one mile to the north. In the village is a Friend's meetinghouse built in 1759. This one-and-a-half-story field stone structure originally stood on what is now the bed of Lake Ontelaunee and was moved to its present site in 1934. It has not been used for many years.

•**MALVERN**, Borough; Chester County; Pop. 2,999; Area Code 215; Zip Code 19355; Elev. 550'; NW suburb of Philadelphia near Paoli, in SE Pennsylvania; residential area.

•**MANCHESTER**, Borough; York County; Pop. 2,027; Area Code 717; Zip Code 17345; Elev. 500'; S Pennsylvania.

Named for the large industrial city in England, Manchester in Pennsylvania has a few industries of its own.

> *Agriculture* - Varied farming
> *Industry/Mfg.* - Lumber, animal feed, wood
>   products

•**MANHEIM**, Borough; Lancaster County; Pop. 5,015; Area Code 717; Zip Code 17545; Elev. 339'; SE Pennsylvania.

Manheim was founded by *Baron Heinrich Wilhelm Stiegel*, it was the center of his glassmaking activities. Glassmaking was one of the country's earliest enterprises, but to *Stiegel* belongs the distinction of making the first fine flint glassware. Four colors predominated: white or clear glass, purple, blue, and green. The blues were the most common and still show remarkable depth, variety, and clearness of coloring. Much of the clear ware was engraved. Enameling in glass was first successfully tried here after *Stiegel* had imported skilled artisans. Specimens of Stiegel glass are in the Philadelphia Museum of Art and in the Metropolitan Museum of Art, New York.

In 1770 *Stiegel* owned all of Manheim. Scheming associates had as much to do with his downfall as did his own prodigality. In 1774 he was thrown into debtor's prison. His valuable Elizabeth Furnace and other properties fell into the hands of *Robert Coleman*, who was making the first of his inroads upon the area. Subsequently *Stiegel* became foreman at the Elizabeth Furnace. He held minor partnership rights, but his creditors were relentless, and he died penniless.

Today, Manheim is a favorite stop for travelers interested in "Pennsylvania Dutch" culture. It is a mainly residential and commercial town.

> *Chamber of Commerce* - 32 N. Main St.
> *Community Event* - Red Rose Festival, Annual, June

•**MANNS CHOICE**, Borough; Bedford County; Pop. 286; Area Code 814; Zip Code 15550; 8 m. SW of Bedford in S Pennsylvania; nearby are the Wonderland Caverns.

•**MANOR**, Borough; Westmoreland County; Pop. 2,235; Area Code 417; Zip Code 15665; Elev. 1,000'; E suburb of Pittsburgh in SW Pennsylvania; named for one of the manors owned by the *Penn* family, which once stood here.

•**MANORVILLE**, Borough; Armstrong County; Pop. 409; Area Code 412; Zip Code 16238; W Pennsylvania; named for Kittaning or Appleby Manor, one of the 40 estates in Pennsylvania belonging to the *Penn* family.

•**MANSFIELD**, Borough; Tioga County; Pop. 3,322; Area Code 717; Zip Code 16933; Elev. 1,174'; 30 m. SW of Elmira, N.Y. in N Pennsylvania; named in 1824 for *Asa Mann*, an early settler.

Today the town revolves around the activities of Mansfield State College.

Agriculture - Poultry, fruit and varied
    farming
Industry/Mfg. - Machine shop, coal, maple
    sugar, dairy products
Higher Education - Mansfield State College
Chamber of Commerce - RD 1, Box 228

•**MAPLETON**, Borough; Huntingdon County; Pop. 591; Area Code 717; Zip Code 17052; Elev. 600'; S central Pennsylvania.

This town was originally a "depot" of the Pennsylvania Railroad when it was first established. maple trees abounded here at the time; hence the name. It did not begin to grow until the Civil War.

•**MARCUS HOOK**, Borough; Delaware County; Pop. 2,638; Area Code 215; Zip Code 19061; Elev. 21'; 2 m. SW of Chester on a "hook" of land into the Delaware River.

The site of Marcus Hook was settled by Swedes in the 1640s, but its name is a corruption of the Dutch "Marreties' Hoeck." No one knows who "Marretie" was, but "Hoeck" is Dutch for a corner or point of land.

Shipbuilding was an important early industry. First port of call for Philadelphia-bound ships, it became, in the late seventeenth and early eighteenth centuries, the haunt of *Blackbeard* and other notorious pirates. Discord Lane earned its name because of their riotous brawls.

Industry/Mfg. - Oil, rugs, shipbuilding

•**MARIANNA**, Borough; Washington County; Pop. 907; Area Code 412; Zip Code 15345; Elev. 1,100';on Ten Mile Creek in SW Pennsylvania.

•**MARIENVILLE**, Village; Forest County; Pop. 900; Elev. 1,719'; occupying one of the high points of Big Level Ridge, was settled in 1833 by *Cyrus Blood* and named for his daughter. The town is set within the Allegheny National Forest preserves.

•**MARIETTA**, Borough; Lancaster County; Pop. 2,740; Area Code 717; Zip Code 17547; Elev. 261'; 22 m. SE of Har-

231

risburg on Susquehanna River in SE Pennsylvania.

Marietta is the center of an area settled by Scotch-Irish pioneers. Early travelers recognized the cabin of a Scotch-Irish settler by its two chimneys, one at each end, and that of the German by its one central chimney. The town was originally two distinct settlements, - New Haven, laid out by *David Cook* in 1803, and Waterford, laid out at "Anderson's Ferry," by *James Anderson* in 1804. In 1812 the two villages were incorporated under one charter as Marietta, a name said to have been compounded of *Mary* and *Etta*, the first names of *Mrs. Cook* and *Mrs. Anderson*, the wives of the two founders.

Antiques dealing is a major business, and several furniture and antique art restorers work here.

> *Industry/Mfg.* - Lumber, medicine, building
> materials, furniture

•**MARION CENTER**, Borough; Indiana County; Pop. 494; Area Code 412; Zip Code 15759; Elev. 1,280'; W central Pennsylvania; crossroads farm trading center.

•**MARION HEIGHTS**, Borough; Northumberland County; Pop. 921; Area Code 717; Zip Code 17832; Elev. 1,360'; E central Pennsylvania; rural.

•**MARKLESBURG**, Borough; Huntingdon County; Pop. 188; Area Code 717; Elev. 900'; S central Pennsylvania; rural.

•**MARKLEYSBURG**, Borough; Fayette County; Pop. 356; Area Code 412; Zip Code 15459; Elev. 1,985'; 1 m. N of Maryland state line in SW Pennsylvania; rural.

•**MARS**, Borough; Butler County; Pop. 1,803; Area Code 412; Zip Code 16046; Elev. 1,031'; NW suburb of Pittsburg in W Pennsylvania.

•**MARSHALL'S CREEK**, Village & Creek; Monroe County; Pop. 50; Area Code 717; Zip Code 18335; Elev. 470'; named for *Edward Marshall*, participant in the Walking Purchase.

•**MARSHALLTON**, Village; Northumberland County; Pop. 1,802; Area Code 717; Elev. 397'; named for *Humphry Marshal* (1722-1801), botanist and stone mason, who in 1785 published a noteworthy botanical essay, *Arbustrum Americanum*. *Marshall*, a cousin of *John Bartram*, the world-famous botanist, built a house and started a garden here in 1773.

POINTS OF INTEREST

BRADFORD FRIENDS MEETINGHOUSE- Built 1765; unusual 4-room meetinghouse plan, typical of early southeastern Pennsylvania meetinghouse architecture.
HUMPHRY MARSHALL HOUSE- Built in 1773 by *Humphry Marshal*, noted American botanist, amateur astronomer and accomplished stonemason.

•**MARTHA FURNACE**, Village; Centre County; Pop. (Rural); named for *Martha* daughter of *Roland Curtin*, one of the owners of the furnace which was started here about 1830, and which formed the nucleus of the village.

•**MARTINSBURG**, Borough; Blair County; Pop. 2,231; Area Code 814; Zip Code 16662; Elev. 1,407'; 20 m. S of Altoona in S central Pennsylvania.

Feed mills here supply large dairy farms nearby.

Agriculture - Grain, fruit and varied farming
Industry/Mfg. - quarrying, animal feed, clothing, dairy products

•**MARYSVILLE**, Borough; Perry County; Pop. 2,452; Area Code 717; Zip Code 17053; Elev.460'; N of Harrisburg, on Susquehanna River in S central Pennsylvania.

•**MASONTOWN**, Borough; Fayette County; Pop. 4,909; Area Code 412; Zip Code 15461; Elev. 1,050'; SW Pennsylvania.

John Mason laid out this town in 1798. Settlers subsequently named it for him. This borough on the Monongahela River has long been an important lumber milling center, and oil refining as well as coal mining have helped build the economy here.

Agriculture - Grain, poultry
Industry/Mfg. - Oil, gas, lumber, dairy
products

•**MASTHOPE**, Village; Pike County; Pop. 500; Area Code 717; name is an anglicization of an Indian word meaning "glass beads." Today it is a ski resort.

•**MATAMORAS**, Borough; Pike County; Pop. 2,111; Area Code 717; Zip Code 18336; Elev. 868'; on the Delaware River, near New York and New Jersey state lines in NE Pennsylvania.

Matamoras, a shaded resort town, roosts on a tableland above the river. The Old Stone Fort, a story and a half structure, was built about 1740 by *Simon Westfael*, one of the earliest Dutch settlers.

•**MAYFIELD**, Borough; Lackawanna County; Pop. 1,812; Area Code 717; Zip Code 18433; Elev. 952'; NE Pennsylvania; was developed prior to 1840 by *John Gibson*, who sold out in 1874 to the Delaware and Hudson Canal Company.

Today it is a coal mining center although this business has declined in recent years.

•**MAYTOWN**, Village; Lancaster County; Pop. 700; Area Code 717; Zip Code 17550; Elev. 402'; is an agricultural village laid out in 1760 near the Susquehanna River.

•**MCADOO**, Borough; Schuylkill County; Pop. 2,940; Area Code 717; Zip Code 18237; Elev. 1,836'; E central Pennsylvania; was founded in 1880 and later named by postal authorities for *William Gibbs McAdoo*. There are collieries in the vicinity, and the predominantly Polish and Lithuanian population finds some additional employment in a paper-box factory and two textile mills.

•**MCCLINTOCK** (alt. McClintockville), Village, Venango County; Pop. 40; Elev. 1,081'.

In McClintock were oil springs well known to the Seneca Indians. Prior to 1860, enterprising settlers soaked blankets in pools of oil water, permitted the water to evaporate, and squeezed out the residue, which they peddled at 25 cents a gill as medicine of rare value.

•**MCCLURE**, Borough; Snyder County; Pop. 1,024; Area Code 717; Zip Code 17841; Elev. 700'; Central Pennsylvania; was founded in 1867 and named for *Alexander Kelley McClure* (1828-1909), journalist, politician, and author. McClure was one of the founders of the Republican Party. The town was formerly called Stricktown for a noted Indian fighter.

> *Community Event* - McClure Bean Soup Festival,
> Annual, September-October

•**MCCONNELLSBURG**, Borough; Seat of Fulton County; Pop. 1,178; Area Code 814; Zip Code 17233; Elev. 955'; 22 m. W of Chamberburg in S Pennsylvania.

McConnellsburg became an important stopping place for overland travelers on the great highway connecting eastern Pennsylvania with the more recent settlements in the region of Pittsburgh.

> *Argriculture* - Varied farming
> *Industry/Mfg.* - Prefab. housing, grain
> milling, clothing
> *Community Event* - Fulton Fall Folk Festival,
> Annual, October

•**MCDONALD**, Borough; Allegheny and Washington Counties; Pop. 2,772; Area Code 412; Zip Code 15057; Elev. 1,020'; 18 m. W of Pittsburgh in SW Pennsylvania.

Coal mining and refining is important here, and there are oil wells in the vicinity.

McDonald was laid out in 1781, and took its name from old Fort McDonald, which was built during the Revolutionary War on the land of *John McDonald*, who settled here in 1775. The western part of the town has grown up on the old McDonald farm.

> *Agriculture* - Varied farming
> *Industry/Mfg.* - Oil, coal, dairy products

•**MCEWENSVILLE**, Borough; Northumberland County; Pop. 247; Area Code 717; Zip Code 17749; Elev. 511'; near the Susquehanna River in E central Pennsylvania; historic Warrior Run Church is nearby as well.

•**MCGEES MILLS**, Village; Clearfield County; Pop. 150; Area Code 814; Zip Code 15755; Elev. 1,307'; a crossroads cluster, was founded in 1826 by the *Reverend James McGee.*

The Covered Bridge, built in 1860, is the only structure of its type remaining along the 200-mile course of the Susquehanna's West Branch.

•**MCKEAN**, Borough; Erie County; Pop. 465; Area Code 814; Zip Code 16426; Elev. 1,040'; 10 m. S of Erie in NW central Pennsylvania; named for *Thomas McKean*, early governor of Pennsylvania.

•**MCKEAN COUNTY**, on March 26, 1804, were formed six new counties, one of which was called McKean County for *Thomas McKean*, then governor of Pennsylvania. McKean was thrice elected governor, beginning his administration in 1799 at the age of sixty-five after serving twenty-two years as chief justice of Pennsylvania. He was the only signer of the Declaration of Independence who sat in the Continental Congress from its beginning until the close of the Revolution, a period of more than eight years. Of Irish parentage, he was handicapped in his administrative work by a somewhat arbitrary manner, an irascible temper, and an occasional outburst of violent language, which raised a spirit of antagonism against him in the legislature. His name should be held in grateful remembrance because he was instrumental in introducing into the Constitution of 1790 a provision "for the establishment of schools throughout the state in such a manner that the poor may be taught gratis."

The name McKean is probably a variant of McKeon or McKeown, "son of John," the Erse form for *John* being *Eoin.* McKean, in Erie County, and McKeansburg, in Schuylkill County, were also named for *Governor McKean.*

•**MCKEE HALF FALLS**, Village; Snyder County; Pop. 35; Area Code 717; Zip Code 17864.

Named for *Thomas McKee*, an Indian trader, who settled at this point on the Susquehanna River in 1752, on a large tract of land extending above and below "the half falls."

•**MCKEESPORT**, City; Allegheny County; Pop. 31,012; Area Code 412; Zip Code 151 + zone; Elev. 750'; 14 m. SE of Pittsburgh in SW Pennsylvania.

McKeesport is at the junction of the Youghiogheny and Monongahea Rivers. *David McKee*, a north country Irishman who settled here in 1755, acquired title to 844 acres and in 1755 obtained ferry privileges from Colonial authorities. *John McKee*, son of *David*, inherited his father's property, and added much to it by numerous purchases. He possessed shrewd business ability, and soon became one of the largest individual landowners in Allegheny County. Judged by the standards of that day, he was a man of wealth. In 1793 he became surety for his brother-in-law, *Judge John Redick*, who was under contract to furnish supplies for the famous Indian expedition of *General Wayne*. *John Redick* failed to fulfill his contract, and his bondsman was required to meet obligations aggregating many thousands of dollars. *McKee's* property was then sold at a great sacrifice by the United States marshal for about $30,000. After losing all this, *John McKee* tried to regain it by laying out a town on the Youghiogheny River, which he named in honor of his father. Mckeesport was a center of conflict during the Whiskey Rebellion in 1794.

A town was laid out in 1795, but it was not until 35 years later, with the opening of coal mines in the vicinity, that it began to grow. It became a borough in 1842.

> *Industry/Mfg.* - Steel products, coal, auto
>   parts
> *Daily Newspaper* - The News, 401-09 Walnut
>   Street
> *Chamber of Commerce* - 307 Union Bank Bldg.

•**MCKEES ROCKS**, Borough; Allegheny County; Pop. 8,742; Area Code 412; Zip Code 15136; Elev. 725'; on Ohio River, 5 m. NW of Pittsburgh in SW Pennsylvania.

McKees Rocks, at the mouth of Chartiers Creek, is an industrial suburb of Pittsburgh. Settled about 1764, it was named for massive rock formations along the Ohio River, and for *Alexander McKee*, an early settler. *Peter Chartiers*, half-breed trader who in 1743 established a post along the stream that bears his name, was the earliest

237

known resident. Ten years later *Christopher Gist*, Ohio Land Company agent, erected a fort at the mouth of the creek.

In 1770, *Washington*, in the journal of his visit to this region, mentions the fact that he "dined with *Mr. Magee*, two miles below the city." This *Mr. Magee* has been identified with *Alexander McKee*, who was a deputy Indian agent at Pittsburgh until 1776. Because of his intimacy with the Tory, *Dr. John Connolly*, who was the active agent of *Lord Dunmore* of Virginia, *Alexander McKee* was suspected of treason, but before he could be brought to justice, he and the infamous *Simon Girty* escaped from Pittsburgh.

McKees Rocks was incorporated as a borough in 1892.

Industry/Mfg. - Shipbuilding, plastics, electronics

•**MCSHERRYSTOWN**, Borough; Adams County; Pop. 2,764; Area Code 717; Zip Code 17344; Elev. 571'; S Pennsylvania; named for an Irish settler, *Patrick McSherry*, who came here in 1765.

•**MCVEYTOWN**, Borough; Mifflin County; Pop. 447; Area Code 717; Zip Code 17051; Elev. 522'; Central Pennsylvania.

McVeytown, formerly Waynesburg, was incorporated as a borough in 1833 and in that capacity assumed "the invaluable perogative is issuing shin-plasters," which were widely circulated during the hard times of 1841-2.

•**MEADVILLE**, City; Seat of Crawford County; Pop. 15,544; Area Code 814; Zip Code 16335; Elev. 1,078'; 87 m. N of Pittsburgh in NW Pennsylvania, on French Creek.

Meadville is in the western foothills of the Alleghenies, was settled in 1788 by *David Mead*, his brothers, and other pioneers from Sunburgh, who made the first white settlement in Northwestern Pennsylvania. They cut a path through the wilderness that was long known as "Mead's Trail," through Clearfield, Jefferson, and to Crawford County to the site of meadville. Home of the first successful slide fastener factory.

POINT OF INTEREST

BALDWIN-REYNOLDS HOUSE- Built in 1843, home of state political leader *Henry Baldwin* ; later belonged to *William Reynolds*, first mayor of Meadville. Museum.

Agriculture - Varied farming
Industry/Mfg. - Iron goods, cloth, machine
    shop, dairy products
Higher Education - Allegheny College
Daily Newspaper - The Tribune, 947 Federal
    Court
Chamber of Commerce - 300 Arch Street, PO
    Box 455

•**MECHANICSBURG**, Borough; Cumberland County; Pop. 9,487; Area Code 717; Zip Code 17055; Elev. 460'; W suburb of Harrisburg in S Pennsylvania.

Named for the large number of mechanics who worked in the foundries and machine shops here.

Agriculture - Varied farming
Industry/Mfg. - Steel products, grain mill-
    ing, auto parts
Chamber of Commerce - Strawberry & Railroad
    Avenue

•**MECHANICSVILLE**, Borough; Schuylkill County; Pop. 519; Area Code 717; Zip Code 18934; Elev. 440'; E central Pennsylvania; named for the number of mechanics who lived here at the time the town was founded.

•**MEDIA**, Borough; Seat of Delaware County; Pop. 6,119; Area Code 215; Zip Code 190 + zone; Elev. 210'; 5 m. NE of Chester in SE Pennsylvania.

Media is the approximate center of Delaware County, hence its name. Quakers early settled in this vicinity, but Media was not officially laid out until 1848 when it was selected as the county seat.

Although many residents commute to work in Philadelphia or Chester, others work in county and other government offices, or in various local industries.

Agriculture - Dairy, fruit and varied
    farming
Industry/Mfg. - Cement products, food
    packing
Higher Education - Delaware County Com-
    munity College

239

Chamber of Commerce - R.D. 6, Box 6765
Community Events -
  Greek Festival, Annual, July
  Indian Heritage Days, Annual, July

•**MERCER COUNTY**, Mercer County, formed from Allegheny in 1800, was named in honor of *General Hugh Mercer*, who was born in Aberdeen, Scotland, in 1720, was educated as a physician at the University of Aberdeen, and served as a surgeon in the army of the Pretender, *Prince Charles Edward*, at the battle of Culloden in 1746. Two years later he emigrated to Pennsylvania and began the practice of medicine in what is now Franklin County, near Mercersburg, which was named for him. He took an active part in the French and Indian War, and was with Washington in the illfated campaign of *General Braddock*. He also served as lieutenant-colonel in *General Forbes's* expedition, and was later commandant of Fort Pitt.

When the Revolutionary struggle began, *Doctor Mercer* was practicing medicine at Fredericksburg, Virginia. He was made a brigadier-general on Washington's recommendation, and in 1777 fought at Trenton and at Princeton, where he fell mortally wounded. His funeral in Philadelphia is said to have been attended by 30,000 people.

•**MERCERSBURG**, Borough; Franklin County; Pop. 1,617; Area Code 717; Zip Code 17236; Elev. 590'; 21 M. NW of Hagerstown, Maryland in S Pennsylvania; was settled in 1729 or 1730, and named for *General Hugh Mercer*, soldier and physician in the Revolution.

The respected Mercersburg Academy is located here. Besides various manufacturing and agricultural pursuits, the town is known for its goldfish hatchery.

POINT OF INTEREST

LANE HOUSE- Birthplace of *Harriet Lane Johnstone*, White House hostess for her uncle, *James Buchanan* from 1857-1861.

Agriculture - Varied farming
Industry/Mfg. - Clothing, lumber, dairy
  products, quarrying
Chamber of Commerce - 113 S. Main Street,
  PO Box 161

•**MESHOPPEN**, Borough; Wyoming County; Pop. 571; Area Code 717; Zip Code 18630; Elev. 1,240'; NE Pennsylvania.

Mesoppen, settled in 1742, was a stagecoach stop until the railroad arrived about 1870; the village is situated between Meshoppen Creek and the Susquehanna. The name is Indian for "glass beads," and comes from a description of the creek.

•**MEYERSDALE**, Borough; Somerset County; Pop. 2,581; Area Code 814; Zip Code 15552; Elev. 2,054'; 18 m. NW of Cumberland, Maryland in S Pennsylvania; was laid out in a valley in 1844 and named for *Peter Meyers*, an early settler who converted his farm into building lots.

> *Agriculture* - Grain, poultry and varied farming
> *Industry/Mfg.* - Clothing, concrete, coal, lumber
> *Community Event* - Pennsylvania Maple Festival Annual, March

•**MIDDLEBURG**, Borough; Seat of Snyder County; Pop. 1,357; Area Code 717; Zip Code 17842; Elev. 515'; Central Pennsylvania; laid out in 1800 by *John Swineford*, it was, for a time, named Swinefordstown.

About 1825, because of its location near Middle Creek, its name was changed. The town today shows much Pennsylvania Dutch influence with its potato chip factory and dress making business.

> *Agriculture* - Fruit and varied farming
> *Industry/Mfg.* - Campers, dairy products

•**MIDDLEPORT**, Borough; Schuylkill County; Pop. 577; Area Code 717; Zip Code 17953; Elev. 721' E central Pennsylvania; was named for its position midway between Pottsville and Tamaqua on the Schuylkill Canal; was founded in 1821.

•**MIDDLETOWN**, Borough; Dauphin County; Pop. 10,122; Area Code 717; Zip Code 17057; Elev. 355'; 8 m. SE of Harrisburg in SE central Pennsylvania, on Susquehanna River.

Middletown, halfway between Lancaster and Carlisle, was founded in 1755. Stubbs Furnace, formerly in the southwestern end of town, is credited with being one of the first steel producers in the United States. It was so named because it was between the old towns of Lancaster and Carlisle, and served as a half-way station for Colonial travelers.

William Penn favored this site, once occupied by an Indian village, for his cherished project of an inland city, but never pushed his plans to completion. Middletown's position at the confluence of Swatara Creek and the Susquehanna River gave it early important in river activities. During the Revolutionary War it was a boatbuilding center. In 1784 *George Washington* outlined to *Governor Harrison* of Virginia a proposed system of canal and river transportation with the town as the center. Later the Pennsylvania Canal and the Union Canal had their junction here and the settlement boomed.

Middletown has accepted the twentieth century readily; a nuclear generating plant supplies the entire area from here. Site of Three Mile Island Nuclear power station, which broke down in March 1979, causing a small leakage of radiation. A study of the area later indicated that the core came within a half hour of major fuel melting, which would have been extremely dangerous.

POINT OF INTEREST

ST. PETER'S KIERCH- Elegant rural example of Georgian design, built in 1767. Lutheran services were held here until 1879.

Industry/Mfg. - Campers, book manufacturing, electronics
Higher Education - Pennsylvania State University
Chamber of Commerce - 25 W. Brown Street
Community Event - Early American Arts and Crafts Fair, Annual, June

•**MIDLAND**, Borough; Beaver County; Pop. 4,310; Area Code 412; Zip Code 15059; Elev. 750'; 7 m. E of east Liverpool, Ohio in W Pennsylvania.

Midland, on the north bank of the Ohio River, is a smoky steel-producing center named for the Midland Steel Company. White men first settled on this early Indian camping ground in the second decade of the nineteenth century. Steel mills and iron foundries were established in 1905. The name was suggested by *J. Ramsey Speer*, vice-president of the steel company, as an appropriate designation both for the new business corporation and for its new industrial town, because of their location midway between Pittsburgh and the Shenango Valley district.

> *Industry/Mfg.* - Steel and related machinery
> *Chamber of Commerce* - PO Box 506

•**MIDWAY**, Borough; Washington County; Pop. 1,187; Area Code 412; Zip Code 15060; Elev. 1,120'; SW Pennsylvania; so named because it is located between Pittsburgh and Steubenville, Ohio.

•**MIFFLIN**, Borough; Juniata County; Pop. 648; Area Code 717; Zip Code 17058; Elev. 500'; S central Pennsylvania; named for *Thomas Mifflin*, who was a Pennsylvania governor in the 1790s.

•**MIFFLIN COUNTY**, in 1789 a new county was taken from Cumberland and Northumberland, and named Mifflin in honor of *General Thomas Mifflin*, then governor of Pennsylvania. To this staunch patriot belongs the distinction of having served as chief executive of the state longer than any other person. He was governor more than eleven years, - from November 5, 1788, to December 17, 1799. He served two years as president of the Supreme Executive Council under the Constitution of 1776; and he was thrice elected governor under the Constitution of 1790.

Thomas Mifflin was born and reared in a prosperous Philadelphia Quaker family, was well educated, and had traveled extensively in Europe. He was an eloquent speaker, a member of the Assembly, president of the Continental Congress at the close of the war, a major-general and Quartermaster-General of the Revolutionary army, one of the framers of the Federal Constitution, and president of the convention that drew up the State Constitution of 1790.

Mifflinville, in Mifflin Township, Columbia County, and Mifflinburg, in Union County, which was long called Youngmanstown for *Elias Youngman (or Jungmann)*, who laid it out in 1783, were both named for *Governor Mifflin*.

243

•**MIFFLINBURG**, Borough; Union County; Pop. 3,151; Area Code 717; Zip Code 17844; Elev. 567'; 20 m. NW of Sunbury in central Pennsylvania.

Mifflinburg, is in the heart of Buffalo Valley in the Seven Mountains region. The name honors *Thomas Mifflin*, first governor of the Commonwealth under the 1790 constitution.

The town was originally called Youngmanstown for *Elias Youngman (or Jungman)*, who laid it out in 1793.

Agriculture - Grain, fruit and varied
    farming
Industry/Mfg. - Cloth, wood products, dairy
    products

•**MIFFLINTOWN**, Borough; Seat of Juniata County; Pop. 783; Area Code 717; Zip Code 17059; Elev. 500'; 35 m. NW of Harrisburg in S central Pennsylvania, on Juniata River.

Mifflintown was laid out in 1791 by *John Harris, Jr.*, on a high plateau overlooking the river, and named for *Thomas Mifflin*, first post-Revolutionary governor of Pennsylvania. Early residents were "bitterly disappointed" when Lewistown was chosen as the seat of Mifflin County, being appeased only when Mifflintown became the seat of newly formed Juniata County in 1831.

A creamery in town takes in the dairy products from the large farms in the area. Quarrying of limestone, brick and shale is also important.

POINT OF INTEREST

TUSCARORA ACADEMY- Church building, built in 1816, later became school building for Tuscarora Academy, first secondary school in the county. Museum.

Agriculture - Varied farming
Industry/Mfg. - Clothing, dairy products,
    quarrying

•**MILESBURG**, Borough; Centre County; Pop. 1,309; Area Code 814; Zip Code 16853; Elev. 700'; Central Pennsylvania; was founded in 1793 by *General Samuel Miles*, Indian fighter, patriot, landowner, iron manufacturer, and onetime mayor of Philadelphia (1790). *Chief Bald Eagle*, whose village occupied this site, was killed by *Cap-

tain Samuel Brady. It is asserted that Brady placed the Indian's body in a canoe, stuck a piece of "johnnycake" between the lips as a gesture of derision and let the craft drift downstream. At the place where it grounded Bald Eagle was buried.

•**MILFORD**, Borough; Seat of Pike County; Pop. 1,143; Area Code 717; Zip Code 18337; Elev. 500'; on Delaware River in NE Pennsylvania.

Milford was laid out about 1796 by *John Biddis*, a Philadelphian of Welsh descent. Before the Revolution the *Wells brothers* had come into this region from Connecticut, built a saw-mill and a grist-mill, and started a ferry across the Delaware River near the mouth of Saw Creek. There is a Milford Haven in Pembrokeshire, Wales, and a Milford in Connecticut; and some have guessed that the name of Milford may have been borrowed from one of these two places. If the name was really borrowed, it seems likely that the founder, *John Biddis*, appropriated the name of the Welsh town.

There is a strong probability, however, that the name of Milford and Milford Township originated independently from an old ford which crossed Saw Creek near its mouth, where the *Wells brothers* had built their mill, and that the juxtaposition of the mill and the ford suggested the name milford.

Today the town is a summer resort of small cottages. Nearby is the Masthope snowskiing area.

> *Industry/Mfg.* - Resort area
> *Chamber of Commerce* - 112 Blackberry Alley
> *Community Event* - Summer Opera Festival,
>   Annual, August

•**MILLBOURNE**, Borough; Delaware County; Pop. 652; Area Code 215; Elev. 100'; SW suburb of Philadelphia in SE Pennsylvania.

•**MILL CREEK**, Borough; Huntingdon County; Pop. 367; Area Code 717; Zip Code 17060; Elev. 603'; S central Pennsylvania.

Mill Creek, site of pre-Revolutionary grit and sawmills, became an iron center in 1838 when Mill Creek Furnace was built. In 1852 the area was known as one of

245

the most extensive iron fields in the world, and was well supplied with water power, timber, and limestone.

•**MILLERSBURG**, Borough; Dauphin County; Pop. 2,770; Area Code 717; Zip Code 17061; Elev. 397'; 28 m. N of Harrisburg in SE central Pennsylvania, on Susquehanna River.

Settlement was made in 1790 by *Daniel* and *John Miller*, brothers, who owned 400 acres here; German and Huguenot emigrants followed.

They plotted the town in 1807. A ferry takes passengers across the river at this point.

Agriculture - Cattle and grain farming
Industry/Mfg. - Dairy products, furniture

•**MILLERSTOWN**, Borough; Perry Bounty; Pop. 550; Area Code 717; Zip Code 17062; Elev. 381'; S central Pennsylvania; founded in 1790, and site of 17 inns during the period the Pennsylvania Canal was being built.

•**MILLERSVILLE**, Borough; Lancaster County; Pop. 7,668; Area Code 717; Zip Code 17551; Elev. 360'; suburb of Lancaster in SE Pennsylvania; site of Millersville State College, with 4,700 students.

Higher Education - Millersville State College
Community Event - Celebration, Annual, June

•**MILL HALL**, Borough; Clinton County; Pop. 1,744; Area Code 717; Zip Code 17751; Elev. 580'; 2 m. SE of Lock Haven in central Pennsylvania, on the West Branch of the Susquehanna River.

•**MILLHEIM**, Borough; Centre County; Pop. 800; Area Code 814; Zip Code 16854; Elev. 851'; 40 m. SW of Williamsport in central Pennsylvania.

Millheim, bisected by Elk Creek, was laid out in 1797 and incorporated as a borough in 1879. It was so named by German settlers, supposedly because it was the "home" of several mills, but perhaps in memory of the old town of Muhlheim in Wurttemberg. Center of a rich agricultural district, which brings poultry, dairy products and grains to market in town.

•**MILLVALE**, Borough; Allegheny County; Pop. 4,754; Area Code 412; Zip Code 15209; Elev. 900'; SW Pennsylvania.

Millvale was in 1844 the property of *John Sample* who sold 164 acres to the Poor Directors of Allegheny County for $1,200. Twenty-three years later, when they decided to move farther from the city, the poor farm was divided into lots and sold for about $300,000. In 1868 when the place was incorporated as a borough, the name Millvale was suggested by the thickly wooded valley of Girty's Run and a local iron mill.

•**MILL VILLAGE**, Borough; Erie County; Pop. 427; Area Code 814; Zip Code 16427; Elev. 1,206'; NW Pennsylvania.

•**MILLVILLE**, Borough; Columbia County; Pop. 975; Area Code 717; Zip Code 17846; Elev. 645'; 15 m. N of Bloomsburg.

Millville, on Little Fishing Creek, has grown around a gristmill founded in 1774 by Quaker *John Eves*. The settlement was destroyed during the raids that followed the Battle of Wyoming, but the settlers had fled; they returned in 1785. The mill, destroyed several times by fire, was, at the time of its last rebuilding in 1913, one of the largest buckwheat flour mills in the United States.

•**MILTON**, Borough; Northumberland County; Pop. 6,730; Area Code 717; Zip Code 17847; Elev. 473'; 23 m. SE of Williamsport in E central Pennsylvania, on the Susquehanna River.

Milton, originally Milltown, is on the east bank of the Susquehanna's West Branch, at the mouth of Limeston Run. On the site of the present post office, near the town center, *Marcus Hulings, Jr.*, agent for the Susquehanna Land Company, erected a log tavern in 1779. *Andrew Straub*, a miller, came to the neighborhood of Milton about 1780, and 12 years later he planned the erection of a mill near the river bank. A spring freshet diverted the course of Limestone Run, which was to furnish him with power, and he was obliged to build his mill "near where the present stone bridge is." Here *Andrew Straub* erected a log mill in 1792, "with a wheel outside and one run of stones." The settlers in all the surrounding country gladly abandoned the long route to the only other mill, located at Warrior's Run, about seven miles distant, and flocked to *Andrew Straub's* place, which they at first called Milltown. A village was soon laid out by *Andrew Straub*, and its name, at the suggestion of the surveyor, was shortened to Milton. The Milton post office was established in 1800.

The community was incorporated as a borough in 1817.

Agriculture - Grain and truck farming
Industry/Mfg. - Clothing, steel products,
  dairy products, furniture
Daily Newspaper - The Standard, 19 Arch St.
Chamber of Commerce - Box 118

•**MINERSVILLE,** Borough; Schuylkill County; Pop. 5,635; Area Code 717; Zip Code 17954; Elev. 820'; E central Pennsylvania.

Named for the fact that a large number of its people have from the beginning been coal miners. The town was started in 1830 by *Titus Bennett*. Like most of the large towns in the anthracite region, Minersville began its existence as three or four distinct and widely separated little clusters of frame houses. These scattered settlements have gradually merged together into one town. Minersville grew rapidly: it was incorporated in about a year after it was founded, and at the end of the first decade its population was 1,265.

•**MODENA,** Borough; Chester County; Pop. 672; Area Code 215; Zip Code 19358; Elev. 300'; SE Pennsylvania.

Named for the *Mode* family. *Alexander Mode,* who settled in East Fallowfield about 1739, used the waters of the Brandywine to run a saw-mill. About 1850, *W.A. Mode* started a papermill here and called the place Modeville, a name that the village retained until about 1873, when the Wilmington and Reading Railroad was built. The railway officials chose the more euphonious name of Modena for their station, and a little later the post office received the same name. They may have had the Italian city of Modena in mind.

•**MOHNTON,** Borough; Berks County; Pop. 2,156; Area Code 215; Zip Code 19540; Elev. 400'; SE Pennsylvania.

Mohnton occupies the farm bought by *Benjamin Mohn* in 1846. Here he erected a mill, in which a store was opened by his cousin, *Samuel Mohn*. In 1857 Mohn's Store post-office was established. Fifty years later, when the village was incorporated, it was renamed Mohnton.

•**MONACA**, Borough; Beaver County; Pop. 7,661; Area Code 412; Zip Code 15061; Elev. 720'; 2 m. S of Beaver in W Pennsylvania.

Monaca was settled in 1813 by an exiled Polish nobleman, *Francis Helvedi*, who raised merino sheep here. In 1832 *Bernhart Mueller* (Count de Leon) and 250 secessionists from the Harmony Society at Economy purchased the site of Monaca from two boatbuilders. By attacking celibacy and openly advocating freedom to marry, *Mueller* split the society's ranks and subsequently declared himself head of the colony. *Father Rapp*, founder and leader of the Harmony movement, protested, and an agreement was eventually reached that *Leon* and his converts were to leave Economy and were to receive $150,000 in full payment of all claims against the society. The Leon following soon disbanded; some migrated to Louisiana and Missouri, and others went into business here. The establishment of the Phoenix Glass Company here in 1880 gave the village impetus. Today the town is mainly a residential suburb.

•**MONESSEN**, City; Westmoreland County; Pop. 11,928; Area Code 417; Zip Code 15062; Elev. 756'; 22 m. S of Pittsburgh in SW Pennsylvania, on Monogaheli River.

Monessen is a steel and tin manufacturing center. The plant of the National Tin Plate Company of Pennsylvania, built in 1897, was the nucleus around which clustered other large industrial concerns. It was incorporated in 1899.

The name Monessen is a curious hybird compound, formed by combining the first syllable of Monongahela with Essen, the name of the greatest iron town in Germany, the home of the famous Krupp works. The original meaning of the name Essen has been lost; it has no connection with *Eisen*, the German word fo *iron*.

Industry/Mfg. - Steel, coal, dairy products, glass, chemicals

Daily Newspaper - The Valley Independent,
    Eastgate 19
Chamber of Commerce - 125 Sixth Street

•**MONONGAHELA**, City; Washington County; Pop. 5,950; Area Code 412; Zip Code 15063 Elev. 754'; 18 m. S of Pittsburgh in SW Pennsylvania, on Monongahela River.

Monongahela is at the mouth of Pigeon Creek. Early named Parkinson's Ferry and later Monongahela City, its charter was granted in 1873. The name "Monongahela" is a form of the Indian *Menaun-gehilla*, meaning "river with the sliding banks."

Agriculture - Fruit, poultry and varied
    farming
Industry/Mfg. - Cement, trucks, steel, coal,
    dairy products
Daily Newspaper - The Herald, 440 W. Main
Chamber of Commerce - 173 W. Main
Community Event - River Festival, Annual,
    July

•**MONONGAHELA RIVER**, River; SW Pennsylvania; flows N approx 130 m. from its source at the confluence of West Fork and the Tygart Rivers in N West Virginia, across Pennsylvania state line and through a twisting, industrial course to mouth at the Allegheny River; forms the Ohio River at Pittsburgh. Navigable in northern reaches.

The name is a corruption of Menaun-gehilla, an Indian phrase meaning "River with sliding banks," since this highbanked river is subject to erosion.

•**MONROE**, Borough; Bradford County; Pop. 627; Area Code 717; Elev. 760'; in a hilly area near Schrader Creek in N Pennsylvania.

•**MONROE COUNTY**, in 1836 a new county was formed from Northampton and Pike, and named Monroe in honor of *James Monroe*, fifth President of the United States, whose title to lasting fame rests on the Monroe Doctrine, which has for a century exerted a powerful influence in shaping the foreign policy of our country. Sixteen states besides Pennsylvania have honored *James Monroe* by naming a county for him. Monroe is a Scotch territorial surname signifying in Gaelic "a dweller at the red bog." The culb-moss, which grows in boggy places, is the appropriated badge of the Monroe clan.

•**MONROEVILLE**, Borough; Allegheny County; Pop. 30,977; Area Code 412; Zip Code 15146; Elev. 1,980'; 13 m. E of Pittsburgh in SW Pennsylvania; residential suburb.

> *Higher Education* - Boyce Campus
> *Chamber of Commerce* - 3753 William Penn Hwy.

•**MONT ALTO**, Borough; Franklin County; Pop. 1,197; Area Code 717; Zip Code 17237; Elev. 850'; S Pennsylvania; name means "High Mountain." Nearby is Mont Alto State Park.

•**MONTGOMERY**, Borough; Lycoming County; Pop. 1,653; Area Code 717; Zip Code 17752; Elev. 500'; N central Pennsylvania.

Montgomery was at first called Montgomery Station in honor of *Robert Montgomery*, who, about 1850, donated land for the railway station and yards. Nearly 40 years later, at the time of its incorporation, the village shortened its name to Montgomery.

•**MONTGOMERY COUNTY**, in 1784 the new county of Montgomery was set apart from old Philadelphia County. The petition presented to the legislature, it is said, did not suggest a name for the proposed county. Less than nine years before, the brave and beloved *General Richard Montgomery*, for whom the new county was named, had fallen in the heroic but vain effort to capture Quebec. His untimely death was one of the severest blows to the American cause during the early days of the Revolution. So popular was he that at the news of his death "the city of Philadelphia was in tears; every person seemed to have lost his nearest friend." It is no wonder that Pennsylvania sought to honor his memory by giving his name to the new county that was taken from the side of Philadelphia.

Richard Montgomery was born in Ireland in 1736. After his graduation from Trinity College, Dublin, he entered the British army as ensign at the age of eighteen, and served under *Wolfe* as ensign at the seige of Louisburg. In 1762 he was promoted to the rank of captain. A year or

251

two later he returned to England, where he became intimate with some of the great liberal leaders, among whom were *Isaac Barre, Charles James Fox,* and *Edmund Burke.* In 1773 he left England forever and came to New York, where he purchased an estate and married *Janet,* the daughter of *Judge Robert R. Livingston.*

At the beginning of the trouble with England he sided with his adopted country and, offering his services to Congress, was made a brigadier-general. With his little army of less than a thousand soldiers he captured two-thirds of Canada. *General Montgomery* was a tall man, "of fine military presence, of graceful address, with a bright, magnetic face, winning manners, and the bearing of a prince."

Some effort has been made to show that Montgomery County was named for *Colonel John Montgomery* of Carlisle, who commanded a Pennsylvania regiment at the battle of Long Island, who was in command of the Pennsylvania militia at Brandywine and Germantown, and who served as a member of the Continental Congress in 1782-3.

Though there can be little doubt that the name of Montgomery County was given with the intention of honoring *General Richard Montgomery,* it would be a mistake to overlook the fact that this name was particularly acceptable to the large number of influential Welsh settlers then living in the new county. As early as 1717 these Welshmen had colonized and organized Montgomery Township, naming it for their native Montgomeryshire. The village of Montgomeryville in this township traces its name to the same source. It is noteworthy also that two of the most active supporters of the bill to establish Montgomery County were *James Montgomery,* of Lancaster County, and *William Montgomery,* of Northumberland. Eighteen counties in the United States and the city of Montgomery, the capital of Alabama, are said to have been named in honor of *General Richard Montgomery.*

The family name Montgomery is derived from Mont Gomerie, a place near Lisieux in Normandy. In 1067 *Roger de Montgomery,* a Norman knight, apparently the first person who is known to have borne the name, was made Earl of Arundel, Sussex, and Shrewsbury.

252

•**MONTGOMERY SQUARE**, Village; Montgomery County; Pop. (incl. with Montgomeryville); Area Code 215; Elev. 440'; has among its scattered old stone buildings, the Blue Jay Tavern, birthplace of *Winfield Scott Hancock* (1824-86), Civil War general and Democratic presidential nominee in 1880.

•**MONTGOMERYVILLE**, Village; Montgomery County; Pop. 800; Area Code 215; Zip Code 18936; Elev. 400'; was founded in 1717; named by Welsh settlers for Montgomeryshire in their native land.

•**MONTOUR COUNTY**, formed from Columbia County in 1850, was named in honor of *Madame Montour*, who has sometimes been represented as a French half-breed, and sometimes as a white woman who had become an Indian by adoption and had remained such from choice. In point of fact, she was three-fourths Indian. In the great mass and maze of conflicting statements that have been published about this extraordinary woman, it has been very difficult to get at what seem to be the correct facts. A good deal that has been written about her is undoubtedly either fiction or guesswork. The essential facts of interest about *Madame Montour* appear to be these:

Madam Montour's father was a half-breed Canadian Indian, "Louis Couc, surnamed Montour," who married a Saco Indian girl, whose Christian name was *Madeleine*. They had at least three children, one of whom was *Madame Montour*, born about 1682. Her first name is generally supposed to have been *Catherine*, though in colonial records she invariably appears as *Madame Montour*, just as if she had no given name. According to her own statement, when ten years old she was captured by some Iroquois and adopted into their tribe.

•**MONTOURSVILLE**, Borough; Lycoming County; Pop. 5,403; Area Code 717; Zip Code 17754; Elev. 525'; near Williamsport in N central Pennsylvania, on Susquehanna River.

The site, once occupied by the Indian village of Otzinachson, was given in 1768 to *Andrew Montour*, a half-breed Indian interpreter, for his loyalty to the provincial government.

•**MONTROSE**, Borough; Seat of Susquehanna County; Pop. 1,980; Area Code 717; Zip Code 18801; Elev. 1,658'; 25 m. SW of Binghamton, N.Y. in NE Pennsylvania.

The borough lies on a summit overlooking the sources of Meshoppen, Wyalusing and Snake Creeks. Founded in 1800, it has many Georgia-Styled buildings. Lumbering and agriculture are important here.

Dr. Robert H. Rose, who came originally from Chester County, bought about 100,000 acres of land in this region, and was one of the most persistent supporters of the Pennsylvania title to this disputed territory. About 1800 the first settlement in what is now Montrose was made by *Captain Barlett Hinds*, who came here with his family from Southampton, Long Island. For the next decade or more the place was known as Hinds' Settlement. In 1812, when the present town was laid out, *Doctor Rose* fashioned a name for it by combining the French word *mont* with his family name *Rose*, which is also the name for an old Scottish town.

> *Agriculture* - Poultry, grain and varied farming
> *Industry/Mfg.* - Wood products. Resort area

•**MOORHEADVILLE**, Village; Erie County; Pop. Rural; Elev. 680'.

Moorville was settled in 1800 by *Thomas Moorhead*, who built in 1810 the two-story red brick Moorhead House, with its white Doric columns and pilasters supporting a low pedimented entrance portico. Unusual features for western Pennsylvania are the parapet walls and double chimneys on the gable ends.

•**MOOSIC**, Borough; Lackawanna County; Pop. 6,068; Area Code 717; Zip Code 18507; Elev. 650'; NE Pennsylvania; named for the great herds of moose that once roamed the Lackawanna River Valley. Suburb of Scranton.

•**MORGANZA**, Village; Washington County; Pop. Rural; Area Code 412; Elev. 936'.

Morganza was named for the Morganza Farm, on which *Colonel George Morgan* (1743-1810) made his home after the Revolutionary War. He was the author of a prize-winning essay, "The Farmyard." While acting as Indian agent at Fort Pitt during the Revolutionary War, *Morgan* was accused of British sympathies, suspended from office, and tried for treason; he was later exonerated and reinstated. In 1806 *Aaron Burr* approached him concerning the scheme to set up an empire in the West, but *Morgan* reported the plot to *President Jefferson*.

•**MORRISVILLE**, Borough; Bucks County; Pop. 9,845; Area Code 215; Zip Code 19067; Elev. 21'; SE Pennsylvania.

Morrisville, first known as Falls of the Delaware, was renamed in honor of *Robert Morris*, financier of the Revolution, who had an imposing mansion here. Morrisville almost became the capital of the Nation. On October 7, 1783, a resolution was introduced in Congress "...that the Federal town should be erected on the banks of the Delaware at the falls near Trenton, on the New Jersey side, or in Pennsylvania on the opposite." The South spoke for Annapolis; *Alexander Hamilton* favored the present site on the Potomac River; Washington advised against Morrisville, but in spite of this formidable opposition, the resolution was defeated by only two votes.

POINTS OF INTEREST

SUMMERSEAT (THOMAS BARCLAY HOUSE)- Home of *George Clymer*, a signer of the Declaration of Independence, member of Continental Congress and delegate to the Constitutional Convention.

PENNSBURY MANOR- Georgian country home from late-17th century, home of *William Penn*.

•**MORTON**, Borough; Delaware County; Pop. 2,412; Area Code 215; Zip Code 19070; Elev. 130'; SW suburb of Philadelphia in SE of Pennsylvania.

Named for *John Morton*, who may have cast the deciding vote from Pennsylvania in favor of the Declaration of Independence, and who signed the historic document.

•**MOSCOW**, Borough; Lackawanna County; Pop. 1,536; Area Code 717; Zip Code 18444; Elev. 1,600'; 12 m. SE of Scranton in NE Pennsylvania.

255

•**MOUNTAIN TOP**, Village; Luzerne County; Pop. 1,800; Area Code 717; Elev. 1,680'; 5 m. S of Wilkes-Barre.

Mountain Top, on the flat summit of Penobscot Mountain, was founded in 1788. Diverse useful products are made here.

> *Agriculture* - Dairy and varied farming
> *Industry/Mfg.* - Building supplies, tires,
>   machine shop

•**MOUNT CARBON**, Borough; Schuylkill County; Pop. 157; Area Code 717; Elev. 600'; near Pottsville in E central Pennsylvania; named for the coal found and mined in the area.

•**MOUNT CARMEL**, Borough; Northumberland County; Pop. 8,190; Area Code 717; Zip Code 17851; Elev. 1,056'; E central Pennsylvania.

Mt. Carmel was settled prior to the Revolution. One of the first settlers erected the Mt. Carmel Inn on the Pottsville-Danville Turnpike. The town's history has been the history of coal; within a radius of five miles are 12 large mines.

The town was named for the mountain in Palestine. No special reason can be given to explain why it received this Biblical name. In 1832 *Felix Lerch*, of Northampton County, leased a two-story log tavern "on the northern side of the turnpike," near the site of the Commercial Hotel. This tavern then bore the name "Mt. Carmel Inn, 1824." It was a busy hostelry and a regular stopping place for stagecoaches plying between Danville and Pottsville, and between Sunbury and Reading.

According to tradition the idea of laying out a town was conceived by *Albert Bradford*, owner of the old Mount Carmel Inn property, who applied the name of the tavern to the town. The earliest town plot bears the title, "Plan of the town of Mt. Carmel in the Middle Coal region, Northumberland County Pennsylvania., 1848." Five years later, when the Mount Carmel post-office was established, the place contained only half a dozen houses. In 1854 Mount Carmel Township was organized. The village of Mount Carmel became an incorporated borough in 1862.

> *Chamber of Commerce* - 23 S. Oak St.

•**MOUNT DAVIS**, Peak; SW Pennsylvania; Elev. 3,213'; Highest point in Pennsylvania; part of the Negro Mountains of the appalachian range.

•**MOUNT GRETNA**, Borough; Lebanon County; Pop. 280; Area Code 717; Zip Code 17064; Elev. 660'; SE central Pennsylvania.

•**MOUNT HOLLY SPRINGS**, Borough; Cumberland County; Pop. 2,068; Area Code 717; Zip Code 17065; Elev. 560'; S Pennsylvania; the town lies along a scenic route near the great Appalachian Trail.

•**MOUNT JEWETT**, Borough; McKean County; Pop. 1,053; Area Code 814; Zip Code 16740; Elev. 2,195'; 21 M. S of Bradford in N Pennsylvania.

Located near the borders of the Allegheny National Forest, the town is popular with tourists seeking the clean air of a mountain resort. Kinzuq State Park is north of town. Clay tile is manufactured in a plant in this town, surveyed in 1883 when a rail line reached this spot.

•**MOUNT JOY**, Borough; Lancaster County; Pop. 5,680; Area Code 717; Zip Code 17552; Elev. 360'; 12 m. W of Lancaster in SE Pennsylvania.

Mount Joy, on Little Chickies Creek, named for one of *Penn's* manor houses, was formed by the merging of Rohrerstown, Richland, and Walleckstown, all settled in the 1760s and 1770s by Scotch-Irish. In July 1938 Mount Joy came into national prominence when the *National Geographic Magazine* revived an old blunder made by *Israel Rupp*, local historian, more than a century ago. *Rupp* mistakenly identified the township of Mount Joy with the hill of that name at Valley Forge and stated that *General Anthony Wayne* had spent the winter of 1777-8 here under sever privation.

POINT OF INTEREST

CENTRAL HOTEL (A. BUBE'S BREWERY)- 1859 complex of adjacent buildings. Museum.

Agriculture - Varied farming
Industry/Mfg. - Confections, footwear,
   quarrying
Chamber of Commerce - PO Box 73

•**MOUNT OLIVER**, Borough; Allegheny County; Pop. 4,576; Area Code 412; Zip Code 15210; Elev. 1,100'; SW Pennsylvania.

The origin of the name "Oliver" is not definitely known, although some think the name is derived from *Oliver Ormsby* who owned several hundred acres of land here in 1840, and the next year it was apportioned among his eight children. The borough was incorporated in 1892.

•**MOUNT PENN**, Borough; Berks County; Pop. 3,025; Area Code 215; Zip Code 19606; Elev. 480'; SE Pennsylvania; laid out in 1884 on Mt. Penn Ridge; named for *William Penn* and the mountains surrounding the town.

•**MOUNT PLEASANT**, Borough; Westmoreland County; Pop. 5,354; Area Code 417; Zip Code 15666; Elev. 1,233'; 12 m. S of Greensburg in SW Pennsylvania.

As to the origin of the name Mount Pleasant, nothing more definite can be given than that it was so called because of its pleasant and commanding location. As early as 1774 the Redstone Presbytery organized the Mount Pleasant Church, which was situated about two miles from the present town; and it is probable, but not certain, that the town took its name from the historic old church. The village was incorporated as early as 1828. In the early days. when the place was a relay station on the Baltimore and Pittsburgh pike, the fighting, thieving gang that loafed about the old inn and stables was so notoriously bad that the place was locally known as Helltown.

Nearby are ski resorts in the Chestnut Ridge.

Agriculture - Truck, grain and varied
   farming
Industry/Mfg. - Concrete, lumber, coal
Chamber of Commerce - Municipal Bldg., Rm 214

•**MOUNT PONOCO**, Borough; Monroe County; Pop. 1,237; Area Code 717; Zip Code 18344; Elev. 1,840'; E Pennsylvania; large snow ski and summer mountain resort area.

•**MOUNT UNION**, Borough; Huntingdon County; Pop. 3,101; Area Code 717; Zip Code 17066; Elev. 600'; 12 m. SE of Huntingdon.

Mount Union, on the Juniata River at the foot of Jack's Mountain, was laid out by a lumbering firm in 1849; a ferry was in service here as early as 1790. The town was named by its first postmaster, *Colonel William Pollock*, who was impressed by "such a number of mountains coming together" near the place. East of town Jack's Mountain and Stone Mountain are United. Ganister rock quarries are nearby.

> *Industry/Mfg.* - Cement products, clothing, quarrying
> *Chamber of Commerce* - Municipal Bldg., PO Box 12

•**MOUNTVILLE**, Borough; Lancaster County; Pop. 1,505; Area Code 717; Zip Code 17554; Elev. 440'; SE Pennsylvania.

Mountville, first named Mount Pleasant, was laid out in 1814 by *Isaac Rohrer*, who owned iron mines in the neighborhood. The depletion of the ore at Ironville and Silver springs, a few miles north, drove part of the population into the large cities, but the remainder stayed to plant the fields with tobacco.

•**MOUNT WOLF**, Borough; York County; Pop. 1,517; Area Code 717; Zip Code 17347; Elev. 420'; Suburb of the city of York in S Pennsylvania.

•**MUNCY**, Borough; Area Code 717; Zip Code 17756; Pop. 497'; 12 m. E of Williamsport on the Susquehanna River in N central Pennsylvania.

Muncy was laid out in 1797, and named for the Munsee Indians. Here the west branch of the Susquehanna flowing through the mountains, turns south for its meeting with the north branch at Northumberland.

The Munsee, Minsis or Monseys were "people of the stony country." In 1826 Muncy was incorporated as Pennsborough because it was built on John Penn's Manor of Muncy; but the next year the name was changed back to Muncy by a legislative act.

Industry/Mfg. - Garments, lumber products, quarrying
Chamber of Commerce - PO Box 119

•**MUNHALL**, Borough; Allegheny County; Pop. 14,532; Area Code 412; Zip Code 15120; Elev. 754'; SW Pennsylvania.

Munhall, an industrial suburb east of Pittsburgh and contiguous to Homestead, is built upon rolling hills and overshadowed by the Carnegie-Illinois Steel Company plant, scene of the 1892 Homestead strike. The first open-hearth furnace in the United States was put into operation here in 1886. In 1786 "Queen' Aliquippa, a celebrated Indian woman, sold 327 acres here for goods valued at $262. Later, *John Munhall*, a native of Pittsburgh, bought coal fields here.

•**MUNICIPALITY OF MURRYSVILLE**, Borough; Westmoreland County; Pop. 16,036; Area Code 417; Zip Code 15668; Elev. 900'; E suburb of Pittsburgh in SW Pennsylvania.

•**MYERSTOWN**, Borough; Area Code 717; Zip Code 17067; Elev. 472'; 8 m. E of Lebanon in SE central Pennsylvania.

Myerstown was laid out in 1768 by *Isaac Myers* along Tulpehocken Creek, enjoyed unusual prosperity during and shortly after construction of the Union Canal.

POINT OF INTEREST

ISAAC MEIER HOMESTEAD- One of the first homes in town; built c. 1750 for town's founder, *Isaac Meier.*

Industry/Mfg. - Grain milling, pharmaceuticals

N

•**NANTICOKE**, City; Luzerne County; Pop. 13,044; Area Code 717; Zip Code 18634; Elev. 640'; Suburb of Wilkes-Barre, on Susquehanna River.

Nanticoke received its name from a tribe of Indians. Nentigo is the form used by the archaeologist *Heckewelder*. The Nanticokes, who were once seated on the eastern shore of Maryland, are "the seashore settlers, or the tidewater people." The first settlement at Nanticoke, which owed its beginning to the water power furnished by the falls, was made about 150 years ago. The town did not begin to grow rapidly until late 1825, when the first coal was mined there.

Community Event - American-Ukrainian
Festival, Annual, August-September

•**NANTY-GLO**, Borough; Cambria County; Pop. 3,936; Area Code 814; Zip Code 15943; Elev. 1,711'; SW central Pennsylvania.

Town was settled by Welsh coal miners, who named it for their native phrase *nant y glo*, or "the coal brook," which is also the name of a town in Wales.

•**NARBETH**, Borough; Montgomery County; Pop. 4,496; Area Code 215; Zip Code 19072; Elev. 285'; NW suburb of Philadelphia in SE Pennsylvania.

Perfumes and metal tableware are made in this residential borough.

•**NAZARETH**, Borough; Northampton County; Pop. 5,443; Area Code 215; Zip Code 18064; Elev. 485'; 13 m. NE of Allentown in E Pennsylvania; Nazareth was the second Moravian settlement in Pennsylvania.

The Whitefield House was begun in 1740 by the *Reverend George Whitefield*, a Methodist preacher from

England. Whitefield purchased 5,000 acres at the forks of the Delaware, where he proposed to establish a school of Blacks and a revivalist headquarters. He employed Moravians, recently from Georgia, to clear the land and erect buildings. Two log cabins and the lower walls of the present building were finished when a dispute arose between Whitefield and the Moravians. They ceased work, acquired a tract nearby, and set up the town of Bethlehem. A year later they bought 500 acres of the original tract and founded Nazareth, named for *Christ's* home in Galilee.

Whitefield, born in England in 1714, became a religious enthusiast early in life, and in 1735 joined the followers of *John* and *Charles Wesley*. He became a successful preacher and acquired fame for the frenzy he aroused in his listeners. His Calvinistic views led to a break with the Wesleys and he became the outstanding Calvinistic Methodist. Touring extensively both here and abroad, and preaching before as many as 20,000 persons at one time, he held most of his revivals in the open. On September 29, 1770, he preached for two hours at Exeter, Massachusetts. The following day he died of asthma.

In 1755, Moravians completed the Whitefield House, or Ephrata, as it was then called. Thoroughly renovated in 1871, it is a three-story Colonial building of native limestone with handhewn timbers, slate-covered gambrel roof, and two stone chimneys. On the same plot is the Gray House, oldest Moravian building in Pennsylvania. Completed in 1740, it is a one-story log and limestone structure with a high attic, steep roof, simple shed dormer, and two chimneys. It has an inside chimney and a "pfortchen," or small hood porch. A school for boys was started here in 1743.

Chamber of Commerce - PO Box 173

•**NESCOPECK**, Borough; Luzerne County; Pop. 1,768; Area Code 717; Zip Code 18635; Elev. 520'; E Pennsylvania; name is Indian for "black, deep and still water."

•**NESHAMINY**, Village; Bucks County; Pop. (Rural); Area Code 215; Zip Code 18976; SE Pennsylvania; near Warrington; named for the Creek nearby, which is called by its Indian name meaning "double stream." An old "Log College" was once located along this stream.

•**NESQUEHONING**, Borough; Carbon County; Pop. 3,346; Area Code 717; Zip Code 18240; Elev. 801'; 28 m. S of Wilkes-Barre in E Pennsylvania.

Nesquehoning is an Indian term meaning "at the black lick," or "narrow valley". It was founded in 1824 by the Lehigh Navigation and Coal Company and early known as "Hell's Kitchen," stretches along the floor of a narrow valley between Pisgah Mountain and Broad Mountain.

Many legends are associated with the discovery of anthracite in Pennsylvania, including the probable one that Indians, building a signal fire on an outcropping, first noted the hard black substance that burned. In 1762 a company of Connecticut pioneers allegedly discovered anthracite near what is now Wilkes-Barre. A blacksmith used it in his forge near Mill Creek as early as 1769; six years later it was used as a fuel in the manufacture of arms in 1769; six years later it was used as a fuel in the manufacture of arms for the Continental Army.

In 1792 a group of Philadelphia businessmen and others organized the Lehigh Coal Mine Company. Facing a skeptical public, the company was forced to give away large quantities of anthracite for trial purposes. Few persons knew how to burn it; and fewer still had proper equipment. Philadelphia authorities were persuaded to try it, but the engineer protested that the coal put out the fire. Only 385 tons a year were mined until 1820.

Meanwhile, however, chance had taken a hand. A workman in *Josiah White's* nail factory in Philadelphia, where coal was being tried with little success, returned to the factory for a forgotten article and found the hard coal fire glowing with intense heat. White's interest was rekindled. In the winter of 1817-18 he set out to investigate the possibilities of the Lehigh River as a waterway for the transportation of coal to Philadelphia. In 1820 the Lehigh Navigation Company and the Lehigh Coal Company, formed two years earlier, were merged as the Lehigh Navigation and Coal Company. The Lehigh Canal, completed in 1829, made cheap shipment possible and marked the beginning of anthracite mining as a large scale industry.

•**NEW ALBANY**, Borough; Bradford County; Pop. 336; Area Code 717; Zip Code 18833; Elev. 1,260'; N Pennsylvania.

•**NEW ALEXANDRIA**, Borough; Westmoreland County; Pop. 697; Area Code 417; Zip Code 15670; Elev. 996'; in SW Pennsylvania.

•**NEW BALTIMORE**, Borough; Somerset County; Pop. 221; Area Code 814; Zip Code 15553; Elev. 1,500'; in S Pennsylvania; named by optimistic early settlers for the older city in Maryland.

•**NEW BEAVER**, Borough; Lawrence County; Pop. 1,885; Area Code 412; suburb of Beaver Falls in W Pennsylvania; incorporated in 1960 from Big Beaver Township.

•**NEW BERLIN**, Borough; Union County; Pop. 783; Area Code 717; Zip Code 17855; Elev. 540'; Central Pennsylvania.
The act of legislature establishing Union County declared the most suitable location for the county-seat to be Longstown, the name of which it changed to New Berlin, because practically all the settlers in this region were Germans. The newly chosen county-seat, which had been laid out in 1792 by *George Long*, did not contain more than half a dozen houses.
In 1855, however, Lewisburg succeeded New Berlin as county seat because it was more than twelve times as large.

POINTS OF INTEREST

NEW BERLIN PRESBYTERIAN CHURCH (NEW BERLIN COMMUNITY CENTER)- Built in 1843; Greek Revival. Donated to city by congregation for use as community center in 1933.

•**NEWBERRYTOWN**, Village; York County; Area Code 717; Zip Code 17319; Elev. 632'; founded in 1791; the manufacture of cigars, now the sole industrial activity, was begun in 1831. Most of the early settlers were Quakers.

•**NEW BETHLEHEM**, Borough; Clarion County; Pop. 1,441; Area Code 814; Zip Code 16242; Elev. 1,075'; 36 m. SE of Oil City in W Pennsylvania.
New Bethlehem, on Red Bank Creek, was incorporated in 1853. Once called Gumtown for an early settler,

it was renamed for the steel center in eastern Pennsylvania.

Industry/Mfg. - Grain milling, coal, oil,
   dairy products
Chamber of Commerce - 428 Broad Street

•**NEW BLOOMFIELD,** Borough; Seat of Perry County; Pop. 1,116; Area Code 717; Zip Code 17068; Elev. 679'; 20 m. NW of Carlisle in an agricultural region.

New Bloomfield (alt. Bloomfield), selected as the seat of Perry County in 1820s, grew around the courthouse. Carson Long Institute, founded in 1837 as New Bloomfield Academy was converted into a military school in 1917.

Agriculture - Grain and varied farming
Industry/Mfg. - Clothing, dairy products

•**NEW BRIGHTON,** Borough; Beaver County; Pop. 7,364; Area Code 412; Zip Code 15066; Elev. 750'; just S of Beaver Falls in W Pennsylvania.

New Brighton, on the east bank of the Beaver River, had its beginning in the Big Beaver Blockhouse erected in 1789.

The town was plotted about 1830 on land which *David Townsend* had bought the year before. It was named New Brighton because it lay just across the Beaver River from "old Brighton," which received its name from the great English seaside resort, 509 miles south of London. Old Brighton is now called Beaver Falls. New Brighton was incorporated in 1838.

•**NEW BRITAIN,** Borough; Bucks County; Pop. 2,519; Area Code 215; Zip Code 18901; Elev. 300'; N suburb of Philadelphia in SE Pennsylvania; named for the industrial city in Connecticut by west-moving pioneers.

•**NEW BUFFALO,** Borough; Perry County; Pop. 156; Area Code 717; Zip Code 17069; Elev. 400'; S central Pennsylvania.

•**NEWBURG,** Borough; Clearfield County; Pop. 132; Area Code 814; Elev. 1,320'; in W central Pennsylvania.

265

•**NEWBURG**, Borough; Cumberland County; Pop. 303; Area Code 717; Zip Code 17240; Elev. 595'; S Pennsylvania.

•**NEW CASTLE**, City; Seat of Lawrence County; Pop. 33,621; Area Code 412; Zip Code 161 + zone; Elev. 806'; 44 m. NW of Pittsburgh in W Pennsylvania, on the Shenango River.

New Castle is at the junction of the Mahoning, Shenango, and Beaver Rivers. An early Indian trading center, this site became the capital of the Delawares of western Pennsylvania after *Colonel John Armstrong* destroyed Kittanning in 1756. In resurveying "donation lands" set aside for Revolutionary soldiers, *John Stewart* discovered and settled on an unassigned 50-acre tract here. He built a charcoal furnace to make pig iron from local ore, and named the spot for Newcastle upon Tyne, the English industrial city, which he desired to duplicate. The Erie Extension Canal, completed between Beaver and New Castle in 1833, stimulated settlement; in 1869 New Castle became a third-class city.

> *Industry/Mfg.* - Varied manufacturing, trade
> and services
> *Daily Newspaper* - The News, 27-35 N. Mercer
> Street
> *Chamber of Commerce* - Room 201-B First
> Federal Plaza

•**NEW CENTERVILLE**, Borough; Somerset County; Pop. 213; Area Code 814; Elev. 2,129'; S Pennsylvania.

•**NEW COLUMBUS**, Borough; Luzerne County; Pop. 214; Area Code 717; Elev. 995'; E Pennsylvania.

•**NEW CUMBERLAND**, Borough; Cumberland County; Pop. 8,051; Area Code 717; Zip Code 17070; Elev. 308'; s Suburb of Harrisburg in S Pennsylvania, on the Susquehanna River.

New Cumberland, at the junction of Yellow Breeches Creek and the Susquehanna River, was the site of a Shawnee village until about 1738. In 1810 it was settled by *Jacob Haldeman* as "Haldeman's Town." It was renamed for the county it sits in, which is Welsh for "land of compatriots."

•**NEW EAGLE**, Borough; Washington County; Pop. 2,617; Area Code 412; Zip Code 15067; Elev. 840'; 16 m. S of Pittsburgh in SW Pennsylvania, on Monogahela River.

•**NEWELL**, Borough; Fayette County; Pop. 629; Area Code 412; Zip Code 15466; Elev. 800'; SE Pennsylvania; incorporated in 1952 from Jefferson Township.

•**NEW FLORENCE**, Borough; Westmoreland County; Pop. 855; Area Code 417; Zip Code 15944; Elev. 1,086'; SW Pennsylvania.

•**NEW FREEDOM**, Borough; York County; Pop. 2,205; Area Code 717; Zip Code 17349; Elev. 820'; S Pennsylvania.

New Freedom was first named Freedom for the *Free* family, who were among the earliest settlers of the town. *E.K. Free* was a member of the first borough council in 1879. The name was changed to New Freedom because there was an older town and post-office called Freedom in Beaver County.

•**NEW GALILEE**, Borough; Beaver County; Pop. 596; Area Code 412; Zip Code 16141; Elev. 960'; suburb of Pittsburgh and Beaver Falls in W Pennsylvania; named by religious settlers for Jesus homeland.

•**NEW GENEVA**, Village; Fayette County; Pop. 350; Area Code 412; Zip Code Zip Code 15467; Elev. 938'.

New Geneva is on the right bank of the Monongahela at the mouth of George Creek. It was named for Geneva, Switzerland, native city of *Albert Gallatin*. The first glass works west of the Alleghenies was established here by Gallatin several years after the Revolutionary War.

Albert Gallatin chased his plantation in this locality in 1785. Here, in partnership with his brother-in-law, *James W. Nicholson*, and the two *Kramer brothers*, *Alber Gallatin* became a pioneer in the manufacture of glass. After Gallatin attained national distinction in public life, he erected a pretentious mansion about two miles from New Geneva. New Geneva is in Nicholson Township, which was named for *James W. Nicholson*.

•**NEW HOLLAND**, Borough; Lancaster County; Pop. 4,147; Area Code 717; Zip Code 17557; Elev. 495'; 13 m. NE of Lancaster in a tobacco and corn farming region.

Agriculture - Tobacco and varied farming
Industry/Mfg. - Cloth, plastics, cement,
dairy products

•**NEW HOPE**, Borough; Bucks County; Pop. 1,473; Area Code 215; Zip Code 18938; Elev. 86'; 16 m. NW of Trenton, New Jersey in SE Pennsylvania.

William Lathrop established in 1900, and such painters as *Edward W. Redfield, Daniel Garber,* and *John F. Folinsbee* are among its members. *Pearl S. Buck, Irina Skariatina, Sam and Bella Spewack, Edwin Justis Mayer, Dorothy Parker, George S. Kaufman, Lester Cohen,* and *George Antheil* lived in the vicinity.

The settlement, once Coryell's Ferry, derives its name from the New Hope Mills built by *Benjamin Parry* after his earlier mill buildings had been destroyed by fire in 1790.

The town lies across the Delaware form Lambertsville, New Jersey, to which it is connected by a bridge. Paper, antiques and art are still the main economic commodities in New Hope.

POINT OF INTEREST

HONEY HOLLOW WATERSHED- First (1939) small watershed development in U.S. on privately owned farmland. Soil and water conservation model. Once part of *William Penn's* land grants, contains three 18th century houses.

Agriculture - Varied farming
Industry/Mfg. - Quarrying

•**NEW KENSINGTON**, City; Westmoreland County; Pop. 17,660; Area Code 417; Zip Code 15068; Elev. 614'; 16 m. NE of Pittsburgh in SW Pennsylvania, on Allegheny River.

New Kensington is one of the largest aluminum producing centers in the country. The aluminum industry came to New Kensington in 1892, one year after the town was laid out on the site of Fort Crawford of the Revolutionary period.

New Kensington probably took its name from the London district of Kensington.

Industry/Mfg. - Aluminum, glass, textiles
Chamber of Commerce - 858 Fourth Ave.

•**NEW LEBANON**, Borough; Mercer County; Pop. 197; Area Code 412; Elev. 1,400'; W Pennsylvania; rural area.

•**NEW LONDON**, Village; Chester County; Pop. 350; Area Code 215; Zip Code 19360; Elev. 470'.

Named directly for the London Company, which once owned about 17,000 acres of land in Chester County, out of which was formed the old township of New London.

•**NEW MILFORD**, Borough; Susquehanna County; Pop. 1,040; Area Code 717; Zip Code 18834; Elev. 1,115'; NE Pennsylvania; named for the industrial town of the same name in Connecticut.

•**NEW OXFORD**, Borough; Adams County; Pop. 1,921; Area Code 717; Zip Code 17350; Elev. 560'; S Pennsylvania; was laid out in 1792. The name was inspired by the English medieval university town.

POINT OF INTEREST

JOHN'S BURNT MILL BRIDGE- Stone bridge, constructed c. 1800, over South Branch of Conewago Creek.

Chamber of Commerce - PO Box 152

•**NEW PARIS**, Borough; Bedford County; Pop. 199; Area Code 814; Zip Code 15554; Elev. 1,280'; S Pennsylvania; named by French settlers for the city in France.

•**NEW PHILADELPHIA**, Borough; Schuylkill County; Pop. 1,341; Area Code 717; Zip Code 17959; Elev. 700'; E central Pennsylvania; the town is also known as Silver Creek.

•**NEWPORT**, Borough; Perry County; Pop. 1,600; Area Code 717; Zip Code 17074; Elev. 400'; 28 m. NW of Harrisburg in S central Pennsylvania, on the Juniata River.

Newport settled in 1789 by *Paul Reider* and successively known as Reider's Ferry and Reidersville. It was named Newport after the quarry is nearby.

Agriculture - Varied farming
Industry/Mfg. - Quarrying, dairy products

•**NEW RINGGOLD**, Borough; Schuylkill County; Pop. 301; Area Code 717; Zip Code 17960; Elev. 560'; E central Pennsylvania; named for *Major Samuel Ringgold*, who was killed in the Mexican War.

•**NEWRY**, Borough; Blair County; Pop. 353; Area Code 814; Zip Code 16665; Elev. 1,040'; S central Pennsylvania.
    Town was founded in 1793 by *Patrick Cassidy*, who had immigrated from Ireland as a British officer's servant. After the Revolution, Cassidy bought 300 acres of land here and laid out the town. He named it for his native city in County Down, Ireland.

•**NEW SALEM**, Borough; York County; Pop. 832; Area Code 717; Zip Code 15468; Elev. 620'; S Pennsylvania.

•**NEW STANTON**, Borough; Westmoreland County; Pop. 2,600; Area Code 417; Zip Code 15672; Elev. 980'; SW Pennsylvania.

•**NEWTON HAMILTON**, Borough; Mifflin County; Pop. 317; Area Code 717; Zip Code 17075; Elev. 600'; Central Pennsylvania.

•**NEWTOWN**, Borough; Bucks County; Pop. 2,419; Area Code 215; Zip Code 18940; Elev. 150'; 22 m. NE of Philadelphia.
    In 1724 the Bucks county seat was moved to a more central location at Newtown, where it remained 88 years. When Newtown Township was laid out, shortly after the formation of Bucks County, there was reserved, near the middle of it, a townstead of 640 acres, on which now stands the borough of Newtown. The name Newtown occures in land conveyances as early as 1683. Just when the townstead began to be built up is not known. As to the origin of the name, tradition tells us that in passing

through this part of the Bucks County wilderness with hs surveyor-general, *Thomas Holme*, *William Penn* remarked, "Here I will lay out my *New town.* "

MAKEFIELD MEETING- 18th century meetinghouse was center of activity for township's early colonial settlement.

Higher Education - Bucks County Community College

•**NEWTOWN SQUARE**, Village; Delaware County; Pop. 11,000; Area Code 215; Elev. 400'; 15 m. W of Philadelphia; residential suburb.

•**NEWVILLE**, Borough; Cumberland County; Pop. 1,370; Area Code 717; Zip Code 17241; Elev. 560'; 11 m. W of Carlisle in a dairy and grain farming region.

Agriculture - Varied farming
Industry/Mfg. - Clothing, dairy products

•**NEW WASHINGTON**, Borough; Clearfield County; Pop. 103; Area Code 814; Elev. 1,660'; W central Pennsylvania.

•**NEW WILMINGTON**, Borough; Lawrence County; Pop. 2,774; Area Code 412; Zip Code 16142; Elev. 950'; 9 m. N of New Castle in W Pennsylvania; on Little Neshannock Creek, was incorporated from Wilmington Township in 1863.

Agriculture - Varied farming
Industry/Mfg. - Dairy products
Higher Education - Westminster College

•**NICHOLSON**, Borough; Wyoming County; Pop. 945; Area Code 717; Zip Code 18446; Elev. 768'; NE Pennsylvania.

Nicholson is at the confluence of Martin's and Tunkhannock Creeks. Nicholson and Nicholson Township were named for *John Nicholson*, comptroller of Pennsylvania from 1782 to 1794. He speculated extensively in wild lands in Pennsylvania, at one time holding title to

3,700,000 acres in 39 counties. In 1797 Pennsylvania held an immense claim against him for unsettled land-warrants and accounts, and his vast holdings reverted to the state. He died in prison n 1800.

Dairy goods production is important in this country town.

•**NOCKAMIXON LAKE**, Reservoir, Bucks County; 40 miles N of Philadelphia in SE Pennsylvania. This reservoir is 10 miles long and 1 mile wide. Formed by the damming of the Nockamixon Creek. The Indians named this place for three houses that once stood here. A state park is located at the southwest tip.

•**NOLO**, Village; Indiana County; Pop. Rural; Area Code 814; ; Elev. 1,900'; SW central Pennsylvania; was founded in 1858 and was named so because it sits on a mountain pinnacle and has no low ground. The place was originally named Stone House for a stage-stop tavern.

•**NORRISTOWN**, Borough; Seat of Montgomery County; Pop. 34,648; Area Code 215; Zip Code 194 + zone; Elev. 83'; located on the Schuylkill River 15 miles NW of Philadelphia in SE Pennsylvania; is in a fertile rolling section of the Schuylkill Valley.

In 1784 the site was known as the Norriton Plantation and Mill Tract. Marble, granite, limestone and iron deposits nearby exerted an important influence on the community's industrial development.

On October 7, 1704, *Isaac Norris* and *William Trent* purchased the land now occupied by the borough for 50 cents an acre and in 1712 Norris acquired Trent's interest and erected a gristmill at the foot of present Water Street. When chartered as a borough in 1812, the population was 500.

Isaac Norris was born in London, England in 1671 and moved to Philadelphia 22 years later. He was an active politician on the governors council and as speaker of the state assembly. He was also mayor of Philadelphia. When he died in 1736, his son *Charles* inherited Norriton Township. *John Bull* bought it from Charles' widow in 1766, and 10 years later, *Dr. William Smith* purchased the site of present day Norristown. His son laid out and renamed the town.

Industry/Mfg. - A Wide variety of products
   and services
Daily Newspaper - Times Herald
   P.O. Box 591, 19404
Chamber of Commerce - 73 E. Main St., 19401
Community Events -
   Freedom Valley Festival Fair, Annual, May
   Worlddance Festival, June-August

•**NORTHAMPTON**, Borough; Northampton County; Pop. 8,240; Area Code 215; Zip Code 18067; Elev. 320'; 5 miles N of Allentown in E Pennsylvania. This borough is named for the county of the same name. Furniture, paint and defense supplies are manufactured in the area. In 1939 Mary Immaculate Catholic Seminary was established here.

•**NORTHAMPTON COUNTY**, E Pennsylvania; Pop. 225,418; Established, October 14, 1751; Seat is Easton.

•**NORTH APOLLO**, Borough; Armstrong County; Pop. 1,487; Area Code 412; Zip Code 15673; Elev. 900'; W Pennsylvania.

•**NORTH BELLE VERNON**, Borough; Westmoreland County; Pop. 2,425; Area Code 417; Zip Code rural; Elev. 900'; SW Pennsylvania.

•**NORTH BEND**, Village; Clinton County; Pop. 700; Area Code ; Zip Code 17660; Elev. 665'; N Pennsylvania; was once known as Young Woman's Town, for nearby Young Woman's Creek, where, it is said, an Indian killed a young woman captive and thereafter avoided the spot in fear of his victim's ghost. Leather tanning is an important trade.

•**NORTH BRADDOCK**, Borough; Allegheny County; Pop. 8,711; Area Code 412; Zip Code ; Elev. 1,220'; 10 miles E of Pittsbuqua in SW Pennsylvania; Incorporated in 1897 and named for its southern neighbor, Braddock. Metal products are manufactured.

•**NORTH CATASAUQUA**, Borough; Northampton County; Pop. 2,554; Area Code 215; Zip Code 18032; Elev. 400'; 1 mile N of Catasaugua in E Pennsylvania; on the Lehigh River.

•NORTH CHARLEROI, Borough; Washington County; Pop. 1,760; Area Code 412; Zip Code 15022; Elev. 1,020'; N of Charleroi in SW Pennsylvania.

•NORTH EAST, Borough; Erie County; Pop. 4,568; Area Code 814; Zip Code 16428; Elev. 800'; 15 miles NE of Erie in NW Pennsylvania on Lake Erie; is bisected by Sixteen Mile Creek. Highway travel between Buffalo and the West in 1809, eight years after settlement, was heavy enough to justify two taverns here.

The town is named for North East Township, which occupies the northeast corner of the Erie Triangle, a wedge-shaped slice of land once claimed by New York, Massachusetts, and Connecticut. In 1792 the federal government sold the tract to Pennsylvania for $151,640. In addition to increasing the state's size, this added 46 miles of frontage on Lake Erie, and, most important of all, gave the commonwealth an excellent harbor.

This lake resort town is also a serious industrial center and there is a winery in town.

> *Agriculture* - Varied farming includes orchard crops
> *Industry/Mfg.* - Metal products, produce packing.
> Resort Area.
> *Chamber of Commerce* - 10765 W. Main Rd., P.O. Box 466

•NORTH IRWIN, Borough; Westmoreland County; Pop. 1,016 ; Area Code 417; Elev. 1,104'; E suburb of Pittsburgh in SW Pennsylvania.

•NORTHUMBERLAND, Borough; Northumberland County; Pop. 3,636; Area Code 717; Zip Code 17857; Elev. 452; 28 miles SE of Williamsport in E central Pennsylvania; On the Susquehanna River; was laid out in 1772 on a wedge of land formed by the junction of the two branches of the Susquehanna River; and was named for the newly-formed county it sits in. *Joseph Priestly*, (1794-1804), scientist and Unitarian theologian, lived here, and his home has been preserved as a historic site.

POINT OF INTEREST

JOSEPH PRIESTLY HOUSE- Georgian home of English chemist Joseph *Priestly.*

•**NORTHUMBERLAND COUNTY**, E central Pennsylvania; Pop. 100,381; Established, March 21, 1772; Seat is Sunbury.

•**NORTH WALES**, Borough; Montgomery County; Pop. 3,391; Area Code 215; Zip Code 19454; Elev. 380'; 20 miles N of Philadelphia in SE Pennsylvania.

Chamber of Commerce - P.O. Box 183

•**NORTH WARREN**, Village; Warren County; Pop. 1,360; Area Code 814; Zip Code 16365; Elev. 1,215'; Just N of Warren, the site of Warren State Hospital. Town lies along the west bank of the Conewago River.

•**NORTH WASHINGTON**, Village; Butler County; Pop. 240; Area Code 412; Zip Code 16048; Elev. 1,490; Named for George Washington.

•**NORTH YORK**, Borough; York County; Pop. 1,755; Area Code 717; Zip Code 17371; Elev. 380'; Just N of the city of York in S Pennsylvania.

•**NORVELT**, Village; Westmoreland County; Pop. 1,800; Area Code 814; Zip Code 15674; Elev. 1,040'; SW Pennsylvania
Norvelt was named by combining the final syllables of *Mrs. Eleanor Roosevelt's* first and last names. Norvelt is the site of Westmoreland Homesteads, an attempt to offset the effects of the "drastic retrenchment of the coal and coke industry in Westmoreland County." In April 1934, the Westmoreland Homesteads was set up on a 1,326-acre tract, with capital borrowed from the federal government. Construction work was handled almost exclusively by homesteaders.

•**NORWOOD**, Borough; Delaware County; Pop. 6,647; Area Code 215; ; Zip Code 19074; Elev. 50'; 9 miles SW of Philadelphia in SE Pennsylvania.

•**NUANGOLA**, Borough; Luzerne County; Pop. 726; Area Code 717; Zip Code 18637; Elev. 1,200'; Suburb of Wilkes-Barre in E Pennsylvania.

•**OAKDALE**, Borough; Allegheny County; Pop. 1,955; Area Code 412; Zip Code 15071; Elev. 900'; S suburb of Susquehanna in SW Pennsylvania.

•**OAKLAND**, Borough; Susquehanna County; Pop. 734; Area Code 717; Zip Code 152+zone; Elev. 1,000'; Near city of Susquehanna in NE Pennsylvania.

•**OAKMONT**, Borough; Allegheny County; Pop. 7,0939; Area Code 412; Zip Code 15139; Elev. 840'; 11 miles NE of Pittsburgh near fruit and dairy farmlands in SW Pennsylvania. Gypsum products and construction materials are made in this suburban borough.

•**OBERLIN**, Village; Dauphin County; Pop. 3,500; Area Code 717; Zip Code 17113; Suburb of Harrisburg near Steelton. Named for the preacher, *Jean F. Oberlin*, who was a preacher in the Alsace-Lorraine region of France.

•**OGONTZ**, Village; Montgomery County; Pop. (incl. with Elkins Park); Named for an Indian chief who converted to Christianity and became a missionary to his people. A campus of Pennsylvania State University is here.

•**OHIOPYLE**, Borough; Fayette County; Pop. 124; Area Code 412; Zip Code 15470; Elev. 1,220'; in SW Pennsylvania; Name is corrupted Indian phrase, approximated as *Ohio-pehelle*, meaning ''Frothy White Water,' since the stream here is whitened and bubbly as it falls over the rocks.

> *Community Event* - Ohiopyle Area Festival,
> Annual, July

•**OHIOVILLE**, Borough; Beaver County; Pop. 4,217; Area Code 412; Elev. 1,100'; 25 miles SW of New Castle in W Pennsylvania; Incorporated in the early 1960s.

•**OIL CITY**, City; Venango County; Pop. 13,881; Area Code 814; Zip Code 16301; Elev. 1,029'; 90 miles N of Pittsburgh in NW Pennsylvania; on the Allegheny River at the mouth of Oil Creek, and once the site of a Seneca village, emerged in 1860 as an important oil center.

It owes its name to the rise and growth of the petroleum business. The first settlement, which was called Oil City, was laid out on the western side of the creek by the Michigan Rock Oil Company about 1860. The new oil town grew so fast that it was incorporated as a borough two years later. In 1863 *William L. Lay* started Laytonia on the south bank of the river. A little later Vandergrift, Forman, and Company laid out an adjacent town and gave it the grand name of Imperial City. In 1866 Laytonia and Imperial City were joined and incorporated as Venango City; and five years after, the two towns of Oil City and Venango City were consolidated under the name Oil City.

Oil is still big business here, and the discovery of natural gas wells has added to the energy-producing capacity of the city. Flooding has plagued Oil City in recent years, however.

> *Agriculture* - Varied produce and dairy farming
> *Industry/Mfg.* - Oil and gas wells. Drilling
>   equipment and supplies
> *Higher Education* - Clarion State College
> *Daily Newspaper* - Derrick, P.O. Box 928
> *Chamber of Commerce* - Transit Mall

•**OIL CREEK**, Creek, NW Pennsylvania; Flows S approx. 50 miles from source in E Crawford County to mouth at Allegheny River in N Venango County, at Oil City. Named when the petroleum industrialists first arrived in the vicinity.

•**OKLAHOMA**, Borough; Westmoreland County; Pop. 1,078; Area Code 417; SW Pennsylvania is named for the 46th state admitted to the union in 1907.

•**OLD FORGE**, Borough; Lackawanna County; Pop. 9,304; Area Code 717; Zip Code 185+zone; 6 miles SW of Scranton in NE Pennsylvania; founded in 1789 when a forge was built by *Dr. William Hooker Smith*, the pioneer physician of this region. *Doctor Smith*, who was the son of a Presbyterian minister, had emigrated to the Wyoming valley from New York in 1772, and had later taken part in the famous Sullivan expedition. The traces of the old forge that he built just above the mouth of Ascension Brook on the rugged edge of the Lackawanna River are still fairly discernible. The iron ore turned out to be poor and scarce, and the business soon had to be abandoned. When a village was started a decade or two later, it naturally took its name from this well-known landmark.

•**OLEONA**, Village; Elev. 1,250'; was the principal site of the colony established in 1852 by the Norwegian violin virtuoso, *Ole Borneman Bull*, who wished "to found a New Norway, consecrated to liberty, baptized with independence, and protected by the Union's mighty flag."

    Bull was born in Bergen, Norway, in 1810; planning to enter the Church, he failed in his examinations and turned to music. His mastery of the violin impressed even the great *Paganini*. In 1831, already celebrated, but overcome with despondency because of the theft of his violin, he stood on a bridge over the Seine contemplating suicide, but was dissuaded by a French girl, *Alexandrine Felice Villeminot*, whom he later married. *Bull* played to large audiences throughout Europe; crowds in Naples, Rome, and Milan responded as they had been taught to do by *Paganini* ; in 1843-4 he made a concert tour of Canada, the United States, and the West Indies. He was big in body, an expert wrestler, and tales of his physical prowess were told, together with stories of his charity toward poor musicians and friends in need.

•**OLYPHANT**, Borough; Lackawanna County; Pop. 5,204; Area Code 717; Zip Code 18447; Elev. 790'; 5 miles NE of Scranton in NE Pennsylvania; *James Ferris* erected the first house here in 1789. Olyphant was named in honor of *George Talbot Olyphant* of New York, who became president of the Delaware and Hudson Canal Company in 1858. In that year the company extended its railroad six miles farther down the valley from Archbald in order to open up some of their undeveloped coal lands. Upon this tract the town of Olyphant was started. It was incorporated in 1876. The name is said to have been suggested by *Thomas Dickson*, who succeeded Olyphant to the presidency of the company in 1869.

Olyphant is usually explained as the Scotch and early English form of elephant.

Today this town is on the southern edge of a mountain resort area. Coal mining is the main activity.

•**ORANGEVILLE**, Borough; Columbia County; Pop. 507; Area Code 717; Zip Code 17859; Elev. 580'; E central Pennsylvania; Named by early settlers for Orange County, New York.

•**ORBISONIA**, Borough; Huntingdon County; Pop. 506; Area Code 717; Zip Code 17243; Elev. 628'; S cen. Pennsylvania; was founded in 1760 and named for *Thomas E. Orbison*, early landowner.

•**OREGON**, Village; Lancaster County; Pop. 100; Area Code 717; Zip Code 17543; Elev. 343'; near Lititz; was formerly called Catfish after the tasty denizens of nearby Lititz Creek.

•**ORRSTOWN**, Borough; Franklin County; Pop. 247; Area Code 717; Zip Code 17244; Elev. 620'; S Pennsylvania.

•**ORWIGSBURG**, Borough; Schuylkill County; Pop. 2,700; Area Code 717; Zip Code 17961; Elev. 640'; 5 miles SE of Pottsville in E central Pennsylvania; Laid out and named by *Peter Orwig* in 1796. It was Schuylkill County seat in 1811 to 1851, when the seat moved to Pottsville.

•**OSBORNE**, Borough; Allegheny County; Pop. 529; Area Code 412; Elev. 760'; NW suburb of Pittsburgh in SW Pennsylvania.

•**OSCEOLA MILLS**, Borough; Clearfield County; Pop. 1,466; Area Code 814; Zip Code 16666; Elev. 1,460'; in W central Pennsylvania.

•**OSTERHOUT**, Village; Wyoming County; Pop. 50; Area Code 717; Elev. 598'; is at the junction with US 309. On the outskirts, is a striking view of the Susquehanna River flowing through gaps in the green mountains. *James Osterhout* founded the town in 1778.

•**OSWAYO**, Borough; Potter County; Pop. 183; Area Code 814; Zip Code 16915; Elev. 1,700'; Near Coudersport in N Pennsylvania; Name is Indian for "the place of flies."

•**OXFORD**, Borough; Chester County; Pop. 3,633; Area Code 215; Zip Code 19363; Elev. 507'; in SE Pennsylvania; founded in 1801 and was named for the English university town.

Agriculture - Varied produce and dairy farming
Industry/Mfg. - Cabinet making, food
   storage supplies
Chamber of Commerce - P.O. Box 4

P

•**PACKERTON**, Village; Carbon County; Pop. 300; Area Code 717; Elev. 500'; is on a bluff high above the Lehigh River, and was named for *Asa Packer*, onetime owner of the Lehigh Valley Railroad, and founder of Lehigh University.

•**PAINT**, Borough; Somerset County; Pop. 1,177; Area Code 814; in S Pennsylvania.

•**PALMERTON**, Borough; Carbon County; Pop. 5,455; Area Code 717; Zip Code 18071; Elev. 420'; 15 miles NW of Allenton in E Pennsylvania; laid out in 1898 by the New Jersey Zinc Company and named for *Stephen J. Palmer*, company president, was incorporated as a borough in 1913. Zinc refining is still the largest industry here.

•**PALMYRA**, Borough; Lebanon County; Pop. 7,228; Area Code 717; Zip Code 17078; Elev. 450'; 15 miles E of Harrisburg in SE cen. Pennsylvania; was settled by *John Palm*, who came to America from Germany in 1749. *Palm* called his settlement Palmstown, but several years later the place was renamed for the ancient Syrian city.

> *Agriculture* - Varied produce and dairy farming
> *Industry/Mfg.* - Clothing, footwear,
>   paper products
> *Chamber of Commerce* - P.O. Box 41

•**PALO ALTO**, Borough; Schuylkill County; Pop. 1,321; Area Code 717; Zip Code 17901; Elev. 680'; Near Pottsville in E cen. Pennsylvania; Name means "high tree" in Spanish.

•**PAOLI**, Village; Chester County; Pop. 5,835; Area Code 215; Zip Code 19301; Elev. 452; 15 miles NW of Philadelphia; took its name from the General Paoli

Tavern, destroyed by fire in 1906, which had been named for *General Pasquale Paoli*, the Corsican patriot. *Paoli* led a successful revolt against the Genoese between 1755 and 1768. His patriotic struggle for independence made him popular in the American colonies. On September 20, 1777, *General Wayne's* little army was taken by surprise and cut to pieces near Paoli in a sudden night attack by a greatly superior force of British and Hessians.

Today, the town is a small industrial center of the Philadelphia metropolitan area, producing cement, office machines and pharmaceutical drugs.

•**PARADISE**, Village; Lancaster County; Pop. 900; Area Code 717; Zip Code 17562; Elev. 353'; was settled about 1800 by Dunkards and Mennonites, many of whose descendants retain century-old customs. Its name was bestowed upon it by early settlers. *Abraham Witman* first built a mill here, and a few years later, he recommended naming the growing settlement Paradise, because that was what he thought of the place.

•**PARKER**, City; Armstrong County; Pop. 808; Area Code 412; Zip Code 16049; Elev. 1,100'; Named for *John Parker*, who surveyed the wilderness here in 1794.

•**PARKESBURG**, Borough; Chester County; Pop. 2,578; Area Code 215; Zip Code 19365; Elev. 539; in SE Pennsylvania; was the site of railroad workshops built for the state-owned Philadelphia & Columbia Railroad, later taken over by the Pennsylvania Railroad. When shop work was transferred to Harrisburg in 1801, accessory enterprises gradually declined until now Parkesburg is primarily a farming town. It was named for the old and influential Parkes family. Wooden and metal skids are made in Parkesburg.

•**PARKSIDE**, Borough; Delaware County; Pop. 2,464; Area Code 215; Elev. 100'; SW suburb of Philadelphia in SE Pennsylvania.

•**PARRYVILLE**, Borough; Carbon County; Pop. 481; Area Code 717; Zip Code 18244; Elev. 440'; in E Pennsylvania; bisected by Pohopoco Creek, was settled in 1780, more than 30 years after the building of the Moravian road from Bethlehem to Gnadenhutten.

•**PARNASSUS**, Borough (defunct); Westmoreland County; 15 miles NE of Pittsburgh on the Allegheny River; Reincorporated with New Kensington in 1931; Old town was named for the Parnassus Church, which in turn was named for the Greek mountain that was sacred to Apollo and the muses in ancient myths.

•**PARSONS**, Village; Luzerne County; Pop. (inc. with Wilkes-Barre); Area Code 717; Zip Code 18701; E Pennsylvania.

Charles Parrish, of the Lehigh and Susquehanna railroad, named this village for *Calvin Parsons*, who owned the town site. It was incorporated as a borough in 1876 and grew rapidly; many years later it was consolidated with Wilkes-Barre.

•**PATTERSON HEIGHTS**, Borough; Beaver County; Pop. 797; Area Code 412; Elev. 1.060'; Suburb of Beaver Falls, in the hills above that city in W Pennsylvania.

•**PATTON**, Borough; Cambria County; Pop. 2,441; Area Code 814; Zip Code 16668; Elev. 1,750'; 20 miles NW of Altoon in SW central Pennsylvania; Named for *Col. John Patton* of Curwensville; The seldom seen Valley Mine is near town; where mining history is preserved and displayed.

> *Agriculture* - Truck and dairy farming
> *Industry/Mfg.* - Lumber, coal mining, mink raising
> *Chamber of Commerce* - R.D. 2, Box 16

•**PAUPACK**, Village; Pike County; Pop. 400; Area Code 717; Zip Code 18451; Elev. 1,540'; E Pennsylvania.

Paupack is a summer resort, with population doubling during vacation months. Named for nearby Wallenpaupack Creek, which dammed to form a small reservoir.

•**PAXINOS**, Village; Northumberland County; Pop. 100; Area Code 717; Zip Code 17860; Elev. 640'; Central Pennsylvania; Named for a Shawnee Indian chief who was friendly to white settlers during the French and Indian War.

283

•**PAXTANG**, Borough; Dauphin County; Pop. 1,646; Area Code 717; Zip Code 17111; Elev. 400'; SE central Pennsylvania.

•**PEN ARGYL**, Borough; Northampton County; Pop. 3,388; Area Code 215; Zip Code 18072; Elev. 831'; 20 miles NE of Allentown in E Pennsylvania. Founded by Welsh slate workers in 1868 and incorporated as a borough in 1882 and is located at the base of the Blue Mountains.

•**PENBROOK**, Borough; Dauphin County; Pop. 1,006; Area Code 717; Zip Code 17103; Elev. 490'; 5 miles Ne of Harrisburg in SE central Pennsylvania.

•**PEN MAR**, Village; Franklin County; Pop. 150; is near Waynesboro; is so named because it lies on the line between Pennsylvania and Maryland.

•**PENN**, Borough; Westmoreland County; Pop. 619; Area Code 417; Zip Code 15675; Elev. 980'; E suburb of Pittsburgh in SW Pennsylvania; Named for William Penn.

•**PENNDEL**, Borough; Bucks County; Pop. 2,703; Area Code 215; Zip Code 19047; Elev. 100'; suburb of Philadelphia in Pennsylvania; Named for William Penn.

•**PENN HILLS**, Urban Township; Allegheny County; Pop. 62,886; Area Code 412; Zip Code 15235; Elev. 1,200'; NE suburban section of Pittsburgh metropolitan area.

Chamber of Commerce - Penn Hills Mall
Suite 106, P.O. Box 10640

•**PENN LAKE PARK**, Borough; Luzerne County; Pop. 217; Area Code 717; Zip Code 18701; newly incorporated suburb of Wilkes-Barre in E Pennsylvania.

•**PENNSBURG**, Borough; Montgomery County; Pop. 2,339; Area Code 215; Zip Code 18073; 40 miles N of Philadelphia in SE Pennsylvania.

POINT OF INTEREST

ANDREAS REITH HOMESTEAD- 18th century stone house and barn, typical of early rural colonial construction in the state.

Agriculture - Varied produce and dairy farming,
   including grain
Industry/Mfg. - Clothing, electronics
Chamber of Commerce - P.O. box 52

•**PENNSBURY VILLAGE**, Borough; Allegheny County; Pop. 798; Area Code 412; Newly incorporated residential suburb of Pittsburgh in SW Pennsylvania.

•**PERKASIE**, Borough; Bucks County; Pop. 5,241; Area Code 215; Zip Code 18944; Elev. 400'; 20 miles SE of Allentown in SE Pennsylvania.

Agriculture - Varied produce and dairy farming
Industry/Mfg. - Electronics, clothing
Chamber of Commerce - 500 Market Street

•**PERKIOMENVILLE**, Montgomery County; Pop. 200; Elev. 200'; N suburb of Philadelphia; Named for the Perkiomen Creek, tributary of the Schuylkill River, which bears an Indian name meaning "place of cranberries."

•**PERRY COUNTY**, S central Pennsylvania; Pop. 35,718; Established, March 22, 1820; Seat is New Bloomfield
    It was set apart from Cumberland in 1820 and named in honor of *Commodore Oliver Hazard Perry*, the hero of the battle of Lake Erie, who seven months before, had died of yellow fever in the island of Trinidad, at the mouth of the Orinoco River. *Perry* was born at South Kingston, Rhode Island, in 1785. In the spring of 1813, in the harbor of Erie, amid many difficulties and hardships, he began to build his little squadron out of timber just cut from the forest. The total tonnage of his nine vessels was 1,671; only two could fairly be called men-of-war. The squadron carried fifty-four guns. *Perry* had a force of 500 landsmen and sailors. His opponent, *Captain Robert H. Barclay*, had an equal force; but his six vessels, with a tonnage of 1,460, carried sixty-three guns.
    In the famous battle that took place on September 10, 1813, the British had the advantage at first, and *Lieutenant Perry* was forced to abandon his flagship, the *Lawrence*, for the *Niagara*. By three o'clock in the afternoon *Perry* had won a complete victory. The British flag was hauled down, and the British squadron was surrendered to a

young man of twenty-eight. *Perry* then sent his famous message to *General William Henry Harrison* : "We have met the enemy, and they are ours."

•**PERRYOPOLIS**, Borough; Fayette County; Pop. 2,139; Area Code 412; Zip Code 15473; Elev. 741'; in SW Pennsylvania; was laid out in 1814 and named for the naval hero, *Oliver Hazard Perry*. The coal and coke industries gave the town its start. *George Washington* bought a 329-acre tract near by in 1769; eventually he owned 1,641 acres in the vicinity; in 1789 he leased the property and later sold it for 4,000 pounds.

POINT OF INTEREST

SEARIGHT'S FULLING MILL- Small rural factory used as fulling mill to produce coarse wool; became obsolete in 1820's. Museum.

Community Event - Pioneer Days, Annual, September-October

•**PETERSBURG**, Borough; Huntingdon County; Pop. 543; Area Code 717; Zip Code 16669; Elev. 700'; in S cen. Pennsylvania; Laid out and named by *Peter Shoenberger* in 1795.

•**PETROLIA**, Borough; Butler County; Pop. 472; Area Code 412; Zip Code 16050; Elev. 1,160'; in W Pennsylvania; The town took its name from the oil industry. In February 1872, the town site was a part of the Bear Creek wilderness. Two months later the "Fannie Jane" well was drilled into the oil land. Soon "the wilderness was filled with an army of excited oil men, and before the close of the year a town, said to contain about 2,000 inhabitants, came into existence." Three years later its population was 5,000 with the dwindling of the oil supply, the boom town declined drastically.

•**PHILADELPHIA**, City & County; Population 1,681,185; Area Code 215; Zip Code 191++; Elevation 110'.
Philadelphia, fourth largest of American cities, is long-recognized as the birthplace of the nation. It was also the first citadel of high finance in the New World and for a

time its largest settlement. William Penn and his early settlers would not recognize the sprawling commercial and industrial giant Philadelphia has become today. Penn's former "greene country towne" now covers over 130 square miles and embraces a number of smaller communities, each with its own distinct characteristics and "neighborhood" feeling.

Conterminous with Philadelphia County, the Quaker City lies along the west bank of the Delaware River and on both sides of the Schuylkill, on terrain rather more typical of the low flatlands of New Jersey and Delaware than of the mountainous remainder of Pennsylvania.

While Penn wasn't able to see his city grow, he was able to plan it. He had soured on England's rigidity and crooked streets, and today the central part of Philadelphia is a neat network of straight north-south and east-west thoroughfares. All points radiate outwards from Broad Street and Market Street, its great axis, which intersect at Penn Square in the area known as "Center City." Nearby are all of the most important government, business and cultural buildings. New luxury apartment and condominium residences are springing up everywhere, especially in the high-rise Square Center across John F. Kennedy Boulevard from City Hall at Penn Square. From this district of canyonlike streets, rectangular blocks of smaller buildings march to the city's boundaries and beyond.

The old city—the Philadelphia of Penn, Franklin, Morris and Girard—lies east of Broad Street and extends a few blocks north and south of Market Street. This is the "towne" of historic shrines, both secular and ecclesiastic, of time-arrested streets and mansions. Around these brick and stone relics are the drab wholesale and retail houses of the nineteenth century, stranded by the westward flow of trade. The industrial development of America had a marked effect on this section of the city. Each succeeding wave of immigrants—Irish, Polish, Italian and Jewish—settled within a stone's throw of the piers at the foot of Washington Avenue, then moved westward to Broad Street and beyond as new arrivals demanded space. Later the blacks made their homes in the places left vacant by the disintegrating foreign groups.

The section east of Broad Street and north of Market presents a conglomeration of commercial establishments, factories and dwellings. As the early city grew it expanded northward. Kensington, the heart of the country's textile trade, flourished in the northeast. Around this center the homes of the workers spread in concentric circles. Shipyards and refineries were built along the Upper Delaware and industrial plants usurped the open spaces. North Broad Street, once a residential avenue of brownstone mansions and carriage blocks, has become an automobile and retail mart.

Northwest from City Hall extends the Benjamin Franklin Parkway. At the far end is the Art Museum, its Ionic architecture in sharp contrast with the eclectic nineteenth-century design of City Hall. Midway between City Hall and the Art Museum is Logan Circle, resplendent with sparkling fountain and flowerbeds, a favorite spot for lovers and strollers and a resting place for weary job-seekers.

Fairmount Park, beyond the Art Museum, is the largest park in the country wholly within a municipality. Areas surrounding the park are predominantly residential. Row houses line the streets, broken here and there by small neighborhood shopping centers. The northern and western extremes are fringed with the finer residential districts of the city.

South and west of City Hall, block upon block of dwelling houses extend to the reeking oil refineries and the maritime activities of the curiving Delaware River on the south, and to Delaware County on the west.

The better shops are on Chestnut and Walnut Streets between 10th and 17th Streets. Market Street is another shopping center, but of a different type. Here are the novelty hawkers, popular-price retail stores and the majority of department stores. The produce center lies close to the Delaware. In the early hours of the morning Dock Street is bedlam as the day's supplies of vegetables, farm produce and poultry are taken from trucks, wagons and boats, to be haggled over and then carted off to the many groceries, hotels and restaurants throughout the city.

West of the Schuylkill is the area known as "University City," where campuses of the University of Pennsylvania, Drexel University, Philadelphia College of Pharmacy and Science, and St. Joseph's College are situated. This area is also dotted with organizations and companies related to university research, and is the site of the federal government's Gateway Building, with Housing, Education and Welfare department offices. A total of 21 colleges are in the city proper, 30 in the metropolitan area. Six of these include medical schools.

A diverse and often divided population of ethnic groups has contributed much to the city. Italians, Irish and Jews still maintain strict neighborhoods in the city, but often live side by side with the descendants of Germans, Slavs and Latin Americans. From the handful of slaves who arrived with the Dutch and Swedish settlers, the black population of Philadelphia has raised considerably. Today, blacks make up the largest ethnic group in the city. An act of legislature in 1870, providing for the gradual abolition of slavery, bore its first fruits in the early 1800s. Blacks, who had been restricted to domestic and manual service, found employment as mechanics, seamen, carpenters and skilled workers in the industries. They became homeowners, supporters of their own schools and welfare societies, and financiers of their own business enterprises. The catering business in Philadelphia was, for a time, monopolized by blacks through the guild of caterers. Here the African Methodist Episcopal Church was founded in 1816 by Richard Allen, one of the most important figures in black church history. As early as 1820 local blacks maintained their own press. Today they have musical and literary circles, and hold exhibitions of the work of black artists.

The city's early history is inseparable from that of the state, and during the Revolutionary period was closely intertwined with that of the nation, for Philadelphia was the first capital.

Long before the coming of William Penn, the Swedes, Dutch and Finns had settled on the tongue of land between the Delaware and Schuylkill Rivers. Only after the Quaker colonizer had acquired the Pennsylvania grant from Charles II in 1681 did Philadelphia come into being. When Penn arrived with his followers late in the autumn of 1682 he found that Thomas Holme had laid out streets and named them for famous persons. Penn, who objected to such "man-worship," promptly gave numbers to those streets running north and south, and renamed the intersecting streets for trees and flowers in the vicinity.

From this originated the jingle:

High, Mulberry, Sassafras, Vine;
Chestnut, Walnut, Spruce and Pine.

The Quakers first lived in caves within the high banks of the Delaware, but this was the "Holy Experiment" and, as the Quaker cave dwellers expressed it, "Better a dugout than a dungeon; better a cave than a loathsome prison." During the first year about 80 houses were erected, and by the following year there were approximately 600 dwellings and business houses. Penn, writing exultingly to England, declared: "I have led the greatest colony into America that ever man did upon a private credit...I will show a province in seven years equal to her neighbors of 40..."

The Quakers grew wealthy from trade and commerce with the colonies and the Caribbean Islands, shiping grain and lumber, tobacco and horses, meants and wool. Increased trade stimulated shipbuilding, and profits were high. They built "brave brick houses" along Front Street, nearly all with balconies overlooking the Delaware, and furnished them with imported luxuries. Women bedecked themselves in elaborate dresses of bright colors, for the Quakers had not yet confined themselves to costumes of drab homespun; the men wore powdered wigs with queues, broadcloth coats with silver or gold lace, knee breeches and low shoes ornamented with large buckles. Amusements were limited to riding, swimming, skating and fishing for the Friends' doctrine prohibited all such "rude or riotous" sports as gambling, fireworks and theatricals. The society, however, did not limit the amount or kind of food its member could eat; consequently meals of the gentry were lavish, and many became known for the Madeira and French wines and the West India turtle they served.

The Quakers established a public grammar school as early as 1689. By the first decade of the eighteenth century Philadelphia was the surgical center of the colonies; portrait painters were at work in the city; on the banks of the Wissahocken a medicinal herb garden had been planted by the pietist Kelpius; his follower, Dr. Christopher Witt, had established in Germantown the first botanical garden in the country.M In the summer of 1723 a young printer arrived in Philadelphia from Boston, with exactly one Dutch dollar and a copper shilling in his pocket. His inconspicuous appearance on the Philadelphia scene contrasts with the acclaim he later received in France and from posterity as a philosopher, statesman, publisher and inventor. The young printer was Benjamin Franklin, who married Deborah Reed and plunged into his lifelong business of self and civic improvement. Franklin had little sympathy with the pietism of the Quakers, and no love was lost between him and Thomas Penn, who had succeeded to the proprietorship. Franklin had a "cordial and thorough contempt" for Penn, while the latter characterized Frankin as a "dangerous man" who was putting wicked ideas about freedom "in the heads of the unthinking multitude."

Poor Richard's Almanac, published by Franklin from 1732 to 1757, appeared in almost every Philadelphia home. Franklin established the debating Junto club in 1727, started America's first circulating library in 1731, organized the American Philosophical Society in 1743 and in 1751 helped found the Pennsylvania Hospital and the Academy for the Education of Youth, which eventually became the University of Pennsylvania. He also saw to it that the streets were paved, lighted and patroled at night by guards. His kite experiment of 1752 proved the relationship of lightning and electricity. Then in 1757, Ben Franklin went to London to represent Pennsylvania.

Quaker control of Philadelphia began to weaken, partly because of Franklin's ascendancy, but chiefly because of the arrival of great numbers of Scotch-Irish and Germans. At least 95 shiploads of Germans came between 1727 and 1742. Unlike the Scotch-Irish, the Germans were not easily assimilated; they set up their own shops with signs printed in German and retained their native language. The Quakers were powerless to suppress this foreign culture; in vain they voiced their disapproval of theaters, fencing academies and dancing assemblies.

The Stamp Act, passed in March 1765, was met by the Philadelphians' resolve to eat no English food, to wear no English clothes, to drink no English beer. John Hughes, whose duty it was to sell the stamps, was expelled from his fire company—a grave disgrace in those days—and a mob threatened to tear down his house unless he gave up the odious assignment. The tax law was repealed in March 1766. When the brig *Minerva* brought the news on May 20, celebration bonfires burned all night, and the well-to-do drank bowls and bowls of punch, rolling kegs of beer into the streets for the poor. But the repeal of the Stamp Act was followed by the passage of the Townshend Act, which levied duties on paper, glass, tea and lead, and again Philadelphians boycotted English products.

News of the Boston Tea Party was received on Christmas Eve, 1773. With Christmas came the report that the tea ship *Polly* had reached Chester and would proceed up the Delaware. Anger reached a high pitch. The committee of action, formed in October, obtained promises from the two Philadelphia tea firms, Thomas & Isaac Wharton and Drinker & and James, to refuse the consignment. On the following Sunday afternoon the *Polly* dropped anchor in the river off Gloucester, New Jersey, and its captain was prevailed upon by the determined committee to continued overland to Philadelphia to observe sentiment there. On Monday morning the State House grounds echoed to the roar of 8,000 citizens demanding that the *Polly* be sent home. Two days later the ship sailed off with its cargo of tea.

As Boston's action in destroying the tea was considered more of an affront to the crown than the procedure of Philadelphia in merely returning it, the Massachusetts city was the first to feel the force of retaliatory measures. Nevertheless, Philadelphia, realizing the gravity of the situation, sent a letter to the Souther colonies with a view to forming a solid colonial front. In May 1774 Paul Revere rode from Boston to Philadelphia with the news that Boston harbor had been closed. Flags were set at half-mast, bells were muffled, shop doors were closed, and townspeople thronged the churches to hear sermons of protest.

To crystallize colonial sentiment against oppression, a meeting to discuss the formation of a "Continental Congress" was held in the State House on June 18, 1774. A committee of correspondence was set up, and the counties were invited to send delegates to a preliminary state conference, which met in Carpenters' Hall on July 15.

On the morning of September 5, 1774, the first Continental Congress opened in Carpenters' Hall, with 12 colonies (Georgia excepted) represented by 55 delegates, among whom were George Washington, Patrick Henry, Peyton Randolph, Richard Henry Lee, and John and

Samuel Adams. Moving cautiously but firmly, this body adopted the Declaration of Rights and issued addresses to the king, to the people of England, and to Canada. A policy of isolation from the mother country was decided upon, and to further this plan an association was formed. This Congress adjourned on October 26, and its proceedings were approved unanimously by the Pennsylvania assembly in December.

The opening months of 1775 were filled with suspense, unending vigilance and frantic preparations against the coming storm, which broke at last when the king's troops clashed with the Minute Men at Lexington on April 19. The news reached Philadelphia five days later. Thousands of angry citizens assembled in the State House Yard to adopt resolutions for the immediate arming and training of recruits. The First City Troop of Cavalry, still in existence, was organized in November.

The Second Continental Congress convened in May 1775. In addition to those who had served actively in the first Congress were Benjamin Franklin and John Hancock. Franklin, just returned from England, was one of the prime movers for independence once it had become evident that temporizing with the king and Parliament could do no good. Hancock succeeded Peyton Randolph as president of the Congress, which sat for two sessions, from May 10, 1775 to December 12, 1776, and assumed to a great extent the responsibility of government.

Philadelphia was now the center of the independence movement. Thomas Paine's pamphlet *Common Sense,* which appeared in January 1776, did much to convince Americans that the time for reconciliation was past. With Congress in session in June, Richard Henry Lee of Virginia presented a motion to sever the bond between the colonies and England. Although his resolution "that these United Colonies are, and of right ought to be, free and independent states," was not adopted until July 2, Thomas Jefferson had been asked to draft the Declaration of Independence. The document was written by him, between excursions to the shops of Philadelphia, in a house that stood on the southwest corner of 7th and Market Streets. It was accepted by Congress on July 4 and read on July 8 to a handful of people gathered in the State House Yard.

The city, with its population of more than 20,000 turned its energies to the assembling of machinery for war.

Before the end of July, Philadelphia had sent five battalions to support Washington's forces around New York, and a committee of safety under Franklin was seeing to the defenses of city and province. Ships of war were built, guns and ammunition were manufactured, while men drilled day and night.

Two Philadelphians, Robert Morris and Benjamin Franklin, did more to finance the Revolution than any other individuals. Morris, a wealthy merchant, obtained loans, even borrowing money on his own personal credit, to supply Washington's army with what necessities he could procure. Franklin's great service was in securing arms, ammunition and unofficial loans from France, and in laying the foundation for the treaty of alliance with that country.

On June 14, 1777, Congress decreed that the American flag should have 13 stripes, alternate red and white, with 13 stars, white on a blue field. This emblem was wildly acclaimed as Philadelphia observed at its first Fourth of July celebration. Guns were fired all day, a public banquet was held in the evening, and at night many Quaker windows were smashed by rioters angered at the society's pacifism.

Though in sympathy with the colonies' viewpoint, the Society of Friends refused to enter the conflict, even with independence at stake. When it was decreed that everyone must take an oath of allegiance to the state or reliquish every privilege, a group of Quakers broke away from the society to take part in the war. These, under the leadership of Samuel Wetherill, were known as Free Quakers until the group dissolved after the Revolution.

The several important battles fought between 1777 and 1779 for possession of the city may be referred to as the Philadelphia Campaign. Washington's defeat by Howe at the Battle of the Brandywine gave Philadelphia to the British, and General Howe with 18,000 soldiers marched in on September 26, 1777. The Battle of Germantown followed in October, but Washington's surprise attack of the city's outskirts failed to dislodge the enemy.

Howe's soldiers, well fed and comfortably quartered, reveled in Philadelphia during that bitter winter when Washington's cold, hungry and ragged forces were encamped close by at Valley Forge. While hospitals in Philadelphia were overflowing with wounded, and

American prisoners crowded in jail, British officers and soldiers amused themselves by attending balls at the City Tavern; there were dinner parties, teas, cockfights and theatricals. The City Tavern, the Bunch of Grapes, and the Indian Queen were packed with boisterous men, and Tory maids flocked into the city in the hope of obtaining British officers asd husbands. Theatricals were the favorite pastime,and Major John Andre, the dashing young officer later hanged for his part in Benedict Arnold's treason, was busy writing script, painting scenery, designing costumes and rehearsing for the *Mischianza,* a farewell pageant to General Howe, given six weeks before the commander sailed for England on May 24, 1778. Soon the British evacuated the city, Congress returned, and General Arnold was placed in command of Philadelphia.

Despite lawbreaking, currency troubles, banishment of many Friends and Tories, and the confiscation of their property, the city's population steadily increased. Estimated at 24,000 in 1777, it numbered 29,000 in 1790. industry and commerce were reestablished. The Bank of North America, the first institution of its kind to be chartered by Congress, was opened in 1782. Robert Morris and his associates had organized the Bank of Pennsylvania two years earlier. In 1786 Dr. Benjamin Rush founded the first American dispensary, and John Fitch applied for a patent on his steamboat. During the following year the prototype of modern chambers of commrce appeared under the name of the Pennsylvania Society for the Encouragement of Manufacturers and the Useful Arts. Mail and stagecoach connections were established with Pittsburgh and Reading.

Delegates to the federal convention, called to revise the Articles of Confederation, met behind closed doors in Independence Hall from May 20 to September 17, 1787. The outcome, the result of many compromises, was the Constitution of the United States, adopted June 21, 1788. Among the delegates to the convention were Franklin, Hamilton, Madison and Washington, who presided.

Philadelphia, the state capital until 1799, was the seat of the national government from 1775 to 1789, when New York succeeded it for a short period. In 1790 Phildelphia became the national capital again, retaining that distinction until the seat of government was moved to Washington in 1800. As the nation's first President,

George Washington gave that high office color and dignity. He tendered formal receptions every other week, attended the theater, and frequently drove through the city in his cream-colored French coach, ornamented with cupids and flowers. Gilbert Stuart, John Trumbull, and Charles Willson Peale were painting portraits of the city's outstanding citizens of the day.

In 1793 a disastrous epidemic of yellow fever broke out. Panic prevailed, and within a month 17,000 persons had fled to other towns or into the country. Corpses were thrown into coffins and buried at night. Persons abroad in the streets held vinegar or camphor-soaked handkerchiefs against their noses in an attempt to ward off the disease. Some smoked one cigar after another, chewed garlic constantly, or carried pieces of tarred rope in the belief that such practices would give them immunity. A period of cold weather put an end to the epidemic after almost 5,000 had died. Many more would have perished had it not been for the heroic work of Dr. Benjamin Rush, one of the great physicians of his time, and Stephen Girard, wealthy merchant, banker and philadnthropist. Rush, who was severly criticized for his method of treating victims of the fever, rejected the usual prescription of quinine; he first bled his patients, then gave them jalap and mercury.

During the first decade of the nineteenth century, such sections as Frankford, Northern Liberties and Moyamensing were absorbed by the growing city. The South Street steam ferry began operations, with boats plying between Philadelphia and kaighn Point, Camden. The Schuylkill Arsenal was contructed in 1800, and Navy Yard, authorized in 1798, was opened in 1801. Though Robert Morris, financier of the Revolution, was in debtors' prison, Philadelphia finance was encouraged by the opning of Stephen Girard's bank, with a capital of $1,200,000, and the establishment of the Pennsylvania Company for Insurances on Lives and Granting Anniuities. The Pennsylvania Academy of the Fine Arts, the Wistar Museum, and the Academy of Natural Sciences were founded.

When war broke out in 1812, many volunteered, and gunboats and forts were contructed for the defense of the Delware, the scene of t a number of engagements. During the next 20 years canals and railroads were built, connecting the city with the trade markets of the West. Philadelphia's first railroad was a six-mile line to Germantown. Within a few years the Camden and Amboy Railroad line connected the city with New York, and the Philadelphia, Wilmington and Baltimore Railroad was built to the southwest.

Commerce, the arts and the sciences meanwhile made progress. The Philadelphia Savings Fund Society was organized in 1816, the Philadelphia College of Pharmacy and Science in 1821, the Historical Society of Pennsylvania and the Franklin Institute in 1824 and Jefferson Medical College in 1825. Medicine continued to battle against epidemics, but when cholera invaded the city in 1832, more than 800 deaths resulted.

The first public school for black children was established on Mary Street in 1822; a second school was opened on Gaskill Street in 1825. In 1834 a mob tore down a black meetinghouse near Wharton Street as a protest against the growing movement for the abolition of slavery. Racial disorders broke out again in 1838; on the night of May 15 a large number of rioters wrecked and them burned Pennsylvania Hall, oon 6th Street above Cherry, which had just been completed and was being dedicated by the abolitionists.

During the 1840s many reforms were effected, including the abolition of imprisonment for debt and the extension of property rights to married women. Bathtubs and other modern conveniences began to make their appearance. The Native American or "Know Nothing" movement, organized during this decade, was directed against the foreign born, particularly those of the Roman Catholic faith. Churches and schools were burned by the rioters, who were quelled by troops, but not before two soldiers and seven civilians had been killed. In 1848 Abraham Lincoln made his first visit to Philadelphia and Zachary Taylor was nominated for the presidency by the Whigs, who held their national convention in the city.

By the Consolidation Act of 1854 the city boundaries were extended to take in the entire county. During that decade the Academy of Music was opened, the Schuylkill Navy organized, the Zoological Society formed and a number of street railways laid down. By the end of the 1850s more than a dozen horsecar lines were operating in the central section and from the city's center to Frankford, Germantown, West Philadelphia and South

297

Philadelphia. Horsecars were supplanted by cable cars in the 1880s, and these in turn gave way to electric trolley systems in the 1890s.

The sentiment of Philadelphians with regard to the South was divided during the years preceding the Civil War, because the city had a lucrative trade with that region. After 1860, however, the feeling changed. The Quakers, hostile to slavery since colonial days, were to a great extent responsible for this. Abraham Lincoln's appearance in Philadelphia as President-elect in February 1861 likewise tended to crystallize public sentiment against slavery.

In the city's Civil War annals the name of Jay Cooke stands out prominently. Cooke established a banking house in 1861. After the defeat of the Union forces at Bull Run, he canvassed every financial institution in the city and in a few days obtained pledges for a loan of $1,737,500 to the federal government. In 1862 he became subscription agent for the national loan.

By 1863 a thorough wartime routine prevailed. When it was learned that Lee's army was marching through Maryland, the city was panic-stricken. President Lincoln issued a call on June 15 for 100,000 militia to be enlisted for six months. All business was suspended, and evry able-bodied man was urged to respond. Not until news of Meade's victory at Gettysburg reached Philadelphia did the city relax. On April 22, 1865, the body of President Lincoln was brought to Philadelphia to lie in state in Independence Hal while more than 85,000 persons filed past the bier.

In the years that followed the war the city spread steadily westward. The opening of the Chestnut Street Bridge in 1866 encouraged development of the west bank of the Schuylkill. During the 1860s, when the fire department was organized, Philadelphia's population increased from 565,529 to 674,022. In 1873 the failure of the banking houses of Jay Cooke & Co. and E. W. Clarke & Co. caused a financial panic and depression, which was followed by strikes for higher wages and the eight hour day.

The Centennial Exhibition in Fairmount Park was held in 1876 in 180 buildings constructed for the purpose. Among the notables attending the opening were President Grant and Dom Pedro, Emperor of Brazil. Representatives of 38 foreign nations and 39 states and territories were present. On Pennsylvania Day, September 28, more thatn 275,000 persons attended the ceremonies. John Wanamaker's Grand Depot, opened in 1876 at 13th and Market Streets, the forerunner of the popular John Wannameker store, stimulated the foundation of other department stores on Market Street, such as Gimbel's, Snellenburg's, Lit's and Strawbridge & Clothier's.

In these years the Quay political machine began to function, with such figures as Matthew Stanley Quay, David and Peter Lane, William R. Leeds and Israel Durham in control. But civic improvements and innovations continued despite political difficulties. The city's first trolley car was installed in 1892, the Reading Railroad Terminal was opened in 1893, and the following year Broad Street was pved. In 1900 the Republican National Convention was held in the city; President McKinley was renominated, and Theodore Roosevelt, then governor of New York, was renominated for vice president. The "horseless carriage," which made its appearance locally during the 1890s, was subjected to good-humored ridicule in the first Mummers' Parade, held on January 1, 1901, to mark the beginning of the new century. The Mummers' Parade has become traditional, and today this impressive New Year's pageant of fantasy and nonsense has upwards of 22,000 participants, with more than 1,000,000 persons from city and nation enjoying it from office windows and roped-off sidewalks.

In the early twentieth century Philadelphia had a population of 1,250,000. A stream of immigrants poured in steadily from Europe, and many blacks came up from the South. The city's skyline, too was mounting. During this period wealthy residents began their exodus to outlying districts, especially along the "Main Line" of the Pennsylvania Railroad. Automobiles, growing in numbers, made the paving of the cobbled streets an urgent necessity.

In 1902 the Philadelphia Rapid Transit Company (now the Philadelphia Transportation Company), which has been involved in many political and municipal controversies, was chartered. The Market Street subway-elevated line was opened in 1907, and additional streetcar lines were built to link the central section with new residential areas remote from City Hall. By 1910 the city had weathered a number of transit strikes and had increased its population to 1,549,008. Powerful figures such as Boies Penrose, James P. McNichol and the Vare brothers had created the "Machine," which failed to function in 1911, however, when Rudolph Blankenburg, independent reform candidate, was elected mayor.

When the United States entered World War I, the production of munitions and war materials for the Allies turned Philadelphia into a hive of industry. On April 10, 1917, a disastrous explosion occurred at the Eddystone Ammunition Works, near Chester, in which more than 100 men and women employees, some of them Philadelphians, were killed; more than 300 were injured and maimed.

A new city charter was adopted in 1920, merging the select and common councils and grouping the wards in councilmanic districts. Philadelphia, with the rest of the nation, now entered an era of prosperity marked by the construction of great public buildings, theaters and apartment houses, and by a general cultural advance. Under the direction of Leopold Stokowski the Philadelphia Orchestra attained prominence in the musical world, while the Free Library, the Art Alliance and similar institutions contributed further to the city's cultural reputation.

During the depression years that followed the stock market crash of 1929, Philadelphia faced the problems of unemployment and want. As a result, in the presidential election three years later, the city rolled up an amazingly large vote for Franklin D. Roosevelt, although it had been strongly Republican since the Civil War. Destitution was alleviated by local relief activities and the allocation of federal funds and the setting up of the Works Progress Administration.

The Quaker City was the scene of the Democratic National Convention in 1936, at which President Roosevelt was renominated. Local Republicanism went down to a crushing defeat with the national ticket in the presidential election that year, when Democrats swept the city with a plurality of 200,000. In the gubernatorial election of 1938, however, the Republican ticket again carried Philadelphia, as it did in the 1939 mayoral campaign.

A degree of slum clearance was accomplished in 1937, with the inauguration of a program for improving substandard areas. Among the famous landmarks that disappeared during 1937 and 1938 were the Broad Street Theater, the old Post Office Building (replaced in 1939 with a new Federal Building), and the massive red brick structures that for years had housed the Baldwin Locomotive Works. In spite of depression many imposing buildings were erected; among them, the new Pennsylvania Railroad station, the Franklin Institute Building with its Fels Planetarium, the Custom House and the Federal Reserve Bank.

Industrially, Philadelphia is known for its cream cheese, scrapple, and ice cream as well as a number of other foods. Textile manufacturing, an important early industry, still the geatest; much of the nation's textiles are produced in its Kensington, Germantown and Manayunk mills. Hatmaking employs thousands, depending on the fashion. Growth of the city's industries was from the first made possible by its nearness to raw materials and its advantageous position 50 miles from the mouth of the Delaware River. The port is second only to New York in point of tonnage of export and import trade.

From the time of Benjamin Rush (1743-1813) to the present, Philadelphia medical men have brought fame to the city. Outstanding contemporaries of Rush were Dr. Thomas Bond (1712-89), who discovered the medicinal value of mercury; Dr. John Morgan (1735-89), who in 1765 founded America's first school of medicine in Philadelphia; and Dr. Philip Syng Physick (1768-1837), "the father of American surgery." The city's first hospital was founded in 1751; by 1940 there were 98.

As World War II drew to a close, Philadelphians turned back to look at how badly deteriorated much of the city had become. In 1945, a Redevelopment Authority was inaugurated, and the first urban renewal project was underway. The 1949 Federal Housing Act provided funds to the city for rebuilding and expanding many turn of the century apartment houses and brownstones, and pockets of the city took on a new look. Under the direction of Mayor Joseph Clark, Jr. (1952-56), badly-needed renovation was begun in all areas of Philadelphia, since there were still large slum areas left over after earlier renewal projects. Clark's comprehensive idea of urban renewal was dubbed "the Philadelphia Approach," and was used by many other aging cities. Since 1958, the Philadelphia Industrial Development Corporation (PIDC), a coalition of business and government leaders, has acquired industrial and commercial land for redevelopment, and supervised the renovation of other areas.

One prominent example of the PIDC's actions has been the development of a formery rotting area along the Delaware River into Penn's Landing, a complex of a marina, restaurants, hotels and apartments. City leaders like to point to the fact that over 375 new restaurants opened in Philadelphia between 1975 and 1980, indicating a "renaissance" in culture and nightlife.

Theater and music are also important to Philadelphia's nightlife. The Walnut Street Theater, built in 1809 and restored in 1971, is the oldest continuing theater in the English-speaking world. The new Annenburg Center at the University of Pennsylvania has two theaters that host drama, music and dance performances.

In all, Philadelphia is not the "slow and conservative" city that comedian W. C. Fields delighted in scorning in the 1930s. It has its problems with race relations, lack of housing, unemployment and crime, to be sure. But there are enough signs of a cosmopolitan liveliness here that it is not so easy to dismiss Philadelphia with a joke. Certainly its history has proved that.

POINTS OF INTEREST

ACADEMY OF MUSIC- Oldest music auditorium in U.S. in continuous use.

ACADEMY OF NATURAL SCIENCES- From 1812; the oldest institution of its kind in the U.S.

AMERICAN PHILOSOPHICAL SOCIETY HALL- Completed in 1789; served as headquarters for the American Philosophical Society led by *Benjamin Franklin.*

ARCH STREET MEETINGHOUSE- Georgian, built in 1804. 19th century religious, social, educational and civic center.

ARCH STREET PRESBYTERIAN CHURCH- *Joseph C. Hoxie,* architect. Greek Revival style, built in 1855.

ATHEUEUM OF PHILADELPHIA- One of earliest and finest American buildings of Renaissance Revival style.

BEGGARSTOWN SCHOOL- Early educational building, from c. 1740, typical of German parish schools of the time.

DANIEL BILLMEYER HOUSE- Original section built 1730, with 1793 addition. Federal style.

MICHAEL BILLMEYER HOUSE- 18th century stone Colonial house once owned by publisher *Michael Billmeyer.* Museum.

CARPENTERS' HALL- Housed the First Continental Congress in 1774. Museum.

CATHEDRAL OF SAINTS PETER AND PAUL- Mid-18th century cathedral in Italian Renaissance Revival style. High altar and interior painting of crucifixion by *Constantino Brumidi.*

CENTENNIAL NATIONAL BANK- One of architect *Frank Furness's* major surviving works; built in 1876.

CHAMOUNIX- One of many country houses built by prominent Philadelphians during post-Revolutionary period when yellow fever was a danger in the city.

CHRIST CHURCH BURIAL GROUND- 18th-19th century cemetery contains graves of many notable Philadelphians, including *Benjamin Franklin.*

CHRIST CHURCH- Excellent 18th Century Georgian church with Palladian details.

CHURCH OF ST. JAMES THE LESS- First church in the U.S. built under direct supervision of the English ecclesiologists of the Cambridge Camden Society.

CHURCH OF THE HOLY TRINITY- Mid-19th century church in Romanesque Revival style, one of several remaining ecclesiastical works of architect *John Notman.*

CLARKSON-WATSON HOUSE- Mid-18th century residence later used as Bank of Germantown. Musuem.

THE CLIFFS- Georgian country house of prominent local Quaker family; built in 1753.

CLINTON STREET HISTORIC DISTRICT- Fairly late display of Federal style in fashionable mid-19th century district.

CLIVEDEN (BENJAMIN CHEW HOUSE)- Built 1763-1764 for *Benjamin Chew,* state's attorney general; occupied as fortress by British during Revolutionary War.

COLONIAL GERMANTOWN HISTORIC DISTRICT- 18th and early-19th century residences, churches, schools and taverns; founded in 1683 by immigrating Netherlanders.

CONYNGHAM-HACKER HOUSE- Mid-18th century house, now a museum.

DESHLER-MORRIS HOUSE- Built in 1772 for shipping merchant *David Deshler* ; residence of President *George Washington* 1793-1794.

EDGAR ALLEN POE HOUSE- Home of author *Edgar Allen Poe* 1842-1844.

EDWIN FORREST HOUSE- Built for noted Shakespearean actor *Edwin Forrest* in 1865; has private theater and art gallery. Later housed the Philadelphia School of Design for Women, which became Moore College of Art.

ELFRETH'S ALLEY HISTORIC DISTRICT- The oldest unchanged and continuously inhabited street in Philadelphia.

FAIRMOUNT PARK- First major and largest (over 4,000 acres) urban park in U.S.; contains numerous noteworthy 18th-20th century structures, buildings remaining from 1876 Centennial Exhibition, many well-known sculptures and America's first zoo.

FIDELITY MUTUAL LIFE INSURANCE COMPANY BUILDING-Built in 1926. Considered one of the most highly articulated commercial buildings designed. Sculpted figures by *Lee Lawrie* regarded as finest commercial work of single most important sculptor of 20th century.

FIRST UNITARIAN CHURCH- High Victorian Gothic; built in 1882.

FORT MIFFLIN- 18th-19th century fort complex containing blacksmith shop, barracks, officers' quarters and other structures.

FOUNDERS HALL, GIRARD COLLEGE- Greek Revival structure built 1833-1847 for the education of fatherless boys.

FRANKFORT ARSENAL- Established in 1815.

FRANKLIN INSTITUTE- Begun in 1824, merged with Jefferson Medical College in 1968. Emphasizes applied science. Public museum.

FREE QUAKER MEETINGHOUSE- Built in 1783 to house Quakers disowned by their own meetings for participating in Revolution. Museum.

FURNESS LIBRARY- One of remaining masterpieces of Philadelphia architect *Frank Furness.*

GLORIA DEI (OLD SWEDES') CHURCH NATIONAL HISTORIC SITE- Begun in 1698, the oldest extant church building in Philadelphia.

GRUMBLETHORPE- First summer house in Germantown. Museum.

HATFIELD HOUSE- Greek Revival style. Built 1760, moved from original location to Fairmount Park 1930.

HEAD HOUSE SQUARE- Commercial and residential district dating from 18th Century.

HOWELL HOUSE- Good example of 18th century Philadelphia row house. Museum.

INDEPENDENCE NATIONAL HISTORIC PARK- Collection of Georgian structures built and used during city's period as principal seat of national government, 1774-1800. Includes Independence Hall, Old City Hall, Congress Hall and other historic buildings.

JOHN BARTRAM HOUSE- Built in 1731 by *John Bartram,* America's first native botanist; property's gardens reflect his work.

JOHN JOHNSON HOUSE- Built for Dutch family in 1768; was a center of fighting during Battle of Germantown. Museum.

MASONIC TEMPLE- Grand Lodge for Pennsylvania Masonry, built in 1873. High Victorian Gothic and Richardsonian Romanesque elements.

MENNONITE MEETINGHOUSE- Built 1770, interior restored, 1952. Present communion table believed used for signing of 1688 Germantown protest against slavery, first attempt by any group in British America to officially disapprove of slavery.

METROPOLITAN OPERA HOUSE- City's second opera house; operated by *Oscar Hammerstein.*

MIKVEH ISRAEL CEMETERY- City's oldest Jewish cemetery; interred here are several Revolutionary soldiers and notables.

THE MONASTERY- Unusually large Georgian house, built 1747.

MOTHER BETHEL A.M.E. CHURCH- Mother Church of the African Methodist Episcopal Church; built in 1889 on site of original 1793 church established by *Richard Allen,* former slave who left the Methodist Church because of its segregated practices.

MOUNT PLEASANT- Notable Georgian style building. Musuem.

MUSIC FUND HALL- Oldest music hall in U.S.

NEW MARKET- Open market space built in 1745 in imitation of Europe's country markets.

OLD CITY HISTORIC DISTRICT- Late 18th-20th century urban district, part of original 1682 plan of Philadelphia; includes commercial, residential and public buildings.

OLD GERMANTOWN ACADEMY AND HEADMASTERS' HOUSES-Constructed for Germantown Academy, est. 1760 as non-sectarian school.

PENNSYLVANIA ACADEMY OF FINE ARTS- Excellent example of High Victorian Gothic. *Furness* and *Hewitt,* architects.

PENNSYLVANIA HOSPITAL- Oldest hospital in the U.S., founded by *Dr. Thomas Bond* and *Benjamin Franklin.*

PHILADELPHIA COLLEGE OF ART- Major 19th century Philadelphia building.

PHILADELPHIA MUSEUM OF ART- Wide range of examples of art throughout history and special collections including much material from Philadelphia and the U.S.

PHILADELPHIA CONTRIBUTIONSHIP- Founded in 1752 by *Benjamin Franklin* ; the oldest continuing fire insurance company in the U.S.

PLAYS AND PLAYERS (THE PLAYHOUSE)- Stage operated since 1922 by local amateur theater group that claims to be oldest little theater group in continuous existence.

READING TERMINAL- Built in 1891, the sole surviving single-span train shed in U.S.; includes farmers' market beneath station on site where market has existed for over 280 years.

SOCIETY HILL HISTORIC DISTRICT- Neighborhood of commercial, residential and religious structures includes original portion of Philadelphia laid out in 1682.

SOUTH FRONT STREET HISTORIC DISTRICT- Well-preserved block; built before 1769 by various master craftsmen of Philadelphia.

SOUTHWARK DISTRICT- Comprises oldest section of Philadelphia, originally settled by Swedes and called Wicaco. Variety of notable and typical structures.

ST. GEORGE'S METHODIST CHURCH- Built in 1767, the world's oldest Methodist Church in continuous use.

STENTON- Built 1727-1730 for *James Logan*, significant for his accomplishments in botany.

THADDEUS KOSCIUSZKO NATIONAL MEMORIAL- House occupied during 1797 and 1798 by *Thaddeus Kosciuszko*, Polish army officer and statesman who served as an American general during the Revolutionary War, and who led the Polish insurrection of 1794.

THOMAS EAKINS HOUSE- Home of American painter *Thomas Eakins* from 1857 until his death in 1916.

U.S. NAVAL HOME- Built in early 19th century to house indigent and elderly sailors. Greek Revival; *William Strickland*, architect.

U.S.S. OLYMPIA- The oldest American steel-hulled naval vessel afloat; built 1890-1893. Retains original engines.

UPSALA- Fine Federal house in Germantown Historic District. Museum.

WALNUT STREET THEATRE- Built in 1809, considered the oldest surviving theater in the U.S.; first operated as a circus.

WOODFORD- Opulent Georgian mansion built in 1756 *William Coleman*, wealthy merchant and judge.

WOODLAND TERRACE- Block-long street of mid-19th century speculative housing designed by noted architect *Samuel Sloan*.

THE WOODLANDS- Built c. 1771, one of best American examples of an Adamesque house.

WYCK HOUSE- Built in 1690 and said to be the oldest house in Germantown. Museum.

Industry/Mfg. - A Wide variety of products and services

Higher Education - Antioch University, Chestnut Hill College, Community College of Philadelphia, Dropsie University, Eastern Baptist Theological Seminary, Gratz College, Hahnemann Medical College, Holy Family College, La Salle College, Lutheran Theological Seminary, Peirce Junior College, Pennsylvania College of Optometry, Philadelphia College of Pharmacy Science, Philadelphia College of Art, Philadelphia College of Tex & Science, Reconstruct Rabinnical College, Reformed Episcopal Theological Seminary, St. Charles Seminary, St. Joseph's University, Temple University,

Thomas Jefferson University,
University of Pennsylvania
Daily Newspaper -
Bulletin, 30th & Market Sts, 19101
Inquirer, 400 N. Broad St., 19101,
Journal, 3010 Market St., 19104,
News, 400 N. Broad St., 19101
Chamber of Commerce - 1346 Chestnut St.,
Suite 800, 19107
Community Events -
Azalea Festival, Annual, May; Chinese New
Year, Annual, January-February; Elfreth's
Alley Day, Annual, June; Embroidery Exhibit
and Demonstration, May; Fairmount Fall
Festival, Annual, September-October;
Festival of Fountains, June or July;
German-American Choral Festival, Annual, May;
Head House Square Arts and Crafts Fair,
Annual, June-August; International Festival
of Short Films, Annual, October; Old Swede's
Church Fair, Annual, June; Philadelphia
Festival, Annual, April; Philadelphia Flea
Market, May-September; Philadelphia Fling,
Annual, June- September; Philadelphia Folk
Fair, Annual, April; Philadelphia Philm
Festival, Annual, Spring; Robin Hood Dell
Concerts, Annual, June-July; Super Sunday,
Annual, October; Temple University Music
Festival, Annual, June-July.

•**PHILADELPHIA COUNTY**, SE Pennsylvania; Pop. 1,688,210; Established, March 10, 1682; Seat is Philadelphia.

•**PHILIPSBURG**, Borough; Centre County; Pop. 3,464; Area Code 814; Zip Code 16866; Elev. 1,433'; 28 miles NE of Altoona in central Pennsylvania; a pleasant town of well-kept houses in a scenic region underlaid with bituminous coal, was founded in 1797 by two Englishmen, *Henry* and *James Phillips*. Moshannon Creek (Ind. "moose stream"), yellowed by clay deposits, flows through the western edge of Philipsburg.

Chamber of Commerce - 14 S. Front Street

•**PHOENIXVILLE**, Borough; Chester County; Pop. 14,165; Area Code 215; Zip Code 19460; Elev. 127'; 10 miles W of Norristown on the Schuylkill River in SE Pennsylvania; at the confluence of French Creek and the Schuylkill River, occupies a site once known as the Manavin Tract, a 1,000-acre parcel of land owned by *David Lloyd* and named for his home in Wales. In 1720 a 650-acre plot was sold to the *Reverend Francis Buckwalter*, a German refugee, who with his followers settled it.

Today, the town is an important iron and steel center that has its roots in *Lewis Wernwag's* "Phoenix Iron Works" of 1813. *Wernwag* was unsuccessful in his iron production, despite the promise of the Egyptian bird that was supposed to be able to rise from its ashes to a new life.

Higher Education - Valley Forge Christian
   College
Daily Newspaper - Phoenix, 225 Bridge Street
Chamber of Commerce - 171 E. Bridge Street,
   P.O. Box 29

•**PICTURE ROCKS**, Borough; Lycoming County; Pop. 615; Area Code 717; Zip Code 17762; Elev. 551'; in N cen. Pennsylvania; takes its name from the Indian rock paintings that formerly decorated the precipice overlooking Muncy Creek about a quarter of a mile from the village. The 'murals' have long since been effaced by rock slides and the weathering of the cliff's wall. The low peaks of Bald Eagle Mountain surround the village.

•**PIGEON**, Forest County; Pop. 50; Near Marienville; so named because it was the site of "the great pigeon roost" of 1868-71, when millions of passenger pigeons, now extinct, flocked to this heavily timbered region in the Allegheny National Forest.

•**PIKE COUNTY**, NE Pennsylvania; Pop. 18,271; Established, March 26, 1814; Seat is Milford. Resort area.

On March 26, 1814, less than a year after *General Zebulon Montgomery Pike* was killed in battle at York (now Toronto), Canada, a new county, formed out of a part of Wayne, was named in his honor. Pike county borders on *General Pike's* native state, New Jersey, and at the time of its organization it joined Northampton County, in which young *Pike* spent his youth at the home of his father, *Captain Zebulon Pike*, in Easton, where the family had moved from Bucks County. At the age of twenty young *Pike* entered the United States Army as ensign in his father's regiment.

308

Shortly after the United States purchased the vast tract known as Louisiana from the French, two important exploring parties were sent out, one under *Captain Meriwether Lewis* and *Lieutenant William Clark*, to trace the Missouri to its source, and the other under the leadership of *Lieutenant Zebulon M. Pike*, to discover the headwaters of the Mississippi. In August, 1805, young *Pike* set out from St. Louis with a party of twenty picked men, and made a wonderful journey of exploration during the following nine months. The next year the intrepid young explorer was sent on a second expedition of discovery into the unknown interior of the Louisiana territory. It was during this journey that he discovered Pike's Peak. After his return to civilization in the mid-summer of 1807 *Captain Pike* received the formal thanks of Congress. In 1810 he published an extended narrative of his two journeys of exploration.

•**PILLOW**, Borough; Dauphin County; Pop. 359; Area Code 717; Zip Code 17080; Elev. 560'; om SE Pennsylvania; name changed from Uniontown in 1965.

•**PINE CREEK**, Creek; Lycoming County; Pine Creek River; N central Pennsylvania, flows E and S through Potter and Lycoming Counties to West Branch of the Susquehanna River, 100 miles long, was called Tiadaghton (Iroquois, "lost") by the Indians. Its passage from the north is through the 'Pennsylvania Grand Canyon'. Billions of feet of white pine have been floated down the creek. For more than three-quarters of a century after the signing of a land treaty with *Chief Widaagh* in 1700, it was not known which of two creeks, Pine or Lycoming, was meant by the reference to 'Tiadaghton' as the western boundary. Squatters, who ignored the question and settled west of Lycoming Creek called themselves the Fair Play Men and set up a tribunal to decide all disputes among themselves and with the Indians. Decisions of the tribunal were enforced by expelling offenders from the territory. After the second Treaty of Fort Stanwix in 1784, the Indians relinquished title to the land, and the Fair Play Men obtained legal claim to their homesteads.

•**PINE CREEK GORGE**, (alt. "Grand Canyon of Pennsylvania"), River gorge, N Pennsylvania; Tioga County, 15 miles SW of Wellsboro; Gorge is 800 feet deep and 50 miles long, with brightly colored rocks and several waterfalls. Best view at Lookout Rock in Leonard Harrison State forest Park or at Colton Point State Park.

•**PINE GROVE**, Borough; Schuylkill County; Pop. 2,244; Area Code 717; ; Zip Code 17963; Elev. 540'; in E cen. Pennsylvania.

•**PINE GROVE MILLS**, Village; Centre County; Area Code 814; Zip Code 16801; Elev. 1,300'; near State College; on Spring Creek, derives its name from a pine grove which stood near early gristmills. Settled about 1810.

•**PIPERSVILLE**, Village; Bucks County; Pop. 140; ; Area Code 215; Zip Code 18947; Elev. 440'; 25 miles SE of Bethlehem; Metal products and clothing are made in this residential hamlet.

•**PITCAIRN**, Borough; Allegheny County; Pop. 4,175; Area Code 412; Zip Code 15140; Elev. 880'; 13 miles E of Pittsburgh in SW Pennsylvania; The borough was laid out in 1892 by the Pennsylvania Railroad Company as the site of its extensive freight yards and car ships. Two years later the new industrial town was incorporated under the name of Pitcairn in honor of *Robert Pitcairn*, then superintendent of the Pittsburgh division of the Pennsylvania Railroad. Pitcairn means "cairn-croft."

•**PITTSBURGH**, City; Pop. 424,205; Area Code 412; Zip Code 152++; Elev. 744'. Pennsylvania's second city of importance and one of the greatest steel centers of the world embraces the forks where the Monongahela and Allegheny Rivers unite to form the Ohio. Named for the great British statesman, the elder *William Pitt*, this city in western Pennsylvania had its origin in a cluster of log cabins built near Fort Pitt after 1758.

The triangle formed by the rivers was once packed with smoke-grimed buildings; from the steel mills came clouds of black smoke that united with the river fog to form Pittsburgh's traditional nuisance, "smog." Some of that pollution remains, although a series of urban renewal measures has pushed most of the heavy industry away from this "Golden Triangle" area which is the core of downtown Pittsburgh. New, steel-girded skyscrapers housing engineering firms and financial institutions rise above a grassy park where industrial plants once stood.

Except for the Golden Triangle and a few outlying sections, the city stretches its length and breadth over hills. Adjoining the Triangle on the east is the formerly cramped Hill District which was little changed from its nineteenth century appearance when it was renovated in the late 1950s. The Oakland neighborhood is mainly residential, and houses the University of Pittsburgh and the Carnegie Institute. East Liberty is like a town in itself, with small businesses and a residential section terminating at the Allegheny River in Highland Park. Several other residential communities have developed slowly over the years in and around the hills. A good view of the entire Pittsburgh area can be obtained from Mount Washington, one mile southwest of the city center, across the Monongahela River. Four large parks grace the city.

The history of Pittsburgh began in 1748 when *George II* of England granted a half-million acres in the upper Ohio region to the Ohio Land Company composed of "gentlemen from Virginia and Maryland." The French also claimed this territory; upon hearing of the grant they sent forces to establish forts and take formal possession. In 1753 *Governor Dinwiddie* of Virginia, who had become a proprietor under the 1748 grant, sent *George Washington* with a letter to the French commandant at Fort Le Boeuf (Waterford), notifying him that this land belonged to the English. *Washington*, then 21 and on his first commission, stated in his Journals: "I spent some time viewing the rivers, and the land in the fork, which I think extremely well situated for a fort, as it has the absolute command of both rivers."

The following February *Captain William Trent* and 70 men, under orders from *Dinwiddie*, began to erect a small fort on the site recommended by *Washington*, but the fort was captured before completion by a strong French force under the *Sieur de Contrecoeur*. *Contrecoeur* rebuilt the fort nearer the Point, christened it Fort Duquesne, and resisted all attacks until *General John Forbes* re-established British supremacy in 1758.

311

Although the city had been founded in the struggle between France and England to gain the Ohio Valley, it was not until *Forbes* had finally expelled the French and named the settlement Pittsburgh that the region was opened to settlers, and not until the Indian warriors of Pontiac had been decisively defeated in 1763 at Bushy Run, near Greensburg, was it safe for settlement. Successive waves of immigration soon swept into the region. English settlers came north from Virginia and Maryland by way of the Monongahela Valley; others arrived from New Jersey, Connecticut, and eastern Pennsylvania. From Europe came Scots, Scotch-Irish, Germans, and a few Huguenots. These pioneers sought freedom from debt, free land, and lower taxes. They sought territory where game from the forest and fish from many streams would supplement produce from garden and farm.

The first cluster of log huts about Fort Pitt-the frontier trading post of 149 civilians who in 1760 had already subscribed 60 pounds to pay a year's salary to a teacher for their 48 children-was torn down in 1763. The inhabitants, forced to take refuge in the fort when attacked by Pontiac's warriors, destroyed their homes in order to deprive the Indians of shelter. The following year *Colonel John Campbell* laid out four new blocks bounded by Water, 2nd, Market, and Ferry Streets. After the Fort Stanwix Treaty of 1768, civil courts were set up by Virginia which claimed the land about the Forks. The controversy between Pennsylvania and Virginia continued until 1780, when the Continental Congress decided in favor of the former. During the years immediately preceding the Revolutionary War there was little need for political organization among a people employed mainly as artisans and farmers. But as conflict with the mother country grew imminent, Pittsburgh settlers prepared for it. On May 16, 1775, they met "to oppose the invaders of American rights and privileges to the utmost extreme." During the war, in addition to furnishing the Eighth Pennsylvania Regiment, they guarded the frontier and kept watch on Tory intrigue in the region. The march of the half-clad, half-starving Pittsburgh regiment through knee-deep snows over the Allegheny Mountains is as heroic a story as that of Valley Forge.

In 1783, when making the first trip westward by wagon, a feat regarded as impossible up to that time, *Dr. Johann Schoepf* described Pittsburgh as a town of "perhaps 60 wooden houses and cabins in which live something more than 100 families. The first stone house was built this summer, but soon many good buildings may be seen because the place reasonably expects to grow large and considerable with the passage of time." The next year *Tench Francis*, agent for the Penns, who still held the manor of Pittsburgh, engaged *George Woods* to survey land between the rivers, bounded by Grant Street and Washington (now 11th) Street, so that it could be sold in lots.

In 1786 *John Scull* and *Joseph Hall* brought a little wooden Ramage press from Philadelphia to the frontier settlement, and on July 29 published the *Gazette*, the first newspaper west of the Alleghenies. The coonskin culture of the frontier village established the Pittsburgh Academy in a log building in *Samuel Ewalt's* field. In 1787 a market house was erected, and regular market days were fixed. Allegheny Town was laid out across the Allegheny River, and in 1788 Allegheny County was organized.

Seven out of nine representatives from the Pittsburgh district opposed the adoption of the federal constitution, feeling that the document favored the mercantile and industrial interests for which *Alexander Hamilton* spoke rather than the interests of the plain people--the artisans, small merchants, and poor farmers-for whom *Thomas Jefferson* was the spokesman.

In 1794, with 400 houses, a fire brigade, a packet-line providing biweekly sailings between the town and Cincinnati, a regular post route to Philadelphia in operation, a post office in *John Scull's* log house, half a dozen taverns, and courthouse, stocks, and pillory, the settlement was incorporated as a borough. Already it was engaged in ropemaking, carpentering, saddlery and harnessmaking, breechesmaking, storekeeping, weaving, salt mining, flourmilling, blacksmithing, cabinetmaking, upholstering, shoemaking, and hatmaking. One of the earliest industries was that of boatbuilding, which had been established in 1760. Nine years later *Jonathan Plummer* erected a distillery and made "excellent whisky," according to *George Washington* , who sampled it while visiting

Fort Pitt in 1770. In 1788 the artisans of the city formed a Mechanical Society to which both employers and employees were admitted. Production remained on a handicraft basis, performed largely at home or in small shops.

In 1804, on his arrival from Philadelphia to engage in the banking business, *John Thaw* noted Pittsburgh as a "fine Country Town" with "tolerable good & cheap markets, dear stores & bad society..." In his opinion it was "a place by no means so Enticeing as Philada. & a person comeing from thence should do it under the conviction of making money & bettering his circumstances, but not of Enjoying the pleasure either of a country or city life. As for speculation there is no chance, landed property being already monopolized by monied men & held at very high prices..."

By 1800 the town had 44 cotton-weaving establishments, a glass works, a large brewery, and several tanyards. A tin factory employed 28 persons, a nail factory 30, and a cotton factory 12; 30 workmen were employed in shipbuilding, about 50 in boatbuilding, and 30 in the ropewalks. Powerdriven machinery was introduced west of the Allegheny Mountains in 1809 when *Oliver Evans* put a steam engine to work in the gristmill run by his son. In 1811 the *New Orleans*, built in Pittsburgh, the first steamboat on western waters, steamed down the rivers to Louisiana, opening a new era of transportation. At the same time turnpikes were built to connect the town with Washington, Greensburg, Wheeling, Butler, and neighboring communities. The Pittsburgh-Harrisburg turnpike was opened in 1817, and during the next 10 years hard-surfaced pikes were laid out along routes followed today. In 1816 the town was incorporated as a city, with *Ebenezer Denny* as its first mayor.

By the 1820's the population had grown to 10,600. Suburbs such as Northern Liberties, Kensington, Birmingham, and Allegheny were flourishing. A bridge had been built over the Allegheny River and another over the Monongahela. Thirty-two attorneys and 16 physicians practiced in the city; the Western University of Pennsylvania developed from Pittsburgh academy, and a high school met in the Unitarian Church. By 1829, with the opening of the western division of the Pennsylvania Canal, Philadelphia was brought within three days' travel of Pittsburgh at a passenger rate of 2¢ a mile; freight was carried between cities in six or seven days for 1¢ a pound.

Important from the beginning as a center for Indian trade, Pittsburgh now became a busy river port and jumping-off place for immigrants moving to the unsettled regions beyond. Arks, keelboats, and flat-bottomed paddle-wheelers plied the rivers. As settlement pushed westward, the need for manufactured products stimulated industry about the Forks. To the production of shoes, saddlery, and cotton goods was added the manufacture of such pioneer necessities as frying pans, knives, nails, axes, and shovels. Foundries and rolling mills grew in size and number as new markets opened up. Such was the grime from industry that visitors commented on the women's practice of wearing black with a white cap or a white frill, which had constantly to be changed. Population figures showed an increase in the number of foreign born, particularly Germans. Freed blacks from Maryland and Virginia became more numerous.

By the fourth decade of the century the city had four daily and 11 weekly newspapers, with 10 other periodicals; 18 printing offices and seven binderies were in operation. The number of church congregations grew from 15 to 76, including four black churches. Tract and Bible societies sprang up; young men's and young ladies' temperance societies took mass pledges and scattered leaflets and tracts. The first high school was erected in 1845; the elder *Booth*, *Charlotte Cushman*, and *Jenny Lind* performed in the local theaters. The Nightingale Ethiopian Opera Company and the Sable Harmonists were organized to satisfy the desire for Negro minstrelsy; an academy of music was founded. Freed Negroes had organized the Theban Literary Society in 1831 and the American Reformed Society in 1837.

Such was the city of which, on April 12, 1845, a minister a few miles down the river wrote in his journal: "Heard that a tremendous fire occurred in Pittsburgh on Thursday, the 10th, by which about 1,000 houses were consumed and an immense amount of property." The great fire raged over 36 acres, destroying 20 blocks of buildings. The property loss amounted to more than $5,000,000 and made 2,000 persons homeless, but only two lives were lost.

The use of steam power increased the transportation

315

of coal on the three rivers; coke ovens were built; crude petroleum from *Lewis Peterson's* salt well at Tarentum was sent to the Hope cotton factory in Allegheny to grease its pindles. *B.F. Jones* sold a profitable canal business and staked his fortunes on a small puddling works on the south bank of the Monongahela. The Jones & Laughlin Steel Company grew to be the largest independent producer of steel in the United States. The Ohio and Pennsylvania Railroad entered the old Allegheny section of the city in 1851. In 1854 the Pennsylvania Railroad completed a line from Philadelphia to Pittsburgh. The subsequent multiplication of railroads speeded the growth of manufacturing establishments, which drew workers in increasing numbers from farms and canal towns.

In 1853 and 1854, after a year of hard times, unions were organized among blacksmiths, bootmakers, bricklayers, cabinetmakers, carpenters, coachmakers, coppersmiths, engineers, machinists, marblecutters, masons, painters, paperhangers, patternmakers, printers, saddlers, tailors, tinners, waiters, and watchmakers. At that time, too, a sojourner in Pittsburgh wrote: "There is a perfect mania here for improvements. Every day somebody commences to tear down an old house and put up a new one with an iron front...One interest, however, is at a standstill, namely steamboating. Ten boats were burnt up and their wrecks lay at the wharf for a month, showing how little demand there is for wharf room." On February 22, 1856, a meeting of the Free Soil Party was held in the city to cement scattered groups from all the Northern States into a national party. During the discussions the party declared that "slavery is a sin against God and a crime against man." A plea was made also for a high protective tariff as "the only permanent guarantee of the life of manufacturing interests and safety from panics." At this convention the formal organization of the Republican party took place. In 1858 the United Sons of Vulcan, parent body of the Amalgamated Association of Iron, Steel and Tin Workers, was organized. The iron business was booming, the quantity of coal mined was increasing every year, and large companies were gradually buying out smaller ones.

During the Civil War Pittsburgh's foundries and factories worked at capacity in producing ammunition, ordance, and equipment for the Union Army. The Civil

War years released the full energies of financiers and industrialists. The volume of business grew so large, and such huge amounts of money were handled, that in 1865 a clearing house was established. At the end of the war Pittsburgh was producing half of the steel manufactured in the country, and one third of the glass.

Panic and crisis struck in 1873, but expansion of business followed. Population increased and 14 wards were added to the city. Gas came into use as a domestic and industrial fuel. This was the period marked with the rise of such steel magnates and captains of industry as *Andrew Carnegie*, *Henry Clay Frick*, and *Charles M. Schwab*. It was an era of amalgamation in industry and finance and of organization of workers in the great basic industries: of the United Mine Workers of America in the coal fields and the Amalgamated Association of Iron, Steel, and Tin Workers in the steel mills.

By 1875 there were a dozen blast furnaces at Pittsburgh, and coal and steel interests were merging with mutual profit. Labor, on the other hand, was having its troubles. In the tumultuous railroad strike of 1877, Philadelphia troops, sent to Pittsburgh when local militia refused to interfere with the strikers, shot into a crowd, killing or injuring about 50 persons. In this and later decades many blacks were brought in during strikes, and by 1901 their number had increased sixfold.

In 1881 eight national trade unions, under the chairmanship of *Samuel Gompers*, met in Pittsburgh to form the Federation of Organized Trades and Labor Unions of the United States and Canada. The organization pledged itself "to work for the benefit of all industrial classes." Six years later it was renamed the American Federation of Labor. During the 1880's efforts were made to correct architectural formlessness, to abate the smoke nuisance, and to improve housing and traffic conditions. The municipality acquired its first park in 1890, when *Mary E. Schenley* donated to the city the tract that bears her name.

In the early years of the twentieth century numerous suburbs developed and traction lines were extended. In 1907 Allegheny, the third largest city in the state, was added to Pittsburgh, bringing with it a population of 150,000. A new filtration plant did much to reduce typhoid fever heretofore prevalent. By 1910 the city's population had reached 534,000, with 80 per cent of the foreign born coming from Austria-Hungary, Italy, Russia, Poland, and the Balkan countries.

During the World War, Pittsburgh industries experienced a boom similar to that of Civil War days, and the peace years that followed likewise were accompanied by prosperity, until the crash of 20 banks between January 28 and October 31, 1929. After 1931, with the deepening of the Depression, bank failures increased and unemployment mounted. Production of pig iron in the Pittsburgh area fell from 8,975,000 gross tons in 1929 to a low of 1,505,000 in 1932. Bituminous coal production fell from 143,516,000 net tons in 1929 to 74,776,000 in 1931. Plate glass dropped from the 1929 figure of 72,143,000 square feet to 21,600,000 in 1932. Department store sales in 1933 had dropped off to 54 per cent of normal volume, and the general business activity index, based on a 1923-25 average, had declined by 1932 to 49.9 per cent.

During the 1930's changes occurred in the character of Pittsburgh's industrial production. Steel shifted from the exclusive production of heavy capital goods to sheet and rolled steel for the automobile and tin can industries. The demand for shatter-proof glass and a new type of rolled glass caused an increase in employment and output in that field, and the autumn of 1939, with much of Europe at war, business in general soared almost to the 1929 level. Steel operations showed a sharp increase as more blast furnaces were lighted, and coal production began to climb rapidly.

Up to the nineteenth century, Pittsburgh's population was composed chiefly of Irish and Scottish, supplemented in the first decades of the nineteenth century by large numbers of English immigrants. During the Civil War there was an influx of Germans; about 95 per cent of all foreign born came from the British Isles and Germany until the 1880's, when development of the coal and steel industries brought thousands of Italians, Poles, Czechs, Slovaks, Hungarians, and Russians.

The decade from 1920 to 1930 was marked by an increase of 57 per cent in the black group and a decrease of six per cent among foreign-born whites. The black, taking the place of the immigrant, has become the city's largest minority group. Twenty percent of Philadelphians are black.

Pittburgh is characterized not only by its mixed populations, but by its varied architectural tone. With the development of commerce and industry, the level ground at the Monongahela and Allegheny Rivers was given over to mills, factories, warehouses, and mercantile establishments, forcing the home builder to the hillsides. As a result of this awkward expansion, the modern city has been troubled with tunnels and inclined planes, steep flights of wooden stairs, a multiplicity of bridges, and thousands of framelings clinging precariously to the slopes above river and mill.

When the St. Patrick's Day flood of 1936 covered almost all of the Triangle, these houses on the slopes--"clingers," as they are picturesquely termed--did not suffer the fate of dwellings on the narrow strips between mill walls and hillsides. The flood waters caused millions of dollars of damage in the Triangle and on lowlands about it.

These annual floods, coupled with continued encroachment of business upon residential areas, unemployment, and property deterioration, caused a number of housing crises after the 1830s. During the early twentieth century, the slum problem was especially acute. In 1929 the Pittsburgh Housing Authority began to plan the rehabilitation of substandard areas as part of a sweeping program leading toward general beautification of the city.

During the 1940s, leaders from major corporations such as Gulf Oil and U.S. Steel joined together to form the Allegheny Conference on Community Development. The group's first goal was to provide flood controls, and afterward it began a vast redevelopment of the city center. Pollution diminished as a result of more stringent controls on industrial emissions, and the "Golden Triangle" began to live up to its namesake, with all of the new office buildings that were erected. The city's most nightmarish and congested areas were cleared for more modern business and cultural centers, as well as public housing.

Although the redevelopment continued during the 1950s and 60s, when such buildings as the Civic Arena and the 64-story U.S. Steel Building were completed, there were still large areas that had deteriorated to uselessness in the outlying areas. The city's population dropped over 15 percent during the 1960s, and 18.5 percent during the 1970s as jobs in the steel, oil and glass industries grew scarcer and residents moved elsewhere to find more pleasant surroundings. A second "renaissance" of community redevelopment began in the late 1970s under the direction of *Mayor Richard Caliguiri*, who has said that "Pittsburgh is going to be the first major city in the Northeast to see actual gains in population." Some of the population is supportive of Pittsburgh's metamorphosis from a sooty steel town into a corporate center, but others, especially from the working class, see the changes doing little for their welfare. Highly technological and financial businesses do not hire many of the largely blue-collar residents of Pittsburgh; a good deal of the employees of new firms in the city are hired from other areas to perform jobs that require special skills.

Still, the metals industry continues to reign in Pittsburgh. Over 5,000 products are manufactured here, including rubber, chemicals, petroleum products, and electrical equipment, as well as ingot steel and glass. West Pennsylvania coal mines supply the raw materials to the great steel industry.

These industries and corporations have been aided by the expansion of transportation facilities in the city. The Port Authority of Allegheny County was created in 1964 to develop and monitor all forms of transit. It oversaw a $60 million mass transit project begun in 1971. New highways, tunnels and bridges, as well as 20 railroads now serve the metropolitan area. The Pittsburgh airport was opened in 1952 and expanded in the mid-1970s.

Pittsburgh, the home or birthplace of such artists as *David Blythe*, *Stephen Foster*, *Willa Cather* and *Gertrude Stein*, has a diverse cultural life. Aside from its many small theaters and community events, the concerts of the Pittsburgh Symphony, Ballet Theater, Opera Society, and Civic Light Opera keep the ornate Heinz Hall (1971) schedule full. The Museum of Art of the Carnegie Institute and the Frick Art Museum have large collections.

POINTS OF INTEREST

ALLEGHENY COUNTY COURTHOUSE AND JAIL- A late and very influential design of *Henry Hobson Richardson*, completed 1888. Gabled dormers, towers, pyramidal roofs. Richardsonian Romanesque.

ALLEGHENY (OLD NORTH) POST OFFICE- Designed by the office of the Architect of the Treasury. Beaux Arts Classicism.

BUHL PLANETERIUM- Dedicated in honor of *Henry Buhl, Jr.* in 1939.

BUTLER STREET GATEHOUSE- Built in 1848; *John Chislett*, architect. Gothic Revival.

BYERS-LYONS HOUSE- Built in late-19th century for industrialist *Alexander Byers.*

CARNEGIE FREE LIBRARY OF ALLEGHENY- First of *Andrew Carnegie* libraries built in Pittsburgh; completed 1890. Richardsonian Romanesque.

CARNEGIE INSTITUTE- Outstanding cultural center includes public library, musuem of fine arts, museum of natural history and Carnegie Music Hall.

EMMANUEL EPISCOPAL CHURCH- Built in 1886, *Henry Hobson Richardson*, architect. Richardsonian Romanesque.

EVERGREEN HAMLET- Remains of communal society founded in 1851. Four houses of frame construction, eclectic and picturesque Gothic Revival.

FORKS OF THE OHIO- Point Park, site of Fort Duquesne and Fort Pitt.

FRICK ART MUSEUM- Large collection includes paintings, furniture, bronzes, tapestries.

HEINZ HALL- Presents concerts of the Pittsburgh Symphony, Ballet Theater, Opera Society and Civic Light Opera.

HIGHLAND PARK- 425 acres overlooking the Allegheny. Contains the city's principal reservoirs, municipal zoo, children's zoo, and aquarium.

MAIN BUILDING, U.S. BUREAU OF MINES- Palmer and Hornbostel, architects. Beaux Arts Classical elements.

MONONGAHELA INCLINE- Railway track and steel drum and cable system; important early transportation link between city's residential hills and industrial area along river; one of the city's 2 inclines still in operation.

PHIPPS CONSERVATORY- Presented to the city in 1893 by *Henry Phipps.*

PITTSBURGH AND LAKE ERIE RAILROAD STATION-Completed 1901; *William George Burns*, architect. Commercial style with external decorative motifs.

RIVERVIEW PARK- Contains the Allegheny Observatory, which was once directed by *Samuel Pierpont Langeley.*

321

ROTUNDA OF THE PENNSYLVANIA RAILROAD STATION-Excellent example of elaborate turn-of-the-century railroad station construction.

SMITHFIELD STREET BRIDGE- One of Pittsburgh's oldest and more picturesque spans, constructed 1883-1889, and one of the country's most significant. One of the earliest steel bridges in the U.S.

SOLDIERS AND SAILORS MEMORIAL HALL- Constructed in 1911 in Beaux Arts Classical style. Built to honor the county's Civil War soldiers, sailors and marines.

ST. JOHN BAPTIST UKRANIAN CATHOLIC CHURCH-Interesting combination of then popular Neo-Classical Revival style and the Byzantine forms preferred by the church; built in 1895.

ST. STANISLAUS KOSTKA ROMAN CATHOLIC CHURCH- Built in late 19th century for the first Polish Catholic parrish in Pittsburgh. High Victorian Romanesque.

UNION TRUST BUILDING- Originally built 1915-1916 as Union Arcade by local industrialist *Henry Clay Frick*. Late Gothic Revival.

Industry/Mfg. - A Wide variety of products and services

Higher Education - Carnegine Mellon University, Chatham College, Community College of Allegheny County, Duquesne University, LaRoche College, Penn Technical Institute, Pittsburgh Theological Seminary, Ref. Presbyterian Theological Seminary, Robert Morris College, Triangle Institute of Technology, University of Pittsburgh

Daily Newspapers - North Hills News Record, P.O. Box 11138, McKnight Br., 15237
Post Gazette, Box 566, 34 Blvd. of the Allies, 15230
Press, Box 566, 34 Blvd. of the Allies, 15230

Chamber of Commerce - 411 Seventh Ave., 15219

Community Events -
Black Week Festival, Annual, November;
Greek Week, Annual, March;
Pittsburgh Folk Festival, May or June;
Square Dance Festival, Annual, Novemver;
Three Rivers Art Festival, May-June;
Women's Cultural Festival, Annual, January.

•**PITTSTON**, City; Luzerne County; Pop. 9,930; Area Code 717; Zip Code 186+zone; Elev. 570'; 10 miles NE of Wilkes-Barre on the Susquehanna River in E Pennsylvania; was named for the elder *William Pitt*, British statesman and friend of the Colonies.

It was built on the site of old Fort Pittston, originally part of Connecticut. It was first settled in 1770, but by 1838, Pittston only had about 10 houses. Not until 1855 was it incorporated as a borough.

Industry/Mfg. - Soft drinks, cloth, electronics
Chamber of Commerce - 7 Broad St., 18640

•**PLATEA**, Borough; Erie County; Pop. 492; Area Code 814; Elev. 876'; in NW Pennsylvania; enjoyed brief prosperity following the construction of the Beaver & Lake Erie Canal in 1844. Named for the ancient Greek city south of Thebes.

•**PLEASANT HILLS**, Borough; Allegheny County; Pop. 9,676; Area Code 412; Zip Code 15236; Elev. 1,160'; S suburb of Pittsburgh in SW Pennsylvania.

•**PLEASANTVILLE**, Borough; Bedford County; Pop. 275; Area Code 814; Zip Code 16341; Elev. 1,240'; in S Pennsylvania; The natural deposits of alum in this area caused this borough's original name of Alum Bank.

•**PLEASANTVILLE**, Borough; Venango County; Pop. 1,099; Area Code 814; Zip Code 16341; Elev. 1,640'; in N Pennsylvania.

•**PLUM**, Borough; Allegheny County; Pop. 25,390; Area Code 412; Zip Code 15239; Elev. 1,100'; E suburb of Pittsburgh in SW Pennsylvania; residential.

•**PLUMVILLE**, Borough; Indiana County; Pop. 431; Area Code 412; ; Zip Code 16246; in W cen. Pennsylvania.

•**PLYMOUTH**, Borough; Luzerne County; Pop. 7,605; Area Code 717; Zip Code 18651; Elev. 540'; W suburb of Wilkes-Barre on the Susquehanna River in E Pennsylvania; named and incorporated from Plymouth Township, one of the five townships formed by the Susquehanna Company on December 28, 1768. Its name was derived from Plymouth in Litchfield County, Connecticut. The Connecticut town was doubtless named for Plymouth in Massachusetts, the oldest settlement in New England. The Pilgrim Fathers called their town Plymouth because the *Mayflower* had sailed from Plymouth in Devonshire, which lies at the mouth of the River Plym. To the early Pennsylvania settlers the little village of Plymouth was known as Shawneetown because it was near the site of an old Shawnee Indian village.

•**PLYMOUTH MEETING**, Village; Montgomery County; Area Code 215; Zip Code 19462; Elev. 180'; in SE Pennsylvania; was founded about 1685. The Plymouth Meetinghouse, with its ivy-covered stone walls and L-shaped porch, was erected between 1710 and 1712. The one-and-a-half-story building was rebuilt after a fire in 1867.

POINTS OF INTEREST

ALAN W. CORSON HOMESTEAD- Pre-1734 stone, stuccoed building. Property used by Quaker *Alan W. Corson* as an early regional nursery with over 2,000 varieties of apple trees, and as a boarding school.

PLYMOUTH FRIENDS MEETINGHOUSE- Township's first school; hospital and gathering place for *George Washington's* troops during Revolutionary War; later used by abolitionists.

PLYMOUTH MEETING HISTORIC DISTRICT- Residential district with dwellings exhibing English and Welsh Quaker influence. Possibly the county's first English settlement; some dwellings present by 1698.

•**POCONOS MOUNTAINS**, Range, E Pennsylvania; Avg. Elev., 1,658'.

Snow skiing and summer lake resorts dot this hilly region only 30 miles from Scranton. In the autumn, fox hunting is a favorite pastime, and a horse show is held in Mt. Pocono annually. Through the deep ravines of this region flow spring-fed streams stocked with trout. This led Henry van Dyke to pose the plaintive question: " Do you remember, father, it seems so long ago, the day we fished together along the Pocono?"

•**POINT MARION**, Borough; Fayette County; Pop. 1,642; Area Code 412; Zip Code 15474; Elev. 815'; 20 miles SW of Uniontown in SW Pennsylvania; at the confluence of the Cheat and Monongahela Rivers, was laid out in 1842, and named for *General Francis Marion*, the "Swamp Fox" of the Revolution.

POINT OF INTEREST

ALBERT GALLATIN HOUSE- Home of *Albert Gallatin* (1788-1832), prominent Secretary of the Treasury and diplomat.

•**POINT PLEASANT**, Village; Bucks County; Pop. 700; Area Code 215; Zip Code 18950; Elev. 132'; 20 miles SW of Uniontown in SE Pennsylvania; a snug village at the mouth of the Tohickon Creek, occupies a site where Indians once quarried argillite for arrowheads and knifeblades. White settlement occurred prior to 1747. Glassware and soft drinks are made in this village, which is near several coal mines.

•**POLK**, Borough; Venango County; Pop. 1,884; Area Code 814; Zip Code 16342; Elev. 1,116'; 15 miles SW of Oil City in NW Pennsylvania; settled about 1798, took form in 1839 when *Aaron McKissick* purchased the site and laid out a village. When incorporated in 1886, it was named for *President James K. Polk*. Today the town is a resort center.

•**PORTAGE**, Borough; Cambria County; Pop. 3,510; Area Code 814; Zip Code 15946; Elev. 1,700'; 20 miles NE of Johnstown in a coal mining region in SW cen. Pennsylvania; named for the old Portage Railroad, which once extended from Hollidaysburg to Johnstown. This unique railroad, completed in 1832 under the patronage of the state, carried the canal boats across the Allegheny Mountains. Thus continuous communication was established between Philadelphia and Pittsburgh. The boats were loaded upon cars, and drawn up and let down inclined planes by means of stationary engines and long wire ropes. The portage-or land passage between waters-consisted of five of these inclines on each side of the mountains. Thus an elevation of more than 1,000 feet was successfully surmounted. The extension of the Pennsylvania Railroad to Pittsburgh in 1852 put an end to the portage system.

•**PORT ALLEGANY**, Borough; McKean County; Pop. 2,593; Area Code 814; Zip Code 16743; Elev. 1,484'; 20 miles SE of Olean, New York on the Allegheny River in N Pennsylvania; was the center of the tremendous lumbering operations along the Allegheny River that reached their peak between 1830 and 1840. Raftsmen thought nothing of returning from Pittsburgh on foot, making as many as 20 such trips a year. Later, when oil was discovered, the rafts were used to convey barreled oil down the Allegheny.

Chamber of Commerce - Main Street

•**PORT CARBON**, Borough; Schuylkill County; Pop. 2,576; Area Code 717; Zip Code 17965; Elev. 720'; 5 miles NE of Pottsville in E cen. Pennsylvania; in the 1830's, great cargoes of coal were shipped from here on the Schuylkill Canal.

•**PORT CLINTON**, Borough; Schuylkill County; Pop. 337; Area Code 717; Zip Code 19549; Elev. 401'; in E cen. Pennsylvania; was founded in 1829, was an important transfer point in canal-boating days; it later boomed as a division junction of the Reading Railroad.

•**PORTERSVILLE**, Borough; Butler County; Pop. 320; Area Code 412; Zip Code 16051; Elev. 1,380'; in W Pennsylvania; (originally Stewartsville), was at the time of its incorporation in 1844 renamed in honor of *David Rittenhouse Porter*, then governor of the Commonwealth.

•**PORTLAND**, Borough; Northampton County; Pop. 540; Area Code 215; Zip Code 18351; Elev. 293'; in E Pennsylvania; was founded in 1845 by *Captain James Ginn*, of Portland, Maine.

•**PORT MATILDA**, Borough; Centre County; Pop. 647; Area Code 814; Zip Code 16870; Elev. 1,015'; 15 miles W of State College on Bald Eagle Creek in central Pennsylvania.

•**PORT ROYAL**, Borough; Juniata County; Pop. 835; Area Code 717; Zip Code 17082; Elev. 445'; 15 miles SE of Lewiston in S central Pennsylvania; located on the Juniata River in a dairy farming area. Lumber is cut in the mills here.

Community Event -
Old Home Days, Annual, July-August.

•**PORT VUE**, Borough; Allegheny County; Pop. 5,316; Area Code 412; Elev. 900; 10 miles SE of Pittsburgh in SW Pennsylvania.

•**POTTER COUNTY**, N Central Pennsylvania; Pop. 17,726; Established, March 26, 1804; Seat is Coudersport.

It was named after *James Potter*. Born in Tyrone, Ireland, in 1729, and came to Pennsylvania in 1741 with his father, *John Potter*, who nine years later became the first sheriff of Cumberland County. *James* was a captain and later a major in the Indian wars. In 1777 he was made a brigadier-general of Pennsylvania troops in the Revolutionary army, serving with distinction almost continuously throughout the war, and receiving a commission as major-general in 1782. In the spring of 1778 *Washington* wrote from Valley Forge: "If the state of *General Potter's* affairs will admit of his returning to the army, I shall be exceedingly glad to see him, as his activity and vigilance have been much wanted during the winter."

In 1781 he was vice-president of Pennsylvania, and in the following year he was *John Dickinson's* strongest rival for the governorship. After the war *General Potter* retired to his estate of 6,000 acres in Penn's Valley, near the present borough of Centre Hall, where, in 1789, he died from injuries received in helping to raise a barn. The surname Potter originated as an occupation name.

•**POTTERS MILLS**, Village; Centre County; Pop. 150; Area Code 814; Elev. 1,257'; in E Pennsylvania; is a crossroads village in Penn's Valley, named for *James Potter*, a brigadier-general under *Washington*, who settled here after the Revolution and built several steel mills.

•**POTTSTOWN**, Borough; Montgomery County; Pop. 22,729; Area Code 215; Zip Code 19464; Elev. 138'; 15 miles SE of Reading in SE Pennsylvania; is at the junction of Manatawny (Ind. "place where we drink") Creek and the Schuylkill River in the heart of a rich agricultural district. From the early eighteenth century when iron forges were built here, Pottstown's industrial character has gradually broadened.

In 1716 *Thomas Rutter*, one time bailiff of Germantown, set up on Manatawny Creek, not far from the present borough limits, the first iron forge in the province. About 1754, *John Potts*, a prominent ironmaster whose father had been asociated with *Rutter*, laid out a town, and in 1815 the place was incorported as the borough of Pottstown.

POINTS OF INTEREST

POTTSTOWN ROLLER MILL- Constructed 1825, one of the earliest gristmills in Pennsylvania, oldest continuing manufacturing company in Pottstown.
POTTSGROVE MANSION- Georgian mansion built 1752-1754 by *John Potts*, founder of Pottstown.

Agriculture - Varied produce and dairy farming
Industry/Mfg. - A Wide variety of products
    and services
Daily Newspaper - Mercury, Hanover & King Sts.
Chamber of Commerce - 1200 High St.
Community Events -
    Mini-Festival, Annual, July;
    Downtown Fair Days, Annual, May.

•POTTSVILLE, City; Seat of Schuylkill County; Pop. 18,195; Area Code 717; Zip Code 17901; Elev. 625'; 35 miles N of Reading on the Schuylkill River in E cen. Pennsylvania; the family of the first settler, *Henry Neyman*, was massacred by Indians 26 years before *John Pott* purchased land here in 1806. The rush to the coal fields from 1824 to 1829 permanently altered *John Pott's* town. Situated at the southern edge of the lower anthracite field, Pottsville proved to have no coal, but some of the newcomers went to work manufacturing machinery, boilers, mine cars, hoisting engines, and pumps needed in the mines. Development continued along this line until the town became the manufacturing and transportation center of the southern or lower anthracite district. By 1840, there were over 4,000 residents.

Pottsville was one of the rallying places of the Molly Maguires, a secret society of miners formed about 1860, and named for an organization that had fought the agents of absentee landlords in Ireland. Even today differences of opinion exist concerning the real nature of this organization. The miners of the period labored under extremely difficult conditions and for small wages; their sporadic strikes were usually beaten down with violence. The Mollies attempted, apparently, to restore a balance. Their methods, carried out on a wide scale according to the

328

version later brought out in court, included threats and violence. A local journal accused the Mollies of perpetrating 50 murders in the four-year period ending March 30, 1867. Between 1862 and 1875 they attained considerable power in the coal regions, especially around Pottsville. After a sensational trial at Pottsville in June 1877, six Mollies were hanged for murder, and many were sentenced to long prison terms. The prosecution's key witness was *James McParlan*, who for more than two years had been simultaneously an active member of the Mollies and a Pinkerton operative, hired by *Franklin B. Gowen*, president of the Philadelphia and Reading Railroad Company, largest mine operator in the anthracite region. In all, 10 Molly Maguires were hanged, and 14 were sentenced to prison in Pottsville, Mauch Chunk, and Bloomsburg. These hangings, coupled with widespread popular opposition, destroyed the Mollies as an organization.

The city was incorporated in the 1920s.

Agriculture - Varied produce and dairy farming
Industry/Mfg. - A Wide variety of products
    and services. Coal mining
Daily Newspaper - Republican, 111 Mahantongo St.
Chamber of Commerce - 201 E. Laurel Blvd.

•**PRINGLE**, Borough; Luzerne County; Pop. 1,221; Area Code 717; Zip Code 18704; Elev. 660'; near Wilkes-Barre in E Pennsylvania.

•**PROMPTON**, Borough; Wayne County; Pop. 249; Area Code 717; Zip Code 18456; Elev. 1,095'; At S end of Prompton Dam and Reservoir in a state park recreational area in NE Pennsylvania.

•**PROSPECT**, Borough; Butler County; Pop. 1,016; Area Code 412; Zip Code 16052; Elev. 1.369'; in W Pennsylvania; in an early agricultural section, first settled in 1796. Today it is a residential suburb of Butler.

•**PROSPECT PARK**, Borough; Delaware County; Pop. 6,593; Area Code 215; Zip Code 19076; Elev. 80'; 5 miles NW of Chester in SE Pennsylvania; the largest industry in this residential suburb is a wire factory.

329

MORTON HOMESTEAD- Two 1-story log cabins connected by stone center, typical of dwellings built by the state's early settlers. Home of *John Morton*, signer of the Declaration of Independence.

•**PUNXSUTAWNEY**, Borough; Jefferson County; Pop. 7,479; Area Code 814; Zip Code 15767; Elev. 1,236'; 80 miles NE of Pittsburgh on Mahoning Creek in W cen. Pennsylvania.

Shawnee wigwam villages once occupied the site. The first civilized settlement was in 1772, when the *Reverend John Ettwein*, a Moravian missionary, arrived with a band of 241 Christianized Delaware. Swarms of gnats, which for years plagued early settlers and their livestock, are blamed for *Ettwein's* failure to establish a permanent settlement. Under date of July 19, 1772, *Ettwein's* journal contains the following entry: "In the evening all joined me, but we could hold no service because the *ponkies* were so excessively annoying that the cattle pressed into the camp to escape their persecutors in the smoke of the fire. These vermin are a plague to man and beast by day and night. In the swamp through which we are now passing their name is legion." Indians called the insects *ponkies* (living dust and ashes), and the village was called *Ponkis Utenink* (land of the ponkies), from which the present name evolved. One of the legends concerning the origin of the term *ponkies* involves an old Indian sorcerer-hermit who had long terrorized the Indians in the region. Eventually he was killed, his body was burned, and the ashes were cast to the winds. The ashes, according to the story, were transformed into minute living things that infested the swamp land. Others account for the term by asserting that the Indians compared the insect bites to burns caused by sparks or hot ashes.

Settlers drawn by lumbering and the discovery of coal eventually exterminated the insects. Shortly after 1850, iron furnaces, glass works, tanneries, and brickyards supplemented mining activity.

Agriculture - Grain and varied produce and
　　dairy farming
Industry/Mfg. - Electronics, shoes, coal mining
Higher Education - Indiana University of Pennsylvania
Daily Newspaper - The Spirit, 111 N. Findley St.
Chamber of Commerce - 123 S. Gilpin St.

•**PYMATUNING RESERVOIR**, Reservoir, Crawford County; NW Pennsylvania; at Ohio state boundary. Formed by a damming of a branch of the Shenango River. A state park is a S tip of lake.

•**QUAKERTOWN**, Borough; Bucks County; Pop. 8,867; Area Code 215; Zip Code 18951; Elev. 499'; 15 miles SE of Allentown in SE Pennsylvania; was founded by Quakers from Gwynedd, Wales in 1715. Its factories--hosiery, clothing, and luggage--have made outward accommodation. Quakertown was a center of the Fries' or "Hot Water" Rebellion. In 1798, when war with France seemed imminent, the federal government endeavored to raise $2,000,000 by levying taxes on land, houses, and black slaves. As there were comparatively few slaves in Pennsylvania, the excise fell heavily on land and houses. The house tax was based on the number and size of windows. The sight of assessors carefully measuring windows so irritated the Pennsylvania German housewives that they frequently greeted federal agents with a dash of hot water. *John Fries* became the chief inciter of the country people, by reason of a vitriolic tongue developed as an auctioneer. When armed opposition against assessors and collectors resulted in the calling of troops, *Fries* disappeared. Soldiers caught him when his dog, Whisky, revealed his hideout. Although found guilty of treason, he was eventually pardoned. One effect of the rebellion was the weaning of the preponderantly German population from the Federalist party to that of Jefferson.

> *Agriculture* - Varied produce and dairy farming, especially potatoes
> *Industry/Mfg.* - A Wide variety of products and services
> *Daily Newspaper* - Free Press, 312 W. Broad St.
> *Chamber of Commerce* - 78 West End Blvd., P.O. Box 484
> *Community Event* - Arts Festival, Annual, September

•**QUARRYVILLE**, Borough; Lancaster County; Pop. 1,558; Area Code 717; Zip Code 17566; Elev. 488'; in SE Pennsylvania; near Stony Hill, lies in the broad fertile Chester Valley, the southern limit of the limestone belt. Development of limestone quarries about 1820 came in time to save profitable farms rapidly becoming sterile. Later, quarrying was discontinued and farming again suffered.

The custom of observing Ground-hog Day begun here in 1907. Annually, on February 2, members of the lodge, clad in picturesque robes, wait before a ground hog hole for the animal to emerge. If the day is sunless, so that the ground hog does not see his shadow, spring is said to be imminent; if the animal does see his shadow, there is bad weather ahead; no record of accuracy has been kept. The occasion is celebrated with a banquet and much gaiety.

POINT OF INTEREST

ROBERT FULTON BIRTHPLACE- Birthplace of *Robert Fulton*, artist and inventor who developed a submarine and the first commercially successful steamboat. Museum.

•**QUINCY**, Village; Franklin County; Pop. 400; Area Code 717; Elev. 710'; in S Pennsylvania; named for *John Quincy Adams*, sixth President of the U.S.

R

•**RADNOR**, Urban Township; Delaware County; Area Code 215; Elev. 250'; in W Pennsylvania; residential suburb.

Settled and named in 1683 by Quakers from Radnorshire, Wales. Cabrini College is located in this town, where over 20 magazines and journals are published.

> *Primarily a residential area*
> *Higher Education* - Cabrini College,
> Pennsylvania State College

•**RAILROAD**, Borough; York County; Pop. 272; Area Code 717; Zip Code 17355; Elev. 740'; in S Pennsylvania.

•**RAINSBURG**, Borough; Bedford County; Pop. 201; Area Code 814; Elev. 1,400'; in S Pennsylvania.

•**RALSTON**, Village; Lycoming County; Pop. 375; Area Code 717; Zip Code 17763; Elev. 852'; in N cen. Pennsylvania; crowded by massive hills, was founded in 1831 by *Matthew C. Ralston*, a wealthy Philadelphian, whose dream of an iron-producing center led him to build a blast furnace here, and to construct a road, and later a railroad, between the settlement and Williamsport. Expenses of the railroad drained *Ralston's* resources, and failure of the iron-mining venture left him almost penniless. Subsequently, lumber mills, a brickyard, a pottery works, and tanneries supported the townspeople.

•**RAMEY**, Borough; Clearfield County; Pop. 568; Area Code 814; Zip Code 16671; Elev. 1,610'; in W cen.Pennsylvania.

•**RANKIN**, Borough; Allegheny County; Pop. 2,892; Area Code 412; Zip Code 15201; Elev. 747'; 5 miles E of Pittsburgh, on the Monongahela River in SW Pennsylvania.

It was on this site and that of Braddock adjoining it,

that *General Edward Braddock's* British and Colonials met defeat at the hands of the French and Indians in 1755. The Carrie Furnace, stretching along the river bank for a mile and extending into the borough limits of Swissvale, was established in 1883. About 1870 a man named *Thomas Rankin* bought a farm, built a house, and lived where the town now stands. At that time Rankin's house was the only one in sight, and the Baltimore and Ohio Railroad made it a stopping place, callin the station Rankin. The present town has grown up about the railway station. The family name Rankin is a diminutive of Rann, or Rand, which has been shortened from Randolf or Randolph, "the shield wolf."

•**READING**, City; Seat of Berks County; Pop. 78,582; Area Code 215; Zip Code 196+zone; Elev. 264'; 70 miles NW of Philadelphia on the Schuylkill River in SE Pennsylvania; on the Schuylkill River's bank in southeastern Pennsylvania, is known to those who have never visited it as the capital of "Pennsylvania German-land" and the second city in the United States to accept socialism. To the stranger within its gates it seems a place of paradoxes. There is the Chinese pagoda on Mount Penn, overlooking the red roofs of the city, the surrounding hills, and the Schuykill. There are more Pennsylvania Germans concentrated here than in any other part of the state.

The Pennsylvania German is known for orderliness and thriftiness, and these traits are reflected in the appearance of Reading. The central section is laid out with gridiron simpicity; urban residential areas are made up of row upon row of red brick houses, and only in the newer suburban districts has complete economy of space been disregarded. The city is bisected from north to south by a belt of large industrial plants. The worker-home-owner sets the economic and cultural standards of the city.

It was the forebears of this worker, the artisans of Germany with their specialized skill in varied sorts of handicraft, who gave impetus to the industrial development of Reading and determined the direction in which it should move. When industrialization had been accomplished, it was the pragmatic, stolid Pennsylvania German who caught the attention of the nation by electing Socialists to operate his city government and to represent him in the state legislature. Led by such figures as *"Jim" Maurer*, active in the labor movement since the days of the Knights of Labor, this political movement drew its support from all workers, even the aristocratic full-fashioned knitters, and from small shopkeepers and some professional people. To them it meant nothing so remote as government ownership of the means of production. They did little theorizing. They accepted the promise of concrete benefits: honest government, higher wages, lower taxes, better schools. Thus, the most revolutionary act of the power plant, and the voters refused this. Yet Reading has a school building program and a wage scale for teachers that exceeds that of comparable cities. Moreover, there is the curious anomaly of progressive educational methods initiated in the center of an area where some older people, many of whose ancestors came here as early as 1748, speak only the Pennsylvania German dialect and cling to the customs of the past.

The Pennsylvania German has been labeled as an unimaginative and exclusively practical being. Yet concerts, opera, and other musical programs enjoy considerable patronage in Reading. Even in the days of scattered settlement, community "sings" were popular and dancing masters established schools. The church choir, then as today, was an important element in the life of the community. One contemporary fete corresponding in some respects to the "sing" is the annual *fersommling*, or folk gathering, one of whose features is the singing of the dialect version of "America" by the 1,500 assembled "Dutchmen":

> *Meland, ich sing fun dir,*
> *Siess is die Freiheet mir,*
> *Do will ich sei . . .*

Professional musical organizations came into existence very early; the 78-piece Reading Symphony Orchestra and the Ringgold Band are among the oldest of their kind in America. Since 1880 the reading choral Society has given public concerts of the great choral works, and in 1934 initiated an annual presentation of the Bach *Mass in B Minor*. There are choral clubs, chamber music ensembles, and regular concerts by visiting artists and groups.

Strangely, it was not Germans but English who began settlement of Reading. William Penn had purchased from the Lenni Lenape Indians a tract extending miles on both sides of the river as far northeast as two full days' journey, and two of his relatives settled here in 1733. Other settlers followed and took up farms. In 1748 the town was laid out by *Nicholas Scull* and *William Parsons* under the supervision of *Thomas Penn*, who had repurchased the land. *Penn* named it for the seat of Berkshire, England, the name of which was derived from the Saxon words *rhedin*, a fern, and *ing*, a meadow. Four years later, when Berks County was established, Reading became the county seat, "having 130 dwellings, 1 store, 41 stables, cabins, huts, and outhouses; 160 families consisting of 379 persons; 3 churches, Lutheran, Reformed, and Friends."

During the French and Indian War the town was at first left unprotected, but later the provincial government established a military base here. In 1758 Reading furnished *General John Forbes* with "fifty-six good Strong Waggons" and "freeholders who have the English and German tolerable well." Already there were so many Germans in the territory that it was a handicap not to know the language.

When the Revolution came, the Berks County Germans threw their support to the rebels, perhaps because they ahd so little kinship with their English rulers. As early as 1774 a citizens' meeting had adopted a resolution of sympathy with Boston and urged action that would "settle with precision the rights of America." In April 1775, two companies of infantry were sent to Massachusetts and participated in action around Cambridge. From 1776 Reading was used as a depot for Continental military supplies and was the site of a camp for British and Hessian prisoners. Forges and furnaces turned out cannon for the army.

By 1783 Reading had a population of 2,100 and was incorporated as a borough; 10 years later a post office was established. Signs of future industrial development were apparent. Iron works were growing rapidly, wool and felt hats were being manufactured, and assorted hosiery made here was underselling similar products imported from England. The hundreds of skilled German craftsmen were finding in the new land raw materials on which they could employ all their artistry.

Industrial development was further accelerated by advances in transportation. Completion of a canal system in 1828 and extension of the Philadelphia and Reading Railroad in 1838 linked the town with other commercial centers. By 1851, four years after it had received its first city charter, Reading was a center of the iron industry, with 41 works operating in its immediate vicinity. The construction of the Schuylkill Valley Division of the Pennsylvania Railroad in 1884 opened up distant markets for the city's many products.

Meanwhile, industrial growth had been accompanied by unionization of labor and some strikes. Formation of an iron molders' union in 1872 was followed rapidly by organization of the cigarmakers, painters, typographical workers, brewery workers, and building trades workers. The most serious labor disturbance reached a bloody climax in July 1877, during the general railroad strike of that year. When 200 militiamen, called in after several days of riot, were greeted with brickbats and jeers as they marched past assembled strike sympathizers, an excited officer gave the order to fire. Ten persons were killed and scores injured.

During the latter decades of the nineteenth century, as expanding industry absorbed an influx of immigrant labor, predominantly German, Reading's population more than doubled. Capital was exploring every avenue to profits, and manufacturing was becoming increasingly diversified. The invention of the "horseless carriage," for instance, brought the pioneer automobile manufacturer, *Charles E. Duryea*, to Reading in 1900 to establish the Duryea Power company plant. *Duryea*, who had previously made automobiles in Springfield, Massachusetts, turned them out in Reading at the rate of one a week for 15 years. Inability to obtain sufficient capital finally compelled him to abandon the enterprise.

Duryea's was only one of many new ventures. By 1940 Reading's products included pretzels, steel, cough drops, shoes, bricks, automobile frames, goggles, gas ranges, paint, wrought-iron pipes, and letter boxes, to cite a few. By far the most important development of the early twentieth century, however, was the rapid emergence of the textile industry as the financial bulwark of the city, due directly to the influx of skilled German workers and to the organizing ability of their leaders. In 1940 at least half the wage earners of Reading and its suburbs worked in textile mills, with full-fashioned hosiery alone employing more than one third.

Since World War II, clothing and hosiery have continued to be major industries, although recent fashion changes have lessened the demand for hosiery somewhat. Auto bodies and other steel products are also made here, and various food specialties of the Pennsylvania Dutch, such as pretzels and beer, are successful industries. However, Reading is experiencing the effects of growing unemployment and a declining population, a problem common to many Pennsylvania cities. The emergence of many factory outlet shops have helped add to the city's economy, since shoppers come from a wide area to find bargains.

Many attractive points of interest are locted in the city or nearby.

POINTS OF INTEREST

ASKEW BRIDGE- So named because its courses of brown stone are laid out in ellipsoidal curves. Constructed 1857, the best U.S. example of a skew bridge.

BERKS COUNTY HISTORICAL SOCIETY- Houses collection of ancient fire-fighting equipment.

CONRAD WEISER HOUSE- Home of German immigrant *Conrad Weiser*, who played an important role in relations between the Indians and the Colonists. Museum.

DANIEL BOONE PARK- Site of famous frontiersman *Daniel Boone's* birthplace and boyhood home.

HOLY TRINITY LUTHERAN CHURCH- Striking in its Colonial and Greek Revival details.

HOPEWELL VILLAGE NATIONAL HISTORIC SITE- Early industrial village dating back to 1770. Restored and reconstructed frame structures, including furnace, charcoal house, blacksmith shop and ironmaster's house.

PAGODA- 1908 reproduction of main tower of the Japanese Battle Castle in Nagoya, Japan. Summer home of politician *William Abbott Witman* ; later adapted for hotel use.

PENN'S COMMONS- The 50-acre park in the center of city contains lawns gardens and receational facilities; resting place of the battleship "Maine's" anchor.

PUBLIC MUSEUM AND ART GALLERY- Ornate Itallian Renaissance design. Contains art and science exhibits; arboretum.

Industry/Mfg. - A Wide variety of products and
services, especially clothing and electronics
Higher Education - Alvernia College,
Pennsylvania State University
Daily Newspapers - Eagle, 345 Penn St., 19601
Times, 345 Penn St., 19601
Chamber of Commerce - 645 Penn St.,
P.O. Box 1698, 19603
Community Event -
Festival of Nations, Annual, November

•**RED HILL**, Borough; Montgomery County; Pop. 1,272; Area Code 215; Zip Code 18076; Elev. 375'; in SE Pennsylvania.

•**RED LION**, Borough; York County; Pop. 5,824; Area Code 717; Zip Code 17356; Elev. 910'; 10 miles SE of York in S Pennsylvania; named for a tavern bult here in colonial times, which had a lion painted red as its emblem.

Chamber of Commerce - P.O. Box 224

•**RENO**, Village; Venango County; Pop. (incl. with Sugar Creek); Area Code 814; Zip Code 16343; Elev. 1,017'; in NW Pennsylvania; had its start in the mind of *C.V. Culver,* who according to his prospectus (1866) foresaw a new oil metropolis. "There is not a particle of doubt of the success of the plan," he declared. Nevertheless the bank that he organized failed, and Reno never shared in the prosperity enjoyed by its neighbors.

•**RENOVO**, Borough; Clinton County; Pop. 1,812; Area Code 717; Zip Code 17764; Elev. 668'; 60 miles NW of Williamsport in central Pennsylvania; located on the Susquehanna River in a soft coal mining region; takes its name from the Latin verb *renovo,* "I renew." The town was laid out in 1862 on a tract of 1,200 acres, one half of which was set aside as a site for the new car shops that the Philadelphia and Erie Railroad had decided to build here. It was these railroad shops, where cars were to be repaired and *renovated,* that brought the town into existence and suggested its name. Renovo became an incorporated borough in 1866.

Agriculture - Varied produce and dairy farming,
especially fruit

Industry/Mfg. - Coal mining
Daily Newspaper - The Record, 129 Fifth St.
Chamber of Commerce - Community Trade Assn., YMCA
Community Event -
 Pennsylvania Flaming Foliage Festival,
 Annual, October

•**REYNOLDSVILLE**, Borough; Jefferson County; Pop. 3,016; Area Code 814; Zip Code 15851; Elev. 1,372'; 10 miles W of DuBois in W central Pennsylvania; *Woodward Reynolds* and his bride came here from Kittanning in 1838 to occupy the 300-acre wedding gift of his father. Their sons, *David* and *Albert*, laid out the town in 1873.

The Soldier Run Mine here was at one time the most productive bituminous coal mine in the world, with a daily output of 8,000 tons.

Agriculture - Varied produce and dairy farming
Industry/Mfg. - Kitchen furniture, soft drinks,
 coal mining
Chamber of Commerce - P.O. Box 157

•**RICES LANDING**, Borough; Greene County; Pop. 516; Area Code 412; Zip Code 15357; Elev. 970'; in SW Pennsylvania.

•**RICHLAND**, Borough; Lebanon County; Pop. 1,470; Area Code 717; Zip Code 17087; Elev. 490'; in SE cen. Pennsylvania.

•**RICHLANDTOWN**, Borough; Bucks County; Pop. 1,180; Area Code 215; Zip Code 18955; Elev. 520'; in SE Pennsylvania.

•**RIDGWAY**, Borough; Seat of Elk County; Pop. 5,604; Area Code 814; Zip Code 15853; Elev. 1,381'; 20 miles N of DuBois in NW cen. Pennsylvania; in a crook of the Clarion River at the mouth of Elk Creek, occupies part of an 80,000-acre tract purchased in 1817 by *Jacob Ridgway*, a prominent Philadelphia Quaker merchant. The town is said to have numbered 17 millionaires among its inhabitants at a time when millionaires were rarites.

Chamber of Commerce - 159 Main St., P.O. Box 357

•**RIDLEY PARK**, Borough; Delaware County; Pop. 7,889; Area Code 215; Zip Code 19078; Elev. 70'; SW suburb of Philadelphia in SE Pennsylvania; a residential community, was established after the route of the Philadelphia, Wilmington & Baltimore Railroad between Philadelphia and Chester was changed in 1870.

Chamber of Commerce - Ward & Cresswell Sts.

•**RIEGELSVILLE**, Borough; Bucks County; Pop. 993; Area Code 215; Zip Code 18077; Elev. 179'; in SE Pennsylvania; founded in 1800, was named for the *Riegel* family, early landowners who established paper mills across the river in New Jersey.

•**RIMERSBURG**, Borough; Clarion County; Pop. 1,096; Area Code 814; Zip Code 16248; Elev. 1,450'; in W Pennsylvania; *John Rimer* settled here in 1829 and later opened a tavern. At that time the southern part of the town was called Pinksville, for *James Pinks*. When the village was incorporated in 1853, a three-cornered fight developed over the name. Apparently the tavern keeper's adherents were more numerous than those of *Pinks* or *Colonel Levi Sloan*, who wanted to call the settlement Sloansville.

Chamber of Commerce - R.D. #2

•**RINGGOLD**, Village; Jefferson County; Pop. 150; Area Code 814; Zip Code 15770; Elev. 1,510'; the village became a post office in 1847, receiving its name from *Major Samuel Ringgold*, who was killed at Palo Alto in 1846 - the first American officer to fall in the Mexican War.

•**RINGTOWN**, Borough; Schuylkill County; Pop. 837; Area Code 717; Zip Code 17967; Elev. 1,140'; in E central Pennsylvania.

•**RIVERSIDE**, Borough; Northumberland County; Pop. 2.266; Area Code 717; Zip Code 17868; Elev. 500'; in E central Pennsylvania; annexed to Gearheart township in 1950.

•**ROARING BRANCH**, Village; Tioga and Lycoming Counties; Pop. 250; Area Code 717; Zip Code 17765; Elev.

1,795'; in NE Pennsylvania; was founded in 1862, consists of a handful of miscellaneous dwellings.

•**ROARING SPRING**, Borough; Blair County; Pop. 2,962; Area Code 814; Zip Code 16673; Elev. 1,260'; 15 miles S of Altoona in S cen. Pennsylvania; in the Lock Mountain Range.

•**ROBESONIA**, Borough; Berks County; Pop. 1,748; Area Code 215; Zip Code 19551; Elev. 453'; in SE Pennsylvania; was founded in 1855 and named for an early settler, *Andrew Robeson. Robeson* was an immigrant from Sweden who eventually became wealthy and powerful in his community.

•**ROCHESTER**, Borough; Beaver County; Pop. 4,759; Area Code 412; Zip Code 15074; Elev. 707'; in W Pennsylvania; at the confluence of the Beaver and Ohio Rivers, where the latter turns southwestward, has been an Indian town, a pioneer settlement, a river town, an industrial center, and a residential borough. This was the site of Logan Town, named for *James Logan*, the Mingo chief, who had his lodge here. In 1773, fear of Indian uprisings spread along the western Pennsylvania frontier. On April 30, while *Logan* was absent, members of his family, including his mother, sister, and brother, were slaughtered by a group of settlers. The chief swore he would take ten scalps for every massacred member of his family.

Rochester's first white settler was the *Reverend Francis Reno*, who built a house in 1799. In the first half of the nineteenth century, westward-bound goods and travelers awaiting passage on the Ohio River packets crowded the town's flimsy river wharves. The name Rochester was not used until 1838, when *Ovid Pinney* named it for his native Rochester, New York.

Chamber of Commerce - 502 Adams St.

•**ROCKHILL FURNACE**, Borough; Huntingdon County; Pop. 472; Area Code 717; Zip Code 17249; Elev. 630'; in S central Pennsylvania.

POINT OF INTEREST

EAST BROAD TOP RAILROAD- Built in 1872; original revived steam engines and cars carry visitors over several miles of track; restored Orbisonia station and roundhouse.

•**ROCKLEDGE,** Borough; Montgomery County; Pop. 2,538; Area Code 215; Zip Code 19111; Elev. 200'; 10 miles NE of Philadelphia in SE Pennsylvania; a large shopping mall graces this residential suburb.

•**ROCKWOOD,** Borough; Somerset County; Pop. 1,058; Area Code 814; Zip Code 15557; Elev. 1,820'; in S Pennsylvania.

•**ROME,** Borough; Bradford County; Pop. 426; Area Code 717; Zip Code 18837; Elev. 830'; in N Pennsylvania; named for the city in New York by the first settlers.

•**ROSCOE,** Borough; Washington County; Pop. 1,123; Area Code 412; Zip Code 15477; Elev. 870'; in SW Pennsylvania.

•**ROSEMONT,** Village; Montgomery County; Area Code 215; in SE Pennsylvania; site of Rosemont College, founded in 1921. Six hundred fifty female students are enrolled.

Primarily a residential area
Higher Education - Rosemont College

•**ROSETO,** Borough; Northampton County; Pop. 1,484; Area Code 215; Zip Code 18013; Elev. 720'; near Bangor in E Pennsylvania.

•**ROSE VALLEY,** Borough; Delaware County; Pop. 1,038; Area Code 215; Elev. 150'; SW suburb of Philadelphia in SE Pennsylvania.

•**ROSEVILLE,** Borough; Tioga County; Pop. 211; Area Code 717; Elev. 1,355'; in N Pennsylvania.

Community Event - Old Home Day, Annual, August

•**ROSSLYN FARMS**, Borough; Allegheny County; Pop. 521; Area Code 412; Zip Code 15106; Elev. 1,060'; S suburb of Pittsburgh near Carnegie in SW Pennsylvania; residential.

•**ROULETTE**, Village; Potter County; Pop. 700; Area Code 814; Zip Code 16746; Elev. 1,568'; 15 miles E of Coudersport on the Allegheny River in N Pennsylvania; named for *Jean Roulette* of the Ceres Land Company, was founded in 1816. For more than 70 years lumbering was the chief, virtually the only, industry, but the last hemlock stand, the Central Pennsylvania tract, was cut in 1912.

•**ROUSEVILLE**, Borough; Venango County; Pop. 734; Area Code 814; Zip Code 16344; Elev. 1,088'; in NW Pennsylvania; was called the Buchanan Farm until February 1861, when it was renamed for *Henry Rouse* who drilled a well that produced 150 barrels a day. In granting subleases *Rouse*, a Warren County schoolteacher, stipulated their forfeiture if intoxicating liquors were sold, and for a brief period the bonanza settlement smarted under enforced abstinence. Between 1870 and 1880 Rouseville's population dropped from 10,000 to 688.

•**ROYALTON**, Borough; Dauphin County; Pop. 981; Area Code 717; Zip Code 17101; Elev. 300'; suburb of Harrisburg in SE cen. Pennsylvania.

•**ROYERSFORD**, Borough; Montgomery County; Pop. 4,243; Area Code 215; Zip Code 19468; Elev. 180'; 5 miles N of Phoenixville in a residential area in SE Pennsylvania.

•**RURAL VALLEY**, Borough; Armstrong County; Pop. 1,033; Area Code 412; Zip Code 16249; Elev. 1,111'; in W Pennsylvania.

•**RUSSELL**, Village; Warren County; Pop. 800; Area Code 814; Elev. 1,233'; 5 miles S of New York state line in NW Pennsylvania; was laid out in 1843 on part of an extensive tract owned by *Robert Russell*.

•**RUTLEDGE**, Borough; Delaware County; Pop. 934; Area Code 215; Zip Code 19070; Elev. 130'; SW suburb of Philadelphia in SE Pennsylvania.

•**SAEGERTOWN**, Borough; Crawford County; Pop. 942; Area Code 814; Zip Code 16433; Elev. 1,120'; in NW Pennsylvania.

•**SADSBURYVILLE**, Village; Chester County; Area Code 215; Zip Code 19369; Elev. 640'; in SE Pennsylvania; named for the town of Sudbury in Suffolk, England.

•**ST. CLAIR**, Borough; Schuylkill County; Pop. 4,037; Area Code 717; Zip Code 17970; Elev. 749'; 5 miles NW of Pottsville in E cen. Pennsylvania; was founded in 1831, once flourished as a result of activity in eight collieries, a number of textile plants, and large railroad yards. Saint Clair took the name of *St. Clair Nichols*, who owned the farm on which the town was built. In 1831 Messrs. *Carey, Lee* and *Hart* bought the Nichols farm, laid out the town, and gave it the name of Saint Clair.

•**ST. CLAIRSVILLE**, Borough; Bedford County; Pop. 90; Area Code 814; Zip Code 16676; Elev. 1,140'; in S Pennsylvania; was named for *General Arthur St. Clair* of the Revolutionary War, who was also an Indian fighter and Governor of the Northwest Territory (1789-1802).

•**ST. LAWRENCE**, Borough; Berks County; Pop. 1,376; Area Code 215; Elev. 360'; in SE Pennsylvania.

•**ST. MARYS**, Borough; Elk County; Pop. 6,417; Area Code 814; Zip Code 15857; Elev. 1,702'; near New York state line in NW central Pennsylvania; a flourishing industrial town had its beginning in 1842 when Philadelphia and Baltimore German Catholics, who had fled the "Know Nothing" persecution, settled on land owned by the German Catholic Brotherhood. As the date of settlement was the feast of the Immaculate Conception of the Virgin Mary, and as the name of the first white woman who set foot on the new town was also Mary, the settlers called the place Saint Mary's. Six years later Saint Mary's was incorporated as a borough. Elk County was formed the year after the founding of Saint Mary's.

> *Agriculture* - Varied produce and dairy farming,
>   especially potatoes and grains
> *Industry/Mfg.* - Wood products, auto parts,
>   coal mining
> *Daily Newspaper* - The Press, P.O. Box 353, 15857
> *Chamber of Commerce* - 10 N. Michael St.,
>   P.O. Box 577, 15857

•**ST. PETERSBURG**, Borough; Clarion County; Pop. 452; Area Code 814; Zip Code 16054; Elev. 1,400'; in W Pennsylvania; the "borough" was first called Petersburg in honor of *Judge Richard Peters* of Philadelphia, who once owned the town site. When the post office was established here in 1862, the postal authorities, to avoid confusion with Petersburg in Huntingdon County, added the prefix "Saint" in imitation of the name of the former capital of Russia.

•**SALISBURY**, Borough; Somerset County; Pop. 817; Area Code 814; Zip Code 15558; Elev. 2,130'; in S Pennsylvania.

•**SALLADASBURG**, Borough; Lycoming County; Pop. 273; Area Code 717; Elev. 650'; in N cen. Pennsylvania; named for founder, *Jacob P. Sallada.*

•**SALTILLO**, Borough; Huntingdon County; Pop. 373; Area Code 717; Zip Code 17253; Elev. 780'; in S cen. Pennsylvania; named for the large city in NE Mexico.

•**SALTSBURG**, Borough; Indiana County; Pop. 964; Area Code 412; Zip Code 15681; Elev. 852'; 30 miles NE of Pittsburgh in W cen. Pennsylvania.
    Tradition credits a *Mrs. Deemer* with the discovery of salt deposits here when she found the food she cooked in water that trickled from rocks along the Conemaugh had a salty taste. Previously, "watching the lick" had been common among hunters who shot deer and other animals as they came to lick the mud or rocks for salt. In any case, a profitable salt industry grew up here after 1813 as the sur-

rounding region was settled. Using a pole with stone chisel attachment as a drill, drillers had to spend a year or two of hard labor to reach the salt deposits. The drilling completed, salt water was then pumped to the surface through a hollow tube, collected in large pans, and boiled over wood fires or left to evaporate in cisterns. For many years, this area of Indiana County was one of the largest inland salt producers in the nation. Soft coal mining is now very important.

•**SANDY LAKE**, Borough; Mercer County; Pop. 779; Area Code 412; Zip Code 16145; Elev. 1,165'; in W Pennsylvania; first settled in 1800, lies in a valley at the eastern end of the lake for which it is named. In addition to a flourishing resort business, it has two small dairies. A few black freedmen settled beside the lake in 1825 and named the spot Liberia, but their community disappeared just before the Civil War.

•**SANKERTOWN**, Borough; Cambria County; Pop. 804; Area Code 814; Elev. 2,070'; in SW cen. Pennsylvania.

•**SAXONBURG**, Borough; Butler County; Pop. 1,336; Area Code 412; Zip Code 16056; Elev. 1,300'; NE suburb of Pittsburgh in W Pennsylvania; is all that now remains of an ambitious German colony, which, in 1831, under the leadership of *Karl* and *Johann A. Roebling*, of Muhlhausen, in Old Saxony, bought 16,000 acres of land in Jefferson Township. Early in 1832 300 families from Muhlhausen left Bremen for their new home; but because of the corrupt activities of colonizing agents at Philadelphia and Baltimore, only a few families found their way to Saxonburg, which was named for their former home in Old Saxony. The founder of this colony, *John A. Roebling*, afterward became a civil engineer and a builder of suspension bridges.

•**SAXTON**, Borough; Bedford County; Pop. 814; Area Code 814; Zip Code 16678; Elev. 900'; in S Pennsylvania; women's clothing is made in town and a lumber sawmill is always busy.

> *Industry/Mfg.* - Clothing, soft drinks, lumber,
> coal mining
> *Chamber of Commerce* - P.O. Box 188, 16678

•**SAYLORSBURG**, Village; Monroe County; Pop. 600; Area Code 717; Zip Code 18353; Elev. 748'; in E Pennsylvania; a lake resort, was laid out about 1825 by *Charles* and *Samuel Saylor*. Saylors Lake known as Paupaunoming to the Indians. Several hundred summer residents come to this town in the green hills each year.

•**SAYRE**, Borough; Bradford County; Pop. 6,951; Area Code 717; Zip Code 18840; Elev. 772'; 20 miles SE of Elmire, New York in N Pennsylvania; was a small railway settlement until the Lehigh Valley Railroad constructed a roundhouse and shops here in 1871 and named the place for *Robert H. Sayre*, superintendent of the road. *Jim Thorpe Sayre*, who was born in Mauch Chunk in 1824, became chief engineer of the Lehigh Valley Railroad in 1852 and for many years afterwards was actively engaged in constructing its main line and its numerous extensions. From 1885 to his retirement in 1898 he was second vice-president of the company. His youngest son, *Francis B. Sayre*, married *President Woodrow Wilson's* daughter.

> *Agriculture* - Varied produce and dairy farming
> *Industry/Mfg.* - Clothing
> *Daily Newspaper* - Times, 201 N. Lehigh Ave.
> *Chamber of Commerce* - 106 W. Lockhart St.

•**SCALP LEVEL**, Borough; Cambria County; Pop. 1,186; Area Code 814; Elev. 1,840'; in SW cen. Pennsylvania.

•**SCHAEFFERSTOWN**, Village; Lebanon County; Pop. 800; Area Code 717; Zip Code 17088; Elev. 600'; in SE cen. Pennsylvania; Settlement was made here in the late seventeenth century by descendants of Brazilian and West Indian Jews. In 1744 *Alexander Schaeffer* laid out a town and called it Heidelberg, but the residents renamed it. On this hill, in 1769, *Stiegel* built a wooden castle, 75 feet high and shaped like a truncated pyramid. The Log Cabin was one of the places where *Stiegel* taught school after his financial reverses.

POINTS OF INTEREST

"BARON" VON STIEGEL'S CASTLE- Ruins of wooden castle builtin 1769.

BRENDLE FARMS- Includes stone "bank" houses with elements illustrating Swiss traditions carried to the New World and one of the best-built stone barns in the county. 18th-19th Century.

MICHTER'S JUG HOUSE- Oldest operating distillery inthe U.S., dating back to 1753. Tours available.

Community Events -
Cherry Fair, Annual, June;
Folk Festival, Annual, July;
Harvest Fair, Annual, September;
Kuch Fescht, Annual, September

•**SCHELLSBURG**, Borough; Bedford County; Pop. 325; Area Code 814; Zip Code 15559; Elev. 1,259'; in S Pennsylvania; on the slope of a ridge, was laid out in 1808 and named for the *Schell* family.

•**SCHNECKSVILLE**, Village; Lehigh County; Pop. 450; Area Code 215; Zip Code 18078; Elev. 669'; in E Pennsylvania; was first built upon property purchased in 1766 by *Adam Schneck.*

Buffalo, palomino horses and deer are allowed to roam wild at the 1,100 acre Trexler-Lehigh County Game Preserve here.

Higher Education - Lehigh County Community College

•**SCHUYLKILL COUNTY**, E Central Pennsylvania; Pop. 160,630; Established, March 1, 1811; Seat is Pottsville.

Formed in 1811 out of Berks and Northampton, it was named for the Schuylkill River, which flows through its territory. This name, which means "hidden stream," was given to the river by the early Dutch explorers because they passed by its mouth at first without seeing it.

•**SCHUYLKILL HAVEN**, Borough; Schuylkill County; Pop. 5,977; Area Code 717; Zip Code 17972; Elev. 526'; 5 miles S of Pottsville in E cen. Pennsylvania; was settled in 1748 by *John Fincher*, a Chester Quaker. Among the earliest settlers were squatters who had trouble with Indians and with later arrivals bearing legal evidence of ownership. The completion in 1825 of the Schuylkill Canal between Philadelphia and a point just north of Schuylkill

Haven gave the town its name and its principal support for six decades. Coal was shipped from here in large quantities.

> *Agriculture* - Varied produce and dairy farming
> *Industry/Mfg.* - Clothing, footwear
> *Higher Education* - Pennsylvania State University
> *Chamber of Commerce* - P.O. Box 203

•**SCHUYLKILL RIVER**, River, SE Pennsylvania; Flows SE approximately 130 miles from source in Schuylkill County, through hilly coal mining country and Reading to the Delaware River, at Philadelphia.

This river was named by Dutch explorers who first passed by its mouth without seeing it. It is a Dutch word for "hidden stream."

•**SCHWENKSVILLE**, Borough; Montgomery County; Pop. 1.041; Area Code 215; Zip Code 19473; Elev. 150'; 10 miles NW of Norristown in SE Pennsylvania; is on the banks of the Perkiomen. The Georgian Colonial Pennypacker Mansion was the home of *Samuel W. Pennypacker* (1843-1916), governor of Pennsylvania from 1903 to 1907. *George Washington* was billeted here at one time during the Revolutionary War; the Pennypacker Mills ground flour for Continental troops quartered in Schwenkville.

Today, the town lies in a quiet residential-resort area.

POINT OF INTEREST

> **CONRAD GRUBB HOMESTEAD**- Rural homestead built 1754 by weaver and farmer *Conrad Grubb* ; house displays variation of common area 3-room plan, originally derived from Germanic traditions. Restored.

> *Primarily a residential area*
> *Community Event* - Philadelphia Folk Festival, Annual, August

•**SCOTTDALE**, Borough; Westmoreland County; Pop. 5,833; Area Code 417; Zip Code 15683; Elev. 1,061'; 15 miles NE of Uniontown in a coal mining and agricultural area in SW Pennsylvania; on Jacobs Creek, originally named Fountain Mills, was renamed for *Thomas A. Scott*, president of the Pennsylvania Railroad, after a spur was extended to the town in 1873. Laid out in 1872, it was incorporated as a borough two years later. Scottdale's pipe works, largest of its kind in the country, was shut down in 1936; many of the coal deposits are exhausted.

Agriculture - Varied produce and dairy farming
Industry/Mfg. - Auto parts, lumber, coal mining
Chamber of Commerce - P.O. Box 276

•SCRANTON,City; Lackawanna County seat; Pop. 87,378; Area Code 717; Zip Code 185++; Elev. 741'. Once the anthracite kingdom of Pennsylvania, Scranton now exists on a wide variety of industries and businesses spread throughout the narrow crescent-shaped Lackawanna Valley. Mountains hem in the city--to the north and east the Moosic Mountains, to the west the West Mountains-- but four federal highways, several railroads, and an international airport keep Scranton from isolation.

Coal has been the theme song of this city in the hills. Coal brought prosperity and also despair. Coal built its mansions, stores, banks, hotels, and hovels; it blackened the beautiful Lackawanna, scarred the mountain sides, made artificial hills of unsightly coal refuse, and undermined the city itself, but it created an anthracite kingdom, the importance of which merits a considerable place in American history. It exalted the hardihood of the Pennsylvania miner and brought into existence one of the most powerful labor unions in the country--the United Mine Workers of America. It did more than any other industry to diversify Pennsylvania's population and to develop its industry and commerce. Today 30 nationalities are represented in Scranton.

Until 1771 the Munsee Indians, under *Chief Capoose*, or *Capouse*, had their wigwams along both banks of the river. About the middle of the eighteenth century white settlers came and lived amicably with the natives, who gradually, between 1758 and 1771, moved westward to the Ohio Valley. The "Wyoming Massacre" at Forty Fort in 1778 spread panic throughout the region, and the valley was depopulated of white settlers; it remained virtually uninhabited until 1788. Then *Philip Abbott*, who had migrated from Connecticut to the Wyoming Valley before the Revolution, came here and built a log hut and gristmill beside Roaring Brook. He was followed some 10 years later by *Ebenezer* and *Benjamin Slocum*. The brothers began to acquire property in the settlement, which they named Unionville, although settlers called it Skunk's Misery. In 1816 they changed its name to Slocum Hollow. The Slocums built a forge and distillery in 1800, and operated both with more or less success-the forge until 1822, the distillery until 1826.

In 1840 two other brothers, *George W.* and *Selden T. Scranton*, came to the settlement from New Jersey. At that time it was a community of five weather-beaten old houses. Attracted by the abundance of iron ore and anthracite nearby, the *Scrantons* and their partners-*William Henry*, *Sanford Grant*, and *Philip Mattes* -organized the firm of Scranton, Grant, and Company, and built a forge here. This firm was the nucleus of the Lackawanna Iron and Steel Company. Despite many discouragements, they finally succeeded in manufacturing iron with anthracite as a fuel. In 1845 the Scrantons named the place Harrison in honor of *President William Henry Harrison*.

With a view to expanding their plant, the Scranton brothers negotiated a loan of $10,000 from a cousin, *Joseph Hand Scranton*, of Georgia. In 1847 the cousin bought out *Sanford Grant's* interest, came north to help the new firm, and soon assumed command of the Lackawanna Iron Works. The post office at Scrantonia was established in 1850. Less than a year later the name of the town and post office was simplified as Scranton. In 1853 the first locomotive of the Delaware and Lackawanna Railroad came in, assuring an outlet for the iron industry. Development of the coal mines attracted thousands of immigrants, and by 1860 the population had reached 9,000.

In 1866 Scranton absorbed the two boroughs of Providence and Hyde Park, and the township of Providence, receiving its city charter in April of that year. In 1886, with a population exceeding 50,000, it introduced electric cars on the streets. The 1880's were also marked by the establishment of the Scranton Steel Company, which rolled the first steel rails in 1883. Eight years later Scranton Steel merged with the Lackawanna Iron and Coal Company, and the consolidated plants thereafter operated under the name of the Lackawanna Iron and Steel Company.

Scranton's first major clash between labor and capital involved the railroad and mining industries. This dispute, which resulted in riot and bloodshed, the call of troops, martial law, and collapse of the miners' union, occurred in 1877. In 1897, however, scattered units were organized into the United Mine Workers of America under the leadership of *John Mitchell*. Striking in 1900 for a 10 percent increase in wages, they attained their objective; and, two years later, after a shutdown of mining operations from May 11 to October 23, they gained other substantial wage increases and better working conditions. Another strike, in 1923, resulted in higher wages and a basic eight-hour day. The longest and most disastrous general strike, from an economic standpoint, was that of 1925-26. It lasted 170 days and its effects were felt for a decade.

In 1902 the city had received a severe setback when the Lackawanna Iron and Steel Company moved its plant to a site near Buffalo, New York, to be closer to the Great Lakes ore supply, but coal mining had already superseded steel as a leading industry, and many manufacturing plants were established here, among them the Scranton Lace Company plant, later one of the largest in the country. In 1914 the board of trade raised $1,000,000 to attract new industrial enterprises, which were soon turning out cotton, silk, woolen goods, shoes, mattresses, furniture, and mining machinery. In 1940 the number of employees in Scranton's 300 and more manufacturing plants exceeded 22,000, as compared with 16,000 at work in the coal industry.

Increasing costs of mining and the availability of other fuels brought the anthracite industry down even further in the next few years. In 1945, a group of Scranton businessmen instituted the Scranton Plan, in which citizens pooled money to purchase industrial sites and plants, build factories and lease them to manufacturers which they lured into the city with good financial incentives. Many new jobs were created with this industrial expansion, and the Scranton Plan became a model for hundreds of other communities who found community action to be the best cure for an ailing economy.

The local fund drives for industry were aided by the completion of interstate highways through the area. Scranton was no longer the provincial coal town it had been in pre-war years, but a large transportation and distribution center. New industrial parks were developed, and

Scranton factories began to produce such diversified products as clothing, electronic parts and various metal goods.

However, even a healthy diversification of industry could no longer stop the effects of a national recession in the late 1970s. Almost 15,000 people left the city during that decade. Some moved only a few miles to a nearby suburb, but many left the industrial Northeast for good to find work in the more prosperous Sun Belt areas of the U.S.

Of those who have remained, many are students in one of the city's seven colleges, including Keystone Junior College, Johnson School of Technology, Lackawanna Junior College, Marywood College, or the State University-Worthington Scranton campus. The University of Scranton was founded for men in 1887, but is now an important co-educational institution. A state school for the deaf is also located here.

The cultural life of Scranton is also flavored by the ethnic mix of its people. Besides its informal events, the city offers entertainment through its concert association, a theater group, and various art and dance associations.

What many Scrantonians boast of is their city's proximity to Poconos Mountains, the site of many summer and winter resorts, and several lakes.

POINTS OF INTEREST

EVERHART MUSEUM OF NATURAL HISTORY, SCIENCE AND ART- Contains natural history displays, American folk art from the 1800's and the world's largest collection of Dorflinger Glass.

NAY AUG PARK- Horticultural gardens, zoo and model mine open to the public.

SCRANTON PUBLIC LIBRARY- Modeled after the Musee de Cluny in Paris.

TERENCE V. POWDERLY HOUSE- Home of labor leader *Terence V. Powderly*, who headed the Knights of Labor in the 1880's.

TRIPP FAMILY HOMESTEAD- The oldest building in Scranton, dating back to about 1812.

Industry/Mfg. - A Wide variety of products and services
Higher Education - Lackawanna Junior College, Marywood College, University of Scranton
Daily Newspapers -
    Scrantonian, 388 N. Washington Ave., 18501
    Times, Penn Ave. at Spruce St., 18503
    Tribune, 388 N. Washington Ave., 18501

Chamber of Commerce - 426 Mulberry St., P.O.
Box 431, 18501
Community Events -
Lackawanna Arts Festival, Annual, September;
Neighborhood Summer Festivals, Annual,
May-July

•**SELINSGROVE**, Borough; Snyder County; Pop. 5,227; Area Code 717; Zip Code 17870; Elev. 445'; 5 miles S of Sunbury on the W banks of the Susquehanna River in central Pennsylvania; was laid out in 1790 by *Anthony Selin*, a Swiss soldier of fortune who accompanied *Lafayette* to America. *Selin's* brother-in-law, *Simon Snyder* moved here in 1784, represented the town in the state legislature, and gave Snyder County its name.

Agriculture - Varied produce, poultry
and dairy farming
Industry/Mfg. - Campers, clothing, wood products
Higher Education - Susquehanna University
Chamber of Commerce - 3 S. Market Street
Community Event -
Summer Festival and Homecoming, Annual, August

•**SELLERSVILLE**, Borough; Bucks County; Pop. 3,143; Area Code 215; Zip Code 18960; Elev. 336'; 20 miles SE of Allentown in SE Pennsylvania; a narrow town founded in 1738, *Samuel Sellers* operated Old Sellers Tavern, a three-story stuccoed stone building that served as an early stage stop along the road to Allentown.

•**SEVEN SPRINGS**, Borough; Fayette and Somerset Counties; Pop. 30; Area Code 814; Elev. 1,480'; in S Pennsylvania; incorporated in 1964.

•**SEVEN VALLEYS**, Borough; York County; Pop. 500; Area Code 717; Zip Code 17360; Elev. 470'; suburb of York in S Pennsylvania.

•**SEWARD**, Borough; Westmoreland County; Pop. 675; Area Code 417; Zip Code 15954; Elev. 1,140'; in SW Pennsylvania.

•**SEWICKLEY**, Borough; Allegheny County; Pop. 4,778; Area Code 412; Zip Code 15143; Elev. 720'; 10 miles NW of Pittsburgh on the Ohio River in SW Pennsylvania; named for an Indian tribe.

Primarily a residential area
Chamber of Commerce - 201 P.N.B. Building

•**SEWICKLEY HEIGHTS,** Borough; Allegheny County; Pop. 899; Area Code 412; Zip Code 15143; Elev. 1,100'; NE of Sewickley on higher ground in SW Pennsylvania.

•**SEWICKLEY HILLS,** Borough; Allegheny County; Pop. 419; Area Code 412; Zip Code 15143; Elev. 1,000'; NE of Sewickley in a hilly area in SW Pennsylvania; incorporated in 1958 from Sewickley Heights Township. Residential.

•**SHADE GAP,** Borough; Huntingdon County; Pop. 141; Area Code 717; Zip Code 17255; Elev. 912'; in S cen. Pennsylvania; is at the eastern end of the Shade Mountain Gap. Early settlers called the vicinity "Shades of Death."
Large growth of hemlock trees surrounds the town.

•**SHAMOKIN,** City; Northumberland County; Pop. 10,357; Area Code 717; Zip Code 17872; Elev. 730'; in E central Pennsylvania; was laid out in 1835, and coal mining on a large scale began in 1840, four years after the Shamokin Coal and Iron Company had been organized.
St. Edward's Roman Catholic Church, Shamokin and Webster Sts., a gray stone building with a sloping roof, erected in 1873, is said to have been the first church in the world lighted by electricity.
Shamokin Creek flows through the town. This stream received its name from the old Indian village that once stood at its mouth, on the present site of Sunbury, 18 miles west of the borough of Shamokin. The Delawares called this village *Schachamekhan*, which signifies "eel stream." Another form of the name was *Schahamokink*, or "the place of eels." Shamokin may also be derived from *Sachem-okhe*, "the place where the chief lived." *Dr. George P. Donehoo* derives Shamokin from *Shumokenk*, "where horns are plentiful." The famous Oneida chieftain, *Shikellamy*, father of *Logan*, ruled over his subjects in the Indian town of Shamokin from 1728 to 1749.

POINT OF INTEREST

ANTHRACITE HERITAGE CENTER- Mining research library and displays of mining equipment.

Agriculture - Varied produce and dairy farming
Industry/Mfg. - Clothing, furniture,
    coal mining
Daily Newspaper - News-Item, 701 N. Rock St.
Chamber of Commerce - 51 E. Lincoln St.

•**SHAMOKIN DAM,** Borough; Snyder County; Pop. 1,622; Area Code 717; Zip Code 17876; in central Pennsylvania.

•**SHANKSVILLE,** Borough; Somerset County; Pop. 273; Area Code 814; Zip Code 15560; Elev. 2,250'; in S Pennsylvania.

•**SHARON,** City; Mercer County; Pop. 19,057; Area Code 412; Zip Code 16146; Elev. 853'; 15 miles NE of Youngstown, Ohio on the Ohio River in W Pennsylvania; is built on a plain in the heart of rich Shenango Valley. A mill, erected on the banks of the Shenango River in 1802, became the nucleus of a settlement that was named, probably, by some Bible-reading pioneer who likened its flat topography to the plain of Sharon in Palestine.

Completion of the Lake Erie extension of the Pennsylvania Canal in 1844 attracted the Sharon Furnace, and after the advent of the railroad in 1863 the town began to grow industrially. A large Italian settlement dates from about 1885 when a pipeline was constructed from the Butler County and Venango County oil fields through Sharon to Youngstown, Ohio. The turn of the century witnessed an expansion of local industry.

The town's population tripled in 1900 to 1940, but in recent years it has declined by the thousands each decade. Much of this is due to the decline in the steel and auto industry.

Industry/Mfg. - Electronics, machine shops
Higher Education - Pennsylvania State University
Daily Newspaper - Herald, 42 S. Dock St.
Chamber of Commerce - One West State St.

•**SHARON HILL,** Borough; Delaware County; Pop. 6,221; Area Code 215; Zip Code 19079; in SE Pennsylvania.

•**SHARPSBURG,** Borough; Allegheny County; Pop. 4,351; Area Code 412; Zip Code 15215; Elev. 741'; 5 miles NE of Pittsburgh on the Allegheny River in SW Pennsylvania; In this community, founded in 1826 by *James Sharp* and incorporated as a borough in 1841, the eight-year-old *Howard J. Heinz* began his billion dollar business by selling the produce of his mother's garden patch. *James Sharp* kept a temperance hotel here until his death in 1861.

For many years, the borough has suffered the haze and grime of the sulphurous fumes from its many industries. Until anti-pollution action was taken in the 1970s, not many trees or plants were able to survive the bad air.

Limestone cliffs along the Allegheny River rise 1,260 feet at this point.

Agriculture - Fruit orchards
Industry/Mfg. - Chemicals, soft drinks
Chamber of Commerce - 905 Main St.

•**SHARPSVILLE**, Borough; Mercer County; Pop. 5,375; Area Code 412; Zip Code 16150; Elev. 950'; 20 miles NW of New Castle in an industrial area in W Pennsylvania; named for *James Sharp*, one of the original owners of the town site.

•**SHEAKLEYVILLE**, Borough; Mercer County; Pop. 155; Area Code 412; Zip Code 16151; Elev. 1.282'; in W Pennsylvania; formerly a somewhat swampy region once overrun with snakes; it is asserted that in the early 1800's a farmer here killed 200 rattlesnakes in one day. A great part of this territory was originally granted, under the Donation Law of the state, to Revolutionary soldiers.

•**SHEFFIELD**, Village; Warren County; Pop. 1,500; Area Code 814; Zip Code ; Elev. 1,336'; 10 miles SE of Warren in NW Pennsylvania; founded in 1864 when tanneries were built along Tionesta Creek, lies in a bowl beside the railroad tracks. Today it is largely residential.

•**SHELOCTA**, Borough; Indiana County; Pop. 139; Area Code 412; Zip Code 15774; Elev. 990'; in W cen. Pennsylvania.

•**SHENANDOAH**, Borough; Schuylkill County; Pop. 7,589; Area Code 717; Zip Code 17976; Elev. 1,300'; 10 miles N of Pottsville in E central Pennsylvania; was first settled in 1835; mining on a large scale began in 1862 when a land

359

company laid out the town. The beginning of the coal industry brought English and Welsh miners, followed by Irish. Subsequent immigrations brough Germans, Poles, Lithuanians, Russians, and other nationality groups. A fire in 1883 virtually reduced the town to ashes. The first Greek Catholic parish in the United States, St. Michael's, was organized here in 1884, and the church was erected three years later.

Shenandoah Creek flows through this valley town.

Agriculture - Varied produce and dairy farming
Industry/Mfg. - Auto parts, plastics,
  coal mining
Daily Newspaper - Herald, Ringtown Rd.
Chamber of Commerce - 121 N. Main St.,
  P.O. Box 187

•**SHENANGO RIVER**, River, W Pennsylvania; flows S approx. 100 miles from source in Crawford County (Pymatuning Reservoir), through Mercer County's coal mining areas, to the confluence with the Mahoning River, SW of New Castle, forming the Beaver River. Dammed in Mercer County to form the Shenengo River Reservoir, N of Sharon, which extends into Ohio.

•**SHICKSHINNY**, Borough; Luzerne County; Pop. 1,192; Area Code 717; Zip Code 18655; Elev. 520'; E Pennsylvania; is named for the indian meaning "five mountains."

•**SHILLINGTON**, Borough; Berks County; Pop. 5,601; Area Code 215; Zip Code 19607; Elev. 350'; 5 miles SW of Reading in SE Pennsylvania. Samuel Shilling laid out this town in 1860 when he decided to locate his 130 acre farm. The town was also named after this earlier farmer a very short time after he settled here.

•**SHIMERVILLE**, Village; Lehigh County; Pop. 85; Area Code 215; Zip Code rural; Elev. 248'; near Emmaus in E Pennsylvania; was laid out on land bought by *John Shimer* in 1792.

•**SHINGLEHOUSE**, Borough; Potter County; Pop. 1,310;; Area Code 814; Zip Code 16748; Elev. 1,490'; located in N Pennsylvania; is named for an old English pioneer clapboard house with shingles, belonging to a French immigrant named *Jaudrie* about 1806.

•**SHIPPENSBURG**, Borough; Cumberland and Franklin Counties; Pop. 5,261; Area Code 717; Zip Code 17257;; Elev. 649'; is located 10 miles N of Chambersburg in S Pennsylvania. Shippensburg is the oldest town in Pennsylvania, with the exception of York that is W of the Susquehanna River. It was founded in 1730 by *Edward Shippen*, who in 1737 was said to have had been the biggest person, the biggest house, and the biggest coach in Philadelphia. Today a few light industries keep this place active. Shippensburg State College, founded in 1871, is located here and is the major focus point of its residents.

> *Agriculture* - Grain farming
> *Industry/Mfg.* - Clothing, grain milling
> *Higher Education* - Shippensburg State College
> *Chamber of Commerce* - 75 W. King Street

•**SHIPPENVILLE**, Borough; Clarion County; Pop. 558; Area Code 814;; Zip Code 16254; Elev. 1,208'; W Pennsylvania; was laid out by *Judge Henry Shippen*, in its early years was known as an iron center.

•**SHIPPINGPORT**, Borough; Beaver County; Pop. 255; Area Code 412; Zip Code 15077; Elev. 780'; is located on the Ohio River in W Pennsylvania; So named because is is a coal shipment point.

•**SHIREMANSTOWN**, Borough; Cumberland County; Pop. 1,179; Area Code 717; Zip Code 17011; Elev. 420'; is a suburb of Harrisburg.

•**SHIRLEYSBURG**, Borough; Huntingdon County; Pop. 147; Area Code 717; Zip Code 17260; Elev. 606'; is located in S central Pennsylvania on the Aughwick Creek, was the site of the Indian town of Aughwick, or Old Town, where the noted Indian trader, *George Croghan*, had an early trading post. The white man's town was founded in 1757 and named for Fort Shirley. Here in 1754 *Conrad Weiser*, Indian interpreter and provincial agent, conferred with the Iroquoian representative, *Tanacharison*, and chiefs of the Shawnee and Delaware.

Community Events -
Fort Shirley Celebration, Annual, May;
Huntingdon County Arts Festival, Annual, June

•**SHOEMAKERSVILLE**, Borough; Berks County; Pop. 1,391; Area Code 215; Zip Code 19555; Elev. 360'; in SE Pennsylvania.

•**SHREWSBURY**, Borough; York County; Pop. 2,688; Area Code 717; Zip Code 17361; Elev. 735'; in S Pennsylvania; a crossroads settlement on the side of a hill, was founded in 1739 by immigrants from Shrewsbury, England. It is near the Mason-Dixon Line.

It has been held by some that "Dixie," romantic name for the South, is a corruption of the name of *Jeremiah Dixon*, with *Charles Mason*, surveyed the Pennsylvania-Maryland boundary, considered the dividing line between the North and the South. Others hold that it came form the nickname of a $10 note issued by the Citizens Bank of New Orleans with a large "dix" (10) inscribed on the reverse. According to another theory, the term may originally have been applied to the North. *Johan Dixie*, so it is said, had tried unsuccessfuly to grow tobacco with slave labor on his Manhattan farm. Disillusioned, he disposed of his blacks to a North Carolina planter. There the slaves, working the year round, looked back with regret on the days of enforced winter idleness in the North. Their lament spread, and whites, hearing it, thought the Blacks pined for a more favored section of the South.

Amid a welter of speculation is the fact that the song "Dixie" was written in 1859 by *Daniel Emmett* and introduced in New York the next day as a "walk around" in *Dan Bryant's* minstrels. Its popularity spread; it was used as a political campaign song in 1860, and Confederate soldiers sang it during the Civil War.

•**SHRINESTOWN**, Village; York County; Pop. 200; Area Code 717; Zip Code ; Elev. 257'; near Manchester in S Pennsylvania; founded in 1800, was for more than 50 years a flourishing cigar-manufacturing center. Once the site of an Indian village, it was named for *John Shrine*, an early settler. Well-kept houses are scattered on a hillside.

•**SILVERDALE**, Borough; Bucks County; Pop. 499; Area Code 215; Zip Code 18962; Elev. 440'; N suburb of Philadelphia in SE Pennsylvania.

•**SINKING SPRING**, Borough; Berks County; Pop. 2,617; Area Code 215; Zip Code 19608; Elev. 345'; 5 miles W of Reading in a red brick residential area in SE Pennsylvania; was founded in 1793 and named for the Sinking Spring, 402 Penn Ave., which fills in each February when water begins to ooze from the frost-packed ground but dries up before summer.

•**SKINNERS EDDY**, Village; Wyoming County; Pop. 60; Area Code 717; Zip Code 18623; Elev. 649'; near Laceyville in NE Pennsylvania; a tavern was erected by *Ebenezer Skinner* in 1792, for an eddy in the Susquehanna made this a convenient stopping place for boatmen.

•**SLATINGTON**, Borough; Lehigh County; Pop. 4,277; Area Code 215; Zip Code 18080; Elev. 367'; 15 miles NW of Allentown in E Pennsylvania; is a slate center where quarrying began in 1845. More than 20 quarries, some with deep ramified tunnels, are in the vicinity.

Chamber of Commerce - 232 Walnut Street

•**SLIGO**, Borough; Clarion County; Pop. 798; Area Code 814; Zip Code 16255; Elev. 769'; in W Pennsylvania; is bisected by Big Licking and Little Licking Creeks. Sligo Furnace, built in 1845 by four men from Sligo, Ireland, was shut down after the panic of 1873.

•**SLIPPERY ROCK**, Borough; Butler County; Pop. 3,047; Area Code 412; Zip Code 16057; Elev. 1,302'; 10 miles NW of Butler in W Pennsylvania; was called Ginger Hill by early settlers from the local tavern keeper's practice of giving away plenty of ginger with the whiskey he sold. Today, this residential community is the site of Slippery Rock State College (1889) with 4,000 students.

Primarily a residential area
Higher Education - Slippery Rock State College
Chamber of Commerce - R.D. 1, P.O. Box 108A
Community Event - Butler County Music and
     Arts Festival, Annual, July

•**SMETHPORT**, Borough; Seat of McKean County; Pop. 1,797; Area Code 814; Zip Code 16749; Elev. 1,486'; 20 miles S of Bradford in N Pennsylvania; was named for *Raymond* and *Theodore de Smeth*, Dutch bankers and business agents of the exiled French nobility in their dealings with the Ceres Land Company.

Oil wells surround Smethport, and natural gas still flows freely from the hills; some oil wells, covered with metal caps, stand in Smethport back yards. In the 1860's mine shafts were sunk more than 1,000 feet in an attempt to mine oil; two of these experiments reputedly had the backing of *J.P. Morgan*. Many residents sold their properties profitably to frantic speculators, and with the bursting of the oil bubble, repossessed them for a pittance.

•**SMICKSBURG**, Borough; Indiana County; Pop. 82; Area Code 412; Zip Code 16256; rural area in W cen. Pennsylvania.

•**SMITHFIELD**, Borough; Fayette County; Pop. 1,084; Area Code 412; Zip Code 25478; Elev. 986'; in SW Pennsylvania; was laid out in 1799 and incorporated as a borough in 1916. Agriculture is the main business here.

•**SMITHTON**, Borough; Westmoreland County; Pop. 559; Area Code 417; Zip Code 15479; Elev. 820'; SE suburb of Pittsburgh in SW Pennsylvania.

•**SNOW SHOE**, Borough; Centre County; Pop. 852; Area Code 814; Zip Code 16874; Elev. 1,572'; S of Clarence in central Pennsylvania; was named for "Snow Shoe Camp Survey," so called, it is supposed, because the surveyor found snowshoes at a deserted Indian camp here in 1773. A few miles west is the Black Moshannon's horeshoe carve, regarded by the Indians as a hoofprint of the great steed of Chettamicco, hero of Indian mythology.

•**S.N.P.J.**, Borough; Lawrence County; Pop. 16; Area Code 412; in W Pennsylvania.

•**SNYDER COUNTY**, Central Pennsylvania; Pop. 33,584; Estabished, March 2, 1855; Seat is Middleburg.

In 1853 a movement was set on foot to divide Union

County and to call the northern division Buffalo County because it comprised the Buffalo Valley. Two years later, however, when the division was made, the northern part retained the name of Union County, and the southern division was called Snyder County, in honor of *Simon Snyder*, the first Pennsylvania governor of German descent, who was chief executive from 1808 to 1817. The new county contained the old town of Selinsgrove, where Simon Snyder lived from 1784 until his death in 1819.

Born in Lancaster in 1759 of German parents, he moved, at the age of twenty-five, to Selinsgrove, which was founded and named by his brother-in-law, *Captain Anthony Seling*, or *Selin*, a veteran of the Revolutionary War. Here the ambitious young Pennsylvania-German opened a store, and began his public career as a justice of the peace, in which capacity he served his pioneer community for twelve years. His first experience in a deliberative body was as delegate to the convention that drew up the state Constitution of 1790. He was a member of the legislature for eleven years, and he was twice elected speaker of the House. Though a man of imperfect education and mediocre ability in comparison with his three predecessors, *Franklin*, *Mifflin*, and *McKean*, he proved himself a popular and public-spirited executive during the trying times of the War of 1812.

The family name *Snyder* is an Americanized form of the common German surname *Schneider*, which means "tailor."

•**SNYDERTOWN**, Borough; Northumberland County; Pop. 358; Area Code 717; Zip Code 17877; Elev. 540'; in E central Pennsylvania.

•**SOLEBURY MOUNTAIN**, Peak, E Pennsylvania; rises behind a group of hills. The Solebury Copper Mine, a puzzle to historians, is nearby. Early settlers heard from the Indians that white men had mined copper in a drift near the river, but not until 1854 was the entrance to the mine rediscovered. Investigation indicated that certain tool marks on the mineral within the shaft had been made at least 200 years before the rediscovery.

•**SOMERSET**, Borough; Seat of Somerset County; Pop. 6,474; Area Code 814; Zip Code 15501; Elev. 2,250'; 30 miles

S of Johnstown in S Pennsylvania; was originally called Brunerstown, after *Ulrich Bruner*, who arrived in 1787. A substantial part of the settlement was destroyed by fire in 1833. Even more ravaging was the conflagration of 1872, which burned more than 150 buildings.

Agriculture - Varied produce and dairy farming
Industry/Mfg. - Cement products, lumber,
    maple syrup. Resort Area.
Daily Newspaper - American, 334 W. Main Street
Chamber of Commerce - 829 N. Center Avenue
Community Events - Mountain Craft Festival,
Annual,
    September; Polish Days, June

•**SOMERSET COUNTY**, S Pennsylvania; Pop. 81,243; Established, April 17, 1795; Seat is Somerset.

The last of the Pennsylvania counties to take its name from an English shire, it was formed from Bedford county on April 17, 1795, and named for Somersetshire in England. On the present site of the town of Somerset, which has a higher elevation than any other county town in Pennsylvania. *Ulrich Bruner* had laid out the village of Brunerstown in 1787.

•**SOUDERTON**, Borough; Montgomery County; Pop. 6,657; Area Code 215; Zip Code 18964; Elev. 428'; 5 miles N of Lansdale in SE Pennsylvania; was founded in 1876 but much older in settlement.

Agriculture - Varied produce and dairy farming
Industry/Mfg. - Auto parts, clothing
Chamber of Commerce - P.O. Box 77

•**SOUTHAMPTON**, Urban Village; Bucks County; Pop. 9,000; Area Code 215; Zip Code 18966; Elev. 260'; 5 miles NE of Philadelphia in SE Pennsylvania; furniture, buttons and boxes are made in this residential suburb.

•**SOUTH BETHLEHEM**, Borough; Armstrong County; Pop. 476; Area Code 412; Zip Code 18015; Elev. 1,080'; near New Bethlehem in W Pennsylvania.

•**SOUTH COATESVILLE**, Borough; Chester County; Pop. 1,359; ; Area Code 215; Zip Code 19320; Elev. 300'; S of Coatesville in SE Pennsylvania.

•**SOUTH CONNELLSVILLE**, Borough; Fayette County; Pop. 2,296; Area Code 412; Zip Code 15425; Elev. 1,00'; adjacent to Connelsville in SW Pennsylvania.

•**SOUTH FORK**, Borough; Cambria County; Pop. 1,401; Area Code 814; Zip Code 15956; Elev. 1,600'; in SW central Pennsylvania.

•**SOUTH GREENSBURG**, Borough; Westmoreland County; Pop. 2,605; Area Code 417; Zip Code 15601; Elev. 1,080'; E suburb of Pittsburgh in SW Pennsylvania; near Greensburg.

•**SOUTH HEIGHTS**, Borough; Beaver County; Pop. 765; Area Code 412; Zip Code 15081; Elev. 745'; residential suburb near Beaver Falls in W Pennsylvania.

•**SOUTHMONT**, Borough; Cambria County; Pop. 2,683; Area Code 814; Zip Code 15901; Elev. 1,540'; suburb of Johnstown in a hilly farming-coal mining area in SW cen. Pennsylvania.

•**SOUTH NEW CASTLE**, Borough; Lawrence County; Pop. 879; Area Code 412; Zip Code 16101; Elev. 1,300'; S suburb of New Castle in W Pennsylvania.

•**SOUTH PHILIPSBURG**, Borough; Centre County; Pop. 523; Area Code 814; Zip Code 16866; Elev. 1,400'; suburb of Philipsburg in central Pennsylvania.

•**SOUTH RENOVO**, Borough; Clinton County; Pop. 663; Area Code 717; Zip Code 17764; Elev. 720'; S of Renovo in cen. Pennsylvania.

•**SOUTH WAVERLY**, Borough; Bradford County; Pop. 1,176; Area Code 717; Zip Code 18471; Elev. 820'; S of Waverly, New York in N Pennsylvania.

•**SOUTHWEST GREENSBURG**, Borough; Westmoreland County; Pop. 2,898; Area Code 417; Zip Code 15601; Elev. 1,080'; SW of Greensburg in SW Pennsylvania; E suburb of Pittsburgh.

•**SOUTH WILLIAMSPORT**, Borough; Lycoming County; Pop. 6,581; Area Code 717; Zip Code 17701; Elev. 540'; adjacent to Williamsport in N central Pennsylvania; nearby is the Little League Baseball World Series Stadium.

Chamber of Commerce - 1550 Riverside Drive

•**SPANGLER**, Borough; Cambria County; Pop. 2,399; Area Code 814; Zip Code 15775; Elev. 1,470'; 20 miles NW of Altoona in a coal mining region in SW Pennsylvania; when it was incorporated in 1893, Spangler was named for *Colonel J.L. Spangler* of Bellefonte.

•**SPARTANSBURG**, Borough; Crawford County; Pop. 403; Area Code 814; Zip Code 16434; Elev. 1,450'; in NW Pennsylvania; named because of the spartan character of the town's early settlers.

•**SPEERS**, Borough; Washington County; Pop. 1,425; Area Code 412; Zip Code 15012; Elev. 767'; W of Belle Vernon in SW Pennsylvania; is on the west bank of the Monongahela River, named for *Apollos Speers*, and closely identified with the early development of the Monongahela Valley.

•**SPRINGBORO**, Borough; Crawford County; Pop. 557; Area Code 814; Zip Code 16435; Elev. 910'; in NW Pennsylvania.

•**SPRING CITY**, Borough; Chester County; Pop. 3,389; Area Code 215; Zip Code 19475; Elev. 150'; 30 miles NW of Philadelphia on the Schuylkill River in SE Pennsylvania; it was at first called Springville from a large spring situated at the corner of Yost and Main Streets. About 1872, when the post office was established and the town incorporated, the name was changed to Spring City because there was already one Springville in Pennsylvania.

Community Event - Craft Fair, Annual, May

•**SPRINGDALE**, Borough; Allegheny County; Pop. 4,418; Area Code 412; Zip Code 15144; Elev. 801'; 15 miles NE of

Pittsburgh on the Allegheny River in SW Pennsylvania; is along a sweeping curve of the Allegheny River. Settled in 1795, it was later named for springs in a nearby hollow. After a glue works had been established here in 1874, the community progressed rapidly.

•**SPRINGFIELD**, Urban Village and Township; Delaware County; Pop. 29,000; Area Code 215; Zip Code 19064; Elev. 220'; 15 miles W of Philadelphia in a residential area in SE Pennsylvania; probably named for Springfield, Massachusetts.

•**SPRING GROVE**, Borough; York County; Pop. 1,832; Area Code 717; Zip Code 17362; Elev. 470'; residential suburb of York in S Pennsylvania.

•**SPRING HOUSE**, Urban Village; Montgomery County; Pop. 900; Area Code 215; Zip Code 19477; Elev. 300'; N suburb of Philadelphia in SE Pennsylvania; has many old houses set in spacious grounds. The Spring House Hotel, a three-story stone structure with mansard roof, built in 1888, stands on the site of an inn that served as headquarters for the Pennsylvania and New Jersey Militia during Fries' Rebellion.

•**SPRING MILLS**, Village; Centre County; Pop. 600; Area Code 814; Zip Code 16875; Elev. 52'; in cen. Pennsylvania; on Penn's Creek, was part of the "Manor of Succoth," held by the Penns until 1791.

•**SPRUCE CREEK**, Village; Huntingdon County; Pop. 140; Area Code 717; Elev. 777'; in S cen. Pennsylvania; at the confluence of Spruce Creek and the Little Juniata River, was settled prior to 1763.

•**STARRUCCA**, Borough; Wayne County; Pop. 216; Area Code 717; Zip Code 18462; Elev. 1,310'; in NE Pennsylvania.

•**STATE COLLEGE**, Borough; Seat of Centre County; Pop. 36,082; Area Code 814; Zip Code 16801; Elev. 1,191'; 50 miles NE of Altoona in central Pennsylvania; located in the Nittany Valley between the Bald Eagle Ridge (NW) and the Seven Mountains (SE).

Community life in State College revolves around the main campus of the Pennsylvania State University, from which the borough received its name. Local enterprise is devoted to supplying the needs of that institution, which is surrounded by impressive mountains.

Pennsylvania State University has grown from a small state-aided farm school, chartered in 1855 into a major institution offering over 100 major fields of study for its 32,500 students. The university has 10 "Commonwealth campuses" for beginning undergraduate work an some fields of graduate study in other cities. Many were established to meet the needs of high school graduates and working persons unable to leave home because of financial or other reasons.

The original Farmers High School was chartered in 1855 to teach better methods of soil cultivation, and the first classes were held in the partially completed Old Main in 1859. In 1862, when *President Lincoln* signed the Morrill Land Grant College Act of Congress, the school became the Agricultural College of Pennsylvania. In 1874, it was named State College, and the borough surrounding it was also incorporated from parts of two townships, Benner and Harris. The University's present name was adopted in 1953.

Near town is the Bald Eagle Lookout, the historic Boal Mansion, and the miles of "fisherman's paradise" of the surrounding hilly countryside.

POINTS OF INTEREST

BOAL MANSION AND MUSEUM AND COLUMBUS CHAPEL- The mansion has been the *Boal* family home since 1789; many original furnishings, tools, etc. A Boal relative brought the 16th century Spanish chapel, which belonged to the family of *Christopher Columbus*, here in 1919.

PENNSYLVANIA STATE UNIVERSITY- Earth and Mineral Sciences Museum, Museum of Art, College of Agriculture Dairy Center.

Agriculture - Varied produce and dairy farming
Higher Education - Pennsylvania State University
Daily Newspaper - Centre Daily Times,
    P.O. Box 89, 3400 E. College Ave., 16801
Chamber of Commerce - 444 E. College Ave.
Community Event - Central Pennsylvania Festival
    of the Arts, Annual, July

•**STEELTON**, Borough; Dauphin County; Pop. 6,484; Area Code 717; Zip Code 17113; Elev. 306'; in SE cen. Pennsylvania; chosen in 1865 as the site for the Pennsylvania Steel Company plant, was formally christened in 1880. The first practical production of Bessemer steel in America was begun here in 1867.

Rudolph and *Henry Kelker*, who owned land adjoining the steel works, first called the town Baldwin in honor of *Matthew Baldwin*, a large stockholder in the steel company. The post office renamed it Steel Works in 1871, and nine years later steel works superintendant *Luther Bent* suggested its present name.

> *Agriculture* - Varied produce and dairy farming,
> especially tobacco, grain.
> *Industry/Mfg.* - Fishing. Stone quarrying.
> *Chamber of Commerce* - 123 N. Front Street

•**STEWARTSTOWN**, Borough; York County; Pop. 1,072; Area Code 717; Zip Code 17363; Elev. 860'; in S Pennsylvania.

•**STILLWATER**, Borough; Columbia County; Pop. 201; Area Code 717; Zip Code 17878; Elev. 700'; in E central Pennsylvania.

•**STOCKDALE**, Borough; Washington County; Pop. 641; Area Code 412; Zip Code 15483; Elev. 765'; in SW Pennsylvania; named for the dairy cows that have grazed on the land here.

•**STOCKERTON**, Borough; Northampton County; Pop. 661; Area Code 215; Zip Code 18083; Elev. 374'; in E Pennsylvania; bisected by Bushkill Creek, was named for *Andrew Stocker*, who laid out the village in 1774.

•**STODDARTSVILLE**, Village; Luzerne and Monroe Counties; Pop. 30; Area Code 717; Elev. 1,589'; a center for hunters, on the west bank of the Lehigh River, was laid out in 1815 by *John Stoddart*.

•**STONEBORO**, Borough; Mercer County; Pop. 1,177; Area Code 412; Zip Code 16153; Elev. 1,185'; in W Pennsylvania.

•**STOYSTOWN**, Borough; Somerset County; Pop. 432; Area Code 814; Zip Code 15563; Elev. 2,000'; 20 miles S of Johnstown in S Pennsylvania; in a rural area.

•**STRASBURG**, Borough; Lancaster County; Pop. 1,999; Area Code 717; Zip Code 17579; Elev. 480'; 10 miles SE of Lancaster in SE Pennsylvania; stone quarrying.

The LeFevres or Ferrees, and other French immigrants settled this town in 1733, naming it for their native Strasbourg in Alsace. A Toy Train museum is in town, run by the Train Collectors Association. The Eagle Museum, west of Strasburg, houses exhibits of colonial guns, toys and fine glassware.

•**STRATTANVILLE**, Borough; Clarion County; Pop. 555; Area Code 814; Zip Code 16258; Elev. 1.480'; in W Pennsylvania.

•**STRAUSSTOWN**, Borough; Berks County; Pop. 377; Area Code 215; Zip Code 19559; Elev. 560'; in SE Pennsylvania.

•**STROUDSBURG**, Borough; Seat of Monroe County; Pop. 5.148; Area Code 717; Zip Code 18360; Elev. 420'; 30 miles N of Easton in E Pennsylvania; lies among the Pocono foothills at the confluence of McMichaels, Pocono, and Brodhead Creeks. In 1776 *Colonel Jacob stroud*, a veteran of the French and Indian War, erected a stockaded house here and called it Fort Penn. In 1778 it served as a haven for survivors of the Wyoming massacre; in the following year *General Sullivan's* punitive expedition rested here. A few years after the Revolution, *Samuel Preston* said of *Stroud*, "He keeps store, tavern, grist mill, and saw mill, besides a large farm...and he has the most hands I ever saw at one place."

Jacob Stroud refused to sell building lots, and he erected only three houses on his land before his death in 1806. Then his son *Daniel* laid out the town, widened the main street, and sold lots on the wise condition that the houses should be set back 30 feet from the street.

Higher Education - Pennsylvania State College
Daily Newspaper - Pocono Record, 511 Lenox St.
Chamber of Commerce - 566 Main St.

•**SUGARCREEK**, Borough; Venango County; Pop. 5,954; Area Code 814; Zip Code 16301; 10 miles W of Oil Creek in NW Pennsylvania; incorporated in 1968.

•**SUGAR GROVE**, Borough; Warren County; Pop. 630; Area Code 814; Zip Code 16350; Elev. 1,400'; in NW Pennsylvania.

•**SUGAR NOTCH**, Borough; Luzerne County; Pop. 1,191; Area Code 717; Zip Code 18706; Elev. 740'; in E Pennsylvania; named for the mountain gap nearby, covered in sugar maples.

•**SULLIVAN COUNTY**, NE Pennsylvania; Pop. 6,349; Established, March 15, 1847; Seat is Laporte.
Set apart from Lycoming in 1847, it was named in honor of *General John Sullivan*, who was born in 1740 at Somersworth, New Hampshire. He studied law, and, when the Revolutionary War broke out, was practicing his profession at Durham, New Hampshire. He was appointed one of the eight brigadier-generals of the Continental army, and in 1776 was commissioned a major-general. He served with credit throughout the war, participating in the battles of Long Island, Brandywine, and Germantown.

•**SUMMERHILL**, Borough; Cambria County; Pop. 725; Area Code 814; Zip Code 15958; Elev. 1,540'; in SW central Pennsylvania; originally named Somerhill for *Joseph* and *David Somer*, two landowners in the area.

•**SUMMERVILLE**, Borough; Jefferson County; Pop. 830 ; Area Code 814; Zip Code 15864; Elev. 1,160'; on Red Bank Creek in W central Pennsylvania; was settled by *Summers Baldwin* in 1812.

•**SUMMIT HILL**, Borough; Carbon County; Pop. 3,418; Area Code 717; Zip Code 18250; Elev. 1,410'; in E Pennsylvania; so named because it is at the summit of Sharp Mountain; an excellent view of the countryside is seen from here.

•**SUNBURY**, City; Seat of Northumberland County; Pop. 12,292; Area Code 717; Zip Code 17801; Elev. 450'; 50 miles N of Harrisburg on the Susquehanna River in E central Pennsylvania; is bounded roughly by the Shamokin Creek and the Susquehanna River.

Sunbury was once the central site of Shamokin, a cluster of three Indian villages, for years the Indian capital of central Pennsylvania. Here, in 1742, *Shikellemy* greeted the first white visitors: *Count von Zinzendorf*, the Moravian, and *Conrad Weiser*, the provincial government's interpreter, land agent, and diplomat. Eventually the Indians abandoned the site, and in 1772 *Governor Richard Penn* ordered a town laid out.

In Sunbury, *Thomas A. Edison* built and operated the first three-wire central station incandescent electric lighting plant in the world. Several advantages induced *Edison* to choose Sunbury as the site of this plant. The gas rate of the town was excessive; it was close to the anthracite fields, making fuel comparatively cheap; and citizens of nearby Williamsport were ready to supply the necessary capital for the enterprise. The plant was built at 4th and Vine Sts., wires were strung to the City Hotel, and on July 4, 1883, the current was turned on. Visitors at the Vine Street Plant, rarely dared to cross the power plant threshold.

Three months after the formation of Northumberland County, *Governor Richard Penn* and the provincial council ordered that "the surveyor-general (John Lukens), with all convenient speed, repair to Fort Augusta on the Susquehanna and with the assistance of *Mr. William Maclay* lay out a town for the county of Northumberland to be called by the name of Sunbury." The county seat was to be located "at the most commodious place between the fort and the mouth of Shamokin Creek." *Richard Penn* borrowed the name of Sunbury from the English village of that name, situated on the Thames about fifteen miles southwest of London.

Etymologically Sunbury signifies "the city of the sun." The new county town grew up on the site of the populous Indian village of Shamokin and about the old pioneer Fort Augusta, erected in 1756, and named, in all likelihood, for the *Princess Augusta*, mother of *George III*. In 1797, twenty-five years after it was formally laid out, Sunbury was incorporated; but it did not attain its growth until many years later, when it was greatly stimulated by the opening of coal mines and the building of the railroad. It received a city charter in 1920.

NORTHUMBERLAND COUNTY COURTHOUSE-
Italianate; painted brick; reputedly based on design
by Philadelphia architect *Samuel Sloan.*

Agriculture - Varied produce and dairy farming,
   especially apples
Industry/Mfg. - Campers, soft drinks
Daily Newspaper - Item, 200 Market Street
Chamber of Commerce -401 Market St.

•**SUSQUEHANNA COUNTY**, E Central Pennsylvania; Pop.
37,876; Established, February 21, 1810; Seat is Montrose.
   The county, which was separated from Luzerne in
1810, owes its name to the fact that within its territory
the Susquehanna River first enters the state.
Heckewelder's explanation of this name is the one that
has generally been accepted: "The word Susquehanna,
properly Sisquehanne, from *sisku,* "mud," and *hanne,* a
"river," was probably, at an early date in the settlement of
this country, overheard by someone while the Indians
were remarking, at the time of a flood or freshet, *"Juh!
Sisquehanne,"* -which is "How muddy the river is!" Thus
Susquehanna is interpreted as meaning "muddy river."
Another interpretation of Susquehanna is that it means
"the long, crooked river," or to phrase it a little more
poetically, "the river of the winding shore." The most recent explanation has been given by *James McKirdy,* who
believes that Susquehanna is derived from the Delaware
Indian word *saskwihanang,* signifying "the place of the
straight river." Susquehanna borough is named for the
county and the river.

•**SUSQUEHANNA DEPOT**, Borough; Susquehanna County; Pop. 1,994; Area Code 717; Elev. 920'; in NE Pennsylvania; named for the county and river flowing through
it. Near New York state line in a farming region.

•**SUSQUEHANNA RIVER**, Central New York, Pennsylvania and Maryland; Flows S approx. 450 miles from
source at Otsego Lake in central New York, through Central and SE Pennsylvania, and into the Chesapeake Bay,
NE Maryland. Navigable for several miles N of mouth.
   West Branch of the Susquehanna flows approx. 200
miles NE and E from source in Central Pennsylvania to

confluence with the main river in Northumberland County at Sunbury.

The word Susquehanna may have come from the Indian words *sisku*, or "mud," and *hanne*, or "river." It may also have been derived from the Lenni-Lenape word *saskwihanang*, meaning "the straight river."

•**SUTERVILLE**, Borough; Westmoreland County; Pop. 863; Area Code 417; Zip Code 15083; Elev. 800'; in SW Pennsylvania.

•**SWARTHMORE**, Borough; Delaware County; Pop. 5,950; Area Code 215; Zip Code 19081; Elev. 190'; 10 miles SW of Philadelphia in SE Pennsylvania; an attractive residential suburb and college town, named for Swarthmore Hall, home of *George Fox* (1624-91), founder of the Society of Friends. Some townspeople are descendants of *Penn's* fellow-passengers on the *Welcome*.

The heart of the community is Swarthmore College, founded by the Hicksite body of Friends in 1864; in 1911 the institution became nonsectarian; enrollment is usually limited to 670 men and 600 women. Swarthmore's important contribution to education in America is its system of honors courses instituted by *Dr. Frank Aydelotte*, former president.

POINT OF INTEREST

BENJAMIN WEST BIRTHPLACE- Birthplace of American artist *Benjamin West* ; located on Swarthmore College campus. Georgian.

Primarily a residential area
Higher Education - Swarthmore College

•**SWISSVALE**, Borough; Allegheny County; Pop. 11,345; Area Code 412; Zip Code 15218; Elev. 920'; 5 miles E of Pittsburgh in SW Pennsylvania; was built up on the farm of *James Swisshelm*, who inherited it from his father, *John*. The name Swissvale is said to have been invented by *Jane Gray Swisshelm*, the wife of the proprietor. When the Pennsylvania Railroad decided to establish a station at this point in 1854, *James Swisshelm* donated half an acre of land for the site, and the railroad company, in recognition of his generosity, adopted the name of Swissvale for the station, around which the present town has sprung up.

Chamber of Commerce - 1319 LaClair Ave.

•**SWOYERSVILLE**, Borough; Luzerne County; Pop. 5,795; Area Code 717; Zip Code 18704; Elev. 840'; 5 miles N of Wilkes-Barre in E Pennsylvania; named for *Henry Swoyer*, early coal operator. The borough was incorporated in 1888. It continues to be an important anthracite coal mining center.

•**SYKESVILLE**, Borough; Jefferson County; Pop. 1,537; Area Code 814; Zip Code 15865; Elev. 1,352'; 5 miles SW of DuBois in a farming area in W central Pennsylvania; settled in 1861 and named for *Jacob Sykes*, sawmill owner of the 1880's, was supported by lumbering until the beginning of the twentieth century; then activity shifted to bituminous coal mining. Lumbering is still practiced to some extent.

•**SYLVANIA**, Borough; Bradford County; Pop. 236; Area Code 717; Zip Code 16945; Elev. 1,280'; in N Pennsylvania; name means "forest land," which is indicative of the terrain here.

T

•**TAMAQUA**, Borough; Schuylkill County; Pop. 8,843; Area Code 717; Zip Code 18252; Elev. 805'; 15 miles NE of Pottsville in E central Pennsylvania; laid out in 1829 by the Lehigh Coal and Navigation Company, Tamaqua was named for the creek flowing by. *Tamaque* was a Delaware Indian word meaning "beaver."

Chamber of Commerce - Broad & Berwick Sts.

•**TARENTUM**, Borough; Allegheny County; Pop. 6,419; Area Code 412; Zip Code 15084; Elev. 737'; in SW Pennsylvania; settled in the last decade of the eighteenth century when a gristmill wa erected on Bull Creek, was laid out in 1829 by *Judge Henry Marie Brackenridge*, and incorporated as a borough in 1842. The Brackenridge farm occupied the site of a Shawnee village known as Chartier's Old Town for the half-breed trader, *Peter Chartier*. Indian artifacts have been unearthed. No one now seems to know why *Judge Brackenridge* bestowed this classical name upon his town. He was a scholar and a student of ancient history and the classical languages, and he may have been attracted by the name of the ancient city in southern Italy which the Romans called Tarentum, and which the Greeks had previously named Taras from the small stream on which the old Greek colony was planted. Tarentum has a large business district, and many houses on the slopes above the river. Discovery of natural gas in 1880 brought rapid expansion.

Chamber of Commerce - 327 E. Sixth Ave.

•**TATAMY**, Borough; Northampton County; Pop. 910; Area Code 215; Zip Code 18085; Elev. 430'; in E Pennsylvania; named for a Delaware Indian chief.

378

•**TAYLOR**, Borough; Lackawanna County; Pop. 7,246; Area Code 717; Zip Code ; Elev. 680'; 5 miles SW of Scranton in NE Pennsylvania; was named for the late *Moses Taylor*, a prominent New York merchant and capitalist, who had extensive business interests in the place that now bears his name. *Moses Taylor* was born in New York in 1806, began his business career as a clerk at the age of 15. He helped finance the Civil War as well as a hospital in Scranton for miners and railroad workers.

•**TELFORD**, Borough; Bucks and Montgomery Counties; Pop. 3,507; Area Code 215; Zip Code 18969; Elev. 420'; 25 miles E of Reading in SE Pennsylvania; brushes, shoes and furniture are manufactured.

•**TEMPLE**, Borough; Berks County; Pop. 1,486; Area Code 215; Zip Code 19560; Elev. 380'; in SE Pennsylvania; near Reading; named for an old hotel sign that bore the words, "Stop at Solomon's Temple." Solomon was the innkeeper's name.

•**TEN MILE CREEK**, Creek, SW Pennsylvania; Flows E approx. 25 miles from source in S Washington County to mouth on the Monongahela River, at Millsboro. So called because it empties into the Monogahela just 10 miles SW of Brownsville, the site of the "Redstone Old Fort," of pioneer days.

•**TERRE HILL**, Borough; Lancaster County; Pop. 1,217; Area Code 717; Zip Code 17581; Elev. 560'; in SE Pennsylvania.

•**THOMAS MILLS**, Village; Somerset County; Pop. 100; Area Code 814; Zip Code 15935; Elev. 1,410'; rural town near Hollsopple in S Pennsylvania; was named for the flour mill erected in 1836 by *John Thomas*.

•**THOMPSON**, Borough; Susquehanna County; Pop. 303; Area Code 717; Zip Code 18465; Elev. 1,640'; in NE Pennsylvania; named for an early settler.

•**THOMPSONTOWN**, Borough; Juniata County; Pop. 593; Area Code 717; Zip Code 17094; Elev. 465'; in S central Pennsylvania; was a mill and tavern site in 1771.

•**THORNBURG**, Borough; Allegheny County; Pop. 526; Area Code 412; Elev. 900'; in SW Pennsylvania.

•**THREE SPRINGS**, Borough; Huntingdon County; Pop. 501; Area Code 717; Zip Code 17264; Elev. 740'; in S central Pennsylvania; named for Three Springs that form a creek of he same name, on a tract purchased by *Col. George Ashman* in 1779.

•**THROOP**, Borough; Lackawanna County; Pop. 4,166; Area Code 717; Zip Code 18512; Elev. 860'; 5 miles NE of Scranton in NE Pennsylvania; was named in honor of *Dr. Benjamin Henry Throop*, the pioneer physician of Scranton. *Doctor Throop* built his modest cottage near Slocum Hollow in 1847, and for many years was the physician of the valley, when Scranton was a mere village and the surrounding country was thinly settled. *Throop* was postmaster of Scranton in 1853. Convinced that coal was destined to be the chief source of wealth in this region, he purchased extensive tracts of valuable coal land. He also added to his great wealth by buying up farms and dividing them into building lots, which he sold at a reasonable price, but always at a handsome profit. He was the founder not only of Throop, but also of Blakely, and was one of the promoters for the formation of Lackawanna County.

•**TIDIOUTE**, Borough; Warren County; Pop. 844; Area Code 814; Zip Code 16351; Elev. 1,115'; in NW Pennsylvania; the name is Indian, and has been translated as "seeing far," straight water," or "cluster of islands."

•**TIMBLIN**, Borough; Jefferson County; Pop. 197; Area Code 814; Zip Code 15778; Elev. 1,270'; in W central Pennsylvania.

•**TIOGA**, Borough; Tioga County; Pop. 613; Area Code 717; Zip Code 16946; Elev. 1,036'; in N Pennsylvania; (ind. "gate or place of entrance"), formerly an outpost of the Six Nations, was settled in 1792 by *Jesse Losey*, a Revolutionary soldier, and named for the river flowing by.

Community Event - Old Home Day, Annual, August

•**TIOGA COUNTY**, N Pennsylvania; Pop. 40,973; Established, March 26, 1804; Seat is Wellsboro.

In 1804 Tioga Township, which had been organized in 1797 as part of Lycoming County, became the new county of Tioga. Both the township and the county took their name from the Tioga River, which flows north into New York and unites with the Cohocton to form the Chemung River. Sweeping about in a semicircle, the Chemung joins the North Branch of the Susquehanna at "old Tioga Point," which is now called Athens.

A few of the earlier forms of Tioga are Diahoga, Diago, Tayego, and Teogo. Several different explanations of this name have been given. There seems now to be little doubt that the word signifies "the forks of a stream," or "the place where two rivers meet"; that is, the gound lying between them. Heckewelder defined the word Tioga as meaning "gateway," explaining that in passing from the Delaware country on the south to the Iroquois country on the north the traveler entered this region as through a gate.

•**TIOGA RIVER**, River, N Pennsylvania and S New York; flows N approx. 40 miles from source in E Tioga County, Pennsylvania across the state line to mouth at the Cohocton River; Forms the Chemung River near Corning.

The river has been called Diahoga, Diago, Tayego and Teogo all derivatives of an Iroquois word meaning "where two rivers meet."

•**TIONESTA**, Borough; Seat of Forest County; Pop. 659; Area Code 814; Zip Code 16353; Elev. 1,073'; 20 miles NE of Oil City on the Allegheny River in NW Pennsylvania; (Ind. "it penetrates the island," or "home of the wolves"), first known as Goshgoshing and later as Saqualinguent (Ind. "place of council"), is at the junction of Tionesta Creek and the Allegheny. Settlement occurred prior to 1790, and its advantageous position made it a lumber center.

The existence of oil in this region was known to *David Zeisberger*, who in 1767 established a short-lived Moravian mission here. *Zeisberger* noted in his journal that oil was used "medicinally for toothache, rheumatism, etc. Sometimes it is taken internally. It is of a brown color and burns well and can be used in lamps."

•**TIONESTA CREEK**, Creek, N Pennsylvania; Flows NE, S and SW from source in Warren County, through the sparsely populated Allegheny National Forest to its mouth along the Allegheny River; Dammed S of village of Tionesta to form Tionesta Creek Lake.

Tionesta is a modification of the Iroquois word *Tiyohwehnoisto*, meaning "it penetrates the island," referring to the way in which the swift current of the stream rushes upon Hunter Island in the Allegheny River.

•**TITUSVILLE**, Borough; Crawford County; Pop. 6,884; Area Code 814; Zip Code 16354; 15 miles N of Oil City in an agricultural region in NW Pennsylvania on Oil Creek; on a suffocating afternoon in August 1859, witnessed the birth of a new industry and a new era. In 1857 an advertisement for Kier's Rock Oil--depicting a derrick over a salt well from which oil was obtained as a by-product--attracted the attention of *George H. Bissel*, part owner of a 100-acre tract near Titusville. *Bissel's* property stretched along Oil Creek-long covered with an oily scum that the Indians had used in mixing their war paints-and he determined to seek the source of the oil. For this purpose the Seneca Oil Company, *Bissel's* syndicate, employed *"Colonel" Edwin L. Drake*, a middle-aged railroad conductor whose chief qualification seemed to be the interest he had shown in oil obtained from a spring in that section.

During the summer of 1858 *Drake* sank several wells by means of pick and shovel, meanwhile working out a method of drilling. Although one of his shallow wells struck a deposit of oil, another encountered an underground spring that filled the shaft so quickly that some of the laborers were nearly drowned. This persuaded *Drake* to try drilling. He hired *"Uncle Billy" Smith*, a Tarentum blacksmith who had had experience with salt wells, and *Smith's* two sons, and in April 1859 began drilling a shaft through solid rock, alongside the creek near Titusville. Idle villagers, discussing the proceedings with amusement, dubbed the project "Drake's Folly."

On August 28 *Uncle Billy* and his son *Sam* saw a dark brown liquid bubbling near the surface after they had raised the bit from an approximate depth of 70 feet. They used a pitcher-pump to fill several barrels, and then *Billy* mounted his mule for the triumphant half-mile ride into Titusville, rousing the townspeople with the cry: "Struck oil! Struck oil!"

Joseph Murray, oil historian, says of this episode: "The news of Drake's discovery was like a clarion call that roused from centuries of sleep or lethargy a mighty giant...The discovery was timed to a psychological moment...as though...the well had spouted a flame that illuminated and dazzled the world, which was ready and waiting for a new light." This was the first well in America drilled for oil exclusively.

The drowsy village soon became a boom town of shady characters, hard life, easy philosophy, and rough democracy. Other towns mushroomed throughout the section as thousands of wells were sunk. Oil gushed from the pitted earth. An endless chain of wagons splashed over deep-rutted roads to the nearest railroad. Hundreds of flatboats, their barrel-stacked decks awash, moved down Oil Creek. Railroads extended spurs in all directions. In 1865 a four-mile pipeline was built near Titusville by *Samuel Van Syckel,* and this was the signal for the first of a series of bloody skirmishes between the oil men and the teamsters who saw their means of livelihood threatened. A pipeline across the Allegheny Mountains to tidewater was begun in 1878.

For 30 years Pennsylvania oil men declared they would "drink every drop of oil found west of the Ohio River."

Today, oil refining is still important, but the electronic components industry is growing steadily.

POINTS OF INTEREST

DRAKE OIL WELL- Site of the world's first oil well, drilled by *Edwin L. Drake* in 1859. Museum.

SITE OF PITHOLE CITY- Site of short-lived (1865-1870) oil boom town, which once had over 10,000 inhabitants.

Agriculture - Varied produce and dairy farming
Industry/Mfg. - Electronics, oil drilling
Higher Education - University of Pittsburg-Titusville
　　University of Pittsburg - Titusville
Daily Newspaper - Herald, 209 W. Spring St.
Chamber of Commerce - 116 W. Central Ave.

•**TOPTON**, Borough; Berks County; Pop. 1,818; Area Code 215; Zip Code 19562; Elev. 480'; in SE Pennsylvania.

•**TOBYHANNA**, Village; Monroe County; Pop. 900; Area Code 717; Zip Code 18466; Elev. 1,940'; in E Pennsylvania; name means "older stream," from an Indian word. The resort's population reaches 2,000 in summer.

•**TOWANDA**, Borough; Seat of Bradford County; Pop. 3,526; Area Code 717; Zip Code 18848; Elev. 837'; 50 miles NW of Wilkes-Barre in a mountainous resort area in N Pennsylvania; (Ind. "where we bury the dead"), occupies a slope on the west shore of the Susquehanna, at the convergence of three valleys. The town's early name, Meansville, for *William Means* who laid it out in 1812, occasioned "considerable animosity," and the present one was adopted in 1828.

On the upper and lower hills are elaborate summer homes of the rich. Some streets here are brick-paved.

Daily Newspaper - Review, 116 Main St.
Chamber of Commerce - P.O. Box 122

•**TOWER CITY**, Borough; Schuylkill County; Pop. 1,667; Area Code 717; Zip Code 17980; Elev. 800'; 25 miles W of Pottsville in E central Pennsylvania; was built on reclaimed marsh lands in 1868 by *Charlemagne Tower.* In 1847 *Tower* had learned from a government geologist that thick coal seams underlay the local hills. Prevented by poverty from exploiting his knowledge, *Tower* guarded it carefully until he had accumulated a small fortune during the Civil War. He purchased Brookside Mountain at $4 an acre and tunneled far into it without success, but eventually he struck coal with a vertical shaft and amassed a large fortune. *Tower's* son later served as U.S. Ambassador to Germany.

Community Event - Celebration, Annual, June

•**TOWNVILLE**, Borough; Crawford County; Pop. 364; Area Code 814; Zip Code 16360; Elev. 1,410'; in NW Pennsylvania; *Noah Town* founded and laid out this town in 1824.

•**TRAFFORD**, Borough; Allegheny and Westmoreland Counties; Pop. 3,662; Area Code 417; Zip Code 15085; Elev. 820'; E suburb of Pittsburgh in SW Pennsylvania.

•**TRAINER**, Borough; Delaware County; Pop. 2,056; Area Code 215; Elev. 29'; SW suburb of Philadelphia in SE Pennsylvania; grew up around grist and saw mills established by *David Trainer*.

•**TRAPPE**, Borough; Montgomery County; Pop. 1,800; Area Code 215; Elev. 300'; in SE Pennsylvania; The origin of the name is uncertain, though many historians declare than an early tavern's high stoop caused it to be called *treppe* (steps) by the German settlers, and that a corrupted form of the word came into popular use as the village name. Another explanation is that the tavern's high steps often became a "trap" for the unsteady feet of steady patrons.

The Augustus Lutheran Church, was built in 1743 by *Dr. Heinrich Melchior Muhlenberg* (1711-87), "Patriarch of the Lutheran Church in America," is a squat building typical of early German rural construction in it is of local stone, with hand-hewn timbers and hand-forged nails, hinges, and door latches. The altar, erected in 1795, is still in place, as are the original pews, some with carved wooden doors and elaborately forged hinges. Another interesting feature is its cut-out balcony railing with its fanciful heart pattern. *Dr. Muhlenberg* was buried in the adjoining graveyard, and his preacher-soldier-layman son, *John Peter*, was buried beside him. It was *J. Peter Muhlenberg* (1746-1807), who, as pastor of a church at Woodstock, Virginia, stirred his congregation at the time of the Revolutionary War by concluding his farewell sermon, "There is a time for all things--a time to preach and a time to fight--and now is the time to fight!" With this he stepped from the pulpit, threw back his ecclesiastical robes, and revealed the uniform of a Continental colonel. He retired from the army in 1783 but never returned to the ministry.

The church building provided shelter for American soldiers before and after the Battle of Germantown.

POINT OF INTEREST

AUGUSTUS LUTHERAN CHURCH- Constructed in 1743 under direction of *Dr. Heinrich Melchior Muhlenberg*, patriarch of Lutheran Church in America.

•**TREMONT**, Borough; Schuylkill County; Pop. 1,796; Area Code 717; Zip Code 17981; Elev. 760'; in E central Pennsylvania.

Chamber of Commerce - 49 E. Line St.

•**TROUTVILLE**, Borough; Clearfield County; Pop. 204; Area Code 814; Zip Code 15866; Elev. 1,560'; in W central Pennsylvania.

•**TROY**, Borough; Bradford County; Pop. 1,381; Area Code 717; Zip Code 16947; Elev. 1,136'; near New York state line in N Pennsylvania; was settled in 1793 by *Nathaniel Allen*, soldier in the Revolution and later a land agent of the Susquehanna Company. Aside from the fire of 1848, which destroyed every business house but one, and the feverish but short-lived hopes of the town when wells were drilled, Troy has enjoyed a placid existence.

This summer resort is now at the center of a tranquil dairy and stock-raising region that once was a hopeful gas and oil field.

•**TRUMBAUERSVILLE**, Borough; Bucks County; Pop. 781; Area Code 215; Zip Code 18970; Elev. 540'; in SE Pennsylvania.

•**TULLYTOWN**, Borough; Bucks County; Pop. 2,277; Area Code 215; Zip Code 19007; Elev. 20'; E suburb of Philadelphia in SE Pennsylvania.

•**TUNKHANNOCK**, Borough; Seat of Wyoming County; Pop. 2,144; Area Code 717; Zip Code 18657; Elev. 613'; 20 miles NW of Scranton in NE Pennsylvania; is at the confluence of Tunkhannock Creek and the Susquehanna's North Branch.   In   1786,   eleven years after its organization, the name of Putnam Township was changed to Tunkhannock Township, and about four years later a

386

settlement was begun where Tunkhannock borough now stands. Half a century after the town was started, Tunkhannock was incorporated as a borough, and in 1842 it became the seat of justice of the new county of Wyoming.

The township and the village of Tunkhannock were named for the Tunkhannock Creek. This name is a corruption of *Tank-hanne*, "a small stream." The earliest form of the name was *Tenkghanacke*, which may be identified with Tagh-ka-nick, an Indian name in New York, and with Taconic in Massachusetts and Connecticut. Tenkghanacke, Taghkanick, and Taconic are all apparently the same Algonquin word in different forms. The common interpretation of this name is "forest, or wilderness."

Timber is still the most important commodity here.

•**TUNNELHILL**, Borough; Blair and Cambria Counties; Pop. 513; Area Code 814; Zip Code 16641; Elev. 2,300'; near Gallitzin in SW Pennsylvania.

•**TURBOTVILLE**, Borough; Northumberland County; Pop. 675; Area Code 717; Zip Code 17772; Elev. 600'; 5 miles E of Watsontown in a residential area in E central Pennsylvania.

•**TURTLE CREEK**, Borough; Allegheny County; Pop. 6,959; Area Code 412; Zip Code 15145; Elev. 900'; in SW Pennsylvania; was settled about 1765. The settlement grew into a pleasant suburban community, stimulated by the laying of the Greensburg turnpike, and was incorporated in 1892. The name is a translation of the Indian words for the place, *Tulpewi-sysu*.

Chamber of Commerce - 1 Fineman & Co.

•**TUSCARORA MOUNTAINS**, Mountain Ridge, S Pennsylvania; Part of the Appalachian Mountains; Extends approx. 100 miles from E Fulton County NE to N Juniata County near the banks of the Susquehanna River.

•**TWILIGHT**, Borough; Washington County; Pop. 298; Area Code 412; Zip Code 15022; Elev. 980'; located near Charleroi in SW Pennsylvania.

•**TYRONE**, Borough; Blair County; Pop. 6,346; Area Code 814; Zip Code 16686; Elev. 909'; 15 miles NE of Altoona in S central Pennsylvania; (Irish, the land of Owen), was settled in 1850, but emigrants from North Ireland had penetrated the region earlier. They named the place for their native county of Tyrone. *Jacob Burley* built the first house here in 1850. In 1852 *Eli Bowen* in his *Pictorial Sketch Book of Pennsylvania* described a nearby forge as the "principal theatre" of the iron industry in this region, and continued: This is a model iron establishment. There are upward of 200 hands regularly employed, averaging 10 dollars per week each, and a more cheerful set of men we never saw...It is so unusual a circumstance to hear overseers complimented by their workers, that for the novelty of the thing we must beg to be excused for mentioning it."

Tyrone became a borough in 1857. It is a shipping center for a large clay and limestone quarrying region.

Agriculture - Varied produce and dairy farming, especially apple orchards
Industry/Mfg. - Clothing, chemicals. Limestone quarrying.
Daily Newspaper - Herald, 1018 Penna Ave.
Chamber of Commerce - 31 W. 11th St.

U

•**ULSTER**, Village; Bradford County; Pop. 400; Area Code 717; Elev. 742'; in N Pennsylvania; was the site of a trading post in 1765. Named by Irish immigrants for their homeland.

•**ULYSSES**, Borough; Potter County; Pop. 654; Area Code 814; Zip Code 16948; Elev. 2,080'; in N Pennsylvania; name was changed from Lewisville in 1960.

Community Event - Harvest Fair, Annual, November

•**UNION CITY**, Borough; Erie County; Pop. 3,263; Area Code 814; Zip Code 16438; Elev. 1,300'; 20 miles SE of Erie in NW Pennsylvania; was diverted from agriculture by the opening of oil refineries in 1862. Long before Drake's well "came in" at Titusville, settlers had been gathering surface oil from the South Branch of French Creek.

Furniture making is important to this essentially Great Lakes town. Dairy and poultry farms surround Union City.

Agriculture - Varied produce and dairy farming
Industry/Mfg. - Lumber, furniture
Chamber of Commerce - 33 N. Main St., P.O. Box 82

•**UNION COUNTY**, Central Pennsylvania; Pop. 32, 870; Established, March 22, 1813; Seat is Lewisburg.

•**UNION DALE**, Borough; Susquehanna County; Pop. 321; Area Code 717; Zip Code 18470; Elev. 1,660'; in NE Pennsylvania.

•**UNIONTOWN**, City; Seat of Fayette County; Pop. 14,023'; Area Code 412; Zip Code 15401; Elev. 1,023'; 45

miles SE of Pittsburgh in SW Pennsylvania; in a wild setting at the foot of the Alleghenies, is one of the bituminous coal center in Pennsylvania.

In 1784, 15 years after the town had been founded by young *Henry Beeson*, a Quaker, *General Ephraim Douglas* wrote: "This Uniontown is the most obscure spot on the face of the globe...The town and its appurtenances consist of...a courthouse and schoolhouse in one, a mill...four taverns, three smith shops, five retail shops, two Tanyards, one saddler's shop, two hatter's shops, one mason, one cake woman, two widows and some reputed maids. To which may be added a distillery." Uniontown, situated on Redstone Creek, was incorporated as a borough in 1796 and as a city in 1916.

POINTS OF INTEREST

FORT NECESSITY NATIONAL BATTLEFIELD- Reconstructed stockade, storehouses and entrenchments of fort constructed by colonial troops under *George Washington.*

SEARIGHTS TOLLHOUSE, NATIONAL ROAD- Built in 1835; restored. Of 6 tollhouses built on the National Road in Pennsylvania, one of only two remaining. Museum.

THOMAS GADDIS HOMESTEAD- Oldest known building in Fayette County, it served as local settlers' fort during the American Revolution. Log construction.

Agriculture - Varied produce and dairy farming
Industry/Mfg. - Clothing, steel products, lumber
Higher Education - Pennsylvania State University
Daily Newspaper - Herald Standard
    8-18 E. Church St.
Chamber of Commerce - 11 Pittsburgh St.
Community Events -
    Fayette County Fall Foliage Festival,
    Annual, October;
    Polish Festival Days, Annual, August;
    Spring Festival, Annual, May

•**UNIONVILLE**, Borough; Centre County; Pop. 361; Area Code 814; Zip Code 19375; Elev. 800'; in central Pennsylvania.

•**UPLAND**, Borough; Delaware County; Pop. 3,458; Area Code 215; Elev. 60'; SW suburb of Philadelphia, near Chester in SE Pennsylvania.

POINTS OF INTEREST

GEORGE K. CROZER MANSION (NETHERLEIGH)- High Victorian Italianate, built in 1869.

OLD MAIN (CROZER THEOLOGICAL SEMINARY, CROZER NORMAL SCHOOL- Built by industrialist *John Price Crozer* in 1850's as Normal Institute for Boys; later used as Civil War hospital and theological seminary.

CALEB PUSEY HOUSE- Early (c. 1683) surviving English-built house, home of *Caleb Pusey,* who emigrated to America and served as member of the Pennsylvania Assembly and Executive Council.

•**UPPER DARBY**, Urban Village; Delaware County; Area Code 215; Zip Code 19082-84; Elev. 100'; adjoins Philadelphia to W in SE Pennsylvania; a large shopping mall makes this the focus of many of Philadelphia's residential suburbs.

•**URSINA**, Borough; Somerset County; Pop. 311; Area Code 814; Zip Code 15485; in S Pennsylvania; named by the town's founder, *Judge William J. Bear* (1868). *Ursina* is a Latin adjective meaning "belonging to a bear.

•**UTICA**, Borough; Venango County; Pop. 255; Area Code 814; Zip Code 16362; Elev. 1,054'; in NW Pennsylvania; named for the New York city.

•**UWCHLAND**, Village; Chester County; Pop. 100; Area Code 215; Zip Code 19480; Elev. 450'; in SE Pennsylvania; name is derived from the Welsh word meaning "upland," or "above the valley."

•**VALENCIA**, Borough; Butler County; Pop. 340; Area Code 412; Zip Code 16059; Elev. 1,100'; NW suburb of Pittsburgh in W Pennsylvania; named for the Spanish city.

•**VALLEY FORGE**, Urban Village; Chester County; Pop. 450; Area Code 215; Zip Code 19481; Elev. 150'; 20 miles NW of Philadelphia in a rural-residential area in SE Pennsylvania; located on the Schuylkill River; was *George Washington's* winter headquarters in 1777-78, a state park commemorates his army's bravery. Today it is the headquarters of the American Baptist Church.

POINTS OF INTEREST

VALLEY FORGE STATE PARK- Includes home of Quaker farmer *Isaac Potts*, which served as headquarters of *Gen. George Washington* at Valley Forge 1777-1778; and headquarters of *Gen. Frederick von Steuben* of the Continental Army.

CRESSBROOK FARM- Farmhouse from c. 1740; headquarters during winter at Valley Forge for French *Brig. Gen. Louis Lebique Duportail*, Chief of Engineers of Continental Forces.

DAVID HARVARD HOUSE- Winter (1777-1778) quarters of *Maj. Gen. Charles Lee* and *Col. William Bradford* who later became 2nd U.S. Attorney General.

LIGHTFOOT MILL- 18th Century combination grist and lumber mill built by *Samuel Lightfoot* who later became active in community affairs.

MAJ. GEN. LORD STIRLING HEADQUARTERS- Good example of 18th century mid-Atlantic farm complex. Occupied by *Maj. Gen. Lord Stirling* of Washington's army.

NICHOLAS EAST HOUSE- Excellent area example of early-19th Century stone farmhouse.

WHARTON ESHERICK STUDIO- Studio complex built deep into hillside. Interior creations in wood by artist-craftsman *Wharton Esherick*. Architect *Louis Kahn* designed separate sawtooth-shaped concrete shop.

393

Community Event - Cherries Jubilee, Annual
February

•**VANDERBILT**, Borough; Fayette County; Pop. 689; Area Code 412; Zip Code 15486; Elev. 900'; in SW Pennsylvania.

•**VANDERGRIFT**, Borough; Westmoreland County; Pop. 6,823; Area Code 417; Zip Code 15690; Elev. 860'; 30 miles NE of Pittsburgh in SW Pennsylvania.

Agriculture - Varied produce and dairy farming,
   especially grain
Industry/Mfg. - Steel milling. Coal mining.
Daily Newspaper - News-Citizen, P.O. Box 90
Chamber of Commerce - P.O. Box 395

•**VANDLING**, Borough; Lackawanna County; Pop. 557; Area Code 717; Zip Code 18421; Elev. 1,600'; near Forest City in NE Pennsylvania.

•**VANPORT**, Village; Beaver County; Area Code 412; suburb of Beaver Falls in W Pennsylvania; named for *Martin Van Buren* during his 1836 presidential campaign.

•**VENANGO**, Borough; Crawford County; Pop. 298; Area Code 814; Zip Code 16440; Elev. 1,130'; in NW Pennsylvania; originally an Indian village; Name means "a tract of level, fertile ground," or "a mink," or "bull thistles."
   About 1757 the French completed a fort at the Indian town of venango, and called it Fort Machault in honor of *Jean Baptiste Machault*, who, in 1745, was comptroller of finance for France. Fort Machault, in 1759, was surrendered to the English, who chose a new site and erected Fort Venango.

•**VENANGO COUNTY**, W Pennsylvania; Pop. 64,444; Established, March 12, 1800; Seat is Franklin.
   The county took its name from the Venango River, which was the name the French used for the stream that has since been more generally called French Creek. The old Indian town of Venango stood at the mouth of this stream. At first the name was spelled Weningo, Wenango, and Vinango. The present spelling first occurs   in

394

Washington's Journal. Venango is said to be a corruption of the Indian word *innungah*, "which had some reference to a rude figure carved upon a tree, which the Senecas found here when they first came to this region." *Gannett* says that *innungah* means "a tract of level, fruitful ground." *Dr. George P. Donehoo* is quoted as saying that Venango is derived from the Indian word *onenge*, meaning "a mink." Many agree with *Charles A. Hanna* that Venango is merely a variant of Chenango or Shenango, which means "bull thistles." The name was popular in the western part of the state and is borne by townships in Butler and Crawford Counties, and also by the borough of Venango in the latter county.

•**VERONA**, Borough; Allegheny County; Pop. 3,179; Area Code 412; Zip Code 15147; Elev. 860'; in SW Pennsylvania; named for the Northern Italian city.

•**VERSAILLES**, Borough; Allegheny County; Pop. 2,150; Area Code 412; Elev. 850'; 15 miles SE of Pittsburgh on the Youghiogheny River in SW Pennsylvania; named for the palace of French kings to commemorate the earliest settlers of western Pennsylvania.

•**VILLANOVA**, Urban Village; Delaware County; Pop. 5,000; Area Code 215; Zip Code 19085; Elev. 430'; 10 miles NW of Philadelphia in a residential area in SE Pennsylvania; Villanova University, with about 8,000 students, is located here. The village's name means "new town."

> *Primarily a residential area*
> *Higher Education -*
> Northeastern Christian Junior College
> Villanova University

•**VINTONDALE**, Borough; Cambria County; Pop. 697; Area Code 814; Zip Code 15961; Elev. 1,440'; 10 miles N of Johnstown in SW central Pennsylvania.

•**VOLANT**, Borough; Lawrence County; Pop. 203; Area Code 412; Zip Code 16156; Elev. 1,050'; in W Pennsylvania; name means "flying."

•**WALL**, Borough; Allegheny County; Pop. 989; Area Code 412; Elev. 800'; E suburb of Pittsburgh in SW Pennsylvania.

•**WALLACETON**, Borough; Clearfield County; Pop. 393; Area Code 814; Zip Code 16876; Elev. 1,740'; in W central Pennsylvania.

•**WALLENPAUPACK LAKE**, Reservoir, NE Pennsylvania; In the Pocono Mountains along the border of Wayne and Pike counties; Formed by a damming of Wallenpaupack Creek; 9 square miles; Name is Indian for "deep, stagnant water."

•**WALLINGFORD**, Urban Village; Delaware County; Pop. 4,000; Area Code 215; Zip Code 19086; Elev. 160'; SW suburb of Philadelphia in SE Pennsylvania; residential; named for town in Connecticut.

POINT OF INTEREST

THOMAS LEIPER ESTATE- Built 1785, home of tobacco and snuff merchant *Thomas Leiper.*

Primarily a residential area
Chamber of Commerce - 214 Sykes Lane

•**WALNUTPORT**, Borough; Northampton County; Pop. 2,007; Area Code 215; Zip Code 18088; Elev. 380'; in E Pennsylvania.

•**WAMPUM**, Borough; Lawrence County; Pop. 851; Area Code 412; Zip Code 16157; Elev. 783'; in W Pennsylvania; settled in 1796 on the Beaver River, was incorporated as a borough in 1876. The name is a contraction of Wampumpeak (Ind. "a string of shell beads").

•**WARMINSTER**, Urban Village; Bucks County; Pop. 37,200; Area Code 215; Zip Code 18974; Elev. 310'; 20 miles NE of Philadelphia in a residential area in SE Pennsylvania; Burpee Seed Company has its national headquarters here, as does the Society for Individual Liberty.

> *Primarily a residential area*
> *Chamber of Commerce* - P.O. Box 123

•**WARREN**, Borough; Seat of Warren County; Pop. 12,146; Area Code 814; Zip Code 16365; Elev. 1,185'; 20 miles S of Jamestown, New York in NW Pennsylvania; near the mouth of the Conewago Creek, on the Allegheny River; was laid out about 1795 by *William Irvine* and *Andrew Ellicott.* Lots were sold at auction in distant communities to speculative bidders, few of whom settled on or paid for their lots. The town grew slowly until lumbering began; in 1860 there was an oil boom. It was incorporated in 1832.

Oil regining is still the main industry here, but the area retains a rural atmosphere.

> *Agriculture* - Varied produce and dairy farming
> *Industry/Mfg.* - Electronics, steel products,
>   oil refining
> *Higher Education* - Edinboro State College
> *Daily Newspaper* - Times Observer, 205 Penna Ave., W.
> *Chamber of Commerce* - 315 Second Ave., P.O. Box 942

•**WARREN COUNTY**, NW Pennsylvania; Pop. 47,449; Established, March 12, 1800; Seat is Warren. Much of the county remains rural.

•**WARRENDALE**, Urban Village; Allegheny County; Pop. 800; Area Code 412; Zip Code 15086; Elev. 1,066'; 20 miles W of Conway in a residential area in SW Pennsylvania; is at the northern limits of the Pittsburgh suburban area. In 1861 an association of farmers drilled for oil on the Warren property but abandoned work at a depth of 190 feet. Twenty-six years later oil was struck here at a depth of 1,455 feet.

•**WARRIOR RUN**, Borough; Luzerne County; Pop. 784; Area Code 717; Zip Code 18701; Elev. 700'; suburb of Wilkes-Barre in E Pennsylvania.

•**WASHINGTON**, City; Seat of Washington County; Pop. 18,363; Area Code 412; Zip Code 15301; Elev. 1,039'; 30 miles SW of Pittsburgh in SW Pennsylvania; The site, once known as Catfish's Camp, was a Delaware Indian village, the headquarters of *Chief Tingoocqua*. A town laid out in 1781 shortly became the county seat of newly created Washington County. Incorporated as a borough in 1810, Washington was chartered as a city in 1924.

Washington and Jefferson College, with 850 students, was founded here in 1780.

POINTS OF INTEREST

WASHINGTON COUNTY COURTHOUSE- Built in 1900; Second Renaissance Revival. In continuous use as courthouse.

WASHINGTON COUNTY JAIL- *F.J. Osterling*, architect. Built 1898-1899, designed with reference to Byzantine architecture; Renaissance Revival and Greek Revival elements.

Agriculture - Varied produce and dairy farming
Industry/Mfg. - Electronics, bottles, cartons.
　　Coal mining. Oil drilling.
Higher Education - Washington & Jefferson College
Daily Newspaper - Observer-Reporter, 122 S. Main St.
Chamber of Commerce - 20 E. Beau St.
Community Event -
　　Washington and Jefferson College National
　　Painting Show, Annual, March-April

•**WASHINGTON COUNTY**, SW Pennsylvania; Pop. 217,074; Established, March 28, 1781; Seat is Washington.

Founded eight years before *George Washington* became President of the United States, was the first Pennsylvania county formed after the Declaration of Independence and the only one organized during the Revolutionary period. At the time of its formation the struggle for independence already showed signs of ending in victory. *George Washington*, as commander-in-chief of the Revolutionary forces, was at the height of his military fame. He was recognized as the leader and the founder of the young republic, and was without doubt the most popular man in America.

Five years before, when he was just entering upon his difficult and heroic leadership, his native Virginia had named a new county in his honor. for nearly thirty years, ever since he had set out on his memorable journey over the rough trails and through the vast wilderness of Pennsylvania in the autumn of 1753, to demand, on behalf of Virginia, an explanation of the French, who were beginning to build a chain of forts from Lake Erie southward to the Ohio, *George Washington*, as explorer, Indian-fighter, and general, had linked his name forever with the history of Pennsylvania.

•**WASHINGTONVILLE**, Borough; Montour County; Pop. 218; Area Code 717; Zip Code 17884; Elev. 540'; in E central Pennsylvania; named for *George Washington*.

•**WATERFORD**, Borough; Erie County; Pop. 1,568; Area Code 814; Zip Code 16441; Elev. 1,192'; in NW Pennsylvania; is a farming and dairying village on Leboeuf Creek. Two blocks south of the central green are the Ruins of Fort Le Boeuf, portions of the stone walls of the last French stronghold in the province. Built in 1753 as one of a chain of forts, it was abandoned by the French in 1759 and occupied shortly afterward by the British. An American blockhouse erected near by in 1797 was destroyed by fire 71 years later.

In the highway opposite the ruins is the Washington Monument, a life-size bronze of *George Washington* as a major in the Virginia militia at the time he visited Forts Le Boeuf and Machault as an emissary of *Governor Dinwiddie*.

The town was laid out in 1795 by *Andrew Ellicott*, and it was named by Irish settlers for their home city and country.

Community Events - Heritage Days, Annual, July

•**WATER STREET**, Village; Huntingdon County; Pop. 25; Area Code 717; Elev. 725'; in S central Pennsylvania; crushed in the embrace of Canoe, Short, and Tussey Mountains, was so named because the early wagon route, as well as the Pennsylvania Canal, passed along the bed of a shallow stream here on its way through the gap in Tussey Mountain.

•**WATSONTOWN**, Borough; Northumberland County; Pop. 2,311; Area Code 717; Zip Code 17777; Elev. 500'; in E central Pennsylvania; named for *John Watson*, who bought 610 acres here in 1792, and two years later laid out the town.

•**WATTSBURG**, Borough; Erie County; Pop. 513; Area Code 814; Zip Code 16442; Elev. 1,286; in NW Pennsylvania; near the branches of French Creek, was founded in 1796 as a fur and supply depot by *William Miles*, who named the place for his wife's family. A weekly mail route was established in 1828 between this place and Jamestown, New York, 30 miles away; for years the carrier walked both ways. In 1853 a plank toll road was laid between Erie and Wattsburg.

•**WAYMART**, Borough; Wayne County; Pop, 1,248; Area Code 717; Zip Code 18472; Elev. 1,400'; in NE Pennsylvania; a state hospital is located outside of town.

•**WAYNE**, Urban Village; Delaware County; Pop. 10,000; Area Code 215; Zip Code 19087; Elev. 494'; 10 miles NW of Philadelphia in SE Pennsylvania; is an attractive, residential town, founded in 1880.
Valley Forge Military Junior College, founded in 1928, is located in town.

Primarily a residential area
Higher Education - Valley Forge Military Academy
Chamber of Commerce - 155 E. Lancaster Ave.

•**WAYNE COUNTY**, E central Pennsylvania; Pop. 35,237; Established, March 21, 1798; Seat is Honesdale.

•**WAYNESBORO**, Borough; Franklin County; Pop. 9,726; Area Code 717; Zip Code 17268; Elev. 713'; 10 miles NE of Hagerstown, Maryland in S Pennsylvania; set in a natural hollow and was laid out in 1797 by *John Wallace*, who had served under *General Anthony Wayne*. On his raid into Pennsylvania, *General Early* entered Waynesboro on July 23, 1863, and demanded that the housewives bake bread for his soldiers.

Agriculture - Varied produce and dairy farming,
especially fruit orchards
Industry/Mfg. - Greeting cards, food packing
Daily Newspaper - Record Herald
Chamber of Commerce - 323 E. Main St.

•**WAYNESBURG**, Borough; Seat of Greene County; Pop. 4,482; Area Code 412; Zip Code 15370; Elev. 1,035'; 50 miles S of Pittsburgh in SW Pennsylvania; was laid out in 1796 and named for *General Anthony Wayne*, whose Indian battles allowed for extensive settlement of western Pennsylvania in the early 1800s. It was incorporated in 1816. One thousand students attend Waynesburg College here.

POINT OF INTEREST

GREENE HILLS FARM- Large area farmhouse, built 1861. Museum.

Agriculture - Varied produce and dairy farming,
    especially apple orchards
Industry/Mfg. - Greeting cards, flour milling
Higher Education - Waynesburg College
Daily Newspaper - Democrat-Messenger, 32 Church St.
Chamber of Commerce - 25 E. High St.
Community Event - Covered Bridge Festival,
    Annual, Spetember

•**WEATHERLY**, Borough; Carbon County; Pop. 2,891; Area Code 717; Zip Code 18255; Elev. 1,095'; 10 miles E of Hazleton in E Pennsylvania; iron and steel castings are made here, but sawmilling and tourism are important trades. The town was settled in 1840 and named for the clockmaker, *David Weatherly.*

•**WEEDVILLE**, Village; Elk County; Pop. 500; Area Code 814; Zip Code 15868; Elev. 1,160'; 55 miles N of Altoona in a farming region in NW central Pennsylvania.

•**WEISSPORT**, Borough; Carbon County; Pop. 486; Area Code 717; Zip Code 18235; Elev. 471'; near Lehighton in E Pennsylvania; was named for *Colonel Jacob Weiss*, wealthy Philadelphian who organized one of the first coal companies.

•**WELLERSBURG**, Borough; Somerset County; Pop. 265; Area Code 814; Zip Code 15564; Elev. 1,340'; in S Pennsylvania.

•**WELLSBORO**, Borough; Seat of Tioga County; Pop. 3,085; Area Code 717; Zip Code 16901; Elev. 1,308; 40 miles SW of Elmira, New York in N Pennsylvania; The town was laid out in 1806 by *Benjamin W. Morris*, a land agent who arrived in 1799 and gave the settlement his wife's maiden name. *Mary Wells Morris* and her brothers promoted their town to be the seat of the new county of Tioga in 1806.

> *Agriculture* - Varied produce and dairy farming
> *Industry/Mfg.* - Electronics, food packaging
> *Chamber of Commerce* - P.O. Box 733
> *Community Events* -
>   Pennsylvania State Laurel Festival, Annual, June;
>   Tioga County Early Days, Annual, July

•**WELLSVILLE**, Borough; York County; Pop. 347; Area Code 717; Zip Code 17365; Elev. 500'; in S Pennsylvania.

•**WERNERSVILLE**, Borough; Berks County; Pop. 1,811; Area Code 215; Zip Code 19565; Elev. 386'; near Reading in SE Pennsylvania; founded in 1854, is a summer and health resort in Lebanon Valley at the foot of South Mountain.

•**WESLEYVILLE**, Borough; Erie County; Pop. 3,998; Area Code 814; Zip Code 165+zone; Elev. 730; in NW Pennsylvania; was laid out by *John Shadduck* in 1828 and named for *John Wesley*, founder of Methodism.

•**WEST ALEXANDER**, Borough; Washington County; Pop. 286; Area Code 412; Zip Code 15376; Elev. 1,450'; near the West Virginia state line in SW Pennsylvania; *Robert Humpl. .y*, who served under Lafayette in the Revolution, founded the town in 1796 and named it for his wife, *Martha Alexander Humphrey*.

•**WEST BROWNSVILLE**, Borough; Washington County; Pop. 1,433; Area Code 412; Zip Code 15417; Elev. 774'; across Monongahela River from Brownsville in SW Pennsylvania; was laid out in 1831 by *Ephraim L. Blaine*. *Ephraim's* son, *James G. Blaine*, born here in 1830, became a noted statesman. As candidate of the Republican party, he almost defeated *Grover Cleveland* for the presidency in 1884.

Coal mining is important here.

•**WEST CHESTER**, Borough; Seat of Chester County; Pop. 17,435; Area Code 215; Zip Code 19380; Elev. 455'; 25

miles W of Philadelphia in SE Pennsylvania; is within cannon sound of Brandywine, Paoli, Valley Forge, and other hallowed places of the Revolution, is the heart of Chester Valley. The *Jeffersonian*, one of the few Northern newspapers to sympathize openly with the South, started publishing in West Chester in 1842.
The rolling hill country outside of town is important for its dairy and grain production.

Agriculture - Varied produce and dairy farming
Industry/Mfg. - Pet foods, auto parts,
  dairy products
Higher Education -West Chester University
Daily Newspaper - Local News, 205 N. Bradford Ave.
Chamber of Commerce - 40 E. Gay St.
Community Event -
  Chester County Day, Annual, October

•**WEST CONSHOHOCKEN**, Borough; Montgomery County; Pop. 1,516; Area Code 215; Zip Code 19428; Elev. 100'; in SE Pennsylvania; adjacent to Conshohocken in a residential area.

•**WEST EASTON**, Borough; Northampton County; Pop. 1,033; Area Code 215; Zip Code 18042; Elev. 360'; adjacent to Easton in E Pennsylvania.

•**WEST ELIZABETH**, Borough; Allegheny County; Pop. 808; Area Code 412; Zip Code 15088; Elev. 760'; SE suburb of Pittsburgh in SW Pennsylvania; adjacent to Elizabeth.

•**WEST FAIRVIEW**, Borough; Cumberland County; Pop. 1,426; Area Code 717; Zip Code 17025; Elev. 360'; 5 miles NW of Harrisburg on the Susquehanna River in S Pennsylvania.

•**WESTFIELD**, Borough; Tioga County; Pop. 1,268; Area Code 717; Zip Code 16950; Elev. 1,370'; 50 miles SW of Elmira, New York in N Pennsylvania; located in a dairy and sheep farming area; named for Westfield, Massachusetts by *Henry Trowbridge*, who established a woolen mill here in the early 1800s.

•**WEST GROVE**, Borough; Chester County; Pop. 1,820; Area Code 215; Zip Code 19390; Elev. 400'; residential suburb of Philadelphia in SE Pennsylvania.

•**WEST HAZLETON**, Borough; Luzerne County; Pop. 4,871; Area Code 717; Zip Code 18201; Elev. 1,700'; adjacent to Hazleton in E Pennsylvania; residential.

Community Event - Folk Festival, Annual, June

•**WEST HOMESTEAD**, Borough; Allegheny County; Pop. 3,128; Area Code 412; Zip Code 15120; Elev. 1,000'; SE suburb of Pittsburgh, adjacent to Homestead in SW Pennsylvania; on the Monongahela River.

•**WEST KITTANNING**, Borough; Armstrong County; Pop. 1,591; Area Code 412; Zip Code 16201; Elev. 980'; W of Kittanning in W Pennsylvania.

•**WEST LAWN**, Borough; Berks County; Pop. 1,686; Area Code 215; Zip Code 19609; Elev. 340'; suburb of Reading in SE Pennsylvania.

•**WEST LEECHBURG**, Borough; Westmoreland County; Pop. 1,395; Area Code 417; Zip Code 15656; Elev. 800'; in SW Pennsylvania.

•**WEST LIBERTY**, Borough; Butler County; Pop. 301; Area Code 412; Zip Code 16105; Elev. 1,190'; 20 miles E of New Castle in W Pennsylvania; near Lake Arthur.

•**WEST MAYFIELD**, Borough; Beaver County; Pop. 1,712; Area Code 412; Zip Code 18433; suburb of Beaver Falls in W Pennsylvania.

•**WEST MIDDLESEX**, Borough; Mercer County; Pop. 1,064; Area Code 412; Zip Code 16159; Elev. 900'; in W Pennsylvania; laid out in 1836 by *James Gilkey*, celebrated for his cultivation of "Gilkies" (Neshannock potatoes), was for many years the center of the Shenango Valley iron industry.

•**WEST MIDDLETOWN**, Borough; Washington County; Pop. 215; Area Code 412; Zip Code 15379; Elev. 1,330'; in SW Pennsylvania.

•**WEST MIFFLIN**, Borough; Allegheny County; Pop. 26,279; Area Code 412; Zip Code 15122; Elev. 1,000'; SE suburb of Pittsburgh in SW Pennsylvania.

Higher Education - Community College of Allegheny County

•**WESTMONT**, Borough; Cambria County; Pop. 6,113; Area Code 814; Zip Code 16603; Elev. 1,795'; near Altoona in a highlands area in SW cen. Pennsylvania.

•**WESTMORELAND COUNTY**, SW central Pennsylvania; Pop. 392,294; Established, February 26, 1773; Seat is Greensburg.

Formed from part of Bedford County, this was the eleventh of the original provincial counties, and the last one organized under the proprietary government. It was named "after the county of Westmoreland in England, a name which geographically describes its situation." Westmoreland has been called "the mother county of western Pennsylvania" because its extensive territory was later divided into a dozen different counties. The meaning of Westmoreland, as applied to the English county, is "the land of the western moors."

•**WEST NEWTON**, Borough; Westmoreland County; Pop. 3,387; Area Code 417; Zip Code 15089; Elev. 770'; 10 miles NE of Monessen on the Youghiogheny River in SW Pennsylvania.

Agriculture - Varied produce and dairy farming, especially grain
Industry/Mfg. - Soft drinks, lumber
Chamber of Commerce - 228 - 1st Street
Community Event - Old Home Week, Annual, August

•**WESTOVER**, Borough; Clearfield County; Pop. 517; Area Code 814; Zip Code 16692; Elev. 1,350'; in W central Pennsylvania.

•**WEST PITTSTON**, Borough; Luzerne County; Pop. 5,980; Area Code 717; Zip Code 18643; Elev. 577'; on the W side of the Susquehanna River, across from Pittston in E Pennsylvania; Jenkins Fort is a small stockade burned by the

British in 1778; the town was known as Jenkins' Fort until 1859, when West Pittston was incorporated. *See also* **Pittston.**

•**WEST READING,** Borough; Berks County; Pop. 4,507; Area Code 215; Zip Code 19611; Elev. 320'; on Schuylkill River, across from Reading in SE Pennsylvania; laid out in 1873 and incorporated in 1907.

Chamber of Commerce - 408 Penn Ave.

•**WEST SUNBURY,** Borough; Butler County; Pop. 203; Area Code 412; Zip Code 16061; Elev. 1,380'; in W Pennsylvania.

•**WEST VIEW,** Borough; Allegheny County; Pop. 7,648; Area Code 412; Zip Code 15229; Elev. 1,200'; 5 miles N of Pittsburgh in SW Pennsylvania; residential suburb.

•**WEST WYOMING,** Borough; Luzerne County; Pop. 3,288; Area Code 717; Zip Code 18644; Elev. 600'; 5 miles N of Wilkes-Barre in E Pennsylvania.

•**WEST YORK,** Borough; York County; Pop. 4,526; Area Code 717; Zip Code 174+zone; Elev. 400'; 5 miles W of York in S Pennsylvania; includes in its 320 acres the 160-acre farm of *Henry Ebert,* for whose ancestors the town was originally named Eberton.

•**WHEATLAND,** Borough; Mercer County; Pop. 1.132; Area Code 412; Zip Code 16161; Elev. 900'; in W Pennsylvania; laid out about 1865 by *James Wood,* a Philadelphia Democrat who named the town for *President James Buchanan's* Lancaster County estate.

•**WHITAKER,** Borough; Allegheny County; Pop. 1,615; Area Code 412; Zip Code 15120; Elev. 1,000'; E suburb of Pittsburgh in SW Pennsylvania.

•**WHITEHALL,** Borough; Allegheny County; Pop. 15,206; Area Code 412; Zip Code 18052; Elev. 1,200'; S suburb of Pittsburgh in SW Pennsylvania.

Chamber of Commerce - 2126 S. 1st. Ave.
Community Event -
Ox Pull Festival, Annual, September

•WHITE HAVEN, Borough; Luzerne County; Pop. 1,217;
Area Code 717; Zip Code 18661; Elev. 1,220'; 15 miles SE of
Wilkes-Barre on the Lehigh River in E Pennsylvania;
settled in 1824 and incorporated in 1842; Named for *Josiah
White*, a Philadelphia coal and railroad investor. Today,
White Haven is a health resort.

Community Event -
Pocono's Bluegrass Folk Festival Annual, July

•WHITEMARSH, Township and Village; Montgomery
County; Pop. 15,886; Area Code 215; Elev. 203'; 15 miles N
of Philadelphia on the Wissahocken Creek in SE Pennsylvania; is St. Thomas Episcopal Church, a simple,
dignified, red stone edifice in English Gothic style. A
crenellated tower rises from the steep slate roof. Three
churches have occupied this site since the first log structure was built in 1698; the present one was begun in 1868.
During the Revolution the church was occupied first by
American, then by Hessian, and finally by British troops. It
is said that tombstones in the adjoining graveyard were
used by soldiers for cooking ranges and for target practice.
Washington and his army stayed here in 1777 before moving on to Valley Forge for the winter.

•WHITE MILLS, Village; Wayne County; Pop. 900; Area
Code 717; Zip Code 18473; Elev. 992'; in the NE corner of
Pennsylvania; was an early transfer point for coal hauled
overland from Carbondale (by sleigh in winter) to be
rafted down Lackawaxen Creek and the Delaware River to
Philadelphia. The difficulty of this course and the greater
desirability of the New York market dictated the construction, in 1826, of a canal from Honesdale to the Hudson
River.

•WHITE OAK, Borough; Allegheny County; Pop. 9,480;
Area Code 412; Zip Code 15131; Elev. 1,100'; S suburb of Pittsburgh in SW Pennsylvania.

•WILCOX, Village; Elk County; Pop. 900; Area Code 814;
Zip Code 15870; Elev. 1,523'; in NW central Pennsylvania;

The Post-War years also saw general prosperity for Wilkes-Barre's miners and industrial workers. However, from the early 1970s onward, the city began to lose population as many people moved to areas of more opportunity and to the outlying suburbs. Still, many products, from swimming pools to electronics components are made here.

Far from being bound by the workaday life, Wilkes-Barre residents are a richly diverse group of people who keep alive their various heritages. Polish and Lithuanian groups hold festivals and classes in cultural education, and publish two journals, the *Bratstvo* and *Garsas* for exchange of news about these communities.

POINTS OF INTEREST

CATLIN HALL, WILKES COLLEGE- Built 1843, good local example of Greek Revival style. Named after *George Catlin,* prominent American painter from Wilkes-Barre. Now serves as residence hall.

McCLINTOCK HALL- Original house from c. 1841 transformed into picturesque villa by architect *F.C. Withers.*

MUNICIPAL CONSERVATORY- Contains rare plants and flowers.

WEISS HALL, WILKES COLLEGE- Original mid-19th Century house with Greek Revival elements encompassed in major remodeling (1886) into fine Queen Anne structure.

WYOMING HISTORICAL AND GEOLOGICAL SOCIETY MUSEUM-Local history and anthracite exhibits.

Agriculture - Varied produce and dairy farming
Industry/Mfg. - A Wide variety of products and services. Coal mining.
Higher Education - Lackawanna Junior College, Kings College, Pennsylvania State University, Wilkes College
Daily Newspaper - Times-Leader
15 N. Main St., 18711
Chamber of Commerce - 92 S. Franklin St., 18701
Community Events -
Cherry Blossom Festival, Annual, May;
Fine Arts Fiesta, Annual, May

•**WILCOX,** Village; Elk County; Pop. 900; Area Code 814; Zip Code 15870; Elev. 1,523'; in NW central Pennsylvania; on the west branch of the Clarion River, was founded in 1858 by *Colonel A.I. Wilcox,* a land agent turned settler.

•**WILKES-BARRE**, City; Seat of Luzerne County; Pop.
51,117; Area Code 717; Zip Code 187+zone; Elev. 575'; 20
miles SW of Scranton in NE Pennsylvania.

Lying on the Susquehanna River's east bank, Wilkes-
Barre is in the heart of Wyoming Valley's anthracite coal
region. A compact little city, its area is confined
topographically by the outlying ranges of the Appalachian
chain, Wilkes-Barre has a rather dense population of over
6,000 per square mile. The city is at the center of a circle
of many major industrial cities. Over one-third of the
population of the United States is within 300 miles of Wilkes-
Barre.

Wilkes-Barre was a strategic point in the long conflict between Pennsylvania and Connecticut over the
Wyoming lands. As early as 1755 the Susquehanna Company from Connecticut tried to colonize the region,
although the Penns claimed ownership under the royal
deed of 1681. Even after the fort Stanwix Treaty of 1768,
when the Indians themselves gave clear title to Pennsylvania proprietors, Connecticut refused to give up its
activity in the valley.

In the summer of 1769 *John Durkee*, veteran of the
French and Indian War, came to Wyoming Valley with a
small band of settlers from Connecticut. He built Fort
Durkee and laid out Wilkes-Barre, naming it for two
members of the British Parliament-*John Wilkes* and *Colonel Isaac Barre* -who as champions of individual rights
were already looked upon as supporters of the American
Colonies in the looming struggle against the Crown. The
erection of Fort Durkee, as much a challenge to the Penns
as a defense against hostile Indians, helped to precipitate
the Pennamite-Yankee War, the first phase of which ended in 1771 with the Connecticut settlers in control of the
valley. In 1774 about 17 settlements, including Wilkes-
Barre, were embraced in the township of Westmoreland
by the Connecticut assembly.

At the outbreak of the Revolutionary War the Continental Congress ordered Pennsylvania and Connecticut
to cease hostilities. During the war, in July 1778, Indians
and Tories swept through the valley, leaving Wilkes-Barre
in smoking ruins. The controversy between the two states
was renewed after Congress, by the Decree of Trenton in
1782, decided in favor of Pennsylvania's claim to the

Wyoming Valley. The second Pennamite War resulted, and the rebuilt Wilkes-Barre was burned to the ground by Connecticut settlers.

There followed in 1785-86 a period of confusion in which Pennsylvania governed a region peopled by settlers loyal in the main to Connecticut. After the failure of a strong movement, directed by New Englanders, to set up an independent state, Connecticut formally released all claims in the valley about 1800.

In the meantime, in 1786, the county of Luzerne was created, and on March 17, 1806, Wilkes-Barre was incorporated as a borough. A few years later, veins of hard coal discovered hereabouts in the early 1760's were recognized as the source of great potential wealth-and the anthracite industry in the Wyoming Valley was born. By 1812 Wilkes-Barre had grown from a mere handful of people to a small town, but it was many years before it changed from a farming to an industrial center. Development of canals and railroads in the second quarter of the century, in addition to the growing demand for hard coal as domestic fuel, gave impetus to the anthracite industry.

Until 1870 all immigration was from the north of Europe, with the Irish predominating. Then mine operators sent representatives to central and southern Europe to induce peasants to come to the American coal fields. Many of the older workers consequently were supplanted by newcomers willing to work for low wages, and bitter conflicts followed. The cleavage along national lines, however, gave to Wilkes-Barre such picturesque sections as Five Points, now East End, where a crowd of miners used to gather nightly on the steps of Mackin Brothers' Store, a scene described by Con Carbon in a popular ballad of the 1890's:

The Far Downs and Connaught men
Fight, and then make up again,
Dutch and Scotch and English men-
All like chickens in a pen.
The powder smoke does be so thick,
You could not cut it with a pick,
The smell of gas would make you sick
In front of Mackin's store.

During the latter decades of the nineteenth century a number of large manufacturing plants, drawn to the Wyoming Valley by cheap coal and extensive shipping facilities, were established in and near Wilkes-Barre. These produced everything from miners' caps to small locomotives and cables. The supply of female labor attracted textile mills; the first lace manufactured in the United States was made in 1885 by the Wilkes-Barre Lace Manufacturing Company, known today for its Nottingham curtains. By 1898, when Wilkes-Barre was made a city of the third class, it had become a center of diversified manufacturing, but the life-blood of the valley continued to flowing the coal veins.

During the first decade of the present century Wilkes-Barre's population increased from 50,000 to 67,000. In 1917 the anthracite industry reached its all-time peak; by 1922 it had dropped one half in production and continued to show a general decline until the start of World War II in 1939.

•WILKINSBURG, Borough; Allegheny County; Pop. 23,669; Area Code 412; Zip Code 15221; Elev. 922'; 10 miles E of Pittsburgh in SW Pennsylvania; settled in 1780 and known successively as McNairsville and Rippeysville, was incorporated in 1887. Its name was changed to honor *Judge William Wilkins*, Minister to Russia and *President Tyler's* Secretary of War. *Wilkens* began his career here when he opened a law office in 1801; he was one of the organizers of the Bank of Pittsburgh. It was incorporated as a borough in 1887.

Today it is a quiet, residential town.

Chamber of Commerce - 727 Penn Ave.

•WILLIAMSBURG, Borough; Blair County; Pop. 1,400; Area Code 814; Zip Code 16693; Elev. 885'; in S central. Pennsylvania.

•WILLIAMSPORT, City; Seat of Lycoming County; Pop. 33,401; Area Code 717; Zip Code 17701; in N central Pennsylvania.

Industry/Mfg. - A Wide variety of products and services

411

Higher Education - Lycoming College,
Williamsport Area Community College
Daily Newspaper - Sun-Gazette, 252 W. 4th St., 17701
Chamber of Commerce - 454 Pine St., 17703
Community Event - Arts Festival, Annual, April

•**WILLIAMSTOWN**, Borough; Dauphin County; Pop. 1,664; Area Code 717; Zip Code 17098; Elev. 1,127'; 25 miles NE of Harrisburg in SE central P⌣ ⌐nsylvania; settled by *Daniel Williams*, the site came into the possession of coal operators in 1826.

•**WILLOW GROVE**, Urban Village; Montgomery County; Pop. 21,000; Area Code 215; Zip Code 19090; Elev. 284'; 15 miles N of Philadelphia in SE Pennsylvania; is Willow Grove Park where *John Philip Sousa*, *Walter Damrosch*, *Arthur Pryor*, *Giuseppe Creatore*, *Nahan Franko*, *Patrick Conway*, and *Victor Herbert* once conducted summer concerts.

Primarily a residential area
Industry/Mfg. - Clothing, electronics
Chamber of Commerce - P.O. Box 100

•**WILMERDING**, Borough; Allegheny County; Pop. 2,421; Area Code 412; Zip Code 15148; Elev. 900'; 10 miles E of Pittsburgh in SW Pennsylvania; was at first a railroad station, built about 1885, on land originally owned by *Major William B. Negley.* The name Wilmerding was suggested by *Robert Pitcairn*, then superintendent of the Pittsburgh division of the Pennsylvania Railroad, Negley's wife, *Joanna Wilmerding Negley.* Wilmerding was the family name of her mother. Several years after the station was established, *George Westinghouse* bought about 500 acres of land in the Turtle Creek valley and organized the East Pittsburgh Improvement Company, which later laid out the town of Wilmerding. When the Westinghouse Air Brake Company built its works here, a movement was started to call the place Westinghouse, but when the town was incorporated in 1890, it borrowed the name of Wilmerding from the railway station.

•**WILMORE**, Borough; Cambria County; Pop. 299; Area Code 814; Zip Code 15962; Elev. 1,560'; in SW central Pennsylvania.

•**WILSON**, Borough; Northampton County; Pop. 7,564; Area Code 215; Zip Code 15025; near Easton in an industrial area in E Pennsylvania.

•**WINDBER**, Borough; Somerset County; Pop. 5,585; Area Code 814; Zip Code 15963; Elev. 1,600'; in S Pennsylvania; was selected by the Pennsylvania Railroad Company in 1897 for its new station at this point. This name, which was suggested by E.J. Berwind, the chief stockholder in the Berwind-White Coal company, was formed by transposing the two syllables of the family name Berwind. Shortly after the station was established, the Wilmore Coal Company, which owned the land, laid out a town under the supervision of their engineer, *James C. Cunningham*. The town then adopted the name of the railway station.

Chamber of Commerce - P.O. Box 460

•**WIND GAP**, Borough; Northampton County; Pop. 2,651; Area Code 215; Zip Code 18091; Elev. 841'; in E Pennsylvania; incorporated as a borough in 1893 and named for the Wind Gap to the north, was settled by Germans and Hollanders. Later, slate quarrying attracted Italian and Welsh immigrants.

The "Wind Gap" in the Blue Mountains is the first notch to the south of the Delaware Water Gap. The gap extends nearly from top to bottom on the mountain here.

•**WINDSOR**, Borough; York County; Pop. 1,205; Area Code 717; Zip Code 17366; Elev. 660'; in S Pennsylvania; named for Windsor, England by *Thomas Armor*, who was justice of the township in the 1750s.

•**WINTERSTOWN**, Borough; York County; Pop. 491; Area Code 717; Elev. 860'; in S Pennsylvania; rural.

•**WOMELSDORF**, Borough; Berks County; Pop. 1,827; Area Code 215; Zip Code 19567; Elev. 434'; in SE Pennsylvania; founded by Germans in 1723, was called Middletown until 1762, when it was renamed for *John Womelsdorf*, leader of emigrants from the German Palatinate.

413

•**WOODBURY**, Borough; Bedford County; Pop. 267; Area Code 814; Zip Code 16695; Elev. 1,290'; in S Pennsylvania.

•**WOODCOCK**, Borough; Crawford County; Pop. 126; Area Code 814; Zip Code rural; Elev. 1,200'; in NW Pennsylvania.

•**WOODWARD**, Township; Lycoming County; Pop. 2,014; Area Code 717; Zip Code 16882; Elev. 794'; in N cen. Pennsylvania; on Pine Creek, is the site of the Woodward Cave, one of the larget dry caverns in Pennsylvania. The cave, in Trenton limestone, is said to have been the haunt of a robber band more than 100 years ago.

•**WORMLEYSBURG**, Borough; Cumberland County; Pop. 2,772; Area Code 717; Zip Code 17043; Elev. 320'; suburb of Harrisburg in S Pennsylvania.

•**WORTHINGTON**, Borough; Armstrong County; Pop. 760; Area Code 412; Zip Code 16262; Elev. 1,120'; in W Pennsylvania; was founded in 1808 on Buffalo Creek.

•**WORTHVILLE**, Borough; Jefferson County; Pop. 87; Area Code 814; Zip Code 15784; Elev. 1,190'; in W central Pennsylvania.

•**WRIGHTSVILLE**, Borough; York County; Pop. 2,365; Area Code 717; Zip Code 17368; Elev. 256'; 10 miles NE of York in S Pennsylvania; on the west bank of of the Susquehanna, is an industrial miniature of Columbia and shares the latter's history. In 1730 surveyors from Maryland attempted to set up a ferry here in opposition to the existing one. *Benjamin Chambers* was "one of the Principal Persons to turn off...*Lord Baltimore's* surveyors, who were chaining up the River Side on *John Wright's* land with a Possey of men not Less than Thirty...which Possey was ordered to take up the Cumpas and Begon, or we would Breake it and make them Begon to their cost." For this and other services to the proprietary government, *Chambers* was rewarded in 1736 with a gift of 400 acres on "Fawlling Spring on Cannogogige," now Chambersburg.

•**WYALUSING**, Borough; Bradford County; Pop. 716; Area Code 717; Zip Code 18853; Elev. 674'; 35 miles NW of Scranton on the Susquehana River in N Pennsylvania;

(Ind. "the place of the old man," or "good hunting grounds"), was settled in the early 1750's by members of the Susquehanna Company, a New England group which claimed most of this area by right of charter and Indian purchases. After the land was sold, the Indians who remained became Moravians as a result of the missionary labors of *David Zeisberger*. But for the zeal of *Chief John Papunhank*, who carried his new faith to neighboring tribes, *Zeisberger's* efforts might have borne less fruit. The Moravians abandoned their settlement at Friedenshutten, June 11, 1772.

This is a favorite tourist stop in the northern, hilly part of Pennsylvania. The Wyalusing Prayer Rocks are east of town, where Indians are believed to have worshipped their gods.

•WYOMING, Borough; Luzerne County; Pop. 3,655; Area Code 717; Zip Code 18644; Elev. 557'; 5 miles NE of Wilkes-Barre on the Susquehanna River in E Pennsylvania; Is the Site of the Battle of Wyoming, where valley settlers fought an invading party of Tories, known as Butler's Rangers, and a band of Iroquois on July 3, 1778. In the spring of 1778, when British forces swooped down upon isolated clearings in the Wyoming district, the valley residents appealed to Congress for the return of two companies that had been levied among them, but were told that they would have to fend for themselves.

Late in June a force of approximately 1,000 Indians and Tories under *Major John Butler* advanced overland upon Wyoming, center of the fertile valley country. Treachery caused the fall of Fort Wintermute on July 2; Jenkins' Fort capitulated the same evening. Settlers had been swarming into Forty Fort, and the following afternoon the Colonists, although outnumbered three to one, marched from Forty Fort against the enemy. *Colonel Zebulon Butler* and *Colonel Nathan Denison* led them. The field of battle was a partially cleared plain; the Colonists' left flank extended into a scrubby swamp, and after the first clash Indians invaded the marsh, enveloped the left wing, and fell upon the rear, turning the battle into a slaughter. Some of the survivors returned to Forty Fort and others fled to Wilkes-Barre.

Women, children, and old men had been left in Forty Fort during the battle, and with the return of the survivors *Colonel Denison* organized the garrison. Articles of capitulation, drawn up when the invaders besieged the fort, stipulated safety for the inhabitants. But when *Major Butler* and his force marched into the fort on July 5, he was unable to restrain his Indian allies, who immediately began to plunder and insult the prisoners in the fort, while a reign of terror was carried on throughout the section. In the battle and ensuing massacre it is estimated that 300 men, women, and children were slain.

Today, coal mining is important in the region. "Wyoming" is derived from an Indian word meaning "extensive plains or fields."

•**WYOMING COUNTY**, E Central Pennsylvania; Pop. 26,433; Established, April 4, 1842; Seat is Tunkhannock.

One of the "seventeen original townships" in the Connecticut county of Westmoreland, which was wholly within the state of Pennsylvania, was Putnam Township, so called in honor of *General Israel Putnam*, the Connecticut hero in the American Revolution. In 1842, when the people of this region, who were for the most part descendants of the early Connecticut settlers, petitioned the legislature to create a new county out of Luzerne, they requested that it might be called Putnam County, for the old township of Putnam and in honor of their beloved hero; but the bitterness engendered by the "Pennamite war" still lingered, and it was apparently to early for Pennsylvania too perform a gracious act by complying with what now seems a reasonable request. In the legislature the member from Luzerne County moved that the name of Wyoming be substituted for Putnam, and thus the new county was named Wyoming.

Originally the name Wyoming, or Wyoming Valley, had been used to designate all the territory which the Susquehanna and the Delaware companies of Connecticut had bought of the Iroquois Indians in 1754, and which is now included in the counties of Luzerne, Lackawanna, Wyoming, Susquehanna, and Wayne. To take the name of Wyoming County from the Wyoming Valley was not inappropriate, because the county forms the northern opening of the exquisitely beautiful valley of Wyoming, famous in history, legend, and literature.

•**WYOMISSING**, Borough; Berks County; Pop. 6,551; Area Code 215; Zip Code 19610; Elev. 320'; 5 miles W of Reading in SE Pennsylvania; residential suburb; name is derived from an Indian phrase meaning "place of flats."

•**WYOMISSING HILLS**, Borough; Berks County; Pop. 2,150; Area Code 215; Zip Code ; Elev. 340'; suburb of Reading near Wyomissing in SE Pennsylvania.

•**WYSOX**, Village; Bradford County; Pop. 450; Area Code 717; Elev. 720'; in N Pennsylvania; name is Indian for "place of grapes."

•**YARDLEY**, Borough; Bucks County; Pop. 2,533; Area Code 215; Zip Code 19067; Elev. 86'; 30 miles NE of Philadelphia in SE Pennsylvania; a leisurely town typical of the vicinity, was settled in 1682. In early days a ferry plied between Yardley and the Jersey shore.

POINT OF INTEREST

WASHINGTON CROSSING STATE PARK- Site where *Gen. George Washington* crossed the Delaware River for the successful surprise raid on Trenton, N.J. in 1776.

•**YATESVILLE**, Borough; Luzerne County; Pop. 555; Area Code 717; Zip Code 18640; Elev. 840'; in E Pennsylvania.

•**YEADON**, Borough; Delaware County; Pop. 11,727; Area Code 215; Zip Code 19050; Elev. 100'; 5 miles SW of Philadelphia in SE Pennsylvania; residential.

•**YELLOW HOUSE**, Village; Berks County; Pop. 100; Area Code 215; Zip Code 19568; Elev. 295'; in SE Pennsylvania; named for the county tavern that has stood here for many years that was painted yellow.

•**YOE**, Borough; York County; Pop. 990; Area Code 717; Zip Code 17313; Elev. 800'; in S Pennsylvania.

•**YORK**, City; Seat of York County; Pop. 44,619; Area Code 717; Zip Code 174+zone; 10 miles WSW of the Susquehanna River in SE Pennsylvania.

First Pennsylvania town founded west of the Susquehanna River, it lies in the basin formed by Codorus Creek as it crosses York Valley. It is the seat of York County, known during the Colonial days as the "breadbasket of America" and still an important agricultural area, exten-

418

ding from Yellow Breeches Creek to the Mason-Dixon line. Noticeable in York are long rows of brick houses under a single continuous roof.

The first military company in Pennsylvania to resist the encroachments of Great Britain was organized in 1774 in York; *James Smith*, who later signed the Declaration of Independence, was captain. From September 1777 to June 1778, during the most crucial days of the Revolution, York's little brick courthouse served as the capitol of the American Colonies. During this time a printing press from the shop of *Benjamin Franklin* was brought from Philadelphia, and upon it were printed the public communications from Congress and $10,000,000 in Continental bills. The *Pennsylvania Gazette* was also printed here for a time.

Here on June 28, 1863, three days before the Battle of Gettysburg, Confederate troops under *General Jubal Early* invaded, demanding $100,000 in cash and stocks of foods and supplies. The town could only raise $28,000 for the invaders, who later left for Gettysburg, 28 miles away.

After the war, York became an industrial community. Inventions brought new enterprises for making turbines, farm machinery, railway coaches and pianos. Metal industries began specializing, and textiles entered upon an era of prosperity. In 1887, with a population of 20,000, York was incorporated as a city whose present existence is dependent upon varied manufacturing interests. York weathered the early 1930s without a single bank loss. However, the recession of the 1970s caused the population to decrease.

POINTS OF INTEREST

COOKES HOUSE (THOMAS PAINE HOUSE)- Earliest stone house in the city, believed to have been the home of *Thomas Paine* when Congress met at York 1777-1778.

GEN. HORATIO GATES HOUSE AND GOLDED PLOUGH TAVERN-Unusual example of mid-18th Century regional construction technique in tavern; house in which *Gen. Horatio Gates* stayed following victory at Saratoga. Museum.

Industry/Mfg. - A Wide variety of products
     and services
Higher Education - Pennsylvania State University,
     York College of Pennsylvania

Daily Newspapers - Dispatch, 15-21 E. Philadelphia
St., 17405
Record, 1750 Industrial Highway, 17402
Chamber of Commerce - 13 E. Market St., 17405
Community Event -
Inter-State Fair, Annual, September

•YORK COUNTY, SE Pennsylvania; Pop. 312,963; Established, October 14, 1748; Seat is York.

This county was probably christened in honor of a royal duke, and the town and county of Bedford received their name from the Duke of Bedford. The only other county in Pennsylvania hearing the name of an English nobleman is Delaware, which was named directly from the Delaware River. Huntingdon County was named in honor of an English noblewoman, the Countess of Huntingdon. In its choice of county names Pennsylvania stands in striking contrast to its aristocratic neighbor, Virginia, thirty-nine of whose one hundred counties were named for English royalty and nobility.

In October, 1741, *Richard, Thomas,* and *John Penn* ordered *Thomas Cookson,* then deputy surveyor of Lancaster County, which included the present territory of York County to "survey and lay off in Monocacy road crosses the stream." They further directed that the town was to be called York, or Yorktown. The *Penns* were the actual owners of the site of York, which was laid out on a part of Springettsbury Manor, which had been named for *Springett Penn,* the oldest son of the founder's son *William.*

Whether the *Penns* named York for the ancient English city of York or for *James Stuart* long the Duke of York and afterwards *King James II,* who had been the friend and patron of both the founder and his father, *Admiral Penn,* is a question that cannot now be definitely answered. In the absence of any direct evidence, all that one can do is to balance the probabilities; and when one considers how much the *Penn* family owed to the favor and friendliness of the Duke, one is inclined to believe that the *Penns* chose the name of York in a desire to honor the memory of the royal patron and benefactor of their family.

In fairness, however, to those who accept the other explanation we must remember that gratitude-especially among the descendants of *William Penn* -was likely to be an evanescent emotion; that the Quaker, *Samuel Blunston,* who, *as the agent for the Penns,* had so

420

much to do with starting and directing the settlements on the western side of the Susquehanna, was a native of Upper Hallam in Yorkshire; and that the English counties of Lancaster and York, like the two Pennsylvania counties, lie side by side. When we consider *Samuel Blunston's* close relations with the *Penns*, we must at least admit the probability that, with his old English home in mind, he may have suggested the name of York and York County.

•**YORKANA**, Borough; York County; Pop. 296; Area Code 717; Zip Code 174+zone; Elev. 660'; in S Pennsylvania.

•**YORKHAVEN**, Borough; York County; Pop. 746; Area Code 717; Zip Code 17370; Elev. 335'; suburb of Harrisburg in S Pennsylvania.

•**YORK SPRINGS**, Borough; Adams County; Pop. 556; Area Code 717; Zip Code 17372; Elev. 620'; in S Pennsylvania.

•**YOUGHIOGHENY RIVER**, S Pennsylvania; Flows N from source in NW Maryland into Pennsylvania, where it is dammed to form a 10mile long lake, to mouth at Monongahela River in McKeesport. Dramatic falls at Ohiopyle and Cucumber Falls, Fayette County. Navigable for 9 miles SE of McKeesport, and in Youghiogheny River Lake.

Name may be derived from the Indian word *Yohoghany*, meaning "a stream flowing in a roundabout course."

•**YOUNGSTOWN**, Borough; Westmoreland County; Pop. 470; Area Code 417; Zip Code 15696; Elev. 1,100'; in SW Pennsylvania.

•**YOUNGSVILLE**, Borough; Warren Borough; 2,006; Area Code 814; Zip Code 16371; Elev. 1,211'; 10 miles W of Warren in NW Pennsylvania; settled in 1795 by *John McKinney*, and named for *Matthew Young*, who taught school from his tent here beginning in 1796. Hunters, fishermen and skiers find lodging in this small town.

•**YOUNGWOOD**, Borough; Westmoreland County; Pop. 3,749; Area Code 417; Zip Code 15697; Elev. 976'; 30 miles E of Pittsburgh in an industrial area in SW Pennsylvania.

Higher Education - Westmoreland County Community College

•**ZELIENOPLE**, Borough; Butler County; Pop. 3,502; Area Code 412; Zip Code 16063; Elev. 906'; 30 miles NW of Pittsburgh, W Pennsylvania; was laid out on Connoquenessing Creek in 1802 by *Baron Dettmar Basse*, who later sold half of his 10,000-acre tract to *Father Rapp* for the latter's Harmony colony. The Baron named the settlement for his daughter, nicknamed *Zelie*. A popular summer resort, Zelienople has been called the "chicken-dinner capital" of western Pennsylvania.

Agriculture - Varied produce and dairy farming
Industry/Mfg. - Molding machinery, coal mining
Chamber of Commerce - P.O. Box 464

Biography Index

Biography Index

Biography Index

430